RELIGION AND CULTURE

AN INTRODUCTION TO ANTHROPOLOGY OF RELIGION

ANNEMARIE DE WAAL MALEFIJT

Department of Anthropology, Hunter College
City University of New York

The Macmillan Company

Collier-Macmillan Limited
LONDON

Third Printing, 1970

Library of Congress catalog card number: 68–12717

THE MACMILLAN COMPANY
866 THIRD AVENUE, NEW YORK, NEW YORK 10022
COLLIER-MACMILLAN CANADA, LTD., TORONTO, ONTARIO

PRINTED IN THE UNITED STATES OF AMERICA

Preface

THIS ANTHROPOLOGICAL STUDY OF RELIGION ATTEMPTS TO GIVE A
broad treatment of the subject. It is directed toward students in
the social and behavioral sciences, but can be profitably read by
anyone interested in human thought and action. Although I have
adhered to traditional anthropological interests in theory and in
integrative analysis of cultural phenomena, I have attempted to
provide an additional dimension by taking into account a much
greater span of time than is usually examined in anthropological
books dealing with religion.

Chapter 1 introduces and defines the topic. Chapters 2–4 trace
the history of the study of religion from Herodotus to the present. In the same historical vein, Chapter 5 discusses those archeological discoveries that have shed light upon the development
of religious consciousness. Chapters 6–11 treat the manifestations
of religion that I believe to be most salient for understanding
the nature of religion. Chapters 12 and 13 deal with religious
functions and religious change, respectively. Throughout the
book, I have emphasized relationships between religion and other
aspects of culture.

Anthropologists have focused their attention on the religions
and cultures of nonliterate peoples, and the descriptive material
in this volume reflects this interest. But, although the book
stresses the religions of nonliterate peoples, the interpretations
are generally valid for religions of all men. By recognizing the
common features of religion wherever it is found, we can enhance

v

our understanding of the religious systems of modern societies.

Whole religious systems are not generally treated here: the descriptions are meant to provide illustrative examples of particular religious phenomena. Reference to the pertinent literature will enable readers to investigate further those religions in which they are particularly interested. Most of the ethnographies mentioned are easily available in libraries and in college bookstores. Many of them are available in inexpensive paperback editions. The bibliography generally cites the newer editions of each work. The year of original publication is usually added.

In writing this book, I have drawn on the knowledge and experience of many colleagues. The extensive bibliography signifies the scope of my indebtedness. I wish to thank Professors Elizabeth Colson, Francis P. Conant, Dorothy Keur, and Baidya Varma for their advice and suggestions. Errors of interpretation, however, are entirely my own responsibility. I thank Hunter College for giving me a George N. Shuster Faculty Fellowship Award to aid in the preparation of the manuscript. I am also grateful to Janet Gilmartin, who made the drawings, to Ellen Gartenfeld for her work on the bibliography, to Gwen Browde and Gail D'Alessio for helping with the typing, and to Robert Zeitlin, without whom I would have missed yet another deadline.

Annemarie de Waal Malefijt

Contents

1

Anthropology and the Study of Religion

RELIGION IS ONE OF THE MOST IMPORTANT ASPECTS OF CULTURE studied by anthropologists and other social scientists. Not only is it found in every known human society, it also significantly interacts with other cultural institutions. It finds expression in material culture, in human behavior, and in value systems, morals, and ethics. It interacts with systems of family organization, marriage, economics, law, and politics; it enters into the realms of medicine, science, and technology; and it has inspired rebellions and wars as well as sublime works of art. No other cultural institution presents so vast a range of expression and implication. Religious concepts and ideas are not constrained by physical environment. Their formulations meet with no other limitations than those of the inquiring spirit of the human mind itself.

The complexity of religious phenomena and their reflection in so many other aspects of life have attracted scholars from many disciplines: historians, philosophers, linguists, and psychologists have analyzed religion each with their own methods. With an already extensive body of literature dealing with various aspects of religion, a question may well be asked: Can anthropology significantly contribute to a further understanding of religion? In one way, this whole book is an answer to this question. In order to show just how and why anthropologists study religion, we must first understand the aims and methods of anthropology as a whole.

1

ANTHROPOLOGY

Anthropology is the study of man and his culture. It aims at an understanding of the totality of man's being—his past and his present existence, both as a biological organism and as a cultural creature. Anthropologists therefore study man's physical and cultural properties and reach backward in time as far as fossil and material remains allow them to go. But anthropologists by no means neglect contemporary human beings. They try to discover the origins, developments, changes, interrelationships, functions, and meanings of every human phenomenon. Anthropology is thus nothing less than an effort to understand humanity through the study of man's biological character as well as his whole social experience.

In the face of so imposing a task, a division of labor and specialization becomes imperative. Accordingly, there are two main divisions in the field: physical anthropology and cultural anthropology. Physical anthropology deals with man's biological aspects and with human evolution, variation, and adaptation. Cultural anthropology is the study of human cultures, their history, their structures, and their functions. Archeology, a subdivision of cultural anthropology, treats primarily those cultures no longer in existence and concerning which no written records have been found. Archeologists try to reconstruct these cultures on the basis of material remains. Linguistics, another subdivision of cultural anthropology, is concerned with language. It has developed into a separate subfield because language although clearly a cultural phenomenon, has many structural aspects that can be investigated independently. Apart from recording, analyzing, and classifying a great number of unwritten languages, many of which are rapidly becoming extinct, anthropological linguists also trace the intimate relationships between language and culture, a branch of study which they have called ethnolinguistics. Ethnology, finally, is the part of cultural anthropology that describes and analyzes human cultures wherever they are found. It investigates the beliefs and activities which people have acquired by virtue of their membership in a group, and those together constitute the "culture" of such a group.

The Concept of Culture

These seemingly diverse topics are united by the principles of anthropological method. One of these principles is that all human phenomena—biological, historical, linguistic, or cultural—must be brought into relation with each other if we are to understand the human whole. Anthropologists have called this their "holistic" approach. The second distinctive feature of anthropology is the concept of culture. The word *culture* is used by anthropologists in two senses. Culture, in a general sense, is the entire social heritage of man; in its specific sense, it is the tradition of a particular human group, a way of living learned from, and shared by, the members of that group. The concept of culture is one of the most significant keys to the understanding of human behavior, and probably the major contribution of anthropology to the understanding of man.

The essence of this concept is that human behavior is acquired and learned behavior, and is thus not instinctive, not inherited through genetic mechanisms, but communicated from generation to generation.

The anthropological approach to the study of religion involves the concept of culture, applied through the use of certain scientific principles. The basic features of the scientific approach to the study of religion are fourfold: universality, empiricism, comparison, and objectivity.

Universality

Universality implies that the anthropological approach encompasses all known religions and religious phenomena, and that it does not exclude any on the basis of "taste," "decency," or similar nonscientific considerations. Ethical and moral standards differ from culture to culture, and it is the scientific task of anthropologists to study them as they actually are encountered.

Empiricism

The study of religion in contemporary anthropology is empirical because it is firmly rooted in field research. The main body of data used for analysis is gathered by anthropologists through direct contact with the carriers of the various cultural traditions. Not only is this method more reliable than one dependent upon reports from untrained observers, but it also affords the field worker an opportunity to examine religion in its total cultural context.

Comparison

Through the systematic comparison of similar religious phenomena, anthropologists seek to achieve a greater or lesser amount of generalization. These comparisons may also reveal historical relationships and evolutionary sequences, or may serve as a basis for deriving typologies.

Objectivity

The anthropological study of religion demands that the investigator remain impartial and unbiased. As an anthropologist, he is not concerned with the possible truth or falsehood of particular religious beliefs, but with the existence and significance of those beliefs.

These four principles, combined with the holistic approach and the application of the concept of culture, constitute the basic anthropological methodology. Anthropologists use these methods not only in their studies of specific groups of people, but also in the many instances where they turn their attention to one specific phenomenon, be it language, kinship organization, or religion. By doing so, they extend their studies well beyond the specific field of investigation. An anthropological study of religion will thus give insights not only into the nature of religion itself, but into many other cultural institutions, into human behavior and interaction patterns, and into human history.

AREA OF STUDY

Although anthropology embraces all human cultures, anthropologists have directed much of their attention to small and homogeneous societies. Anthropological theory was forged out of the encounter with simple or primitive societies, which taught fieldworkers to view familiar phenomena in a new light.[1] An-

[1] Until quite recently, the term *primitive* was commonly used by anthropologists and nonanthropologists alike to refer to the cultures and the religions of simple non-Western societies. There is, however, an ever-increasing

thropologists have found that the study of nonliterate societies has a number of distinct advantages.

Increase in Knowledge About Human Phenomena

Anthropologists have added thousands of examples of religious phenomena to the store of common knowledge by studying little-known, nonliterate societies. These examples have increased the knowledge about the great variety of religious expression, provided more comparative data, and generally broadened the scholar's outlook.

Increase in Objectivity

The discovery of the wide range of cultural diversity has led the anthropologist to realize that there are many possible ways of life and that his own culture is neither normative for others, nor superior. Exposure to foreign cultures thus makes him consider his own more objectively. Moreover, it is easier to make objective observations in cultures unlike his own, because the newness engages his attention, and he is less emotionally involved with other people's value systems.

Growth of Complexity

One task of cultural anthropology is to study the interrelationships of social institutions within their total cultural framework. It is obviously much easier to begin with those cultures which are structurally less complex and culturally more homogeneous, with relatively few conflicting values or beliefs. Such cultures can be directly viewed as wholes, and a study of these cultures prepares the way for the understanding of the more complex societies.

---

concern among anthropologists about the derogatory connotations of this word. These connotations contradict the anthropological principle of objectivity, even if most anthropologists who used the word were probably the last persons to attach a degrading meaning to it. But the fact remains that no one likes to be called a "primitive," and since anthropological books are not written exclusively for other anthropologists or students, but are of interest to many people, including non-Western ones, the term should be avoided. Several alternative terms have been proposed, none yet wholly satisfactory. In this book we shall use such terms as *nonliterate, tribal, simple, small-scale,* or *homogeneous.*

Record of Vanishing Cultures
A final reason for studying nonliterate societies is that many of them are rapidly being transformed, or are disappearing altogether. The recording of these cultural and religious systems not only adds to the understanding of cultural phenomena by adding comparative material, but preserves knowledge of these unique ways of life for posterity.

Although anthropology adheres to the scientific principle of universality, it does not follow that the anthropologist studies "everything." The universal approach implies that he takes all pertinent data into account and does not suppress any knowledge that may bias his definitions. But anthropological methods are not, for instance, designed to lead to aesthetic judgments, nor can they determine the ultimate truth or falsehood of religious beliefs. The individual anthropologist will usually make such judgments, but these are derived from his own cultural experience and background, not from anthropology.

Although philosophy and theology indulge in speculations about the existence of the supernatural, and aesthetics attempts to establish criteria for beauty, anthropology looks for the manifestations of religious beliefs in patterned cultural and social behavior. Thus anthropological studies of religion are cultural rather than philosophical, theological, or aesthetic inquiries.

RELIGION AS CULTURE

Religion, like culture itself, consists of systematic patterns of beliefs, values, and behavior, acquired by man as a member of his society. These patterns are systematic because their manifestations are regular in occurrence and expression: they are shared by members of a group. But regularity is not to be confused with homogeneity. In all religions there are differences of interpretation of principles and meanings. There will be found dissenters and believers, innovators and traditionalists. Dissenters and innovators do not, however, deny regularity: they merely protest against it. When active and successful, they will establish new regularities, to be challenged by others in their turn. In smaller societies, all members share the same cultural and religious traditions, while in heterogeneous societies different religious traditions exist side by side, often correlating with ethnic background or social status.

Religion is acquired by man as a member of his society, in part through conscious instruction, in part through imitation of others. Much of this learning takes place in childhood. Children come to see the world through their particular culture, and if they are not confronted with conflicting evidence later in life, they will generally not question the principles of their culture and religion, but will accept them as self-understood.

Anthropologists studying religion as a cultural institution will begin their research by recording the regularities of its expression within a given culture. When enough data are at hand, cross-cultural comparisons can be made, and the similarities and differences thus revealed be analyzed. Viewing religion as a cultural phenomenon also directs attention to change. This may begin anywhere—an increase in population, or technological innovations, economic improvements, or the visions of a prophet. Because culture is a complex whole, each change is reflected in other cultural institutions and throughout the cultural structure.

Social Aspects of Religion

The concepts *cultural* and *social* represent alternate but related ways of looking at the same phenomena. When we characterized religion as "cultural," we saw it as an ordered system of meanings, values, and beliefs by which individuals define their world. These individuals themselves form a society, an aggregate of persons who act and interact on the basis of a given cultural way of life. The specific modes of social interaction based upon religious beliefs give rise to the existence of religious roles and social status and stratification.

It would not be necessary to distinguish between the social and cultural aspects of religion if people acted in blind obedience to cultural rules. If such were the case, it could only be observed how culture maintained society, but there would be no explanation for varieties of behavior, and no explanation for change. Culture often makes conflicting demands upon people, and they react as human beings, not as robots. Culture provides a necessary guide in the affairs of life, and is a prerequisite for the proper functioning of any society—but it is only a guide.

Every person remains a distinct entity with individual needs and motivations, capable of independent thought and action. No environment is completely static and no two individuals have identical social experiences. When the conflicts between the norms of culture and the demands of society increase, the traditional religious systems will fail to provide satisfaction and will cease to function properly. It is in this manner that we must attempt to understand both cultural and social change.

Religion as a System of Symbols

Symbolic thought and behavior are among the most characteristic features of human life. The ability to assign symbolic meanings is uniquely human. Animals can deal only with their immediate environment, but man can transcend his physical surroundings through the principle of symbolization. Human beings do not need physical experience in order to acquire knowledge about something. For example, no presently living individual has met Socrates in person, but through the use of linguistic symbols we have maintained our links with the past. Symbols can refer to things present or absent, past or future, experienced or not directly observed. Concepts such as *love, freedom,* or *duty* have no physical or temporal limits.

Words are the most important symbols, but not the only ones: gestures, objects, actions, and events are also used to express human values. Because symbolic behavior is learned behavior, each culture possesses its own symbolic system. In one culture, respect for the sacred powers may be symbolically expressed by covering one's head; in others by uncovering it. Individuals born into a culture will learn the cultural symbol systems and their meanings. The common understanding of these symbol systems provides avenues for communication and interaction on an abstract level. No matter what its form, a symbol can refer to something beyond experience. And it is this capacity to create symbols that makes it possible for man to think in religious terms.

Religious symbols are not intrinsically different from other cultural symbols. Myths, ritual behavior, and sacred images and objects are symbolic in the same sense in which symbols of status, of political office, or of mourning are symbolic: each is endowed with meaning and communicates common values. Symbols are as vital to religion as they are to culture as a whole. They help to maintain culture and its institutions, and make it possible to pass on its basic values to new generations.

Religion and the Supernatural

So far, religion has been characterized as a cultural system and a social system, but no criteria have yet been provided to differentiate religion from other cultural institutions. One criterion may be found in the fact that religion assumes, and refers to, the existence of powers beyond human power and outside the regular processes of nature. These powers, often conceptualized as beings, are called supernatural or superhuman. Their forms and functions vary, but these higher powers are usually conceived as capable of perception. They are thus believed to be aware of human actions: they "hear" man's words uttered in prayer, "notice" man's ritual observances, "receive" offerings and sacrifice. Thus human actions are believed to be potentially capable of influencing the supernatural, of evoking supernatural responses of some sort. Clearly, then, religious systems depict the relationship between man and the supernatural as a social one. Man's interactions with his gods and spirits are modeled upon human forms of interaction. Like human beings, supernatural powers not only have knowledge of human behavior in the abstract, but they also judge the appropriateness of such conduct. Although evil supernatural spirits are also believed to exist, in general gods are conceptualized as taking an interest in the welfare of human communities. If human behavior receives approval, the supernatural will generally be inclined to maintain human welfare, while deviant and disapproved behavior is subject to punishment. Religion, then, is concerned with the expression of the values of a society, and attempts to safeguard them by endowing them with divine sanctions.

Religion and the Sacred

Another distinctive aspect of religion is that it deals with, or has reference to, the sacred. Émile Durkheim (1961:52), in formulating this distinction, maintained that everywhere man classified things into two opposing categories: the sacred and the profane. The sacred is attended by prohibitions, dispensations, and prescriptions which do not usually apply to the secular elements of culture, while the profane is the everyday world, dealt with in a practical and matter-of-fact manner.

Durkheim's study of religion thus emphasizes human attitudes and behavior. Indeed, most anthropological fieldworkers have reported that people act at times in special ways, motivated by the posited existence of culturally conceived sacred categories. The distinction is thus not spurious, but is quite difficult to handle because almost every form of human behavior can be invested with religious meaning. Religious behavior thus cannot be identified outside its cultural context or its religious setting. Religious attitudes and emotions are not necessarily different from any other secular attitudes and emotions. Prayer is often offered in everyday speech; it becomes religious language only when it is directed to culturally posited supernatural powers. Music, dancing, and singing become sacred when they are performed to communicate with, or please, the gods. Some cultures have distinctive styles of music for religious occasions, but there is nothing in these musical modes to make them intrinsically sacred. Eating and drinking are profane activities which become religious only in a ritual setting. Neither are there any specific religious emotions: awe, reverence, fear, respect, love, and hatred can and do appear both in secular and in religious contexts. Although every culture prescribes certain emotional attitudes as most appropriate in the presence of supernatural entities, no emotion can be said to be uniquely religious.

The criterion of the sacred, then, becomes significant only in its religious setting. It is the supernatural which is sacred, and which evokes certain actions and emotions, but the specific forms which these actions and emotions assume are culturally learned responses.

The Social Functions of Religion

The social functions of religion, like those of any other cultural institution, are its effects within a given society. These effects may be integrative or disruptive, implicit or explicit (see Chap. 12). The functional properties of religion are crucial to an anthropology of religion, for religion is never isolated from other institutions. It has significant influence upon economics, politics, family patterns, technology, and all other important areas of life. This influence is always mutual: these secular institutions, in turn, affect religious forms, values, and beliefs. When a society moves from agriculture to industry, its religion will undergo significant changes, but the religious structure itself will also modify and shape the patterns of urban living.

Cultural institutions thus cannot be fully understood if their mutual functions are not taken into account. Religion is particularly important in this respect, because it codifies and expresses the cultural values of the society as a whole. Any functional analysis of religion therefore involves the study of all cultural institutions. We must ask not only, "What is the function of religion?" but also, "Of which other cultural elements is religion itself a function?"

Religion as a Universal Phenomenon

Systems of belief and action involving the supernatural exist in all known human societies. (Some modern societies attempt to repudiate the supernatural, but it is doubtful that they have repressed religion altogether.) The universality or near-universality of religion suggests that it corresponds to important social and individual needs. It supplies answers to otherwise unanswerable questions; it reinforces social values by divine sanctions; it provides hope and consolation.

Religion as a System of Belief and Action

Early anthropologists tended to concentrate on the belief systems of religion, neglecting its behavioral aspects. Tylor defined religion as "the belief in Spiritual Beings" (1958:II, 8), and many of his followers continued to focus upon the cognitive aspects of religion. Now the situation is almost reversed: studies of religious behavior patterns outnumber by far those dealing with beliefs.

Belief systems and action systems are so intimately related that the one cannot be fully understood without the other. Religious behavior verifies religious belief. If, in a given culture, a ritual is performed for the purpose of inducing rain, there must be a belief in the supernatural control of rainfall and which can be affected by human action. This observation does not necessarily reveal the degrees of individual acceptance of this belief. Belief systems are cultural, but individual acceptance or rejection is social. The interaction between religion as a cultural system and the social behavior of the religious actors poses problems well worth studying, because they highlight the dynamics of religious change and draw attention to the secular functions of religion.

Religion Defined

William James defined religion as "the feelings, acts, and experiences of individual men in their solitude, so far as they apprehend themselves to stand in relation to whatever they may consider the divine" (1961:42).

It should be clear from our previous discussions that this definition reflects a viewpoint entirely different from that of anthropology. James was an experimental psychologist, and to him the individual varieties of people and emotions were more fascinating than their similarities. Anthropology, without denying the importance of religion to "men in their solitude," is more concerned with men in their cultural environment.

Once we have understood that religion is both social and cultural, we may define religion as "a system of actions and interactions based upon culturally shared beliefs in sacred supernatural powers." The definition is descriptive rather than structural, but it contains all that is necessary for an anthropology of religion.

MAGIC AND RELIGION

Anthropological literature abounds in attempts to make meaningful and clear-cut distinctions between magic and religion. None has been fully successful, partly because of the complexity of religious phenomena. Furthermore, nineteenth-century anthropologists, who initiated the discussions, regularly compared "magic" with Western "religion," judging the former as "primitive" and the latter as "civilized." Tylor (1958:I, 133) called magic a "monstrous farrago"; Frazer considered it to be a "pseudo-science"; Durkheim (1961:58) characterized it as "thoroughly antireligious"; and Lévy-Bruhl (1966) saw it as a product of "prelogical mentality." Although modern anthropologists do not support these views, they must contend with the criteria set down by their predecessors (cf. Wax and Wax, 1963, on recent discussions). The definitions have been made sharper and more objective, but there is no unanimity about the results. Radcliffe-Brown (1952:138), noting the lack of agreement, advocated deleting the term *magic* from anthropological language. Nevertheless, the term continues to appear in most textbooks and ethnographies dealing with religious phenomena. Some writers, noting the basic similarities between magic and religion, have sought a compromise in labeling all beliefs and actions related to the supernatural as *magico-religious.* Yet they hesitate to apply the term to Christianity, Judaism, or Buddhism.

Manipulation-Supplication

One of the major distinctions made by nineteenth-century anthropologists between magic and religion was based on the concept of "manipulation" and "supplication." According to this distinction, magic involves the attempt to manipulate the higher powers, while religion relies on supplication. Magic, then, would compel the supernatural to bend to man's wishes, and success is seen as inevitable—provided one knows the right ritual or formula. Religion, on the other hand, assumes that the supernatural powers are free agents that may or may not grant requests. According to Frazer, religion is born of the realization that man himself is powerless. Later scholars, although rejecting Frazer's evolutionary implications, found that some ritual acts are indeed carried out with greater conviction of success than others. They have tended to call the former *manipulative* and thus *magical;* the latter, *supplicative* and thus *religious.*

Utility and Celebration

Malinowski proposed a distinction between magic and religion based on utility. In his detailed studies of the Trobriand Islands, Malinowski noted that Trobriand men sometimes fish in the inner lagoon of the island, and sometimes venture out in the open sea. Because lagoon fishing is not dangerous, no ritual is associated with it. Open-sea fishing, however, because of the danger it involves, is accompanied by an extensive ritual designed to assure safety and success (1954:30–31). Thus the ritual has an immediately useful purpose in the eyes of the people. Religion, on the other hand, is "an end in itself," according to Malinowski, and its rituals "have no purpose to a subsequent event" (*ibid.*:38). Religious rituals are actually statements of fact: they celebrate the birth of a child, mark the passage from childhood to maturity, affirm the bonds of marriage, or mourn the passing of the dead.

Personal and Communal

Durkheim stressed the social circumstances surrounding magic and religion when he stated that magic has no church and no congregation (1961:60). Practitioners of magic carry out their functions on an individual basis, much like a doctor treating patients. The persons "treated" form no lasting bonds among themselves. Religion, on the other hand, is communal, it is not directed at single individuals, but carried out for the benefit of the whole community.

Natural and Social Environment

A number of more modern writers prefer to classify religious behavior on the basis of the goals of ritual behavior. Aberle (1966b:221–30) divided these into those dealing with the natural environment and those dealing with the social environment. Some rituals, which may be termed *magical,* attempt to establish man's control over nature. These include attempts to control the weather, to increase crops or catches of fish, to multiply the herds of wild or domesticated animals, or to attain good health. Other ritual acts, which may be termed *religious,* attempt to overcome social conflicts, to protect codes of behavior, to avoid or resolve power clashes, and so on. In other words, religion is directed toward the attempts to overcome the gap between the existence of social rules and man's inability to abide by them at all times. There is no society in which the moral code is not broken from time to time. Religious ritual, in this view, serves to mend the social disturbances caused by violation of social norms.

CONCLUSIONS

Any attempt to make clear-cut distinctions between magic and religion is bound to fail. Criteria used by various scholars to delineate the supposed realms of magic and religion are not mutually exclusive. Manipulation and supplication, utility and celebration, and individual and communal purposes subtly shade into one another; rituals directed toward coping with nature always include social overtones. No single criterion has been found to define magic as an intrinsically different category of religious behavior.

The criteria can, however, be useful as guidelines for identification of ritual attitudes, motivations, and goals. No two religious systems are identical: each possesses its own ideals, patterns of belief, and concepts of the supernatural. These contrasting elements are manifested in ritual attitudes and their emotional qualities. The mere labeling of certain ritual acts as magical or religious has no purpose in itself, but the recognition of differences in ritual behavior patterns should lead to an investigation of their meanings in their own cultural settings.

2

History of the Study of Religion

IT HAS BECOME CONVENTIONAL TO PLACE THE BEGINNINGS OF THE study of religion in the middle of the nineteenth century, and to name Tylor or Frazer or Max Müller as its founder or originator. Such treatment creates the mistaken impression that this study was of no great concern to scholars before that time. Actually scholars of many different disciplines have observed and analyzed religious phenomena and institutions throughout the entire history of the Western world.

GREEK AND ROMAN SCHOLARS

Apart from the fact that intellectual history is fascinating in itself, an inquiry into the past has several advantages. First, knowledge of older humanistic and scientific traditions provides greater insights into contemporary theories of religion. Second, the various theories of religion which try to explain the practices and beliefs of nonliterate man will give many glimpses of the ever-changing "image of the savage." Finally, the descriptive data have "preserved" many ancient religions which would otherwise have long since been forgotten. It is impossible to make a complete survey of all developments that took place prior to the nineteenth century within this limited space, because the source material is very rich. But it is possible to sketch the major contributions to the field.

Herodotus (c. 484–c. 425 B.C.)

Early evidence of interest in religions of "foreign" peoples is found in the writings of Herodotus. An ardent traveler, this ancient Greek historian visited more than fifty different nations and tribes, and he recorded—often in remarkable detail—many of their habits and customs, both secular and religious.

Herodotus did not travel abroad in order to "prove" the superiority of his native culture and religion, although he wrote: "All men, if asked to choose the best way of ordering life, would choose their own." As a Greek, he felt that his own culture was the best way of ordering life, and he followed the convention of his time by calling all non-Greeks *barbarians*. His works indicate that he often maintained a healthy skepticism: "In the highest tower of Babylon, in the topmost chamber, there is a great couch on which the god himself is reported to sleep. So the priests told me, but I do not believe it." But his treatment of other peoples is not unsympathetic. For example, he praised the Scythians for their piety, temperance, and morality, and he honored the Egyptians—"the most religious people in the world"—for their pyramids, temples and elaborate rituals.

Although Herodotus' writings show a greater concern for recording data than for explaining them, he made a number of contributions to subsequent studies of religion. He established, for instance, the principle of "the equivalence of gods," which later became known as the *Interpretatio Romana*. Using what would now be called *the comparative method,* he showed how gods in different religious systems and with different names and attributes actually had very similar functions. Struck by these similarities, he maintained that such gods could be equated; thus the Egyptian Bupastis is the Greek Artemis, Horus is Apollo, and Osiris is Dionysius (Book II). Those gods for whom he could not find equivalents he considered to be truly barbarian.

Herodotus' canon of the equivalence of gods also led him to note diffusion: he remarks that the Persians had borrowed the worship of Aphrodite from the Assyrian cult of Astarte. He also observed that Babylonian funeral songs so strongly resembled those of the Egyptians that "imitation must have played a role," and that the Abystae had copied the religious practices of the Cyrenians.

Herodotus did not formulate a theory of comparative religion, but he does offer a three-stage theory of historical development: the age of gods, the age of heroes, and the age of men. He does not elaborate this theory however. Nor does he speculate about the origins of the gods or of religion in general. About the Greek gods he has this to say:

> Where the gods come from, whether they always existed, what they looked like, was, so to speak, unknown until yesterday. Homer and Hesiod lived not more than four hundred years ago and it was they who made the gods for the Greeks and gave them their names and shapes. (quoted by Hamilton, 1942:94–95).

Herodotus used many techniques which are still considered important in the study of religion. He was quite objective; he tried to be universal (he traveled through almost the whole known world of his time); and many of his data were empirical. Unfortunately, his good qualities were lost sight of and were not rediscovered until relatively recently.

Euhemerus (c. 330–c. 260 B.C.)

Herodotus only hinted at the human origins of the gods, but the Sicilian philosopher Euhemerus developed this idea into a full-fledged theory. He wrote in his work *Sacred History:*

> With respect to the gods, too, our ancestors believed carelessly, credulously, with untrained simplicity; while worshipping their kings religiously, desiring to look upon them when dead in outward forms, anxious to preserve their memories in statues, these things became sacred.

In other words, he believed that gods were originally human rulers who were gradually deified by their subjects. Myths, in this view, were the glorified accounts of the deeds of these great men and of the events relating to their lives, births, and deaths. This principle of interpretation is now known as *euhemerism* and it has been utilized by later thinkers. In the early Christian era for example, the Church Fathers eagerly applied the principles of euhemerism to all religions except their own. As late as the nineteenth century, Herbert Spencer used euhemerism to account for the origin of religion. According to Spencer, all gods were ancestors, founders of tribes, war chiefs famed for strength and bravery, medicine men of great repute, or inventors. These human beings, regarded with awe and fear during their lifetimes, were feared even more after death, so that the propitiation of their ghosts became necessary and inevitable. Thus, says Spencer, ancestor worship is the root of every religion (1885:I, 411).

From Berossus to Pausanias

After Euhemerus, there developed two basic approaches to the study of religion: the historical and the theoretical-philosophical. The historians recorded the religions which they encountered on their travels or reconstructed older religions on the basis of original documents, often comparing these beliefs and practices with those of their own culture. The theory-oriented scholars investigated the origins and meanings of religious beliefs, and frequently sought these meanings in what would now be called *social functions*.

The Chaldean priest Berossus (c. 280 B.C.) was primarily a historian, although he did not neglect theoretical considerations. He collected Assyrian myths and described Assyrian religious practices, probably on the basis of information derived from inscriptions or other original documents. He also wrote extensively on astrology, thus contributing to the rapid spread of this art.

The Roman scholar Marcus Terentius Varro (116–27 B.C.), is usually called a historian. His book, *Antiquitatus Rerum Divinarium (On the Antiquity of Divine Beings)*, is a storehouse of information about ancient religions. Parts of his work are lost, but fortunately St. Augustine quoted liberally from Varro in his polemics against paganism, so that a fairly complete record exists after all.

Marcus Tullius Cicero (106–43 B.C.), a friend of Varro, was an equally prolific writer. Trained as a lawyer, he was also very active in politics, and he became one of the greatest orators of antiquity. His writings reflect the wide variety of his interests. Well-versed in Roman law, he was particularly interested in its relationship to religion. Laws were, in his view, basically of two types: some were made by men; others were of divine origin. Man-made laws were products of government and based upon convention. They differed from nation to nation, because they had to fit the specific political configurations of the particular society. Divine laws, on the other hand, were eternal and universal, valid everywhere and at all times, even though religious beliefs and practices might differ.

Cicero's best-known books on religion are *De Natura Deorum* (*On the Nature of the Gods*), *De Divinatione* (*On Divination*), and *De Fato* (*On Fate*). In the first, he shows clear insight into the function of religion as a disciplinary, ethical, and integrative force:

> In all probability the disappearance of piety toward the gods will entail the disappearance of loyalty and social union among men as well, and of justice itself, the queen of all virtues. (*De Natura Deorum*, I, 4).

In *De Divinatione*, Cicero criticized and even ridiculed the many divinatory practices of Rome, although he himself was an official augur. His recognition of the abuses and misuses of these practices in his own day made him eager to separate divination from other religious institutions and practices.

Cicero lived in a period during which the public religion had lost much of its authority, and Cicero himself appears to have been a skeptic. Although in a letter to his wife, Terentia, he seriously implored her to offer sacrifice to Apollo and Aesculapius in gratitude for the recovery of his health, it is fairly clear from his writings that religion held very little personal and emotional value for him. He viewed it, rather, as a valuable social institution.

This attitude is reflected in his well-known etymology of the word *religion*, in which he maintains that the Latin word *religio* is derived from *re-ligere*, "to execute painstakingly and by repeated efforts." The later Apologist, Lactantius (c. 260–c. 340), believed the word derived from *re-ligare*, "to bind" or "to hold together." Although there is no certainty about the correctness of either derivation, the latter is the more generally accepted. It was adopted by St. Augustine, and dominated the theological views of the Middle Ages.

Julius Caesar (c. 100–44 B.C.) provides the earliest known descriptions of Germanic and Celtic paganism. The seven books of the *Gallic Wars* were commentaries on Roman military tactics, but they also contained factual information about the customs of the peoples whom he encountered during his campaigns.

The great geographer Strabo (c. 63 B.C.–A.D. 21), in his seventeen-volume work, *The Geography*, provides careful descriptions of Greek and non-Greek tribal religions. He also presents one of the earliest social typologies, distinguishing three basic forms of society: the pastoral-nomadic, the sedentary-agricultural, and the city-state. In contrasting the different types of social structure found in each, he implies that each will develop a set of religious institutions suitable to its specific mode of life.

Several important works have survived from the early Christian era, such as Plutarch's (c. 48–120) *De Iside et Osiride* (*On Isis and Osiris*) and Lucian's (c. 125–c. 150) *De Dea Syria* (*On the Syrian Gods*). Plutarch deals extensively with the Osiris mythology, comparing its different versions. As a Stoic, he was opposed to euhemerism, attributing the origin of the gods to the deification of natural phenomena. Lucian was an exponent of skepticism and moral relativity, but he gave very valuable information about Syrian forms of religion.

An excellent report of a great many different religions is found in the writings of the Greek traveler and historian Pausanias (c. A.D. 150). So detailed and precise were his accounts of gods and deities that medieval sculptors and painters used them as the basis for their work.

CHRISTIAN SCHOLARS

Although most Greek and Roman writers had a fairly objective attitude toward foreign religion (and were often skeptical enough of their own), early Christian writers were convinced that theirs was the only true religion. They relied strongly on euhemerism to prove the falseness of non-Christian religions. Thus Clement of Alexandria (c. 150–c. 215) declared to the infidel: "Those to whom you bow were once men like yourselves." Lactantius (c. 260–c. 340) states triumphantly in his *Divinae Institutiones* that the pagan gods are mortals, deified through the idolatry of their contemporaries. The argument is repeated again and again—in *De Idolorum Vanitate* of St. Cyprian (c. 200–258), in the *De Idolatria* of Tertullian (c. 155–c. 230), in the *Ad-*

versus Nationes of Arnobius (fl. 284–305), and in the *De Civitate Dei* (VII, 18; VIII, 26) of St. Augustine (354–430). Eusebius (c. 263–c. 339) explains in his *Ecclesiastical History* that the Babylonian god Baal was in reality the first king of the Assyrians, who lived at the time of the war between the Giants and the Titans (quoted by Seznec, 1961:12–14).

Ironically, these lengthy denunciations helped to preserve knowledge about many ancient religions. St. Augustine, for example, is a major source of information about many aspects of Greek, Roman, and Persian religion—especially because many of the original works which he so liberally quotes have since been lost.

In the sixth and seventh centuries, the euhemeristic tradition begins to lose much of its polemic venom. Instead, it came to be used to unravel the past, including ancient myths and legends, in order to reconstruct Christian history. Thus, Isidore of Seville (c. 560–636), in the *Etymologiae,* attempts to place all pagan gods (on the principle that they once were men) in one of six periods of world history: from the Creation to the Flood, from the Flood to Abraham, from Abraham to David, from David to the Babylonian Captivity, from the Captivity to the Birth of Christ, and from the Nativity onward. Isidore's erudition enriches this scheme with a wealth of detail concerning the religions of Egypt, Assyria, Greece, and Rome. Drawing on Varro and on many other sources, he reconstructed dynasties, singled out leaders and pioneers, slayers of monsters, founders of cities, and discoverers and innovators. As a result, the pagan gods were restored to dignity: as benefactors of humanity, they had the right to be gratefully remembered. They could be ranked together with the patriarchs, judges, and prophets of the Biblical tradition even if they were of a different lineage (Seznec, 1961:14–15).

St. Ado of Vienne (799–874) is one of many who carried on the work of Isidore. In his *Chronicle of the Six Ages of the World,* he refers to Moses and the Greek and Roman gods in one breath:

> In those days [*i.e.,* of Moses], it is said, lived Prometheus, who is believed to have fashioned men out of clay; his brother, Atlas, living at the same time, was regarded as a great astrologer; the grandson of Atlas, Mercury, was a sage skilled in several arts. For this reason, the vain error of his

contemporaries placed him after his death among the gods (quoted by Seznec, 1961:15).

Several centuries later, Peter Comestor (fl. 1148–78), dean of the church of Notre Dame at Troyes, and later chancellor of Notre Dame at Paris, was still writing in the same tradition. In his *Historia Scholastica* (c. 1160), he equates many non-Christian and Biblical personages, recognizing in each category men of superior stature, wisdom, and knowledge: Zoroaster invented magic and inscribed the Seven Arts on four columns, Isis taught the art of writing to the Egyptians, Minerva taught weaving, and Prometheus instructed the ignorant. Surely they are as worthy of veneration as are the patriarchs and prophets.

Friar John and Friar William

The Biblical command to preach the Gospel to all nations gave rise to missionary activity early in the Christian era. Missionaries were sent not only to European countries, but also to parts of Mesopotamia, Arabia, Armenia, India, and Africa. It soon became clear that the missionaries' work could be facilitated by a knowledge of the cultures, and particularly of the religions, of the peoples they were trying to convert. The attempt to meet this need produced a number of quite accurate descriptions, among them those of two Franciscan friars, Carpini and Rubruquis.

Giovanni de Plano Carpini (c. 1182–1252), better known as "Friar John," was sent out as a missionary to the Mongols, but one of his main tasks was to write a first-hand account of Asiatic cultures. His *Historia Mongolorum* (1247) describes the physical appearance, the economy, the political organization, and the laws of the peoples among whom he worked, and contains detailed information about their "superstitious traditions."

Several years later (c. 1253) William de Rubruquis (or Rubrouck), generally known as "Friar William" (c. 1215–c. 1270), was sent on a similar mission. He was even more informative than his predecessors. In his *Itinerarium* (c. 1256), he makes many comparisons between "idolatrous" practices and Christian ritual: he saw the "pagans" carrying strings of beads, much like rosaries, "altars" with winged images resembling the archangel Michael, priests in sacerdotal vestments who offered oblations of bread and fruit to the people, and so on. Also, his descriptions of burial rites are very detailed and probably quite correct.

Other missionaries who furnished written reports include Ricoldo da Monte Croce (1243–1320), Ordorico da Pordenone (1286–1331), Giordano Catalani (fl. 1330), and many others (Slotkin, 1965b: 8). Together they provided much valuable information on religious practices in Asia and other parts of the world.

Marco Polo (c. 1254–c. 1323)

Another source of ethnographic information is found in the writings of traders and travelers of the period. Although they were not, like the missionaries, obliged to tell the truth, some were rather factual and objective. Marco Polo, for one, wrote well, and his reports appear to be relatively truthful. Although most interested in the trading conditions, the natural resources, the value of currency, and the products of the countries he visited he also provides accounts of religious customs in China, Japan, Siberia, India, Burma, and many other countries which were relatively unknown in the Europe of his time.

It may be mentioned at this point that Asian scholars, too, studied the religions of Asia. The Chinese descriptions of Indian religions made by Buddhistic pilgrims such as Fah-hien (fifth century) and Hiuen-Tsiang (seventh century) are among the earliest known accounts.

Somewhat later, Arabian historians and geographers began to roam the Asian continent to collect data of an ethnographic nature. Although primarily interested in forms of Buddhism, Brahmanism, and Manichaeism, they also gathered data about tribal religions. Some of the better known of these Arabian travelers are Tabari (838–923), Ma'sudi (d. 956), and Albiruni (973–1050).

Perhaps the first systematic comparative history of religion was produced by the Moslem scholar Shahrastani (d. 1153). After comparing "all known religions" (but not including tribal religions), he set up a fourfold typology: Islam; literary religions (Judaism); quasi-literary religions (Zoroastrianism and Manichaeism); and philosophical and "self-willed" religions (Buddhism and Hinduism).

Roger Bacon (c. 1214–1294)

Though Bacon was a contemporary of the Friars and of Marco Polo, he lived in an entirely different intellectual milieu. Born in England, he studied at the University of Oxford and of Paris, later teaching at Oxford. His publications include books on astrology, alchemy, geography, optics, comparative philology, mathematics, and the nature and utility of science. His was indeed a more scientific mind, and, like his later namesake, Francis Bacon (1561–1626), he emphasized observation and experimentation rather than reliance upon the writings of the ancient Greeks.

Roger Bacon applied his "scientific method" to the study of religion. Rather than attempting historical reconstructions, he was the first European scholar to write a comparative history of religion, and, like his predecessor Shahrastani, he sets up a typology which is meant to cover all religions of the world: pagans (those who worship objects in nature and natural phenomena); idol-worshippers (polytheists and Buddhists); Mongols, who combine monotheism with magic and fire worship; Saracens (Moslems); and Jews.

Bacon's objectivity toward religion is noteworthy. Confronted with many different forms of religion, he asks himself what the criteria of "true" religion might be. He does not rely upon the authority of the Church for his answer, but applies the democratic principle of consensus. During Bacon's lifetime, the Mongolian emperor Mangu Khan (1207–1259) had called a religious council, at which Mongolians, Moslems, Jews, and Christians had come to the unanimous conclusion that monotheism was the right form of religion. Although Bacon undoubtedly believed that Christianity was more correct than the others, he was willing to consider that non-Christian religions might also be valid in their own right.

The purpose of Mangu Khan's council was more political than religious: he was eager to establish a degree of agreement among his subjects. Akbar of Hindustan (1542–1605) called an even larger religious council, in a similar effort to unify the many different sects in his large domain. Bacon's writings, and the efforts toward unification, are new phenomena in the development of the study of religion because they betoken a relative absence of hostility which opened the way to greater objectivity.

THE RENAISSANCE AND THE ENLIGHTENMENT

Giovanni Boccaccio (1313–75) provides a link between the Middle Ages and the Renaissance with his *Genealogy of the Gods* (c. 1360). This work, which was not dissimilar to Frazer's *Golden Bough,* both in scope and in method, was an attempt to systematize the whole known classical mythology. Reprinted at least a dozen times during the next century, this work attracted much public attention. New compendiums by such writers as Buccardo, Stamler, Pictorius, Comes, Batman, Cartari, and many others were often expanded to include Oriental gods, as well as Celtic, Germanic, and other "savage" deities. Cartari (c. 1520–c. 1570), in his *Images of the Gods of Antiquity* (1556), even added a few examples of the "barbarous and butcherly" religions of recently discovered South American Indians.

Boccaccio's *Genealogy* has been severely criticized by later scholars for its uncritical use of sources and for its plagiarism (Seznec, 1961:221). Nevertheless, it foreshadowed the more rationalistic treatments of religion of future centuries.

Lord Herbert of Cherbury (1583–1648)

Clearly then, the interest in comparative religion did not begin with the writings of Lord Herbert of Cherbury, as is so often maintained (*cf.* Bouquet, 1941:17; and Slotkin, 1965b:xiv, 143). Nevertheless, Lord Herbert is important as an example of the critical spirit of his times. Scientific advances in astronomy and physics had made it necessary to modify the conception of God, who could no longer be visualized as a mere Creator. The complexity of nature and of the cosmos made sixteenth- and seventeenth-century scholars aware that there must be a law of the universe to keep it operating. God became a law-giving being, a view more suitable to the requirements of the Newtonian cosmic perspective. Moreover, God's functions in the Universe were now considered to be beneficial, not only for certain select groups, but for all peoples at all places and at all times. Lord Herbert was one of the first rationalists to state systematically the principles of this deistic form of religion. Basic to his theories were the related ideas of "natural instinct" and "common notion." He explains: ". . . natural instincts are expressions of those faculties which are found in every normal man, through which the Common Notions touching the internal conformity of things . . . are brought into conformity independently of discursive thought" (1624:52–53). Religion must thus be a common notion, because it is found in all periods and all nations. If a comparison of religions reveals certain principles common to all of them, these must be the principles of the true religion.

Herbert deduces five "undeniable" principles of religion that all mankind must acknowledge. They are

1. There is one divine Numen (or a supreme God).
2. This Numen must be worshipped.
3. Virtue, piety (or the promotion of better living), is the chief end of worship.
4. Better living must be preceded by the repentance of sins.
5. The Divine Goodness rewards and punishes both in this life and after it in accordance with a person's daily behavior here on earth.

Herbert's theories are significant in the history of the study of religion because, from his time onward, this study became gradually more scientific and more objective. Rationalists in general were willing to grant reason to people of all times and ages, including early and nonliterate men.

Thomas Hobbes (1588–1679)

Nevertheless, religion remained a sensitive point, and only skeptics dared to treat it as a more or less neutral datum. The British philosopher, Thomas Hobbes, was such a skeptic, but he was less concerned with religion than with the development of the state and of society. Nevertheless, he constructed a theory of the origin of religion, using psychological criteria. Religion, according to Hobbes' analysis, is not related to a primary drive such as the need for sex, sleep, nourishment, and elimination. Yet, it is a very powerful drive since it is rooted in fear. In Hobbes' estimation, early man was wise enough to know that everything has a cause, but he did not always know the cause. More specifically, early man was ignorant about the cause of illness, death, and the other calamities that befell him. Because fear and anxiety increase when their causes are unknown, man attempts to fix them on something. Gradually, he invents invisible powers. This is the inception of religion, "which, by reason of the different fancies, judgments, and passions of several men, hath grown up into ceremonies so different, that those which are used by one man, are for the most part ridiculous to another" (1955, Chap. 12).

The theory that religion springs from human fears was not new: it had already been stated by Lucretius (c. 99–55 B.C.) in his *De Rerum Natura* (*On the Nature of Things*) and by Petronius (c. A.D. 66) in the *Satyricon*. But speculations about the origin of religion were virtually absent in the Christian era up until this time because religion was considered to be revealed truth. Coupled to the belief that all men descended from Adam, all but Judeo-Christian religions were, at best, corruptions of the "original" truth. Hobbes called into question the ultimate truth of any and all religious doctrines, and declared that no revelation is capable of proof.

Hobbes was also one of the first to use ethnographic data to bolster scientific theory. Available information on nonliterate peoples had hitherto been used in a variety of ways, most often in comparison with European cultures. In these treatments, the nonliterates were denounced as "barbaric" and "inferior," or evaluated on their comparative merits, or used to illustrate the nobility of the ancient mind. But the descriptions were not used as a body of empirical knowledge which could help to demonstrate or uphold some general scientific argument. Hobbes is by no means accurate in his employment of ethnographic data, but that is another matter.

Bernard le Bouvier de Fontenelle (1657–1757)

Deism, rationalism, and skepticism tended to create an intellectual climate responsive to cultural relativism. The "natural" religion of the deists denied revelation and based religion in general upon "universally valid" criteria; rationalism saw man as a reasonable being, so that religion might thus well be a reasonable human invention; skepticism denied the primacy of Christianity over other religions.

But this trend was intercepted by the ideology of progress, which found its early expression in the writings of Fontenelle, and which held the intellectual mind spellbound until the beginning of the twentieth century. A belief in limitless progress implies that early cultures are, by definition, less advanced than later cultures. Recorded history, however, could not provide sufficient proof of this theory, for it begins with the literate cultures of Sumer, Egypt, and Greece. Contemporary nonliterate tribes seemed to represent a close approximation of prehistoric man. It was then that the unfortunate equation of contemporary nonliterates with early man was born, and became almost axiomatic.

Fontenelle may be said to have formulated the first systematic theory of progress. In his *Digression on the Ancients and the Moderns* (1688), he formulated two fundamental principles: (1) that men were relatively equal in their mental capacities and, because natural processes had not changed, the minds of men must have remained of similar quality; (2) that progress in the fields of science and technology is cumulative and, since experience also increases, progress is endless and the latest men of science must be the most competent.

Fontenelle did not explicitly apply his theory of progress to religion. In his *History of Oracles* (1687), he deals mainly with Greece, and his main argument here is similar to that of Hobbes: Greek religion was not the work of the devil, but had become what it was through sacerdotal imposture. He was also quite interested in mythology, and compared ancient Greek mythology with the myths and legends of nonliterate peoples. He denied that these legends were corrupt versions of Biblical accounts, and saw them instead as products of human fantasy. As such, they could reveal important facts about human nature, and their similarities became understandable because human nature is basically the same everywhere. Fontenelle thus brought his myth analysis in line with his theory about the equality of human minds.

Giambattista Vico (1668–1744)

Vico was a contemporary of Fontenelle, but, although Vico's influence was greater and more enduring, he was scarcely known in his own day. His monumental work, the *New Science* (1725), was a synthesis of many older theories. The "new science" may be summed up as the secularization of human history, including the history of human religion. It has been said (Löwith, 1949:

115–16) that Vico himself was hardly aware of the revolutionary implications of his writings, and his contemporaries certainly were not. He was far ahead of his time, anticipating the social theories of Hegel, Comte, Marx, de Coulanges, and Müller.

The basic theme of the *New Science* is that the world of civic society was made and molded by men, not by God. Vico reserves a place for God in his scheme by saying that everything man did was, in the final analysis, under Divine Providence, but he made it clear that the study of man's history is not an inquiry into this Divine Providence but the subject matter of science. According to Vico, this new science could, through diligent research, discover and reconstruct man's total social and religious history and trace it back to its beginnings.

The changes which are forever taking place in human history are man-made changes, Vico believed, and the differences among contemporary social and religious systems are not willed by God but caused by the changing mind and will of man himself. There is neither absolute progress nor absolute degeneration in Vico's theory. A certain regularity is demonstrated in the law of oscillation, of *corso* and *ricorso,* "flux" and "reflux," or what Hegel later called a process of dialectics. This process gives rise to three successive ages in the development of human history: that of the gods, that of heroes, and that of men. Vico admittedly borrowed these stages from Herodotus, but Herodotus' scheme included prehuman history, with no explanation of how the changes could have taken place. Vico's scheme begins with human history, and all changes are caused and conditioned by human forces.

The divine stage marks the beginning of human society; this period gave rise to language, the family, the burial of the dead, and religion. These were the primary social institutions from which all others were eventually derived. Family patterns, for example, led to a patriarchal form of government, which had already begun to evolve in the divine stage.

Like many of his contemporaries, Vico is very interested in the origin of religion, and he describes it thus:

> . . . at last the sky fearfully rolled with thunder and flashed with lightning, as could not but follow from the bursting upon the air for the first time of an impression so violent.

Thereupon a few giants, who must have been the most ro-
bust, and who were dispersed through the forests on the
mountain heights where the strongest beasts have their
dens, were frightened and astonished by the great effect
whose cause they did not know, and raised their eyes and
became aware of the sky. And because in such a case the
nature of the human mind leads it to attribute its own
nature to the effect . . . they pictured the sky to themselves
as a great animated body, which in that aspect they called
Jove, the first god of the so-called greater gentes, who meant
to tell them something by the hiss of his bolts and the clap
of his thunder. And thus they began to exercize that natural
curiosity which is the daughter of ignorance and the mother
of knowledge, and which, opening the mind of man, gives
birth to wonder . . . (1961:75–76)

The second age, that of the heroes, came into existence when
patriarchal rulers began to extend their powers over other
groups. This effort gave rise to political and social inequalities,
class struggles, and constant warfare. Finally, mythical language,
predominant in the divine stage, now became metaphorical.

In the last stage, that of man, an alphabet is developed, and
language becomes positive and more precise. In this period, too,
myths fade away, and religion acquires the function of upholding
the moral principles of society. Simultaneously, religion is subjected to the pressure of growing skepticism, and is eventually
replaced by philosophy.

But the human age has no permanency. Its refinements lead to
the corruption of the wealthy and the envy of the poor. In Vico's
scheme, these discords among the classes are either resolved by a
strong ruler or obliterated by a barbarian conquest made possible
by this internal dissension. If the latter comes to pass, the refinements of the human age deteriorate rapidly, and the cycle begins
anew. Not all the accomplishments of the previous cycles are
lost, however, for the memory of basic inventions and primary
institutions does endure. Thus, although the cycle begins anew,
there is a form of progress—which would not be shown in a
straight line but as a spiral (cf. Bury, 1955:67–68).

Vico's attempts to reconstruct the earlier phases of human
history, and particularly of religion, took into account the po-

tentialities of language and myth. Thoroughly familiar with
Greek and Latin, he believed that these languages, like the
"vulgar tongues" of European peasants, had been developed
in the heroic or divine stages, and that they therefore could
furnish evidence of what the past had been like. Myths, too, he
considered an important source of knowledge: they reflected the
civil histories of the first nations, and represented the political
struggles of the early societies. (In his application of etymology,
Vico anticipates Max Müller; in his myth analysis, he harks back
to Euhemerus.)

The significance of Vico's work certainly does not rest upon
his often fanciful reconstructions. Neither was his method entirely new: it had already been applied in the fields of mathematics, physics, biology, and medicine. But Vico's ambition was
to create a science of human society, and he correctly noted that
such a study could not be scientific as long as it was based upon
the theological concept of "God's will." Social science, as Vico
envisaged it, should be a history of form and order, universal and
eternal, bound by a chain of causes. These causes were to be
found in men.

Vico, as a practicing Catholic, had to overcome one objection:
according to the Judeo-Christian view of history, the basic secular and sacred institutions were established by God. Vico meets
this objection by excluding the Hebrew-Christian tradition and
its institutions from the range within which the "new science"
could claim competence.

Joseph François Lafitau (1681–1746)

The growing conviction that progress was a permanent characteristic of the human process intensified the pejorative context
in which nonliterate peoples were viewed. Religious institutions
constituted an important cultural standard. However, it was soon
realized that Europe itself had had non-Christian beginnings,
and there was evidence that some rude peasants had not yet done
away with their idols and magic. Alexander Ross (1591–1654),
for instance, wrote that ancient Europeans had possessed the
same idolatrous form of religion as contemporary barbarians and
savages, and that this idolatry "was yet professed in Lapland,
Finland, and in parts of Norway and Lithuania" (1653).

Adherents of this position observed that the ancient Greeks had also been pagans, and concluded that they must have been far behind modern men in cultural as well as in religious development. One of the deeper issues involved was that of progress versus degeneration: if the ancients had indeed been as illustrious as Renaissance scholars had depicted them, it became almost impossible to argue in favor of progress.

It soon became popular to equate European peasants with Greeks, Romans, Egyptians, and Chinese, and all of these in turn, with Africans, American Indians, and other pagan savage peoples, wherever they were found. In 1700, Père Noël Alexandre wrote on the similarities between Chinese ceremonies and Greek and Roman idolatry. In 1704, M. de la Créquinière pointed out parallels between the customs of the Indians and those of the Jews and other ancient peoples. Twenty years later, Lafitau's influential *Moeurs des Sauvages Amériquains Comparées aux Moeurs des Premiers Temps* (1724) appeared. This is perhaps the most famous book of this type, and it was more profusely and authoritatively documented than any of its predecessors. Dissatisfied with the fragmentary reports provided by casual observers and travelers, Lafitau, who had worked many years as a missionary among the Iroquois Indians, declared:

> I was not content with knowing the nature of the savages and with learning of their customs and practices. I sought to find in these practices and customs vestiges of the most remote antiquity. I have read carefully those earliest authors who have dealt with the customs, laws, and usages of the peoples with whom they had some acquaintance. I have compared these customs, one with another, and I confess that while the ancient authors have given me support for several happy conjectures concerning the savages, the customs of the savages themselves have thrown much more light on the ancient authors (cited by Hodgen, 1964:348).

This was the common method: the investigator compared isolated fragments of culture, stressed similarities, overlooked differences, and concluded that the existence of certain parallels was proof of identical origins.

Lafitau shows that the religion of the Iroquois (and, by implication, that of all savages) was very much the same as the religion of the Greeks (and, by implication, that of all ancients). The American Indians deified everything in nature that was beyond their feeble powers of comprehension; and the Greek gods were also only nature gods. Many rites and practices of the two types of culture are cited in order to demonstrate the "striking resemblances" and "close correspondences" between them.

Although Lafitau's main interest was religion, he also studied other cultural institutions in order to bolster his argument. The comparison of cultural traits other than the religious gave great credibility to Lafitau's theory, and he was widely quoted in his own time as well as in the following century. His arguments were made even more convincing by the addition of carefully drawn illustrations showing the similarities between the religious symbols of American Indians and those of the ancient Greeks and Romans, between the canoes of the Eskimoes and the boats engraved upon Egyptian monuments, and so on.

The conclusion that all pagan cultures are nearly identical, and inherently different from Christian civilizations, could neither contribute to understanding of the nature of culture nor assist in a reconstruction of human history. Nevertheless, the realization that cultural and religious similarities do exist was important for later developments in comparative religion.

François Marie Arouet de Voltaire (1694–1778) and David Hume (1711–76)

Vico explicitly excepted Judaism and Christianity from secular interpretations; Lafitau took it for granted that his own religion was intrinsically different from paganism. No such restrictions were made by the scholars of the early eighteenth century. This was a period in which conscious efforts were made to secularize every aspect of human life and thought; in a sense, it marked an organized revolt against religion, which was considered an unfortunate vestige of earlier, less enlightened ages.

This was a condemnation of early man—and thus also of contemporary nonliterates—even stronger than that implied by the ideology of progress. The theory of progress merely contended that, in earlier stages of human development, technology was still in its infancy and social institutions more primitive. Most rationalists acknowledged, however, that the important inventions—language, family, political organization, religion—had been made in prehistoric times; early man was thus considered to possess the same reasoning power as modern man, though much less experience. Eighteenth-century scholars stripped early man of his faculty for logical thinking, and claimed that religion had come into existence through the irrationality of early man's thought processes.

The French philosopher Voltaire regarded himself as the leader of the crusade against religion. Yet Voltaire also considered religion to be necessary for the nonenlightened common man, who (he believed) would otherwise be incapable of moral behavior. Voltaire was not very much interested in nonliterate peoples, and his discussion of history in the *Essay on the Manners and Spirit of Nations* (1756) begins with China.

David Hume presents a full-fledged theory about the origin of religion and the development of monotheism. Hume's opposition to religion was as sharp as Voltaire's, although he denied being an atheist. The title of his essay *The Natural History of Religion* (1757) implied that there was a natural history of religion, just as there was a natural history of flora and fauna. Religion could be analyzed as an aspect of human nature, and the scientific principles of observation and generalization could be applied to religion as to physics, biology, and medicine. Hume was indifferent to the traditional adaptations of sacred history, and did not exclude any form of religion from his considerations.

He begins with an investigation of origins. Hume denies that early man had an innate sense of religion, for such a hypothesis assumes a form of divine revelation. Neither was religion born of reason, for even if prehistoric man were capable of reason, he had neither the leisure nor the necessary knowledge to develop it. Man was at first a "barbarous, necessitous animal," so pressured by needs and desires that he has no curiosity about natural phenomena. It is in these needs that the origins of religious beliefs lie—"the anxious concern for happiness, the dread of future misery, the terror of death, the thirst for revenge, the appetite for food and other necessaries" (1964:39). Gods, according to Hume, were originally created and evoked in connection with specific events of life, and, as a result, early man had many gods. Early man could only react to immediate, real experiences, and he sought direct, immediate answers. Storms, sickness, birth, death—each was explained by assigning its cause to a separate, imaginary being.

Gods are creations of human fears arising from the necessity of human emotions. The early gods themselves were imperfect: each had very limited jurisdiction. Nature itself was viewed as being full of contradictions:

> Storms and tempests ruin what is nourished by the sun. The sun destroys what is fostered by dews and rain. War may be favorable to a nation whom the inclemency of the seasons afflicts with famine. Sickness and pestilence may depopulate a kingdom, amidst the most profuse plenty. . . . (1964:30)

When each of these contradictory events is believed to be the work of a particular supernatural power, religion itself becomes contradictory, inconsistent, confused, and irrational.

In Hume's view, man's progress toward monotheism was born, not of reason, but of statistical necessity. Each generation of man added gods to the pantheon, until the number reached infinity. All gods then become amalgamated into one. Polytheism and monotheism were thus both based upon false world views, both unacceptable to the philosopher.

It is curious that Hume nevertheless denied being an atheist. Yet the monotheistic God he described in the *Natural History* was not Hume's concept but that of the overwhelming majority of common people. Hume looks objectively at the religious behavior and beliefs of the masses, viewing them as a reality of conduct rather than as an approach to truth. By doing so, he separates theology from "natural history," and although he does not deny the existence of God, he does not find in "natural history" any scientific evidence for or against this idea.

Charles de Brosses (1709–77)

Charles de Brosses, a friend of Hume and an enemy of Voltaire, was neither a creative genius nor an original thinker. He would scarcely be remembered at all, were it not for his book *Du culte des dieux fétiches, ou, parallèle de l'ancienne religion de l'Egypte avec la religion actuelle de Nigritie* (1760). In this work, he introduced the term *fetishism* into the languages of Europe, thereby influencing among others, Saint-Simon, Marx,

Comte, and Tylor. The latter even calls him "a most original thinker" (1958:II, 230). His "originality" consisted of substituting the word *fetishism* for Hume's *polytheism* in an otherwise almost literal translation of Hume's theory of the origin of religion. The remainder of de Brosses' work, however, is different. Where Hume focused upon Greek and Roman polytheism, de Brosses used Egyptian animal worship as his type case. These animals were, in de Brosses' term *fetishes*. Fetishism was a form of religion involving the worship of objects, animate or inanimate. These objects had been made sacred by early man, so that fetishism was both the earliest form of religion and the most nearly universal. A profusion of fetish objects existed even in Biblical times: Abraham had a sacred grove; Jacob anointed a sacred stone at Beth-el; and Moses erected a fiery serpent of brass upon a pole. De Brosses conjectured that even the Holy Cross might be of fetishist origin. Thus de Brosses' contribution to the study of religion was the realization that Judaism and Christianity possess elements of other religions and are, in this sense, syncretistic.

Johann Gottfried Herder (1744–1803)

Johann Gottfried Herder—philosopher, poet, and critic—passionately opposed the cool rationalism of the eighteenth century. He believed that the origin and development of religion was a matter of culture or of society—what he called the *Volk*. Each *Volk* had enacted a unique version of the religious drama, because external factors were different everywhere. These factors did not merely consist of "climate," or physical environment, but each nation had its own complex of psychic forces, its own *Geist*. Although this elusive German term can be rendered in English as *spirit* or *genius,* Herder was actually suggesting something which we would now call *national character*—the specific organizing powers of culture. Neither did Herder discount diffusion or migration, for both demanded adaptation to a changed environment, an adaptation possible only if the *Geist* of the people were brought into harmony with their environment.

Herder is remarkably free from ethnocentricity. As a true romanticist, he values the past, and sets out to discover the special values of early cultures. He believes that every *Volk* perceived the beauty of nature and the goodness of its powers somewhat differently, but that all religion was a total creation, not a partial one.

Herder did not view Egyptian animal worship as repulsive. He observed that the early Egyptians lived in such proximity to their beasts that it was not astonishing that they should make them sacred. City dwellers, he maintained, cannot understand the relationship between man and beast, and do not know that they are "brothers who understand each other, who teach each other and live together as equals" (1883:370). To Herder, then, the gods were spontaneous emanations of social reality and physical environment.

THE NINETEENTH CENTURY

Auguste Comte (1798–1857)

Comte is often credited with creating the concept of sociology (*cf.* Parsons, 1961:645), although all the fundamental ideas of his system can be found in the writings of Saint–Simon (1760–1825). The latter had insisted that the study of societies should be the subject matter of a separate science; Comte named this science *sociology*. But he was not satisfied with stating the need for such a discipline; he set out to create it.

In Comte's view, sociology could be scientific because societies were, in many respects, similar to biological organisms, except that biological organisms are essentially immutable while societies are capable of immense improvements. The governing principle of social progress was to be found in Comte's famous "law of the three stages of intellectual advance." The first stage is theological; the second, metaphysical; the third, scientific or positivistic.

Religion, according to Comte, could not form a stable and permanent part of society; it would eventually be replaced by science. Every society, however, had to pass through the first two stages in order to reach the third.

During the theological stage, several forms of religion developed. The first was fetishism, characterized by concern for, and worship of, familiar objects. As man began to cast his glance to farther objects, there developed the worship of the stars (astrolatry). This form of worship demanded the presence of a priest, skilled in the interpretation of the different constellations. The deification of multiple stars was but a step toward polytheism, the third form of religion.

Although Comte characterized fetishism as "a feeble instrument of civilization" (1896:II, 549), he nevertheless was convinced of its importance in the development and progress of society in the theological stage. Fetishism, because it endowed the whole universe with life, favored the expansion of imagination and gave rise to poetry and art. It established the permanent use of clothing, "one of the chief marks of nascent civilization." Through its system of taboo, it effected the first consolidation of territorial property. Fetishism also provided the basis for social discipline and ethics, gave rise to the early form of the state, inspired law, and finally brought about "the institution of agricultural life, without which no further human progress would have been possible." (*ibid.*: 545–64). Comte stressed that fetishism involved the worship of those objects which were nearest and most common—and what is nearer to man than his native soil? Driven by the desire to remain near his domestic gods then, man invented a method of subsistence which enabled him to lead a sedentary life.

According to Comte, the theological stage extended to the end of the Middle Ages, when it finally gave way to the metaphysical stage, which corresponded to the "Western revolution." In this period, women became more influential, industrial improvements took place, the state developed while the church decayed, art flourished, and law was adapted to the needs of the time. Metaphysicians replaced the invisible divinities of the theologians with a "logos" or "reason" as determinants of the world order, but they, too, hindered progress by their many controversies. The "positive" stage is finally reached when science is recognized as the only source of genuine knowledge.

In his later years, Comte regarded his own philosophy as providing a basis for a new "religion of humanity," suitable to the mentality of men in the age of science. In the last years of his life, when he displayed a degree of emotional disturbance, he considered himself to be a veritable prophet, and the high priest of his new religion.

Hegel, Creuzer, and Schelling

The literary movement known as Romanticism was characterized by an interest in, and glorification of, the past. Many writers
of the late eighteenth century felt that civilization had corrupted
man, that his original benevolence was to be found only among
simple peasants and nonliterate peoples, who lived close to nature
and were still untainted by the evils of civilization. To some
authors, they became "noble savages," happy and innocent children of nature, with an innate sense for the poetic and the
mystic.

Debates about their religions were, for a time, out of fashion.
Students of religion either philosophized about religion in general, without specific reference to the beliefs of nonliterates, or
concentrated on mythology.

George Friedrich Wilhelm Hegel (1770–1831) provides an important example of the philosophical attitude. Religion, to
Hegel, is a historical manifestation, and its growth and development represent a logical process. In analyzing this historical process, he sets up a scale to show how the unfolding of religion
correlates with that of the human spirit.

He places nature religions at the beginning of the scale,
because he considers them spontaneous realizations of the religious idea. Religions of spiritual individuality, according to Hegel,
begin to develop when conscious thought starts to take control
over natural emotions. Several forms of religion may be distinguished within this type. One is the religion of majesty, in which
the thinking mind is overwhelmed by the contemplation of the
manifestation of the Divine. Another is the religion of beauty
which combines the religions of the natural and the spiritual.
A third form appears when the idea of religion, now fully conscious and determined by human thought, comes to include the
recognition of the purposes served by the powers of nature and
by the supernatural powers or gods themselves.

Both Schelling and Creuzer focus their attention mainly upon
mythology. Friedrich Wilhelm Joseph von Schelling (1775–
1854) differs from Hegel in that he recognizes only two forms of
religion: mythology and revelation. In his scheme, mythology
represents the mental world; revelation, the practical. He is much
more interested in the mental world of mythology, and sees it as

a reflection of the evolution of human nature. His aim was not to resolve the logical contradictions. In his own words, he wanted "to do justice to the subject, not to level it down, simplify or garble it, just to make it easier" (1957:136). Simplify he did not: his arguments are ponderous and perplexing. His importance in the study of mythology rests in his attempts to adjust his own philosophy and outlook, rather than the myths themselves in a vain effort to make them conform to current systems of belief.

George Friedrich Creuzer (1771–1858) is an exponent of the changed view of nonliterate man. The philosophers of the Enlightenment had explained the origin of religion as an error which had arisen from the uncritical and infantile mind of early man. Creuzer, however, explained the origin of mythology as early man's *Urweisheit,* or primeval wisdom (1816–22).

CONCLUSION

This review of some of the more important scholars of religion who wrote before the rise of anthropology as an independent discipline reveals that there is no dominant trend in their writings. Romanticism did give rise to a more positive attitude toward nonliterate peoples, but this trend was to be reversed once more with the writings of early anthropologists.

3

The Science of
Religion

IT HAS BEEN SEEN THAT INTEREST IN HISTORICAL AND COMPARATIVE religion reaches back at least as far as the fifth century B.C. The science of religion (*Religionswissenschaft*), however, did not become an independent discipline until the latter half of the nineteenth century. The term appeared first almost casually in the writings of some German authors, but it was Max Müller who first used it in a stricter sense, because he felt that the science of religion should be modeled after the science of language:

> During the last fifty years the accumulation of new and authentic material for the study of the religions of the world has been most extraordinary; but such are the difficulties in mastering these materials that I doubt whether the time has yet come for attempting to trace, after the model of the Science of language, the definite outlines of the Science of Religion (1872:xi).

But the time *was* ripe. In 1873 Geneva established the first academic Chair of Religion in Europe; three years later the Netherlands established four; in 1879 the Collège de France at Paris endowed one; and in 1885 the Sorbonne founded the first independent Faculty of Religion. In the early part of the twentieth century, courses of study in religon (as distinguished from theology) were offered at nearly every important university in Europe. In 1888, M. Vernes began to publish the *Revue de l'histoire des religions;* in 1898 the *Archiv für Religionswissenschaft* first appeared; and a number of other periodicals dealing exclusively with the study of religion came out soon afterward. The first international congress devoted to the findings of the science of religion took place in Stockholm in 1897, and such meetings, both national and international, became regular events thereafter.

The new discipline had three basic aims: to analyze the common elements among different religions and myths; to study the development or evolution of religion; and to discover the origin of religion.

It was particularly the last point that fired the enthusiasm and also the imagination of many nineteenth-century scholars. Many of their methods, neither new nor original, would now be considered unscientific. They were given to wild speculation and implicit ethnocentrism, and also tended to jump from hypothesis to conclusions while making an uncritical and eclectic use of data.

The most important aspect of the new science of religion was not its methodology, but its acknowledgement of a new and independent framework of thought, separate from theology. It came to be realized that theology could not be truly comparative, because it dealt with a single religion only. There were Christian, Jewish, Islamic, Buddhistic theologies, each analyzing and often defending its own doctrinal position.

The professionalization of the science of religion resulted in a sharper focus upon important questions and a clearer statement of aims. It was also discovered that its findings could be brought to bear upon a number of other new disciplines: linguistics, sociology, anthropology, archeology, and psychology. Moreover, the methods of each of these disciplines could be meaningfully applied to the study of religion, and the interrelatedness of these studies was expressed by such terms as *sociology of religion, anthropology of religion,* and *psychology of religion.*

Even though the search for absolute origins has been abandoned, and views on cultural evolution and cultural reconstruction have become more modest, current theories and methods were not developed merely through the repudiation of the work of nineteenth-century scholars. The process was, rather, one of modification; later scientists examined problems inherent in traditional methods, eliminating questions that appeared to be unanswerable, and slowly applying newer insights and the findings of related disciplines. The problem of evolution, so central in the nineteenth century, has not lost its importance, but contemporary nonliterate peoples are no longer considered the living prototypes of prehistoric man. This was the fundamental error of the nineteenth century, when the concept was a natural concomitant of the prevailing belief in the inevitable progress of the human race. The cultural practices of contemporary nonliterate peoples were thus not only seen as representative of those of early man but they were also necessarily believed to be less developed than their Western equivalents. Such a conceptual framework naturally imposed severe limitations upon otherwise serious treatments of religion.

Another handicap was the lack of reliable data about nonliterate societies. None of the most influential scholars, not even the anthropologists among them, had done any fieldwork. They therefore could not appreciate the living qualities of the religions about which they wrote. Their information came from ancient historical documents or from the anecdotal and superficial reports of untrained observers. It is not surprising that the study of religion started rather unscientifically. It is a tribute to the intellectual powers of the authors whose theories we shall now examine that they were able to introduce a new discipline and inspire so many scholars after them.

LINGUISTIC THEORIES

As an independent discipline, the science of language is not much older than the science of religion. Shortly before 1800, Sir William Jones observed that the ancient literary language of India, Sanskrit, was related to Greek and Latin and to contemporary European tongues. Soon afterward, scholars began systematic comparisons of these languages, and their work led to the development of historical linguistics as a discipline. Not only did they attempt to trace the relationships among languages, but they were hopeful that they could reconstruct the "original" Proto-Indo-European tongue, the "parent language" from which all others supposedly were derived. Some scholars combined this interest with another favorite nineteenth-century topic, mythology. If it seemed possible to reconstruct the proto-language, it appeared equally possible to recover the original proto-myths, and thereby to gain insight into the origin of religious thought.

Jakob and Wilhelm Grimm

The brothers Jakob (1785–1863) and Wilhelm (1786–1859) Grimm were among those who combined linguistic and mythological interests. They collected legends, folktales, superstitions, riddles, and proverbs from all over Europe, and were struck by the remarkable similarities among them. Moreover, certain recurring motifs seemed also to be present in the *Rig-Veda,* the most ancient literary document among the sacred Hinduistic scriptures in the Sanskrit language, dating not later than the second millennium B.C.

Using these discoveries, the Grimm brothers developed two theories: (1) contemporary folktales are corrupted myths of the past, and can be understood only by proper analysis of the original myths; and (2) most present-day Indo-European folktales derive from a common ancient source.

Friedrich Max Müller

It was on these and similar principles that Friedrich Max Müller (1823–1900) continued to build. Born in Germany, he had studied both philology and comparative mythology before going to teach at Oxford in 1846. In 1856 he published his well-known *Comparative Mythology,* outlining the principles of the explication of myth through comparative philology. Max Müller begins his analysis by pointing out that the otherwise advanced civilization of the ancient Greeks contained many absurd and irrational myths. He maintains that the Greeks themselves did not understand their mythology, and cites many Greek philosophers whose attempts to explain myth led to contradictory conclusions. Müller's own conclusion is that the myths were not invented by the Greeks, but by the speakers of a hypothetical Proto-Indo-European language from which Greek was derived. He conjectures that, in the earliest stage of human development, man could express his observations of nature only anthropomorphically. Instead of *It is night,* early man could only say *The moon (silene) has kissed the setting sun (endymion) into sleep. Sunrise* was *the sun-embracing dawn.* These and similar expressions were "mytho-poetic," but meant literally. Succeeding generations forgot those literal meanings, but kept the terms. The moon "became" a woman (Silene), and the setting sun "became" a young man (Endymion). Myth was therefore born of early man's inability to distinguish between concrete and abstract meanings: it was a "disease of thought."

As these original myths were handed down from generation to generation, linguistic changes rendered them less and less understandable. Comparative linguistics, particularly the etymology of the names of the gods, could provide a rational explanation. Thus the story of Daphne fleeing from Apollo and changing into a laurel tree was based upon a linguistic error which had taken place in the transmission from Sanskrit to Greek. The Greek word *daphne* meant *laurel* and it is quite similar in sound to the Sanskrit word *ahana* which meant *dawn*. The original myth may thus have involved only the pursuit by the sun, Apollo, of his bride, dawn, and the inconsequential laurel tree was merely a matter of mistaken transmission and of folk-etymology. Myth, beginning as a "disease of thought," continued to exist through a "disease of language."

After having thus explained the origin and persistence of myth, it was no longer difficult for Müller to understand the origin of religion. Religion was based, he said, upon the belief in a human soul. Early man noticed that dead people do not breathe, and the concrete term *breath* came to denote the principle of life. Later generations again made the concrete abstract, personifying *breath,* and extending it to mean *soul* and *mind,* as the Greek word *psyche* (breath, air) clearly showed.

Not yet satisfied, Müller now sought to pinpoint a specific phenomenon which had set all mythology in motion, and he came to believe that the sun was this catalyst. He writes:

> I look upon the sunrise and sunset, on the daily return of day and night, on the battle between light and darkness, on the whole solar drama in all its details that is acted every day, every month, every year, in heaven and on earth, as the principal subject of early mythology (1870:537).

Eventually, he came to include almost every legend, folktale, and song—as well as Christmas and New Year celebrations—as part of a corrupted solar myth.

Other comparative philologists advanced rival origins. Kelly and Kuhn believed that stormclouds and thunder had been the catalytic phenomenon. For Ehrenreich it was the moon; for Preller, the sky; for Winckler, the stars. Max Müller's following stretched even across the Atlantic. Daniel Brinton (1837–99), a specialist on American Indian cultures and languages, also began to use linguistic analysis in his attempts to show that both North and South American Indian myths were largely inspired by the sun. One example would be found among the Algonquian Indians, who worshipped the "Great Hare," Michabo or Manabozho, a word which Brinton believed to have been derived from an Algonquian root *wab,* meaning both *rabbit* and *white. White* was, in turn, *dawn, light, morning, East, day,* and thus also *sun;* and the term became confused with its other meaning, *hare* (1868:109).

Max Müller's theories were sharply attacked by many of his contemporaries as well as by later generations. Probably the most outspoken of his contemporary critics was Andrew Lang (1844–1912). He pointed out, correctly, that all nonliterate peoples had myths, and that the speakers of the hypothetical Proto-Indo-European language could not therefore have been the original inventors of all myths. Moreover, he found it very unlikely that mytho-poetic man would remember phrases, but utterly forget their meanings. Another critic, W. Mannhardt (1831–80), showed that myths and folktales were still very meaningful among European peasants. If myth was a linguistic error, it would not have persisted—and certainly not in any meaningful form. The wittiest criticism came from the French folklorist H. Gaidoz (1842–1932), who used Müller's linguistic methods to prove that Müller himself was not real, but a mere solar myth, as were also Oxford and his German place of birth (1884:II, 73–90).

Yet, Müller had greater insight into the nature of contemporary nonliterate societies than many anthropological writers of his time. He wrote:

When we read some of the more recent works on anthropology, the primordial savage seems to be not unlike one of those hideous India-rubber dolls that can be squeezed into every possible shape and made to utter every possible noise. . . .

Contemporary "savages" have lived as long as civilized races, and are nothing like primitive man. (1885:111).

Indeed, although Müller is an evolutionist, he does not equate contemporary nonliterates with prehistoric man. His theory was rooted in linguistic reconstructions, and if these were often spurious and wrongly applied, the method itself was not to blame. The errors he made were those inherent in the nineteenth-century intellectual climate, with its interest in absolute origins, its confidence in the historical method and in the possibility of reconstructing the past, and its lack of experience in applying scientific methods to the humanities.

The great American anthropologist-linguist Edward Sapir (1884–1939) continued to use linguistics as a tool for the analysis of religion, but his aim was more modest and therefore more realistic than Müller's: namely, to show patterns of diffusion. One example he cited was that of the Nootka Indians, who performed a ritual in which the wolf plays a central role. The ritual is called *tlokwana,* a word foreign to the Nootka language. The neighboring Kwakiutl Indians, Sapir found, also have a wolf ritual, called *dlogwala,* a term indigenous in Kwakiutl language. Because of similarities between the two terms, Sapir concluded that at least certain elements of the Kwakiutl ritual, together with its name, had been taken over by the Nootka (Sapir, 1949: 446–48).

RATIONALISTIC THEORIES

Rationalism is the acceptance of human reason as the ultimate source of knowledge. Applied to the nineteenth-century study of religion, it meant the conviction that prehistoric man reasoned out his beliefs in an almost scientific manner, but arrived at the wrong conclusions because he lacked knowledge and experience and the opportunity for scientific observation.

It is quite unwarranted to attribute to early man the same kind of scientific curiosity as modern man. Human cultures differ not in terms of mental capacity but in the type of questions that are culturally important. Rationalistic explanations of the origin of religion are, moreover, necessarily speculative. Most nineteenth-century writers attempted to describe how they themselves would have reasoned if they were "primitive" and did not yet know anything about religion or science. Their arguments are not only *a priori*, but they fail to account for the fact that the beliefs and practices based upon such "fallacious" reasoning are still held by many literate people of our own day and age.

Edward Burnett Tylor

Edward Burnett Tylor (1832–1917) was a rationalist in the sense just described. His minimum definition of religion was "the belief in Spiritual Beings," and he called this early belief *animism*. Like Max Müller, he felt that the belief in spiritual beings derived from the concept of the soul. His theories and doctrines were backed up by illustrations from contemporary cultures, both nonliterate and literate. He explained the beliefs and practices in literate cultures as survivals from earlier times. "Survivals," in Tylor's terminology, were cultural habits which had lost their original meaning and purpose, but were retained from the force of habit.

Tylor's scheme of the origin and development of religion is a logical construction, but it is a creation of his own mind and without proof. He begins by stating that animism consists of two great dogmas, one concerning the souls of individual creatures capable of continued existence after death, and the other concerning other spirits, including powerful deities (1958:II, 10). Early men were deeply impressed by the difference between a living body and a dead one, and the causes of waking, sleep, trance, disease, and death. They concluded that man had not only a material body but also life and a phantom. Life enabled the body to feel and think and act; the phantom was its image or second self. Both were separable from the body: life went away at death, the phantom could appear to people at a distance. Since life and phantom appeared connected, prehistoric man combined the two, and together they became the "apparitional soul." This soul sometimes left the body during sleep, wandering to distant places and appearing to other people in their dreams. After death, the soul left the body permanently. But since the dead also appeared in dreams, acting as if they were alive, the belief grew up that the ghost-soul continued to live after the death of the body. This belief in souls was easily extended to include animals, plants, and inanimate objects since they, too, appeared in dreams.

Tylor realized, however, that a mere belief in souls does not constitute religion. Religion becomes a social institution only if the beliefs give rise to communal ritual. The transition from belief to action took place, according to Tylor, because early man recognized that the ghost-soul is superior to the body. The soul, the principle of life, survives the body, has physical power, can flash swiftly from place to place. After death, the ghost-souls became *manes,* and the living first admired their powers and then began to worship them. According to Tylor, the principles of *manes* worship are not difficult to understand:

> The dead ancestor, now passed into a deity, simply goes on protecting his own family and receiving suit and service from them as of old; the dead chief still watches over his own tribe, still holds the authority by helping friends and harming enemies, still rewards the right and sharply punishes the wrong *(ibid.:199)*.

Once having established the origin of religion, Tylor continues to outline its development by a number of successive theories which he calls "doctrines." According to the "doctrine of Continuance," the idea that departed souls and spirits must reside somewhere gave rise to the belief in an after life. The "doctrine of Embodiment" accounts for the fact that souls and spirits, free to flit around in the world, can also enter other bodies and objects at will. This in turn leads to the "doctrine of Possession": when an evil or foreign spirit enters a person, it will make him ill, and from this it logically follows that man will resort to exorcism *(ibid.:209–28)*.

The beliefs in embodiment and possession give rise to the "doctrine of Fetishism." Since spirits are believed capable of entering material objects, such objects acquire a special power and are treated as having personal consciousness. They are carried around to fend off enemies and disease, manipulated to man's advantage, and worshipped. Fetishism becomes idolatry when a fetish object is altered in a material way to indicate its special function as the residence for a spirit. It then becomes an idol, combining the properties of a portrait or image with those of a fetish, and it takes on a human personality *(ibid.:255)*. The spirits now become the personal forces of the world and of nature (*ibid.:*270). All nature becomes possessed, pervaded, crowded with spiritual beings, both good and evil. Spirits are then elevated to the rank of gods—of the forests, the earth, the water, the sky, and later also of agriculture, of war and peace, of childbirth, and life and death. This is the great stage of polytheism.

When there are so many different gods, they cannot possibly all be of the same rank and importance. A hierarchy soon emerges, with one god becoming the supreme deity. All minor gods and spirits recede in the background and finally disappear altogether in the last stage of development, monotheism.

The rationalistic concepts of Tylor are implicit in this scheme. Religion is explained as an intellectual effort which has no other purposes than to understand biological events and natural phenomena. Early man is a logician, analyzing the universe, but coming to wrong conclusions.

Tylor's approach is also individualistic, which means that he attempts to explain religion as individual action rather than as a social phenomenon. Such treatment leaves many questions unanswered. Individual experience differs according to sex, age, status and personality. How do these variant experiences become unified, and so strong a social force? Also, if religious activities are individual experiences, why do other members of the group accept them? W. Goode neatly summed up Tylor's shortcomings:

> The rationalistic approach, then, fails to take into account the emotional, obligatory character of these beliefs and practices. The individualistic approach fails in its attempts to explain the integrative character of religion, as well as the integrated character of the social structure. This means, concretely, failing to see the close connection between religious activities and the moral aspects of behavior. In addition, this means that Tylor does not see religion as *analytically necessary.* There is merely evidence that religion is a universal social phenomenon, an entirely different matter (Goode, 1951:244).

Herbert Spencer

The same criticisms hold true for the theories of Herbert Spencer (1820–1903). His approach was similar to Tylor's even if his conclusions were apparently independently reached. The principal difference was that Spencer stressed the belief in ghosts, and felt that the concept of a personal soul was a much later development. According to Spencer, the changes that occur in nature—from night into day, from sunshine to storm, from winter to summer—must have suggested to early man a basic duality in nature. By extension, man posits a duality in his own nature, a notion reinforced by dreams and swoons. Death is first seen as a temporary absence of the ghost from the body, and reanimation, the belief in the return of the ghost to the deceased body, is one of the earliest forms of religion. Reanimation explains the concern of nonliterate peoples with the protection of the body after death, and gives rise to such burial practices as embalming and the provision of food, implements, and clothing for the deceased. When it became clear that the dead never come back to life, man concluded that the ghosts must inhabit another world, and only then did the concept of a soul come into being. The ancestral spirits were believed to live in a world separate from, but similar to, that of the living. When man became more sophisticated about natural events, and asked for their causes, the ancestral spirit world became the logical choice for a reasonable explanation. In this manner, spirits become important to man, since they can control life and death as well as bring sickness and health, abundance or poverty. The ghosts become gods, and they are feared. Since they retain their human character, and their human needs and vanities, they can be influenced by offerings, sacrifices, flattery, and propitiation. Thus the demand arises for specialists in the art of ritual: medicine men and priests, who themselves often assume supernatural properties (1885:I, 411).

Andrew Lang and R. R. Marett

The evolutionary schemes of Tylor and Spencer attracted a great deal of attention, and inevitably invited criticism. Among those who accepted parts of Tylor's theories and attacked others were two of his own pupils, Andrew Lang and R. R. Marett.

Andrew Lang (1844–1912) agreed with Tylor that a belief in souls may well have arisen from dreams and visions, but he refused to accept the idea that gods developed from notions of ghosts and spirits. Lang pointed out that a number of extremely simple tribes had a conception of a moral and all-powerful creator-god, a supreme deity. Moreover, in many cases the supreme being is not thought of as a spirit, but as a person. He considered it unlikely that the conception of God had evolved from that of ghosts (1898:2). Rather, Lang believed that available evidence pointed to monotheism as preceding animism, the latter representing a corruption and degeneration of the original concept.

R. R. Marett (1866–1943), Tylor's successor at Oxford, argued along different lines. He, too, denied that animism was the earliest stage of religion. Following Tylor's own reasoning that whatever was simplest was also likely to be earliest in development, Marett posited a pre-animistic stage where belief in *mana* prevailed. Mana, a Polynesian word, refers to an impersonal, nonanthropomorphized power. Marett felt that a belief in mana is much simpler than the ideas of phantom, soul, and spirit, and it must thus have preceded animism. Earliest man simply recognized the powers present in nature or in certain objects, and reacted with emotions of awe, fear, wonder, respect, and admiration. These feelings were not so much thought out as danced out (1909:xxxi). Marett calls the belief in mana *animatism*.

Sir James George Frazer

Within the latter part of what Lowie calls the "Tylorian period" fall the theories of Sir James George Frazer (1854–1941). While Tylor, Spencer, and Lang conceived of early man as a kind of philosopher, and Marett saw him as a creature swayed by his emotions, Frazer wrote:

Primitive man looks at the world from such a different point of view from us, that what seems simple and obvious to us almost certainly did not seem so to him; and vice versa what seems simple and obvious to him is almost always so entirely remote from our ways of thought that we should never have dreamt of it. Accordingly, any explanations of the origin of religion or society which commend themselves to us as entirely argeeable to reason ought always, in my opinion, to be regarded with the greatest distrust. (Quoted by Kardiner and Preble, 1963:81.)

Frazer was indeed a rationalist of a different order. According to him, man passes through three stages of intellectual development: from magic to religion to science.

During the magical period man was not yet reasonable, but merely superstitious. Reason gave rise to religion, and later also to science. Magic was a kind of pseudoscience by which early man attempted to manipulate nature. His attempts were based upon erroneous correlations between cause and effect. The two fallacious "laws" underlying magic were the "law of similarity" and the "law of contact or contagion." The law of similarity presupposes that "like produces like" or "effect resembles cause," and the application of this principle is what Frazer calls *homeopathic magic*. His best-known example is the injury or destruction of an image resembling an enemy in the belief that the person it is modeled upon will suffer the same effects. The law of contact or contagion implies that things which have once been in contact continue to act upon each other, and the type of magic associated with this principle is known as *contagious magic*. When a person takes possession of the hair- or nail-cuttings of an enemy, or anything else that has been part of his body, he believes he has acquired the power to harm their former owner.

Both "laws" derive from a false conception of natural law (1959:7), and are the basis of all magical ceremonies and spells. The magician does not supplicate any higher supernatural power; he feels that he himself can control nature. Such beliefs and actions, Frazer believes, cannot possibly be equated with religion.

Religion is not a continuation of magic, but a departure from it. When man began to realize that he was not quite so powerful, that magic did not always have the desired results, it occurred to him that there must be higher powers: demons, ancestor spirits, or gods. Religion was born when man appealed to these higher beings with offerings and sacrifices. It could emerge only after man had reached a state of higher intelligence—when he could reason correctly and recognize the errors of his past.

Frazer's evolutionary scheme is more contrary to fact than any other theory discussed so far. Tylor and others used ethnographic materials to support their theories, although they erred in their chronologies and time perspectives. Frazer, however, misinterpreted the data themselves. Ethnological evidence shows clearly that religion and magic do not exist as separate categories. Even in the religions of literate civilizations magical elements appear side by side with worship and supplication. In nonliterate societies, magical rites are commonly carried out in a spirit of reverence and respect and involve a belief in gods and deities.

Nevertheless, Frazer's treatment of magic and religion contributed to the understanding of these topics and inspired much later research. He brought religion into relation with political organization by attempting to prove that early kings were often magicians and priests. There must have been, according to Frazer, early specialists in the art of magic, one of whose significant functions was weather control—especially the insurance of an adequate rainfall. These rainmakers became important in early nonliterate societies, and some of them attained the positions of chiefs or kings, or even were regarded as gods (*ibid.*:54, 61).

Assessments of Frazer's contributions must account for the fact that he was never very interested in theories. He was an evolutionist and a firm believer in comparative method, but he did not explicitly state his own position. He was most fascinated by facts, which he collected from field reports of ethnologists and travelers. He also sent out questionnaires, but never did fieldwork. In the preface to the third edition of *The Golden Bough* he says:

> . . . it is the fate of theories to be washed away . . . and I am not so presumptuous as to expect or desire for mine an exemption from the common lot. I hold them all very lightly, and have used them chiefly as convenient pegs on which to hang my collection of facts.

Frazer is best known for his thirteen-volume *The Golden Bough* (1890–1915), but he also wrote on a variety of topics of interest to anthropology, including burial customs, totemism, exogamy, taboo, folklore, and the fear of death. The amount of ethnographic material he amassed and used is truly awe-inspiring, but much of it is unreliable, and not placed within its proper cultural framework.

SOCIOLOGICAL THEORIES

The evolutionary theories discussed all tend to neglect the functional aspects of religion. Sociological theories differ in that they question the roles that beliefs and practices play and their relationship to other cultural institutions. The earliest sociological theories combined the quest for origins with an interest in functions. Later on, the focus shifted away from origins.

Fustel de Coulanges

One nineteenth-century scholar with an interest in the social aspects of religion, Fustel de Coulanges (1830–89), was himself a historian by profession. His most famous work, *The Ancient City* (1864), presents us with a remarkably modern and comprehensive sociological study of religion. The societies selected for his analysis were those of the ancient Greeks and Romans. He did not seek the ultimate origins of religion, but he was interested in the origin of those religious ideas which gave rise to early Greek societies. His main purpose was, however, to investigate "upon what principles and by what rules Greek and Roman society was governed" (1956:11). He found that the social institutions of the ancients were intimately related to their religions. He believed that the earliest form of belief among the Greeks was merely that death was not a dissolution of being, but simply a change of life. The departed soul continued to live near men, but underground. From this belief arose the necessity for burial and the need (since the spirits were still human) for periodic offerings of food and drink. It was the duty of the living to satisfy these needs, and nothing was more natural than that the living relatives of the deceased should take up these responsibilities. Religion thus became a domestic concern and the basis for the strong patrilineal families that were the foundation of society as a whole. The father acted as priest in the daily rituals and held a very powerful position. The family became identified with the cult: the ancestors were both the gods and the symbols of family unity. Religiously governed family groups could function properly only under certain social conditions, so that the religious system was strongly interrelated with specific rules of marriage (lineage exogamy), residence (patrilocality), the order of relationships (patri-

having the social function of strengthening group integratic
Later forms of Hebrew sacrifice developed out of this totem.
feast.

Even if his analysis was directed only to a certain group of
people, Smith implied that his theory was generally true for all
nonliterate societies. Early religions, he felt, had no dogmas or
creeds, but consisted entirely of ritual acts. There is, of course, no
evidence of the truth of this theory, and it is even quite doubtful
that it is true for early Semitic religions.

Émile Durkheim

Important contributions to the sociological study of religion
came from Émile Durkheim (1858–1917). He took several of his
ideas from Fustel de Coulanges and Robertson Smith, but he is
also, more clearly than most scholars of his time, true to the
positivist position. Positivism can be traced back, in France, to
Descartes (1596–1650); it was applied to the study of society by
Montesquieu (1689–1755) and further developed by such scholars
as d'Alembert (1717–83), Turgot (1727–81), Condorcet (1743–94),
Saint-Simon (1760–1825) and Comte (1798–1857). These writers
have in common a certain awareness of the concepts of science,
even if in their theories they did not always remain faithful to the
principles they so admired. The tenets of positivist social science
were set down by Montesquieu, who declared that social phenomena, like natural phenomena, have a fixed and necessary order
and are governed by rational laws discoverable by the human
mind. Turgot, Condorcet, and Comte formulated these laws in
terms of stages of development. Turgot's stages were the ani-
mistic, the metaphysical, and the scientific, a formulation closely
resembling Comte's theological, metaphysical, and positive or
scientific stages. In these views, religion was characteristic of a
stage of development. Comte stated explicitly that progress
depends on the atrophy of both religion and philosophy.

Durkheim was convinced that religious phenomena are ruled
by observable scientific facts. The phenomena are then related
to one another, and, like all other social facts, are subject to
real and natural laws. Therefore, he concluded, the methods of
physical science are applicable to the study of society and of
religion:

lineality), and property and inheritance (*ibid.*:13). Whe
cities became more powerful, family-oriented worship w
placed by state religion. Family integration broke down, h
city brought new forms of political organization and pub
private law, both powerfully upheld by religious beli
practices.

Fustel de Coulanges has been criticized by classici
showed that his reconstructions were not entirely correc
anthropologists, who felt that he overstressed the causal
religion. One can understand the importance of
only by keeping in mind that *The Ancient City* was pu
early as 1864, when the archeological record was still v
plete and not many good ethnological reports were ir
De Coulanges' insight into the social nature of religic
remarkable, and he was the first modern writer to pr
"structural" theory of religion.

W. Robertson Smith

Another example of sociological analysis of rel
found in the writings of W. Robertson Smith
Scottish philologist, physicist, archeologist, and Bil
took the more dangerous path of applying objec
Semitic peoples, including the Hebrews of the Ol
show the "pagan" origins of many of their sacred
and other "heresies," he was removed from his
Aberdeen Free Church College, but he was we
bridge as professor of Arabic.

In his descriptions of Semitic societies, he s
identity was equated with religious identity.
small groups had its own gods, and these
physical creators and fathers, so that gods a
one blood. The gods were originally totemi
species of animal. The relationship between
sealed and strengthened by the fact that kin
to time to eat the totem in a sacred ritual. In
ilated the gods within themselves, reinforci
relationship not only between gods and me
human participants in the ritual. By ritual
they maintained and guaranteed their c
munal ties. Religious rites were thus prir

Our principle, then, implies no metaphysical conception, no speculation about the fundamental nature of beings. What it demands is that the sociologist put himself in the same state of mind as the physicist, chemist, or physiologist when he probes into a still unexplored region of the scientific domain (1958:xlv).

Durkheim, however, does not take the position of Comte and other positivists who held that religion was a thing of the past and an obstacle to progress. Durkheim sees religion as a very ueseful institution, both for society and for the sociologist, for it is "better adapted than any other institution . . . to show us an essential and permanent aspect of humanity" (1961:13). The universality of religion, according to Durkheim, contradicts the idea that it is a mere fallacy of reasoning on the part of early man.

Durkheim also rejects all definitions of religion as a belief in the supernatural. He feels that early man's dreams cannot possibly account for the origin of the concepts of souls and spirits. The absolute origin of religion can never be found, Durkheim maintains; at most we can describe "the most simple social condition that is actually known, beyond which we cannot go at present" (ibid.:20n). The most significant topics in Durkheim's treatment of religion center on problems of definition, possible distinctions between magic and religion, and attempts to account for the origin of religion as a function of society itself.

The core of Durkheim's definition of religion is his distinction between the sacred and the profane. Religion, according to Durkheim, is a system of belief and practices pertaining to the sacred (ibid.:62). The sacred is a realm apart from the profane. Profane things may occasionally be transferred to the sacred realm, but only through elaborate ritual: changes of this nature cannot be incidental. Evans-Pritchard (1965:65), for one, has shown that such sharp dichotomies cannot always be drawn, and that transitions from the sacred are often casually made. He cites as an example the sacred ancestor shrines that stand in the middle of the courtyards of the Azande tribe: Azande men often use them to rest their spears against, and the shrines are treated with reverence only during rituals.

Durkheim emphasizes that religion cannot be studied merely

as a system of beliefs. Sociological analysis must, in his view, rely on sense data. Beliefs can neither be observed nor verified unless they are expressed in ritual action. Ritual, moreover, involves the society, and in Durkheim's view sociology is not interested in individuals, but in society as a whole. This is why Durkheim is less interested in magic than in religion. Magical practices are individualistic: magicians offer their services to clients with personal problems, and these clients might not even know one another. Magic therefore cannot create social solidarity (*ibid.:*60). Religious beliefs, on the other hand, are always group beliefs, shared by members of a society and preserving their unity. Religion, everywhere, has a "Church": a place where people come together for shared social action; but there is no Church of magic.

Nevertheless, in Durkheim's theory magic shows certain similarities to religion because it is derived from religion. Unlike Frazer, Durkheim maintains that religion appeared before magic. Religion, according to Durkheim, addressed itself to the sacred supernatural for the material and moral benefit of the whole group. Only later were religious rituals taken over by specialists in magic, who diverted the communal benefits to private functions of curing and divination. Magic addresses itself to the same sacred entities, and contains religious elements, because it is born of religion (*ibid.:*405).

Stressing the social meaning of religion, Durkheim seeks its origins on the social, rather than on the individual level. He limits his analysis to a few Australian aboriginal groups, using the descriptions of Grey (1841), Spencer and Gillin (1899 and 1904), and Strehlow (1907–20) as his principal sources. His selection is motivated by the desire to study "the most primitive and simple religion it was possible to find" (*ibid.:*115), and he assumes that such a religion can only be found among people with the simplest technology and social organization. In fact, however, there is no such correlation between technological development and religious complexity. Furthermore, Durkheim eschews comparative method, justifying his position by saying that "one single fact may make a law appear, while a multitude of imprecise and vague observations would only produce confusion" (*ibid.:*115).

The hunting-and-gathering peoples in Australia lived in small nomadic groups, called *hordes*. Several hordes considered themselves related by bonds of kinship, and this larger social unit was the *clan*. Each clan had a name, taken from a species of animal or plant. This species was the clan's totem: it was sacred to the group, and might not be eaten or harmed by its members. The visible representation of the totem species became an emblem, a means of identification of the clan and its unity. Totemic designs were carved on *churinga*, wooden or stone slabs which were then held very sacred. Profane persons—women and uninitiated young men—were not permitted to set eyes upon them. The *churinga* owed their sacredness to the totemic emblems carved upon them. Members of the clan acquired sacred aspects only by virtue of resemblance to the totem, so that scarifications were made on the human body to resemble the patterns of the *churinga*.

The totem was above all a symbol, representing the supernatural protector, the god of the group, and the group itself. It follows, in Durkheim's reasoning, that the god and the group were identical:

> The god of the clan, the totemic principle, can therefore be nothing else than the clan itself, personified and represented to the imagination under the visible form of the animal or vegetable which serves as totem. (*ibid.:* 236).

He then attempts to demonstrate how these identifications might have originated. The hordes that were members of a clan did not regularly reside together. Periodically, however, they came together for ritual and ceremony, in order to increase the species to which they had a sacred relationship. The true function of these gatherings was the reinforcement of clan solidarity. They were always festive and exciting, forming a sharp contrast to the anxieties of the daily quest for food:

> When they are once come together, a sort of electricity is formed by their collecting which quickly transports them to an extraordinary degree of exaltation. Every sentiment expressed finds a place without resistance in all the minds, which are very open to outside impressions; each re-echoes the others, and is re-echoed by the others. The initial impulse thus proceeds, growing as it goes, as an avalanche grows in its advance. And as such active passions so free from all

control could not fail to burst out, on every side one sees
nothing but violent gestures, cries, veritable howls, and
deafening noises of every sort, which aid in intensifying still
more the state of mind which they manifest. And since a
collective sentiment cannot express itself collectively except
on the condition of observing a certain order permitting
cooperation and movements in unison, these gestures and
cries naturally tend to become rhythmic and regular; hence
become songs and dances. (*ibid.*:247).

In this state of elation, people no longer recognize themselves,
and they become convinced that there exist two different and
mutually incorporable worlds: the profane of the daily life, and
the sacred of clan meetings. The clan creates the sacred because
it *is* sacred:

So it is in the midst of these effervescent social environments
and out of this effervescence itself that the religious idea
seems to be born (*ibid.*:250).

Because religion is born out of the social, it follows that both
have moral authority. Society submits man to many incon-
veniences, it constrains and compels him. But it also protects
him, for man cannot survive alone. Because society both domi-
nates man and protects him, he respects it. The gods of society
have the same power and the same moral authority. The individual, knowing that he is part of society, will believe that the
sacred forces are present in him, and he can thus approach the
world with confidence and energy.

This summary sketch of Durkheim's analysis of religion cannot do justice to its profundity. Although his reasoning methods
are now largely unacceptable, there is no doubt about his
fundamental insight into the symbolic content of religion and
into its social and human meanings. Durkheim showed that religion was not to be explained as something based on errors and
lies, but as a social reality which answers to the given conditions
of human existence (*ibid.*:15). He noted the close integration
between religion and other cultural institutions, and between
religion and societal value systems. Without neglecting the cognitive aspects of religion overstressed by the British evolutionists,

he brought these aspects to bear upon ritual and other socially patterned actions.

Durkheim's starting points were sound; his shortcomings rest mainly in the logical applications of his principles and in his misunderstanding of the nature of society. Much of this misunderstanding derives from the fact that Durkeim had not done field work, and the ethnographies upon which he had to rely were not completely reliable, and certainly were not adequate bases for his generalizations.

Nevertheless, Durkheim gave new directions and perspectives to sociology and to the study of religion. His influence is widespread, and he found many enthusiastic disciples to carry on and expand his work. Of his own contemporaries we may mention his nephew, Marcel Mauss (1872–1950), who applied Durkheim's theory of religion to Eskimo society (1906). Together with Henri Hubert, Mauss also wrote an important essay on sacrifice (1899), and the same two scholars collaborated on a study of magic (1904).

Lucien Lévy-Bruhl

Another contemporary of Durkheim was the French philosopher Lucien Lévy-Bruhl (1857–1939). His fundamental conceptions, like Durkheim's, were sociological, but his analysis of nonliterate societies was built upon different premises, and he did not identify himself with the Durkheimian school. Perhaps no other scholar dealing with early man has been more maligned by anthropologists, particularly in America. Lévy-Bruhl declared that primitive people possess a mentality different not only in degree but also in quality from that of civilized people: they were "prelogical." His statement shakes the very foundations of anthropological field work and analysis. If the mind of nonliterate man is of a different quality from that of civilized man, we can never fully grasp its workings. All modern ethnographies would be erroneous, for field workers have assumed that their data can be meaningfully analyzed in terms of our own culture.

Yet, his critics misunderstand Lévy-Bruhl's aims and interests. He felt that cultures and societies can legitimately be studied by analyzing how patterned modes of thinking give rise to patterned social behavior. In this respect, he has much in common with the personality-and-culture school of modern anthropological analysis, and he may indeed be called one of the pioneers of this important movement. Lévy-Bruhl was doing nothing less than attempting to investigate systematically the unproven assumptions of Max Müller, Tylor, Spencer, Frazer, and all others who had built imposing schemes of origin and evolution. Like them, Lévy-Bruhl misrepresented nonliterate peoples. Although anthropologists tend to plead extenuating circumstances for other scholars, no excuses are made for Lévy-Bruhl.

Lévy-Bruhl begins his discussion by observing that each society has its own type of mentality, closely associated with the predominant values of its social institutions. This idea is not dissimilar from the more modern concept of "national character." But unlike the adherents of the latter concept, Lévy-Bruhl distinguishes only two types of society: the primitive and the civilized. *Civilized,* in Lévy-Bruhl's terminology, means *scientific.* Those societies whose collective representations include the notion of science will, according to Lévy-Bruhl, seek scientific explanations for all natural phenomena. It is assumed that such an explanation does exist and that diligent research will eventually discover it. Basic to the scientific world-view, Lévy-Bruhl adds, is "the law of contradiction," which means that science is predicated by the concept that a thing cannot simultaneously be itself *and* something else (1966:90).

Primitive (*i.e.,* nonscientific) societies differ in that their collective representations do not demand causal explanations in terms of natural law. Instead, nonliterate man thinks and acts in accordance with "the law of participation": a thing *can* be itself *and* something else at the same time (*ibid.*:101).

Lévy-Bruhl stresses the fact that *prelogical* is not the same as *antilogical* or *alogical* (1966:79), and that nonliterate man is not incapable of reason or opposed to it, but merely that he has different categories of logic.

Early man's prelogical modes of thinking, according to Lévy-Bruhl, are most clearly demonstrated by his magico-religious beliefs (Lévy-Bruhl does not differentiate between magic and religion). Early man's collective representations are "mystical," *i.e.,* concerned with forces, influences, and actions imperceptible to the senses, though nonetheless real. The reality in which primitive man moves is itself mystical, and as such it is also religious: there are mystical participations between man and his shadow, and it becomes his soul; between man and his totem, and it becomes his god. Lévy-Bruhl does not speculate about the origin of religion, but merely tries to show how religious ideas evidence a distinctive mentality.

In a way, Lévy-Bruhl became his own best critic. In his posthumous *Carnets* (1949), he declares that primitive mentality does not mean the acceptance of logical contradictions, as he first believed, but merely that early or nonliterate man accepted ideas which had later been proven to be unacceptable (1949:9). In other words, it was not a matter of logic, but of knowledge. In this manner, Lévy-Bruhl himself undermined the concept of prelogical mentality. It is undoubtedly true that many ancient religious beliefs have been disqualified by later scientific discoveries, but this is a theological question which cannot be solved by anthropology.

Adolf Bastian

The German scholar Adolf Bastian (1826–1905) is generally classed as an anthropologist rather than a sociologist, perhaps because he was an ardent traveler and met many "primitives" in the flesh. Yet, he was not a field worker in the modern sense of the word. Although he recorded many cultural traits and habits, he did not place them in their proper context, and he was more of a globetrotter than an ethnologist. He found that cultures all over the world showed "an appalling monotony of the fundamental ideas of mankind." In other words, Bastian was more alert to similarities than to differences.

This tendency was useful in his time, because Bastian stressed that nonliterate peoples were not very different from literate peoples. His main thesis was that human nature is basically one, and that the workings of the human mind are uniform. He calls this principle *"the psychic unity of mankind."* People everywhere had the same "elementary ideas" (*Elementargedanken*), because they reacted in similar ways to similar circumstances; any differences could be explained by differing environmental stimuli, and cultures grouped themselves into "geographical provinces." The two interacting forces, elementary ideas and environment, produced for every province its own "ethnic ideas" (*Völkergedanken*).

Bastian applies this scheme also to religion. He maintains that people everywhere will use those implements with which they have most incidental success. Although the implements differ from culture to culture, the reaction will be identical: lucky implements will be assigned a special supernatural power. The "land of the shadows" is, in many places, located in the west, thus suggesting the "elementary idea" of locating it where the sun is setting. Many people use masks: it is an "elementary idea" that man wants to deceive the spirits.

Bastian does not deal with religion as a total cultural phenomenon; he dissects it into small pieces which he then tries to explain. It is, of course, entirely untrue that similar practices have identical meanings. Masks, for instance, are only rarely used for deception; more often they are used to identify man with the gods or to represent a deity, but they have also many other ritual or secular functions.

MIGRATION AND DIFFUSION THEORIES

Bastian's theory implied that most cultural traits, including religion, originated independently of each other. A reaction against this view—which was not Bastian's alone—came from members of the Austrian culture-circle school (*Kulturkreislehre*), who maintained that the similarities among cultures and religions are to be explained by migration or diffusion. They postulated that early men lived in small groups in different parts of the world, with each group developing its own early culture (*Urkultur*). When the groups grew in size, and means of travel improved, people spread out, taking along their basic culture traits and thus forming a culture-circle (*Kulturkreis*). In some cases these circles fused with one another, forming "secondary cultures."

Fritz Gräbner and Father Wilhelm Schmidt

The task of ethnographers of this conviction was to reconstruct the original cultures by noting the trait distributions and setting up schemes of development. The main exponents of these ideas were Fritz Gräbner (1877–1934) and Father Wilhelm Schmidt (1868–1954). Father Schmidt is also known for his extensive treatment of the religion of nonliterate peoples. He considered the African pygmy tribes to be the best present-day representatives of original African culture. He noted that several of these tribes were both monotheistic and monogamous, and he concluded that monotheism had been the original form of religion in the *Urkreis.*

Schmidt found the idea of an all-father or a sky-god to be present among the most primitive peoples everywhere in the world, and he wrote a twelve-volume book (*Der Ursprung der Gottesidee* [1926–55]) to prove his point. Coupled with the idea of original monotheism was that of original morality, which was, in Schmidt's view, eminently demonstrated by monogamy. All forms of totemism, animism, magic, fetishism, and polytheism, according to his theory, were subsequent developments, as was polygamy.

Father Schmidt's theories corresponded with the Catholic belief that man is created perfect and later falls away from grace. Yet, Schmidt attempts to remain objective, and does not, as one might expect, postulate primeval revelation. Early man, according to Schmidt, discovered his god in a rational manner—seeking an explanation of the world in which he lives, the most logical and most simple conclusion seemed to be that it was created by one powerful force, an omnipotent and omniscient deity, who, moreover, cared for his creation.

Schmidt's theories cannot be upheld in view of present knowledge. Anthropological field work has shown that some nonliterate peoples are polytheistic. There is no proven correlation between complexity of culture and the number of deities worshipped. The *Kulturkreis* school became nearly defunct after Father Schmidt's death, and its chronological reconstructions are no longer accepted.

G. Elliot Smith and E. J. Perry

At about the same time, there formed in England a group of "extreme diffusionists." Their theories are too far-fetched to warrant extensive discussion. The main proponents were G. Elliot Smith (1871–1937) and his disciple, E. J. Perry. Smith (1928) wrote that "natural man" (*i.e.,* nonliterate man) possessed nothing that was worthy of the name of culture—no religion, no burial practices, no arts or crafts worth mentioning, no huts or shelters. He lived essentially like the anthropoid apes. Civilization was born in Egypt, according to Smith, when the early Egyptians cultivated the wild barley that grew in that country, and thus invented agriculture. Then, imitating the inundations of the Nile, they added irrigation. Having thus acquired surplus food they had to invent pottery and granaries to store it. Those who could predict the inundations of the Nile eventually became king-priests, and they acquired so much power that their people, in an effort to retain them, mummified them after death. The belief in continued existence, Smith argues, gave rise to religion. The practices performed to insure the well-being of the royal corpse gave rise to ritual, drama, theater, dancing, and music, as well as stimulating architecture and carpentry (1928:83). From this center of civilization, culture slowly diffused into Europe and parts of Asia, all traits somehow changing and degenerating in the process. This was the "Pan-Egyptian" theory, and even the mild Father Schmidt said of Perry and Smith that their lack of any real method was so complete that it could bring only discredit to anthropology.

PSYCHOLOGICAL THEORIES

Sigmund Freud

Nearly all theories discussed so far include some psychological variables, mainly in the form of speculations on the degree of rationality of the minds of early and nonliterate peoples. These deliberations were, most often, presumptive, because the true dimensions of the human mind were still unknown. All this changed with the momentous discoveries of Sigmund Freud (1856–1939). Known chiefly for his innovations in psychology and as the founder of psychoanalysis, Freud also wrote on religion and society, including those of nonliterate man. In fact, some aspects of his theories of the mind have a direct bearing upon his treatment of religion.

Starting his career as a physician, Freud found that many physical ailments had a psychic background. First using hypnosis, then free association, he soon found that most people resisted the recollection of certain events, particularly those which violated the moral imperatives implanted by parents and parent-surrogates during early childhood. These conventions, internalized by the rewards and punishments bestowed by the childhood authorities, gave rise to a personal "censor" in the individual, his *superego,* which privately rewards and punishes according to cultural standards. Symptoms of illness are one manifestation of self-punishment.

When Freud began to search not only for individual causes of psychic disturbances, but for general ones as well, he found that culture itself created most of the difficulties, for it is superimposed upon man's animal nature, his pleasure-seeking *id.* Animals, for example, usually mate as soon as they are sexually mature, but culture prevents man from gratifying his sexual desires at will. The energy associated with the sexual instinct, the *libido,* must seek alternate modes of expression, and makes compromises compatible with cultural demands.

One such adjustment is the resolution of the Oedipus complex. In the early phases of libidinal development, a child has inevitable sexual desires toward the parent of the opposite sex and feels fear and hostility toward the parent of the same sex. As he becomes socialized, the individual learns to repress these unpleasant and unattainable wishes, and later to direct them toward culturally approved nonincestuous relationships. Or he may learn to direct this repressed energy into such nonsexual channels as science, art, politics, or friendship—again, in conformity with cultural norms. It is this concept of adaptation which led Freud to his writings about culture and religion.

The four major works in these fields are: *Totem and Taboo* (1913), *The Future of an Illusion* (1928), *Civilization and its Discontents* (1930), and *Moses and Monotheism* (1939). Since Freud was seeking evidence for the universality of the Oedipus complex, he diligently began to read the available anthropological literature.

The basic assumptions that determined his view of nonliterate man were that nonliterate peoples represent a well-preserved stage of human development, and that the behavior and thoughts of neurotics and primitives are fundamentally similar. In Freud's thinking the two notions are not unrelated. Ernst Häckel (1834–1919), an influential German biologist, had stated that the biological development of human individuals reflected, in microcosm, the evolution of the species. Although this notion was

refuted during Freud's own lifetime, Freud extended it to include cultural and psychological evolution.

With these presuppositions, Freud set out to find the origins
of culture and religion. In *Totem and Taboo,* his thesis is that
"the beginnings of religion, ethics, society, and art meet in the
Oedipus complex" (1938c:872). Like Durkheim, he selects the
Australian aborigines as his primary example because they are
"the most backward and wretched," and thus, according to his
theory, at the earliest stage of psychic childhood. Freud is particularly intrigued by two aspects of totemism: the exogamy of
totemic clans, and the notion that the totem species may not be
eaten or killed except on ritual occasions. Before society was
organized, Freud explains, men lived in "primitive hordes" dominated by a father who keeps all females for himself and drives
away the growing sons:

> One day the expelled brothers joined forces, slew and ate the
> father, and thus put an end to the father horde. Together
> they dared and accomplished what would have remained
> impossible for them singly. . . . Of course these cannibalistic
> savages ate their victim. This violent primal father had
> surely been the envied and feared model for each of the
> brothers. Now they accomplished their identification with
> him by devouring him and each acquired part of his
> strength. . . . They hated the father who stood so power-
> fully in the way of their sexual demands and their desire
> for power, but they also loved and admired him. After they
> had satisfied their hate by his removal and had carried out
> their wish for identification with him, the suppressed tender
> impulses had to assert themselves. This took place in the
> form of remorse, a sense of guilt was formed which coincided
> here with the remorse generally felt. The dead now became
> stronger than the living had been, even as we observe it
> today in the destinies of men. What the father's presence
> had formerly prevented they themselves now prohibited in
> the psychic situation of "subsequent obedience" which we
> know so well from psychoanalysis. They undid their deed by
> declaring that the killing of the father substitute, the totem,
> was not allowed, and denounced the fruits of their deed
> by denying themselves the liberated women. Thus they cre-

ated two fundamental taboos of totemism out of the sense of guilt of the son, and for this very reason these had to correspond with the two repressed wishes of the Oedipus complex" (*ibid.*: 915–17).

Thus, according to Freud, the Oedipus complex gave rise to totemism, incest taboos, exogamy, the ritual totem meal, and society itself. The totem animal is the father—feared, envied, and yet also loved. Freud now sets up an evolutionary developmental scheme: every religious sacrifice is the old totem meal, and the god in every case is modeled after the father (*ibid.*:919). The totem animal loses its sacred nature in time, and the rite becomes a simple offering to the deity. This deity, in turn, becomes more and more exalted, until ordinary man can no longer directly communicate with him and a priesthood must be created (*ibid.*: 921–22).

The theme that religion originated in frustration and remorse (and is therefore basically an obsessional neurosis) is further elaborated in *The Future of an Illusion* and in *Civilization and its Discontents*. Religion (not totemism) comes into being, Freud maintains, as a psychological necessity. Helpless against nature's forces, man must take a stand against them in order to define his position. Therefore he assigns human qualities to storms, earthquakes, and other frightening phenomena, and relieves his tensions by reacting against these personified forces with anger and rage. But again, the gods are mere father figures, because anthropomorphy is always based upon phylogenetic experiences. The most powerful of these experiences, man's ungratified desire for his mother, is frustrated by the presence of the father. Thus the primal father, frightening in thunder and earthquakes, is the prototype of god. Religion is, then, "an infantile obsessional neurosis," and the future of this illusion is, hopefully but not certainly, that man will outgrow the need for it (1928:Chap. 10).

In *Moses and Monotheism*, Freud applied his analysis to Judaism. According to Freud, Jewish monotheism derives from the innovations of Amenhotep IV, the Egyptian pharaoh who inaugurated the worship of one supreme god, Aton. One of his loyal followers was Moses, an Egyptian prince, who would not abandon his religion after the pharaoh's death (about 1369 B.C.) and the reinstatement of polytheism. In his loneliness and disappoint-

ment, Moses turned to the Jews, a Semitic tribe that had im-
migrated to Egypt a few generations earlier. Leaving Egypt with
this group, he hallowed them by the custom of circumcision,
gave them laws, and introduced them to the worship of Aton,
who becomes the Jewish Adonai (1955:74). But the Jews, a stub-
born and unruly group, may have found the laws of Moses even
more restrictive than those of the Egyptians. At this point, Freud
finds some very obscure evidence to support his contention that
the rebellious Jews killed Moses, rejected the new religion, and
adopted a tribal god of the Midianites, Jahve. The parallel with
Totem and Taboo now becomes clear: Moses, the "father" of
the Jews in exodus, is slayed by his rebellious "children." Later,
guilt feelings impel the "children" to resume allegiance to his
laws and his god, and thus Jahve and Adonai become one.

It is not difficult to criticize Freud's theories on religion, but
it would be, as Kroeber says, "breaking a butterfly on the wheel"
(1939:446). Nevertheless, Freud's reconstructions were based on
fancy and not on fact. Exogamy and totem-abstinence are not
universal in totemism, blood-sacrifice is not universal, and the
persistence of "totemic guilt" from early times to the present is
highly conjectural. But most other theories about the origin of
religion were based upon wrong presuppositions and unfounded
speculations. The problem here is that Freud's great authority
in psychology and psychoanalysis has led many subsequent investigators to accept his views on nonliterate society and religion.
His unfortunate equation of children, neurotics and nonliterates
still plague many contemporary anthropologists and psychologists. Actually, every culture, literate or not, has its own adult
normality, its own varieties of childhood, and its own neuroses.
Every culture has its own valid set of norms and standards to
which its members are trained to conform. Nonliterate societies,
therefore, represent neither infantile stages of mankind nor arrested deviations from Western cultural norms, but a complete
way of mature human living.

Freud's work on psychology has been of greater value to anthropology, by adding the dimension of man to the study of
culture and providing insight into the influence of childhood
and child-rearing practices upon the formation of personality.
And even if his theories about the nature and origin of religion

are now unacceptable, his discovery that the gods are often the projection of man's ordinary life is certainly important.

PHENOMENOLOGICAL THEORIES

Little attention has been given in America to the attempts to apply phenomenology to the study of religion. Yet, phenomenology and anthropology have much in common, for both seek objectivity and both the explanation of human beliefs and actions in terms of what they actually mean to those who hold them. The principal exponents of phenomenology were William Dilthey (1833–1911) and Edmund Husserl (1859–1938).

Phenomenology means *the study of phenomena,* and the term *phenomenon* is taken in its original Greek meaning as *that which reveals itself.* Phenomenology holds that all facts and experiences can and must speak for themselves, and show their "intentions." But their intentions can be discerned only if nothing else interferes, so that all preconceived schemes—historical, philosophical, psychological, or sociological—must be abandoned. When, for instance, we investigate religious belief with, say, history in mind, we will discover aspects of history; but this is not the "intention" of religion. All phenomena have their own intentions, and they all intend "something." It is this "something" which the phenomenologist tries to discover, meanwhile suspending all inquiries into problems of truth, and "bracketing" all relations to the empirical world. Phenomenologists contend that the outside empirical world must be "bracketed"—temporarily disregarded in order to see, hear, and sense the phenomena and their essential meanings. They do not claim that other approaches are invalid, but they feel that these approaches have concentrated on the discovery of relationships, thereby overlooking essence. The task of a phenomenologist is not the deduction of the rational, but the description of the conceivable—that which comes from "inconvertibly given evidence." The phenomena then become "pure consciousness," and their meanings are grasped through the logic of "intuition."

Phenomenology itself has taken many different directions, and there is no firm agreement about its principles or applications. In practice, the principle of "bracketing" has been the most difficult to apply. Most phenomenologists work within their own—and therefore preconceived—conceptual frameworks. Yet, the method has been applied, with interesting results, to the analysis of value-systems, ethics, ontology, psychology, language, and religion.

Rudolf Otto

Its application to the study of religion is exemplified by the writings of the German philosopher and theologian, Rudolf Otto (1869–1937), whose book, *The Idea of the Holy,* has been very influential. Otto declares that it is necessary to articulate the nature of religious experience before investigating religious expression, because experience must have preceded expression. Religious experience is experience of the Holy, which is always endowed with power, reason, purpose, love, and good will. But before anything can acquire such rational attributes, its existence must be discovered or perceived, and this discovery itself is nonrational.

Man discovers the Holy through the recognition that there is something else beside him. The nature of this something is only gradually learned; at first it is merely felt as a transcendent presence. The manifestation of this something can be learned only from man's reactions toward it. Originally and everywhere man reacts with dread and fascination toward the mystery of the "other presence." These human reactions then give us the clues about the nature of the Holy: it is the *Mysterium Tremendum* and the *Mysterium Fascinans. Tremendum* plays on both meanings of the term—that which is tremendous and overpowering, and which makes man tremble. Man trembles, however, not with fear (which, in Otto's terminology, is rational) but with the nonrational feelings of dread or awe (1958:16). At the same time, the mystery also draws man toward itself in mystical communion.

Otto gives many examples of man's expressions of dread and fascination, most of them taken from literate societies rather than from ethnographic sources. Yet he feels that the "fantastic idols" of nonliterate man demonstrate his dread, while their profusion shows his fascination. Otto attacks all theories of animism that present religion as deriving from fear of the dead, or from mana. Even if man feared the dead, he argues, such feelings could not have given rise to the concept of the Holy. Otto applies the term *numinous* to the state of mind in which man approaches the Holy, a state in which man recognizes the mystery of the "wholly other," and develops a feeling of dependence, of smallness, which Otto calls *creature feeling* or *creature consciousness*.

Religion arises, then, out of emotions, but the emotions are caused by the nature of the Holy. Emotions are, to Otto, *sui generis* (i.e., they are given, natural categories, phenomena which cannot be further reduced). Fear, respect, love, and dread are all emotions, but dread forms a separate category because it alone is nonrational.

From the numinous state of mind arises first the concept of demons. Because man cannot grasp the nature of the Holy, he must anthropomorphize it. He assigns rational human qualities to the Holy, and demons eventually become the centers of worship, still later evolving into gods or God.

Otto's explanation, like Tylor's, is individualistic, and leaves open the question of how individual experiences become communal and social. Otto is aware of this problem, and he seeks a not very convincing solution. He maintains that a prophet or seer is assigned to each *numen,* and it is he who experiences the Holy at first hand. When such a person reveals the numen, forms of worship and a common cult arise (*ibid.:*122).

Otto's theory is interesting, and he avoids a number of pitfalls by insisting upon the nonrational nature of religious experience. Also, Otto was more interested in the nature of the Holy than in evolution. Yet he presents theories of both origin and evolution which find no support in current knowledge about nonliterate peoples' reactions to the sacred. Some do react with "dread," but others treat their deities with great familiarity or irreverence, sometimes even scolding or threatening them. Otto would undoubtedly reply that these were secondary and rational developments, arising only after "dread" had established the presence of the Holy, but he would be unable to prove this contention. As long as he does take ethnographic material into account, he should provide an answer for its variations. But it appears that Otto did not sufficiently "bracket" his preconceptions, and he bases his concept of primeval dread upon his own introspective feelings toward God.

A more serious criticism is that he fails to relate the concept of the Holy to the facts and requirements of everyday life. It is not that he neglects these aspects of religion, but rather that his type of analysis renders them inexplicable.

RELIGION AND CULTURE

Max Weber (1864–1920)

The major link between the study of religion in the nineteenth century and that in the twentieth can be found in the works of Max Weber. A contemporary of Durkheim, and, like Durkheim, a sociologist, Weber displays the nineteenth-century interest in origin and evolution, but departs radically from the modes of thought that prevailed among his contemporaries.

Weber stressed the relationship of religion to other cultural institutions, especially economics. With Durkheim he shared an interest in the place of religion in society. Rather than explaining it in terms of society as a whole, Weber saw a causal significance of religious ideas in their interaction with other social institutions. While Durkheim had drawn his data from non-literate societies, Weber turned to Confucianism, Taoism, Hinduism, and ancient Judaism. He was not greatly influenced by the anthropological speculations of his time, for he relied more upon the study of classics, history, philosophy, and economics. His work in the sociology of religion became famous through his essay, *The Protestant Ethic and the Spirit of Capitalism* (1904–5), the well-known thesis of which is that Calvinistic Protestantism preconditioned the rise of capitalism.

In this essay as in later writings, Weber successfully combined the historical approach with a functional one. In *The Protestant Ethic,* Weber achieves historical depth by describing the cumulative interactions between religion and economy. By using this approach, Weber can account for culture change in a much more meaningful way than is possible in an exclusively functional approach.

Although *The Protestant Ethic* constituted a departure in the sociology of religion, Weber soon realized that comparative studies were necessary. Although he had found that one form of religion could shape man's secular actions, he did not conclude that this must be the case everywhere. Later, he stressed the necessity for intensive cultural studies. Unlike Durkheim, who had stated: "One single case may make a law appear" (1961:115), Weber turned to the study of the religions of China and India as well as ancient Judaism, and he had planned comparable studies of Islam, of early Christianity, and of medieval Catholicism.

But although Weber insisted that every culture be studied intensively and separately, he did not become a cultural relativist. Instead, he found *comparable* aspects between cultures and their institutions, and made some of these aspects generalizable through his principle of the "ideal type."

In Weber's terminology, an "ideal type" is constructed from the study of different expressions of personality, institutions, or culture, resulting in (respectively) an ideal personality type, an ideal institutional type, and an ideal cultural type. Such types are rarely, if ever, found in a "pure" form, but they reveal dominant modes—not, as Weber stressed, statistical averages (1958:200, n. 28). Ideal types are thus deliberate accentuations of historical reality, which make possible scientific control over that reality. Weber acutely observed the many differences, both temporal and spatial, among cultures, as well as the manifold expressions of individual character and temperament within each culture. He saw, correctly, that all meaningful comparisons must allow both generalization and abstraction. Comparative studies had, of course, been made long before Weber's time, but the unit of comparison was frequently left unclear. Even if disagreement exists about what constitutes an "ideal type" in one culture or another, the isolation and delineation of what is being compared is in itself clarifying and makes comparisons much more meaningful. Ideal types are thus useful devices, reflecting the full particularity of history or of individuals but formulated in such a way that the particularity can be at least partially generalized.

One such an "ideal type," for example, is the "charismatic religious leader." In certain cultures, under certain circumstances, religious leadership is typified by an extraordinary quality of personality, or an ability to exert authority to which others submit (Gerth and Mills, 1958:295). Once this type had been constructed—in the awareness of individual and cultural variations of charismatic behavior—it became possible to look for the presence of such leaders in other cultures. Even if they are not found, their absence is a significant negative trait for which subsequent explanations can be sought.

Weber also deals with the origin and evolution of religion, dominant nineteenth-century concerns. However, even his treatment of evolution was "modern." Nineteenth-century evolutionism was predominantly unilineal; that is, cultural development was considered in general and worldwide terms—"from homogeneity to heterogeneity" (Spencer), "from animism to monotheism" (Tylor), or from savagery to barbarism to civilization (Tylor, Morgan, et al.). This approach was eventually replaced by the concept of multilineal evolution. Multilineal evolutionists recognize that cultural traditions may be wholly or partially distinctive, and although they attempt to make historical reconstructions wherever possible, they do not classify these in universal stages. Instead, they compare cultures and cultural developments in order to find possible significant regularities (Steward, 1953:313–26). Multilineal evolutionists do not search for ultimate origins, and, although Weber made such an effort, he did not attempt to pinpoint the origin of religion at a specific time or place. Neither did he start with preconceived ideas about early man's rationality or lack of it. Observing that religion in every known culture has economic implications, he posited that this had always been true, that the most elementary forms of religion were oriented towards this world rather than the beyond (1964:1). Religion, according to Weber, was first purposive, and nonsymbolic. The soul, for instance, was not conceived as a personal or impersonal entity; it was directly identified with something that, like the heartbeat or the breath, disappears after death. The essential change in religion is the introduction of symbolism:

> Transitions from preanimistic naturalism to symbolism were altogether variable as regards specific details. When the primitive tears out the heart of a slain foe, or wrenches the sexual organs from the body of his victim, or extracts the brain from the skull and then mounts the skull in his home or esteems it as the most precious of bridal presents, or eats parts of the bodies of slain foes or the bodies of especially powerful animals—he really believes that he is coming into possession, in a naturalistic fashion, of the various powers

attributed to these physical organs. The war dance is in the first instance a mixture of fury and fear before the battle, and it directly produces a heroic frenzy; to this extent it too is naturalistic rather than symbolic. But insofar as the war dance, in the pattern of manipulations by sympathetic magic, mimetically anticipates victory and seeks to insure it by magical means, ... the transition to symbolism is at hand (1964:9).

Weber, then, did not seek one specific origin of religion; he left open the possibility of multiple origins. He also implied that economic concerns precede religious ones. Although scientific verification of this theory is not possible, it is not unreasonable; animals must "make a living," but they do not have anything even vaguely resembling religion. In the process of humanization, through which man became a "cultured animal," subsistence activities were carried over, but religion had to be created.

In his discussions of the further developments of religions, Weber emphasizes differentiation. Again and again he demonstrates how religious developments are influenced by specific historical, cultural, and economic circumstances. Yet, all religious systems express man's conception of himself, his place in the universe, and the normative order of his society. Social order, however, is not constant, because man is always attempting to clarify it intellectually. The thinking process—rationalization—is, according to Weber, one of the primary factors of change. In this, he again exhibits a nineteenth-century influence. Yet Weber's rationalism was tempered by his insistence upon the dynamic interaction between historical circumstances and social structure as concomitant factors in cultural change.

In the course of his work, Weber found that not all instances of change yielded to this type of analysis. Certain cultural permutations seemed totally unpredictable. He called such changes *breakthroughs*. In the historical development of any culture, crucial moments appear where two alternative directions can be taken: one will reinforce the existing order; the other, alter it. The latter constitutes a breakthrough, and Weber makes it clear that such a process is initiated by those individuals who are unable or unwilling to accept the existing order. One of

Weber's examples is Buddha, who, though born a prince, was not satisfied by the Brahmin philosophy in which he was raised. Renouncing his family, he became a homeless wanderer until he found "enlightenment," and then began to teach his new doctrines. A social breakthrough of this type, however, depends upon at least two factors: the charisma of the individual leader, and a change—political, economic, or other—in social conditions.

It is not possible to do justice to the tremendous scope of Weber's insights and contributions within so brief a discussion. Although his theories have not gone unchallenged, his writings have done more than those of perhaps any other scholar, to overcome the dogmatism of nineteenth-century evolutionists and positivists.

CONCLUSION

The nineteenth century exhibited a strong interest in religious phenomena and a great variety in theory. Juxtaposition of such names as Frazer and Weber, Tylor and Durkheim, Freud and Wilhelm Schmidt shows at once that there were differences not only in theoretical outlook, but also in background and method. It is difficult to find one representative theme with which all scholars were centrally concerned. Nevertheless, they held in common an interest in origin and historical development.

Any theory about the genesis of religion must remain speculative. No historical or archeological records provide evidence of the thought processes of early men. Criticism of nineteenth-century theorists should not, however, be directed to their speculations but to the fact that they continued to build upon them. Scientific method does not preclude speculation, but it cannot permit the construction of vast systems based upon assumptions. This was precisely the flaw in the nineteenth-century "science" of religion.

Nevertheless, the questions with which nineteenth-century scholars were concerned were valid. The broad framework of theoretical propositions to which the scholars attempted to find answers and explanations played an essential role in shaping the further developments of the study of religion.

4

Twentieth-Century Theories of Religion

TWENTIETH-CENTURY SCHOLARSHIP REFLECTS AN EVER-INCREASING awareness of the inadequacy of older methods. The new generation of investigators became keenly aware of the great need for better data, and thus for first-hand observations. They soon discovered that magic, animism, fetishism, or totemism were not the clear-cut concepts their predecessors had imagined them to be. Historical reconstructions gave little guidance, and proved impossible in many cases. One early fieldworker wrote:

> It was largely from this [historical] point of view that I approached the study of the Andaman Islanders and attempted by an investigation of physical character, language, and culture to make a hypothetical reconstruction of the Andamans. . . . During the course of my work a systematic examination of the methods available for such reconstructions of the unknown past convinced me that it is only in extremely rare instances that we can ever approach demonstrable conclusions and that speculative history cannot give us results of any real importance for the understanding of human life and culture (Radcliffe-Brown, 1964:vii).

It was not surprising, therefore, that many twentieth-century investigators abandoned historical considerations. Instead, they discovered that the customs and beliefs of nonliterate societies played important roles in these societies and had meaning for the people in them. The emphasis shifted from the past to the

81

present, from history to function. Functionalism, as this school
of thought came to be called, replaced evolutionism. Only later,
particularly in the United States, was it concluded that functionalists had gone too far in the rejection of history and evolution.
Even if ultimate origins could not be found, it was often possible
to make limited reconstructions based upon existing records,
archeological findings, the recollections of older informants, and
known patterns of diffusion.

BRITISH THEORIES

Although the new functionalists rejected evolutionism, they
remained indebted to the insights of those who had studied
culture and religion before them. In England, it was not Tylor,
but Émile Durkheim who became the central figure in the
subsequent development of social anthropology. He directly influenced both Radcliffe-Brown and Malinowski, the men who
shaped social anthropology in that country.

Alfred Reginald Radcliffe-Brown
Of the two, it was Alfred Reginald Radcliffe-Brown (1881–
1945) who most clearly and persistently laid down the principles
of functionalism. Trained at Cambridge by Alfred Cort Haddon
(1855–1940) and William Halsey R. Rivers (1865–1922), he
acquired their sense of the urgency of field work.

The two older men had participated in the 1898 Cambridge
Torres Strait Expeditions, the first in which a *team* of scientists
collaborated in the study of various aspects of culture. Rivers,
moreover, published a valuable book on the Todas of southern
India (1906) and another on the Melanesian peoples (1914). Both
works were based upon his own first-hand observations. None of
the early fieldworkers dealt extensively with religion. Haddon, a
zoologist, concentrated upon technology and art, while Rivers,
medically trained, made important contributions to the study
of kinship and social organization. He was also the first to ad-
minister psychological tests to nonliterate peoples.

Radcliffe-Brown's field work included research in the Andaman
Islands (1906–8), Australia (1910–12), and South Africa. He
brought his theories to America, teaching at the University of

Chicago from 1931 to 1937. His most important contributions to anthropology come from his theories rather than from his ethnographies. In his formulations of functionalism, he draws heavily upon analogies between social life and organic life (1952:178). His three key words—*structure, process* and *function* —are borrowed from biology, and their application to social life is first explained in biological terms:

> A complex organism, such as a human body, has a structure as an arrangement of organs and tissues and fluids. . . . An organism also has a life, and by this we refer to a process. The concept of organic function is one that is used to refer to the connection between the structure of an organism and the life processes of that organism. The processes that go on within a human body while it is living are dependent on the organic structure. It is the function of the heart to pump blood through the body. The organic structure, as a living structure, depends for its continued existence upon the processes that make up the total life processes. If the heart ceases to perform its function the life process comes to an end and the structure as a living structure also comes to an end. Thus process is dependent on structure and continuity of structure is dependent upon process (*ibid.:*12).

Social systems, too, have a structure. The interrelatedness of their customs and institutions gives them "life." Social function is, then, the relation between social structure and the processes of social life. Each of the separate features of social life has a function which contributes to the maintenance of structural continuity and thus to the coherence and perpetuation of the society as a whole. Like the human body, each society possesses a degree of functional unity because all parts of the system work together without producing persistent conflicts (*ibid.:*181). Radcliffe-Brown calls this *the working hypothesis* of functionalism, and it becomes the task of the investigator to establish the functions of the social activities encountered in his field work. Once sufficient data have been collected, cross-cultural comparisons must be made. These will reveal cross-cultural regularities, or, in Radcliffe-Brown's terms, *social laws.*

Radcliffe-Brown carefully points out that not everything in the life of a community has structure and function. Moreover, he guards against oversimplifications by stressing that apparently identical social usages in two or more cultures may well have very different functions.

In applying these principles to the study of religion, Radcliffe-Brown acknowledges his indebtedness to Durkheim. He avoided Durkheim's explanations of the origin of religion, but adopted his view that religious ritual is an expression of the unity of society, and that its function is to affirm and strengthen the sentiments upon which social solidarity, and therefore the social order itself, depends (*ibid.*:165). Using his field work in Australia, Radcliffe-Brown demonstrated that Durkheim and his followers erred in considering totemism as a single phenomenon, although their thesis of the social function of totemic ritual is basically correct and valid. Australian totemic rituals function not only to express and recreate the sentiments upon which the social order depends, but also reveal a close correspondence to the form of the wider social structure, such as kinship patterns. Thus when Australian informants said, "The kangaroo [totem] is my elder brother," they meant that the kangaroo species, conceived as a totemic entity, stood to them in a social relationship analogous to that in which men stand to their elder brothers in the kinship system (*ibid.*:169). In the account of his field work among the Andaman Islanders, Radcliffe-Brown applies the same methods in order to demonstrate that both myth and ritual are essential to their society, because they express sentiments upon which the very existence of the Andaman culture depends. Through regular expression in ritual, these important principles are kept alive and passed from generation to generation (1964:404).

Bronislaw Malinowski

Among present-day anthropologists, Bronislaw Malinowski (1884–1942) is considered particularly important because of his contributions to field work methodology. In his writings, particularly those dealing with the Trobriand Islanders, he gave new dimensions to ethnography. People were no longer treated as anonymous informants, but as living human beings with human likes and dislikes, with opinions and ideas. Malinowski recognized that the best documentation must remain barren if it is not filled out by commentaries from people about their own actions and beliefs. He added to his descriptions of cultural insti-

tutions what he called the "imponderabilia" of everyday life, including—among other things—the routine of a man's working
day, the details of his care of the body, the tone of the conversations around the village fires, the friendships and hostilities
among peoples. These conditions, and many others as well, are
part of the social fabric (1961:18–19).

Malinowski is also distinguished as a theorist. Like Radcliffe-
Brown, he is a functionalist, and the two men are usually
credited with founding this important school of thought. Yet,
Malinowski's concepts of function are somewhat different from
those of Radcliffe-Brown. Radcliffe-Brown uses the term function primarily in its biological sense, as that which contributes
to life. For Malinowski, function was more often equated with
purpose. While Radcliffe-Brown saw social institutions mainly
as parts contributing to the whole, Malinowski considered
society as something that can survive only if its basic needs are
fulfilled. In an organism, nutrition, breathing, and excretion aid
survival, but in a social system it is culture itself that is essential
to life: "Culture is a specifically human form of biological adjustment" (1960:75). Family organization is, in this view, a cultural response to the basic biological and social need for
reproduction, while the building of shelters answers the need
for physical protection. What is then the function of religion?

In order to answer this question, it becomes necessary to
explain Malinowski's theory of religion. Like Frazer and Durkheim, he makes a clear-cut distinction between magic and religion, and indeed sees them as having somewhat different
functions, although he also notes their similarities. Magic and
religion are alike in that both arise from universally experienced
emotional stress—man's realization of his inability to control
nature. Both, also, are based upon mythological tradition, and
both are surrounded by taboos which set them apart as sacred
(1954:87–88). But whereas magic is utilitarian and instrumental,
always directed to a clearly stated end, religion has no utility
but is an end in itself. According to Malinowski:

> While in the magical act the underlying idea and aim is
> always clear, straightforward, and definite, in the religious
> ceremony there is no purpose directed toward a subsequent
> event. It is only possible for the sociologist to establish the

function, the sociological *raison d'être* of the act. The native can always state the end of the magical rite, but he will say of a religious ceremony that it is done because such is the usage, or because it has been ordained, or he will narrate an explanatory myth (*ibid.*:38).

Magic, moreover, can be evil as well as good (black and white magic), while religion is essentially moral (*ibid.*:89). Marriage ceremonies, for instance, are typically religious. They are held not to create the union between husband and wife, but to demonstrate it. The same is true for initiation rites: they do not produce maturity, but herald it. Rituals held during pregnancy, on the other hand, have a definite and practical purpose— namely, to prevent death in childbed—and they are thus of a magical nature (*ibid.*:37–38).

Although Malinowski's distinction as well as his examples are open to criticism, he supplies the important insight that many ritual activities are carried out in situations in which the outcome of human undertakings is uncertain. Nonliterate man does not have a generalized "magical worldview," nor does he confuse magic with logic. The Trobriand Islanders had at least two distinct procedures for dealing with their physical world. They had at their command an impressive amount of sound and practical knowledge which they successfully applied to the business of making a living. But there were limits to their skills and knowledge. In spite of all efforts, the crops would sometimes fail because of droughts, blights, or other unforseeable and uncontrollable events. In these instances they would resort to magic.

Magic, then, is neither a form of primitive and mistaken science, as Tylor and Frazer had maintained, nor a confusion of the natural and the supernatural, as Lévy-Bruhl would have it. Magic is, to Malinowski, a complement to rational systems of thought and knowledge. Nonliterate man never relies upon magic alone, but "clings to it whenever he has to recognize the impotence of his knowledge and of his rational technique" (*ibid.*: 32). The function of magic is to supply man with a "definite and practical technique which serves to bridge over the dangerous gap in every important pursuit or critical situation" (*ibid.*:90).

In Malinowski's view, the function of religion lies in a different area. Religious rituals, like magical ones, are carried out in situations of emotional stress, but they are not expected to bring clearly definable, direct results. When death occurs, the Trobriand people know as well as anyone else that rituals cannot restore life. Death, moreover, reminds the living of their own mortality, and is thus doubly disturbing and emotionally upsetting. Because man cannot face the idea of annihilation, he creates a comforting belief in spiritual continuity and an afterlife. Mourning rituals do not achieve immortality; they express it. As such they are "ends in themselves," but they also fulfill important "biological" functions. In small communities, the death of a member "breaks the normal course of life and shakes the moral foundations of society" (ibid.:53). Even when the loss does not immediately affect every member of a society, the rituals remain communal. Bereaved members of the group, overcome by sorrow, are unable to carry out the religious rituals, so society steps in to lead the stricken individuals through the comforting experiences of religious ceremony (ibid.:62–63).

Religion, like magic, thus represents an escape from human uncertainties and frustrations. But religious ritual is also a public statement of religious dogma, which in turn contains the value structure upon which the proper functioning of society depends. Particularly among nonliterate peoples, it is essential that the society's doctrines be regularly acted out in order that they may be safeguarded and transmitted to succeeding generations (ibid.: 67–68).

In his functional analysis of magic and religion, Malinowski is more creative and more explicit than Radcliffe-Brown, but he is also more dogmatic. Although Radcliffe-Brown had been careful to note that "what appears to be the same social usage in two societies may have different functions in the two" (1952:184), Malinowski states categorically: "Magic fulfills an indispensable function within culture. It satisfies a definite need which cannot be satisfied by any other factors of primitive civilization" (1926: 136). This "postulate of indispensability," as Merton called it (1957:32ff), provoked much criticism. It appears to exclude the possibility of functional alternatives. Moreover, it implies that magic in the Trobriand Islands is typical of magic all over the world. Nadel (1964:190) comments that Malinowski's thoughts seemed to move on two levels only: that of the Trobrianders

and that of society at large. This seemed to have happened
particularly in Malinowski's theories of magic. Without giving
specific examples, Malinowski feels that magic is "unchanging
and timeless," similar everywhere:

> Primitive magic—every field anthropologist knows it to his
> cost—is extremely monotonous and unexciting, strictly
> limited in its means of action, circumscribed in its beliefs,
> stunted in its fundamental assumptions. Follow one rite,
> study one spell, grasp the principles of magical belief, art,
> and sociology in one case, and you will know not only all
> the acts of the tribe, but, adding a variant here and there,
> you will be able to settle as a magical practitioner in any
> part of the world . . ." (1954:70).

Also, according to Malinowski, the functions of magic do not
significantly differ from place to place. It is "the standardization
of optimism" (1954:90; 1960:202), and such optimism is necessary
—indeed, indispensable—to man's biological need for safety
(1962:226). Magic alone provides man with the necessary confidence to "carry out his important tasks, to maintain his poise
and his mental integrity in fits of anger, in the throes of hate, of
unrequited love, of despair and anxiety" (1954:90). Magic becomes in Malinowski's hands the cure for a variety of human
ills.

Although magic occasionally plays such a role, it is obvious
that other institutions—such as education, art, sports, and so
on—often serve the same purposes. It is also very clear that
religion may serve the same functions as magic. But since
Malinowski has made a strict distinction between the two, he is
forced to assign a somewhat different task to religion. He posits,
first, that magic precedes religion, since its function is more
stringent, more directly related to survival.

> Then, once man develops the need of building up systems of
> knowledge and anticipation, he is bound to inquire into the
> origins of humanity, into its destinies, and into the problem
> of life, death, and the universe. Hence, as a direct result of
> man's need to build systems and to organize knowledge,
> there emerges also the need for religion (1960:202).

Malinowski overlooks the fact, however, that magic too is able to "systematize knowledge," and many secular institutions can do so equally well. Furthermore, these views cannot account for the negative sides of magic and religion. Both can cause tensions as well as alleviate them, cause insecurities as well as relieve them, and produce social disintegration as well as cohesion.

Nevertheless, Malinowski made substantial contributions to the understanding of magic and religion. It is obviously sounder to reason from the intimate and empirical knowledge of at least one culture than to theorize without any such experience. As Redfield remarked:

> The criticism so often leveled at Malinowski . . . loses much of its force if the assumption may be admitted that there are a common human nature and a universal culture pattern. . . . We may learn much of all societies from a single society, of all men from a few men, if unusual insight is combined with patient and prolonged study of what other students have written about other societies (1954:10).

Malinowski himself suggested that his critics encourage parallel inquiries into other cultures, and admitted that further testing is necessary (quoted by Lowie, 1937:240–41).

Furthermore, Malinowski often went beyond his own utilitarian theory. Particularly in his ethnographic descriptions, in which he was not immediately concerned with theory, he repeatedly demonstrated important interrelations between magic, religion and other institutions. Thus he notes how the magic rites accompanying the Trobriand agricultural cycle function to regulate and systematize the work, and carry it through its successive stages (1961:59–60). The magician acquires, through his functions, an authority which carries over in secular areas. Magic also allows for the organization and systematization of economic effort in the trading system known as the Kula ring (*ibid.*:392–427), and, among the Trobriand, magic is inherited along specific kinship lines, and is closely related to kinship rules and family organizations (*ibid.*:426). Religious ceremonies can have definite legal and economic implications, and even the weeping and wailing of a bereaved widow may be substantially rewarded by her dead husband's kinsmen in the form of ritual payment (1959:33–34).

Malinowski makes an interesting linguistic analysis of magical terminology (1961:428–63). Above all, he kept in mind that the various magical and religious observances had direct and often profound meanings for the Trobriand Islanders. Malinowski's practice rises above his theories, and he goes well beyond the abstract idea that religious institutions serve mainly to integrate societies.

AMERICAN THEORIES

In one sense, the development of anthropology in America parallels that in Europe. American scholars of the nineteenth century, like their European counterparts, were evolutionists. But American scholars placed far greater emphasis upon the need for first-hand observations. Such observations were facilitated by the proximity of the American Indians, and often fostered by other than anthropological considerations. Thomas Jefferson (1743–1826), in promoting the Lewis and Clark expedition (1804–6), certainly was not motivated by an interest in the American Indian culture *per se*. Yet, the results of the expedition stimulated Jefferson to encourage a systematic collection of ethnographic and linguistic data by the Philosophical Society. The president of that organization, Samuel Stanhope Smith (1750–1819), had already outlined a future anthropology when he wrote:

As the character, and manners, and state of society among the savages would make a very important part of the history of human nature, it appears to me to be an object that merits the attention of literary societies, not less than the discovery of new islands and seas. . . . I conceive it would not be unworthy of societies established for extending human knowledge, to employ good philosophers, who should be hardy enough for the undertaking, to travel among their remotest nations, which have never had any intercourse with Europeans; to reside among them on a familiar footing; to dress and live as they do; and to observe them when they should be under no bias or constraint. . . . Above all we should discover the nature and extent of their religious ideas, which have been ascertained with less accuracy than others, by travelers who have not known to set a proper value upon them (quoted by Hallowell, 1960:34–35).

One of the best-known early students of Indian myth and legend was Henry Rowe Schoolcraft (1793–1864). An Indian agent, he discovered (to his amazement) that the Ojibwa and other Indian tribes possessed a traditional oral literature. (Schoolcraft's famous collections later became the inspiration for Longfellow's long poem, *Hiawatha*.) With the establishment of the American Ethnological Society in 1842, and under the influence of such scholars as John Wesley Powell (1834–1902), the number of excellent collections rapidly increased.

Lewis Henry Morgan

Because of the emphasis on field work, there was relatively little theorizing either about myth or religion. Lewis Henry Morgan (1818–81), lawyer by profession, became interested in the Iroquois Indians, and eventually worked out a vast and ambitious scheme of human evolution. Although he was primarily interested in kinship organization, he extended his theories to many other cultural institutions—but he did not include religion. However, he does treat the influence of totemism upon kinship (1963:81; 1962:182).

The growth of religious ideas is environed with such intrinsic difficulties that it may never receive a perfectly satisfactory exposition. Religion deals so largely with the imaginative and emotional nature, and consequently with such uncertain elements of knowledge, that all primitive religions are grotesque and to some extent unintelligible (1963:5).

Nevertheless, Morgan's writings on kinship and kinship terminology blazed the trail for important avenues of research in these areas. And, although his direct influence upon the development of anthropology in America is relatively small, his work was to prove interesting and useful to Karl Marx and Friedrich Engels. (Engels used Morgan's writings as the foundation of his own book: *The Origin of the Family, Private Property, and the State in the Light of the Researches of Lewis Henry Morgan*.)

Franz Boas

It was Franz Boas (1858–1942) who greatly shaped the course of anthropology in the United States. Although most of the scholars discussed thus far can be categorized according to their dominant views, Boas cannot. Not only was his range of interest very wide, but his theoretical standpoints were anything but consistent. Kardiner epitomized Boas' position when he wrote: "He can be associated with almost all theories, but can be identified with none" (1963:138). Boas was rather impatient with theoretical speculations, and his contributions consisted more in the critical clarification of earlier doctrines than in the addition of new ones.

With Boas, anthropology became firmly rooted in empiricism. Keenly aware that many nonliterate cultures were fast disappearing, he viewed the collecting of objective data as a task of the utmost urgency. Among the fruits of his labors were the voluminous collections of myths, legends, and folktales from a large number of Indian tribes (Chinook, 1894; Bella Coola, 1898; Tsimshian, 1902, 1912, 1916; Kwakiutl, 1905, 1906, 1910, 1935; and many others). Many of these were rendered both in English and in the original language, so that they are also of great value to linguistic analysis.

Boas' theoretical contributions in the fields of mythology and religion were comparatively small. His theoretical emphasis is on diffusion, but he saw clearly that the borrowing of myths and folktales was never automatic, and that the themes were usually adapted to the cultural circumstances of the borrowers. Nor does Boas deny the possibility of independent inventions:

Two rules have been laid down as necessary for cautious progress. First, the tale or formula, the distribution of which is investigated and is to be explained as due to historical contact, must be so complex that an independent origin of the sequence of nonrelated elements seems to be improbable. . . . The second rule is that, for a satisfactory proof of dissemination, continuous distribution is required. The simpler the tale, the greater must be our insistence upon this condition (1940:458–59).

In comparing the myths of different Indian tribes, Boas attempted to trace every historical connection so as to determine what was peculiar to one group and what was borrowed. But he tended to minimize the distinctions between folktales and myths, indicating that he was less interested in the religious character of the latter. Boas sees myth mainly as a story with a plot, consisting of a number of elements or traits. These elements lend themselves to cross-cultural comparison more readily than the whole, and their historical connections can be discovered much more easily.

This same attitude governs his approach to religion. In studying totemism, for instance, Boas focuses on its component traits rather than on its overall meaning or function. Noting that the elements of different totemic systems are quite distinct, he shows clearly that totemism is anything but a simple and unified concept. Conspicuous similarities between the totemic systems of neighboring tribes, according to Boas, are most probably the result of diffusion; they do not reflect universally similar historical or psychological origins. A variety of beginnings or origins are possible—the observation of nature, artistic feelings, philosophical considerations, linguistic forms, and so on (1940: 316–23). Such considerations give rise to questions concerning the validity of the comparative method, and these questions plagued Boas more and more during his lifetime.

There is no "Boasian school" of anthropology today, nor is there any theory closely associated with his name. Yet, his influence is generally acknowledged by those who studied under him. He was able to communicate to them the urgency of anthropological research "not by preachments," as Margaret Mead put it, "but by tempo, tone, and gesture, and this urgency remained with us" (1959:43).

Leslie Spier

A number of Boas' students pursued his distribution and diffusion studies. One who dealt with religion was Leslie Spier (1893–1961). In his book, *The Prophet Dance of the Northwest and its Derivatives: The Source of the Ghost Dance* (1935), he compared these two religious cults and found significant similarities in content, but he also showed that the older Prophet Dance is nearer to the native culture of the Indian tribes who practiced it. Using extensive documentation, he plotted the geographic distribution of the two cults, as well as that of the Shaker cult. The Prophet Dance was by far the most widespread, extending farther south, east, and north than the Ghost Dance, thus indicating, with the support of known chronology, that the latter developed on the older foundation laid by the Prophet cult. The Shaker cult extends along the border of the Pacific, from the northern fringe of South California to Puget Sound, and seems to represent a western extension of the older native cults.

Spier's type of treatment retains an interest in historical questions. This remained true for most subsequent studies, and it is perhaps one of the most significant differences between American and British anthropology. Even when functional and psychological explanations came to prevail in the United States, the historical perspective was seldom lost. Attempts to reconstruct the past became, of course, much more modest. Not only had Boas critically exposed the weaknesses of evolutionary theories, but rapidly mounting evidence of archeology and paleontology pushed the beginnings of man and his culture to such distant ages that any hope to recover absolute origins had to be abandoned. Furthermore, the emphasis on empirical and objective data restricted speculative thought. Nevertheless, it was found that limited reconstructions of specific cultural items were both feasible and useful.

Alexander Goldenweiser

Alexander Goldenweiser (1880–1940), for instance, dealt with the origin of totemism (1931:363–92) as one socioreligious phenomenon, rather than seeking an absolute beginning of religion or magic. Although many earlier theorists had treated totemism as a clear-cut, uniform phenomenon, Goldenweiser noted that the alleged totemic criteria were by no means universal. With impressive documentation he showed that exogamy, which had been hailed by Frazer and others as the hallmark of totemism, was absent in a number of tribes. Other "totemic" traits—such as the group's belief in descent from a totem, taboos centered around it, the naming of the groups after their totem, clan organization, and so on—were often wanting, so that no feature appeared to be either necessary or specific.

This discovery did not lead Goldenweiser to conclude that there was no connection between the various forms of totemism. Rather, he stressed that connections should not be sought in traits, but in structure. He found that there were two constant elements in totemism: a defined social group, and emotional value. Furthermore, since social grouping is a universal phenomenon and totemism is not, it may be assumed that the former is the older. Totemic beliefs were thus superimposed upon existing social systems. As Goldenweiser put it:

> In a community subdivided into social units, such as clans, the first demand is for some kind of classifiers, preferably names, which would identify the separate units and yet signify their equivalence by belonging to one category. Again, hereditary kinship groups, such as clans, with a strong feeling of common interest and solidarity tend, so sociopsychological experience shows, to project their community spirit into some concrete thing which henceforth stands for the unity of the group and readily acquires a certain halo of sanctity. It often happens with such objects that certain rules of behavior develop with reference to them, both positive and negative rules, prescriptions, and restrictions. Such objects thus become symbols of the social values of the group (1931:381).

Totemism has, according to Goldenweiser, a logical origin— the desire of certain groups to distinguish themselves from other groups. But there might well have been groups that had no such desire or chose other forms of distinction.

Because the phenomena were so heterogeneous, Goldenweiser concluded that they had no common historical or psychological origin. Totemic ideas were independently conceived at different times and in different parts of the world, and adapted to the specific social circumstances. From these various points diffusion of the ideas took place. If the underlying social structures were similar, the totemic complexes would, in all likelihood, also be similar.

Goldenweiser's theories have not remained unchallenged. Lowie, for instance, questioned even the universality of the emotional value of the totems (1947:142). He was forced to the conclusion that "totemism can only be studied as a series of specific problems *not* related to one another," except when it appears in a continuous area where it can be clearly proven that the elements were borrowed.

Goldenweiser contributed the important insight that totemism, or any other system of religion, cannot be derived from any one of its specific features. Totemism, whatever else it may be, is a cultural phenomenon to be understood in its cultural setting. As Goldenweiser put it: "Neither the sociopsychological nature of totemism, nor its geographical distribution, nor its historic role can be understood without a proper appraisal of the underlying social skeleton" (1942:327).

Paul Radin

While Leslie Spier followed up Boas' idea on diffusion, and Goldenweiser elaborated on his method of historical reconstruction, another one of Boas' students, Paul Radin (1883–1959), applied his technique of using literate Indians to record aspects of their own culture. Radin's principal field work was done with the Winnebago Indians, and his focus was on myth and religion. His many publications include the autobiography of a Winnebago Indian, Crashing Thunder (1920). This work gave a penetrating view of a culture "from within," and showed how great differences may exist between cultural and religious rules and their interpretation and acceptance by individuals.

Earlier, it had been taken more or less for granted that nonliterate cultures formed homogeneous collective unities, and that religious beliefs were not critically examined. Crashing Thunder showed that this was not so. In the Winnebago culture it was important that young men seek a vision, often by means of prolonged fasting, which gave them a certain mystical power. Crashing Thunder was a skeptic, and admitted that he only pretended to have a vision. Luck seemed to confirm his power. But the cultural value system had its consequences nevertheless: he realized that a faked vision could only give false power. He reacted by antisocial behavior—drinking, debauchery, fraud, and murder. Only later, when the Peyote cult reached the Winnebago, did he have "genuine" visions brought on by the ingestion of the hallucinatory peyote plants. His personality became reoriented, and he was henceforth an important and respected member of his society.

The recognition of such cultural deviance led Radin to an

interest in personality and in psychology. Probably to the great disappointment of Boas, Radin believed that psychology could help in the reconstruction of the origin and evolution of magic and religion. In his book, *Primitive Religion: Its Nature and Origin* (1937), he revived the old theory that religion originated in fear. This fear, according to Radin, was not inspired by natural phenomena or by dreams or death, but by the lack of economic security. Early man, said Radin, lived in an inimical physical environment and lacked the means by which to defend himself or to make a satisfactory living. Although early man's mentality was largely dominated by "animal characteristics," Radin assures us that he desired "happiness, success, and a long life" (1957:6). The conflict between what man wanted but could not attain "naturally led to a disorientation and disintegration of the ego. The mental correlate for such a condition is subjectivism, and subjectivism means the dominance of magic and of the most elementary forms of coercive rites" (*ibid.*:7).

Once magic was established, it evolved into religion in four stages: the completely coercive, the incompletely coercive, the reciprocally coercive, and the noncoercive (*ibid.*:7–8). This is a modified version of Freud's theory of religious origin. Radin agrees with Freud that religion is a "compensation fantasy," but he believes it stems from economic insecurity rather than from the Oedipus conflict.

Radin's theory is not only conjectural, but also rather implausible. There is no evidence that early man was economically insecure, and his success as a species seems to contradict this presupposition. Furthermore, economic insecurity does not necessarily lead to a "disintegration of the ego"; it sometimes inspires greater efforts. Moreover, one might well ask how this utterly insane humanity ever became sane again.

Radin's answer was, in a way, that some people were more religious-minded than others. Personalities differ, and each is one of two types: the "philosopher-thinker-artist" type and the "layman" type. The former is interested in the analysis of religious phenomena; the latter, only in its results. The "thinkers" became religious specialists: shamans, medicinemen, and priests: and "the fundamental trait of all shamans and medicinemen everywhere . . . [is that] they must be disoriented . . ." (*ibid.*:107). These neurotic thinkers were, according to Radin, the only people sufficiently articulate to describe to others what they felt and saw. The reality they described was that of people neurotically susceptible to all inward stirrings, physical and mental (*ibid.*:107). Together with their liability to trances and epileptic fits, they became "eminently suitable to become religious leaders. At their hands, magical rites and observances received a voluminous and loving elaboration" (*ibid.*:133). Later, when the emoluments of office increased, normal individuals were also attracted to the priesthood (*ibid.*:131). By that time, however, the neurotic pattern of religious behavior had "become fixed, and the nonneurotic shaman had to accept the formulation which owed its origin and its initial development to his neurotic predecessors and colleagues" (*ibid.*:132).

Radin presents what he calls "concrete illustrations" in an effort to show both "the universality and the persistence of certain neurotic-epileptoid features in even the most complicated civilizations where the priest has become a figure of an entirely different order from the simple magician or shaman" (*ibid.*:110). These illustrations consist of accounts given by native shamans and priests in nine different societies of the details of initiation into the religious profession. The accounts may well strike uninformed Western readers as neurotic, but no serious psychiatrist would venture to make such a diagnosis on the basis of some highly symbolic statements taken out of religious and cultural context. Any such judgment, if it is to be scientific, must take into account the full personality of the individual concerned as well as the social environment in which it developed. Radin neglects these important scientific procedures, and judges the native testimonies on the basis of Western symbolism. Moreover, he is certainly stretching a point when he infers from only nine statements that "neurotic" features are universal concomitants of religious office.

Robert Lowie

This does not mean that psychological approaches to the study of religion are useless. Robert Lowie (1883–1957), in an early work on religion showed that psychology could be used in combination with other anthropological techniques. This is now considered so obvious as to be hardly worth mentioning, but at the time Lowie wrote his book, *Primitive Religion* (1924), it was a novel thought. Psychological interpretations had been made before, of course, but anthropologists had generally overlooked the possibility that the two disciplines might complement each other.

Lowie does not fall into the error of assigning neurotic qualities to religion and its leaders. He is careful to stress that psychological interpretations cannot be made in isolation from cultural constellations and their histories. Like several of his predecessors, he uses the Ghost Dance to illustrate his method. Combining historical, anthropological, and psychological insights, he gives some important clues toward the explanation of the rapid but irregular diffusion of this cult (1952:188–200). The Ghost Dance originated among the Paiute Indians in Nevada, when a prophet, Wovoka, announced that visions had revealed to him that the deceased ancestors would return to life, and that the tribesmen should prepare themselves for this event by attending specific ritual dances. The Ghost Dance spread to a large number of other tribes, including the Plains Indian Teton, who accepted it around 1890.

A scholar using psychology as his only tool would tend to explain the acceptance of this religion by describing the longing for the deceased as a phenomenon of universal occurrence, a human motive that requires no further explanation (ibid.:199). But Lowie correctly observes that this explanation begs the question, because this supposedly universal longing had never before produced a belief in the return of the dead among the Teton. Acceptance of the new dogma demands additional explanation, and this can be found both in the history of the group and in its changed cultural conditions. Historically, the older forms of religion included a strong belief in the power of visions. The fact that the messengers of the prophet told the Teton Indians that he had received his revelations in a vision made it possible for them to accept those revelations. The message itself was psychologically welcome, because the ancestors would, upon their alleged return, also destroy the white invaders. At least three elements are thus necessary for understanding the diffusion of the Ghost Dance: the historical background (the acceptability of visions); the changed cultural conditions (the presence of the whites was felt more strongly), and psychological readiness.

Lowie maintains that certain psychological qualities are pre-requisite to leadership in religion as others are essential to leadership in politics (*ibid.*:247), and that not every individual possesses the necessary mental qualifications. However, it is a misunderstanding to think that only those psychologically most suitable will become religious leaders. Religious office may be a hereditary privilege, or it may be tied to political office, or it may be bestowed as a favor by political leaders. "Even when we are bent on determining the individual mentality, we are thus obliged to examine constantly the social concomitants" (*ibid.*: 222).

Ruth Fulton Benedict

Still a different use of psychology was made by Ruth Fulton Benedict (1887–1948). Like Lowie, she emphasizes culture rather than individuals, as her influential book, *Patterns of Culture,* clearly shows. She describes and contrasts three nonliterate groups: the Pueblo Indians (chiefly the Zuni), the Kwakiutl Indians of the Northwest Coast, and the Melanesian Dobu. She finds significant cultural and emotional differences among them. In terms borrowed from the German philosopher Nietzsche, the Pueblos are typified as Apollonian, while the Kwakiutl and Dobu are Dionysian. *Dionysian* denotes a cultural emphasis on violent experiences, emotional excess, frenzy, and intoxication. *Apollonian* denotes a distrust of excess, and an inclination for the middle of the road, the peaceful, the harmonious, and the sober (1946:79).

Benedict also maintained that every culture has a psychological unity that gives rise to a certain congruence in the behavior patterns of the members of the group. In the course of socialization, the child learns the forms of conduct acceptable to its society, and thus tends to be molded into the type of person considered desirable by the other members. No two cultures are exactly alike in this respect:

> The cultural pattern of any civilization makes use of a certain segment of the great arc of potential human purposes and motivations, just as . . . any culture makes use of certain selected material techniques or cultural traits. The great arc

58939

along which all the possible human behaviors are distributed is far too immense and too full of contradictions for
any one culture to utilize even any considerable portion of
it. Selection is the first requirement. Without selection no
culture could even achieve intelligibility, and the intentions
it selects and makes its own are a much more important
matter than the particular detail of technology or the marriage formality that it also selects in similar fashion" (ibid.:
219).

Selectivity is therefore a key concept in Benedict's theory of
cultural configuration. Selection proceeds basically along lines
of psychological harmony, which may, of course, be upset "by
exposure to contradictory influences" such as the introduction of
alien culture elements, or migration.

If the culture is relatively stable and well-integrated, however,
it will tend to reject elements antagonistic to the dominant
configuration, or adapt them to the existing cultural situation.
The Apollonian character of the Pueblos led them to reject the
"Dionysian" Ghost Dance religion, and helps to explain the absence of shamanistic trances, frenzied lamentations at funerals,
self-torture in the vision quest, and the ceremonial use of drugs
and alcohol. All these elements may be found among many of
the neighboring tribes. An example of reinterpretation of a
Dionysian trait into an Apollonian one is found in fasting, which
among the Zuni is never severe, but a means of assuring ceremonial cleanliness, while in the Plains tribes it was carried out
to attain the half-conscious state conducive to visionary experiences.

It has been said that Benedict exaggerated the features of the
groups under description, and subsequent fieldworkers had no
difficulty in detecting Dionysian features in the Apollonian Pueblos, and Apollonian tendencies among the Kwakiutl and the
Dobu (cf. Barnouw, 1963:39–57). These observations, undoubtedly correct, do not detract from the significance of Benedict's
insights. She herself warned against the danger of cutting down
every culture "to the Procrustean bed of some catchword characterization." But the knowledge that many cultures possess
deep-seated guiding principles governing the lives of its members

is of the greatest importance to the understanding of cultural behavior in general and religious behavior in particular. Benedict stressed the necessity for studying human behavior in its cultural context, and this is particularly important for the study of religious behavior, because religion—more, perhaps, than any other institution—helps to express, uphold, and reinforce the cultural configuration and its dominant values.

Although many more American scholars than those discussed here wrote on religious topics, the focus shifted in subsequent years. A survey of the anthropological literature published between 1930 and 1960 shows that books and articles dealing with religion were radically outnumbered by those on kinship, economy, and political organization. But there is evidence that research and interest in religion are again on the increase, both in the United States and in Europe. Among the recent trends the following may be mentioned:

1. An interest in societies undergoing rapid change (Sundkler, 1961; Worsley, 1957; Sierksma, 1961; Lanternari, 1965; Lewis, 1964; Lawrence, 1964).
2. The application of anthropological methods to the study of religion in complex and literate societies (Geertz, 1960; Anesaki, 1961; Ekvall, 1964; Harper, 1964; Bellah, 1965).
3. The analysis of symbolism in religion and myth (Warner, 1961; Wolf, 1958 and 1964; Turner, 1962; Lévi-Strauss, 1963a).
4. Attempts to develop new and more precise methods for the study of religion and myth: structural analysis (Leach, 1961 and 1967; Lévi-Strauss, 1960, 1962, and 1963b; Frake, 1964; Goldman, 1964); and cross-cultural and statistical analysis (B. B. Whiting, 1950; J. Whiting et al., 1958; Burton and Whiting, 1961; Young, 1962 and 1965; Lenski, 1963).
5. The application of new fields in anthropology to the study of religious phenomena: ethnomedicine (Lieban, 1967; Metzger and Williams, 1963); and ethnolinguistics (Sebeok, 1964; S. Newman, 1964).

The older interests in function, history, and psychological aspects are generally maintained in these studies, although with varying degrees of emphasis.

CONCLUSION

The development of the study of religion in the twentieth century is characterized by an increasing emphasis on the necessity of reliable data collected by trained fieldworkers. Results of these investigations have challenged assumptions about religious absolutes. The wider perspectives thus gained have brought about many refinements in theory. No agreement has been reached, however, about the *raison d'être* of religion and the role it plays in the functioning of human societies.

The greatest accomplishment of twentieth-century anthropology is the establishment of a clear distinction between man as a biological organism and man as the creator and bearer of culture and thus also of religion. The importance of this distinction cannot be overestimated.

5

Prehistoric Religion

TYLOR OPENS HIS FAMOUS CHAPTER ON ANIMISM WITH A QUESTION: "Are there, or have there been, tribes of men so low in culture as to have no religious conceptions whatever?" (1958:II,1). The question was not a rhetorical one. Missionaries, traders, and other travelers reported encountering such tribes. Tylor observed correctly that many of these authors contradicted themselves, for although they categorically denied that some of the peoples they described had any idea about religion, they simultaneously gave evidence that these same people carried out sacrifices, believed in spirits, and buried their dead with grave goods. Tylor's own position was a very careful one:

> The assertion that rude nonreligious tribes have been known in actual existence, though in theory possible, and perhaps in fact true, does not at present rest on that sufficient proof which, for an exceptional state of things, we are entitled to demand (*ibid.*:2).

In other words, Tylor felt that logically and historically the assumption was not unreasonable, but he found no evidence that societies devoid of all religion did exist. From this empirical observation Tylor concludes that religion was probably a universal culture trait, and an integral part of society that was as old as man himself.

Darwin recapitulated Tylor's position, and pointed out—even

more clearly than Tylor—the semantic and ethnocentric error made by earlier observers, who equated religion with monotheism:

> There is no evidence that man was aboriginally endowed with the ennobling belief in the existence of an Omnipotent God. . . . If, however, we include under the term *religion* the belief in unseen spiritual agencies, the case is wholly different; for this belief seems to be universal with the less civilized races (468–69).

Twentieth-century ethnography has upheld the theory of the universality of religion in existing nonliterate cultures, while modern archaeology has uncovered evidence that religious phenomena are of great antiquity. When Tylor wrote *Primitive Culture,* he could not have known how old human culture really was. Although there is still no definite answer to this question, it is certain that human culture is a great deal older than Tylor ever dreamed.

No branch of anthropology requires more inference, more weighing of imponderables, than prehistoric archaeology. The reconstruction of religious phenomena is a particularly difficult task, for religion has more symbolic content than any other cultural institution, and the meanings of artifacts and other material remains have to be interpreted without benefit of written documents.

In spite of these difficulties, archeologists have provided important insights into man's cultural and religious development. Perhaps the most startling fact to emerge from archeological reconstruction is that Tylor was apparently quite right when he speculated that religious phenomena are as old as man himself. There is, of course, no way of knowing whether these phenomena were institutionalized or random in the early stages of human development, so that the term *religion* must be given the broadest possible interpretation in this discussion.

It will be useful to discuss briefly the archeological divisions of man's evolution so as to provide a chronological context for the various findings.

THE PALEOLITHIC PERIOD

Several now extinct species and varieties of hominids preceded *Homo sapiens*. Although their classification is subject to great controversy, Buettner-Janusch (1966:26) presents three hominid forms: Australopithecines, Pithecanthropines, and *Homo sapiens*, each of which had various subspecies. Knowledge of the existence of early hominids is derived from their skeletal remains and their artifacts. The oldest of these artifacts were made of stone, and although it is possible that other materials (such as bone or wood) were also used, only stone tools survived. Each of these tools falls into one of the three divisions of the Stone Age: the Paleolithic, the Mesolithic, and the Neolithic. These divisions are not based upon geological criteria, but on the appearance of certain types of human artifacts. Because the artifacts appeared at different times in different places, these periods cannot be uniformly dated. But everywhere the Paleolithic was the longest in duration, and it is subdivided in Lower, Middle, and Upper Paleolithic.

In Europe, the various archaeological periods roughly coincided with geological periods as follows (after Buettner-Janusch, 1966:26):

Recent (postglacial) period:	Neolithic and Mesolithic
Upper Pleistocene	Upper and Middle Paleolithic
Middle and Lower Pleistocene:	Lower Paleolithic

Man's place in the Pleistocene may thus be represented:

Australopithecines:	Beginning Lower Pleistocene
	Extinct before end of Lower Pleistocene
Pithecanthropines:	Beginning late Lower Pleistocene
	Extinct during Middle Pleistocene
Homo sapiens:	Beginning late Middle Pleistocene
	Not extinct

Lower Paleolithic

Leakey, whose work at Olduvai (Kenya) over the last thirty-five years has won world renown, discovered the oldest known hominids. If his dates and interpretations are correct, the age of the hominid line is much closer to 2 million years than to the previously estimated 500,000 years (Leakey, 1965). Leakey, however, has not made any inference about the possible existence of religious beliefs among the early hominids. It is different in the case of Peking man (*Sinanthropus pekinensis*), a tool-making creature who lived roughly 500,000 years ago and is classified as a Pithecanthropine. Fragments of at least forty individuals of both sexes were recovered from a cave near Chou Kou Tien, about forty miles from Peking. Numerous crude stone implements were also found, together with evidence of the use and control of fire. When tools of a standard type are intentionally and purposely made for future use, the individuals who made them must have been capable of forming mental images of the ends to which these tools were to be used. This is a form of conceptual thinking, of foresight, of an ability to abstract from the immediate situation, the existence of which is not easily demonstrable among animals. Deliberate and systematic tool-making is one of the criteria used to decide if a fossil form is human and belongs to the hominidae—although physiological criteria also play a role.

Peking man was definitely human, and he was also probably a cannibal. All skulls and skullcaps found in the cave of Chou Kou Tien were broken precisely at the foramen magnum, the opening in the occipital bone that forms the passage to the brain. This seems to indicate that the brains were extracted and possibly also consumed. The long bones, too, were split open, presumably to get at the marrow.

What has all this to do with religion? The traces of blows on the skulls, the broken arm and leg bones, and the evidence of decapitation and preservation of skulls—all this has been regarded by some as the earliest evidence of ritual treatment of the dead (James, 1957:18). A more interesting analysis is made by von Koenigswald (1956:202), who observed that Sinanthropus must have been a very able and successful hunter, because of the enormous number of bones of large and ferocious animals found in and around the cave site. Because Sinanthropus' cannibalism was not apparently motivated by hunger, it may have had—according to von Koenigswald—magical implications. Sinanthropus must have formed the idea, however dimly, that man's power and life resided in the brain. They may have believed that the consumption of the brains of the dead resulted in a transference of their power. If the interpretation is correct, the cannibalism of Sinanthropus would represent a form of sympathetic magic.

Many have found this interpretation far-fetched, and it may well be so, for it is not even certain that Sinanthropus was, in fact, a cannibal. Yet von Koenigwald's theory is possibly supported by findings about more recent societies. Some of these societies used stone tools not unlike those used in the Paleolithic Period, and it is possible to make some inferences about similar parallels in beliefs and practices.

Ritual cannibalism and head hunting, for example, are found in a number of contemporary cultures. The South American Jívaro take the heads of their enemies in order to acquire their souls as well (Harner, 1962:258–72). The South American Amahuaca grind up the bones of their deceased and drink the powder in a mixture of corn gruel (Dole, 1962:567–74). Some Pamoan groups consume the flesh of their dead (*ibid.*:570), and other examples of similar practices could be found. In most cases, the reasons given for these practices are of a supernatural nature: to banish or appease the spirit of the deceased, to prevent it from reoccupying the body, or to acquire the good qualities and powers of the deceased. In the light of these findings, von Koenigswald's theory about Sinanthropus' magical cannibalism gains somewhat in credibility.

Middle Paleolithic

In the Middle Paleolithic period there appeared in several parts of Europe, Africa, and western Asia the best known of our fossil ancestors: Neanderthal men. These are considered to belong to a subspecies of *Homo sapiens,* and are officially known as *Homo sapiens neanderthalensis.* They are much closer to modern man than Sinanthropus was, both in time and in physical appearance.

The many stone tools left behind by Neanderthal man belong

to the Mousterian tool complex. These tools were often well made, and certainly less crude than those associated with Sinanthropus.

Many Neanderthals lived in rock shelters and the mouths of caves for varying periods, although their mode of life was likely to have been predominantly nomadic. Since agriculture was then completely unknown, they had to follow the game upon which their lives depended. Most Neanderthal remains, both artifacts and bones, were found in caves, for these offered protection from weather and predatory animals.

What is most interesting about Neanderthal man is that he often carefully and deliberately buried his dead. (The bones and skulls of Peking man were carelessly scattered about, although it is possible that this scattering was the result of a later disturbance.) Neanderthal burials often included the careful placement of tools and animal bones, indicating that the bodies of the deceased may have received ritual treatment. Sometimes only the skull was preserved. One was found in one of the smaller, inner rooms of a cave near Monte Circeo in Italy. It was surrounded by a circle of stones and by the bones of different types of animals. Some of these bones were partly charred, and while some were scattered around the cave, most were neatly piled up along the walls. The skull, like those of Sinanthropus, was broken at the base, so that it is possible that the brains were extracted and consumed.

Another example of deliberate burial was found in a cave near the French village La Chapelle-aux-Saints. Here a skeleton of an old man was found buried in a pit hollowed out of the marly soil of the grotto. The body had been buried in a contracted position, with the knees drawn toward the chin. The skull had not been forcibly detached from the body, and the foramen magnum had not been enlarged. However, at least one interpreter (Coon, 1962:532–33) noted that the nose bones were missing at the time of discovery, and he believes that the brains might have been withdrawn from that aperture. The area around the grave was very rich in Mousterian implements, including excellent scrapers and crystal flakes of various colors. A great number of animal bones were also present, among them those of the woolly rhinoceros, the reindeer, the ibex, the bison, the cave hyena, and the marmot (Boule and Vallois, 1957:204). Some of the flint tools had never been used; others were broken near the point and showed traces of having been used at the place they were found. Many of the animal bones were split open; others were partially charred. The great number and variety of the bones suggests that people returned frequently to the burial site, bringing in the animals captured in the hunt and possibly consuming them in a ritual feast.

Still another good example of Neanderthal burial was found in a cave near La Ferrassie, also in France. A man and a woman were found buried side by side; nearby the remains of two children were discovered, and under a tiny mound those of a baby. A fourth child was buried in a shallow pit which had been dug in the floor and covered with a stone slab. The cup-shaped depressions carved on the underside of the slab have given rise to much speculation (see Figure 1). Some interpreters felt that these

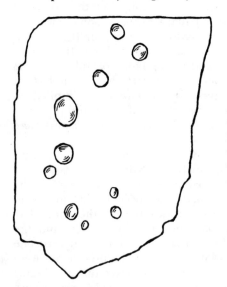

Figure 1. Cup-shaped depressions in a stone slab covering the grave of a Neanderthal child, La Ferrassie, France.

depressions might have held food intended to sustain the dead in the next world: others see them as the first manifestations of artistic activity (Capitan and Peyrony, 1921:382ff). Both adult skeletons were covered with stone flakes and protected by stone slabs. In front of the graves of the children there lay a deposit of bones and ashes.

Even more significant evidence of ritual treatment of the dead was uncovered at Mugharet es-Shkül, Mount Carmel, Palestine, where the skeletons of nine adults and one child were found. Of great interest is a later discovery of a child burial in the cave of Teshik-Tash, Uzbekistan. The child's head was surrounded by six pairs of horns of the Siberian mountain goat; the horns had evidently stood upright in a circle, still attached to their frontal bones (Clark, 1961:44).

The so-called bear cult stems from the same period. In the Alpine region of Germany and Austria, caves were discovered in which the skeletal remains of bears—especially skulls and the adjacent first and second cervical vertebrae—had been systematically stored between the walls, against which had often been built parallel lower walls of stone.

Sometimes, the skulls were placed in four-sided stone chests of undressed stone, which were covered with stone slabs. The discoverers of these caves concluded that bears must have been the center of ritualistic cults. Certainly bears were singled out from among other animals for ritual treatment and burial; they constitute 99.5 per cent of the faunal remains (Bächler, 1940).

These and other examples of burials in this period make it seem likely that supernatural beliefs of some sort existed among the Neanderthals. The preparation of a grave demands time and effort, and this indicates social concern and presumably some sort of funeral ritual. When the bodies are protected by stone slabs and provided with offerings of food and stone tools, it seems possible that the survivors believed that the dead could somehow use these items—in other words, that there was a "soul" that continued to live. Evidence of graves, burial rituals, and funeral offerings is usually considered to reflect the origin of religion. Such evidence also provides more information about the life and beliefs of Paleolithic man than most other types of archeological findings. The reason is that burials are usually found in their original condition, not worn down by use—unless grave robbers found them first.

Upper Paleolithic

In the Upper Paleolithic Period, the ice fields of the Würm glaciation began to retreat. The Neanderthal population disappeared, and for the first time in Europe there appeared modern man.

The cause and nature of this change, as well as the exact relationship between Neanderthal man and the newer forms of *Homo sapiens* are still the subject of much disagreement. It is certain, however, that there were differences. The new stone tools were better made, sometimes beautifully worked, and more varied in form. Ivory, antlers, and bones of all kinds were extensively used, and in this period true art makes its first appearance. Several classifications of the various skeletal remains have been made, for they were considered by many to represent various species and races. Later investigators agreed that all were true *Homo sapiens,* displaying no greater differences from contemporary man than those normally existing between different human breeding populations. In order to make a taxonomic distinction between them and *Homo sapiens neanderthalensis,* they were classified as *Homo sapiens sapiens.*

In Europe, three major successive Upper Paleolithic cultural traditions are usually distinguished: the Aurignacian, the Solutrean, and the Magdalenian. The burials of this period become increasingly more careful: the dead are not only accompanied by tools, but are frequently stained, and decorated with ornaments of different types, and objects usually believed to be amulets make their first appearance.

Cro Magnon is a community in the Dordogne region of France where, in 1868, railroad workmen found several human skeletons under a sheltering rock. The archeologists who were called in eventually unearthed five skeletons grouped at the back of the shelter under conditions suggestive of deliberate burial. Beside them were about three hundred shells, all perforated and clearly prepared for making necklaces or other ornaments. Several round and oval ivory pendants, also pierced, probably were part of this ancient jewelry. Many stone tools and worked reindeer horn were also found (Luquet, 1930:45).

Perhaps the most famous Aurignacian burial site is near Grimaldi, where a number of skeletons were discovered in nine caves. Like those found at Cro Magnon, these were surrounded by a whole series of objects—among them, quantities of pierced shells. Later explorations in the cave, which had been named *Grotte des Enfants* (two skeletons of children had been found there), revealed more skeletons at deeper layers, and on the lowest level two skeletons were buried side by side in a grave about thirty inches deep. One was that of a boy about sixteen to eighteen years old; the other one, that of a much older woman. The boy lay on his right side, with his legs folded under in a kneeling position. The skeleton was stained with red ochre, and there were four rows of pierced shells around the head. The woman's arms were doubled up under her chin, and her knees were drawn up to her shoulders. The shell bracelets that circled the arms of the skeleton were stained red, but the rest of the skeleton was not colored. The heads of the two skeletons were close together and were protected by a flat stone slab supported by upright stones, the interstices filled with iron peroxide. The fact that all the bones were in strict anatomical order indicates that they had been buried at the same time. Many speculations have been made as to why the old woman and the young boy should be thus united in death. They may have been married, or mother and son, or it may be that one was a servant buried to serve the other in the next world.

In a layer above this pair was found the skeleton of a tall man. He was lying in an extended position, and he too wore a crown of shells, while his thorax was covered with a great number of shells of the same type, all perforated, and perhaps originally attached to a garment. Protective stones had been placed over his body, and his head rested on a stone pillow stained with red dye. Stone tools of the Aurignacian type were lying nearby in a kind of hearth.

Similar types of burial were found in many other parts of Europe. In South Wales, for instance, a skeleton stained bright red was discovered: it was accompanied by shells, a few bean-shaped pendants, and a quantity of stone and bone implements. A great number of bones of woolly rhinoceros, bear, bison, and hyena were lying around, including the entire head of a mammoth, still armed with its tusks. Popularly known as "The Red Lady of Paviland," this find was later more scientifically classified as "parts of a male skeleton minus skull."

A burial site at Brno (Brünn) also yielded shell ornaments. More than 600 shells were worked so that they formed conical tubes (some still inserted one into another) which could have constituted a kind of breastplate. There were also big, perforated discs of stone, smaller discs engraved with circles, three discs of mammoth rib, three discs cut out of mammoth molars, and a carved ivory figurine of a man, of which only the head, torso, and left arm remain. The figurine is one of the earliest examples of sculptures of the human figure, and for art historians it is of particular interest that the remaining arm is well detached from the trunk. The skeleton itself and several objects were partially covered with red ochre.

Cro Magnon, Grimaldi, Paviland, and Brno belong to the Aurignacian Period. In the following Solutrean and Magdalenian Periods, artistic activities increased, but burials retained the same general characteristics. At Raymonden, near Chancelade, France, a skeleton was found lying on its left side. The arms were raised, with the left hand under the head and the right hand under the lower jaw, and the knees were just touching the mandible. Iron ore colored red not only the bones, but the surrounding earth as well (Boule and Vallois, 1957:302). Magdalenian-type implements were also found.

The characteristics of Upper Paleolithic burials may be now summed up: burial was careful; attempts were made to protect the bodies by partially covering them with stone slabs; the skeletons were stained with red ochre; animal bones were placed near the bodies, as were tools and ornaments (the latter usually of shell), and small stone discs to which no utilitarian function can be assigned. The skeletons are either in extended or flexed positions, some with the knees almost touching the chin, others with the legs drawn up in a more natural position.

The presence of animal bones, tools, ornaments, and discs indicates something more than mere respect for the dead. Burial with ornaments, tools, and food is frequent in contemporary nonliterate societies, as it was also in the literate civilizations of Egypt, Sumer, and Greece. In these instances the burial objects have most often the stated purpose of serving the dead in the afterlife. It is possible to conclude that such beliefs might have existed in Paleolithic times, and most interpreters agree that this was the case.

There is, however, considerable disagreement about the more detailed meanings of the animal bones, the red ochre, the shell ornaments, and the positions of the skeletons. The animal bones found in association with the skeletons were clearly not all deposited at the same time. Some might well have been placed there at the time of burial, serving perhaps as provisions for the

journey to the realm of the dead. Another interpretation holds
that food was placed near the body in the expectation that it
would restore the dead to life. But both theories are too conjectural. The condition of the bones, the partially charred remains, the ashes, and the used tools indicate that the flesh of the
animals was consumed at the gravesite by the survivors. The
variety and quantity of the bones show, moreover, that people returned to the burial site with their quarry, and a likely interpretation is that they took part in ritual feasts in the presence of
the dead.

The coloring of bones with red ochre has also given rise to a
number of speculations. Early interpreters were unwilling to
believe that Paleolithic man could have been so "sophisticated"
as to stain the dead bodies and believed that the coloring had
occurred accidentally. At Chancelade, for example, a layer of
peroxide iron is believed to have spread over the whole body,
coloring the bones brick red, and in places violet. Although the
peroxide was found at the burial site in the greatest quantity,
other deposits were found much farther away at the same level.
According to the discoverer: "It is not impossible that in one
of the floods, the traces of which the station exhibits, this diluted
iron was spread everywhere" (Hardy, 1891:50). It is possible that
this may have happened once or twice, but available evidence
shows clearly that the color was generally applied deliberately.
Thus, in a higher layer of Grimaldi, well above the old woman
and the young man, a skeleton was found only the skull of which
had a thick coating of red ochre, much like a skull cap (Luquet,
1930:163). Most other known remains point clearly to the inten-
tional use of coloring material.

Another theory held that Paleolithic man had no knowledge
about the permanency and irreversibility of death. The bodies
of the dead were painted the color of blood, the life-giving fluid,
in the naïve expectation that they would return to life. This
interpretation has found little favor with anthropologists, for
there are no parallel beliefs among any known peoples, and the
separation of skulls from the rest of the body (as, for instance,
in the Paviland case) speaks against this theory.

The most plausible—but equally unprovable—theory is that
the coloring of the bones, together with the offering of tools

and ornaments, was meant to aid and prepare the dead for another realm of existence. Macalister remarked that:

> If the dead man was to live again in his own body, of
> which the bones were the framework, to paint them with
> the ruddy coloring of life was the nearest thing to mummi-
> fication that the Paleolithic people knew; it was an attempt
> to make the body again serviceable for its owner's use
> (1921:502).

Much discussion has centered around the position of the body,
particularly the flexed position, which resembled both the sleeping posture and that of the unborn fetus. It was concluded that
Paleolithic man considered death as a temporary sleep, a prelude
to another awakening in a new world. James (1957:29) rejects
this interpretation on the grounds that Paleolithic man could
not have had any knowledge of embryology. But early man's
close association with animals certainly could have taught him
something of prenatal development, and there is no reason to
suppose that he was totally unaware of the human fetal position.
Others conjectured that the bodies were folded merely for
lack of space, or to reduce the difficulties of digging graves with
the stone tools of that time. This hypothesis cannot have general validity, although it might occasionally have been true. In
some instances there was certainly enough space, and no pits
were dug, and yet the body was flexed. In the cave near La
Ferrassie a male skeleton was placed in a long and narrow natural depression which would easily have accomodated it at full
length, but it was found in the fetal position.
Still another theory holds that the bodies were bent to prevent the spirits of the dead returning to earth to haunt the living. The ditches and tombs would then not have been designed
to shelter the dead, but rather to restrain them. A number of
skeletons were found in so unnaturally flexed a position that it
seems likely that the corpse was firmly bound at the time of its
burial. The custom of binding the dead is found in a number
of contemporary cultures. The Hopi place their dead in squatting positions and wrap them tightly in a mat. Similar practices
have been reported for the Inca, Nama Hottentots, and a
number of North and South American Indian tribes. In a few
cases the reason given for the practice is fear of the returning

spirits; one Peruvian account points out that it is impossible for the spirits to walk in such a position.

But this type of explanation is not wholly satisfying. Why were not all the dead buried in a flexed position? Were some spirits considered more dangerous than others? Or did some people fear the return of spirits while others did not? To these and many other questions no answer has yet been found.

The presence of shells in Paleolithic graves is another topic of interest and speculation. Although the shell bracelets and crownlets are often seen as mere "ornamentation" of the dead, in a number of burials they seem to have a larger significance. In the cave of Placard a woman's skull, complete with mandible, was found placed on a rock and surrounded by 170 pierced and unpierced shells of different species (Luquet, 1930:168). The cave of Cavillon produced one male skeleton and 7,868 marine shells, 857 of them pierced (*ibid.:*165). On the body of the "Crushed Man" of Laugerie-Basse in the Dordogne region, four shells were found on the forehead, two at each elbow, two below each knee, and two on each foot.

It is not certain that the choice of shells to accompany the dead has any specific meaning. But they were not selected simply because they were plentiful or near at hand. Most of the shell species are of maritime origin, and since the burial sites are usually miles away from the sea, some conscious effort must have been made to collect and transport them.

Scholars who view the flexed position of the skeletons as part of a rebirth motif point out that shells—which, in Freudian psychology, represent the female principle—represent another variation of the same theme. Others believe the shells were fertility charms, for they "resembled the portal through which a child enters the world" (Jackson, 1917:130ff).

It is tempting for anthropologists to speculate about possible social differences reflected by the greater or lesser elaborateness of burial treatment, but there is no proof of such a social stratification. It may be noted that women, at least after death, appear to have been treated in the same manner as men. But the only possible objective statement about Upper Paleolithic burials is that they were not subject to any fixed rules, and that the differences in position, ornamentation, and so on, cannot be correlated with differences in epoch, social status, sex, or age.

The number of skeletons discovered in graves is very small compared to the total population size in Upper Paleolithic times. Large quantities of stone tools have been discovered in many different parts of the Old World, and not merely in cave sites. Many bodies must have been buried in the open—placed perhaps in shallow graves, or simply abandoned.

Upper Paleolithic Art

Additional clues to the supernatural beliefs of Upper Paleolithic men are provided by the various manifestations of artistic activity.

There is no evidence of such activity in the cultural remains of Middle and Lower Paleolithic, unless stone implements be considered works of art. Boas was one of those who held that technical excellence and perfection in technical form *is* art (1955: 10ff). Some writers see artistic intent in the cupshaped depressions of the stone slab at La Ferrassie (Levy, 1963:6, 41), but inspection reveals that these markings are neither "artistic" nor representational, and may even have been accidental (see Figure 1, p. 110). Even if they were not, they are the only ones of their kind.

Only with the Aurignacian period do true art forms—statues, engravings, and paintings—begin. French scholars have given the name *art mobilier* to the various portable art objects found in prehistoric cave sites, while they call paintings on rocks or cave walls *art immobilier*. Burkitt made an additional distinction between *home art* and *cave art* (1963:162ff). Home art is found in sites that show evidence of everyday occupation—the "living rooms" of the cave, so to say—and in open sites that were inhabited for continuous periods. Cave art is found in the inner grottos, often not easily accessible, or in other places where people did not regularly live.

Upper Paleolithic art includes figurines, engravings, and paintings. True sculptures regularly appear in the Aurignacian period, and particularly noteworthy are the so-called Venuses. These are true sculptures in the round, and although they vary, most of them strongly emphasize secondary sex characteristics. The heads, arms, and legs of the figures are almost negated. Perhaps the most famous is the Venus of Willendorf (see Figure 2), found in a village of that name not far from Vienna. It is carved of fine-grained limestone, some four and a half inches high. The

*Figure 2. Venus of Willen-
dorf, Austria (c. 4½ inches).*

breasts are extremely heavy and full, extending to the navel; the
abdomen is prominent, as in pregnancy; the hips are broad and
the buttocks round and protruding. The arms are barely indicated by a narrow kind of ridge, with some dots on the forearm
that seem to represent a bracelet, and two tiny hands that rest
upon the gigantic breasts. The thighs are heavy, but the lower
limbs are unfinished. There are no facial features: the head is
decorated all around with carvings that seem to resemble braids,
even where the face should be.

Similar figurines have been found elsewhere. Sometimes they
were worked in ivory, as was the "Venus of Lespugue," found
in the Grotte des Rideaux in the Haute Garonne (see Figure 3).

This statuette, almost six inches in height, is similar to the Willen-dorf Venus: long, full breasts hanging over the abdomen, enor-mous buttocks and thighs, tapered legs, a small head covered with short hair that partially hides a featureless face. This statuette is distinguished from all others by a sort of garment that covers the

Figure 3. Venus of Lespugue, France (c. 6 inches).

back of the thighs below the buttocks. It seems to be made of verti-cal strips suspended from a horizontal cord, and ends in a fringe (Boule and Vallois, 1957:313). In Laussel, France, the same fe-male type is found carved in bas-relief on a flat piece of stone about fifteen inches long (see Figure 4). In her right hand the nude holds an object resembling the horn of a bison. Also her face is feature-

Figure 4. Bas-relief from Laussel, France (c. 15 inches).

less, although the head is turned in profile. Again, the breasts
are elongated and enormous; the abdomen is prominent; and
the external labia are carefully drawn. The legs are short and
slender; the arms are very thin but well modeled; and the fingers
are indicated.

Two other Venuses were found at the same site, together with
a very curious bas-relief representing two persons lying down and
facing each other. The details of this last piece are very unclear
—some believe that it represents copulation, while others see in
it a woman in childbirth.

At Brassempouy, in southwestern France, two cave sites have been explored, the Grotte du Pape and the Grotte des Hyènes. Examples of both Aurignacian and Solutrian art were found here. Apart from the "Venus" statuettes, there was also the head of a young woman—the "hooded figure" (see Figure 5). About two inches in height, it is carved in the round from mammoth ivory. It has eyes, a nose, a mouth, and shoulder-length braided hair. In the same cave the "belted figure" was discovered, which probably represents the lower part of a male body.

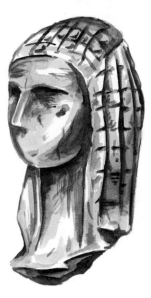

Figure 5. Head of a young woman, Brassempouy, France (less than 2 inches).

Male figures are, however, extremely rare. The "Venus" woman is predominant in Aurignacian sculpture. All in all, some fifty different "Venuses" have been found. Apart from those in France and Austria, some have been discovered near Mainz in Germany, in Savignano, Italy, and quite a few in the Soviet Union near Mizyn, Kostienki, and Gagarino. Two thousand miles further east, in Siberia, about ten female bone figurines were unearthed, but they were much more slender than their European counterparts.

What is the meaning of these statuettes? And why are they

discussed in a book dealing with religion? Although the Aurignacian men who produced these statues may have been pre-
occupied with sex, it does not follow that the Venuses therefore
"were not cult objects, but characteristic products of unregenerate
male imagination," as Clark would have it (1953:56). The most
widely accepted theory is that they were fertility charms. The
main purpose of these art objects seems to be the promotion and
conservation of life in and through the outward signs of female
fecundity. Frazer's principle of homeopathic magic—"like produces like"—may well be applied here.

Until fairly recently it was believed that painting was little
developed in the Aurignacian period. During World War II,
however, the now famous Lascaux cave paintings were accidentally discovered by two boys. First believed by scholars to be
either Solutrian or early Magdalenian, the paintings have now
been dated back to the Aurignacian. They depict various kinds
of animals: oxen, stags, horses, bison, mammoth, and many
others. The paintings reflect skilled technique, masterly realism,
and above all a real aesthetic sense. Although animals clearly
predominate, there are a few human stick figures and some other
patterns. In style and probable significance this Aurignacian cave
art shows great similarities to the later Magdalenian forms.

The Solutrean period appears to indicate a temporary decline
in artistic activity, although it is quite possible that examples
have yet to be discovered. One of the most impressive Solutrean
finds, in a home-site cave at Le Roc, France, is a circle composed of
large blocks of stone on which a number of animals were carved in
high relief. The animals depicted include reindeer, oxen, birds,
ibex, and bison, and there is also a man facing a musk ox. There
is no special reason to infer supernatural beliefs from this art.
The frieze may have been purely decorative, created by the
owner of the shelter in the wish to embellish his abode (Burkitt,
1963:178).

The most impressive Upper Paleolithic art is Magdalenian.
Sculpture, however, had declined. There are a few Magdalenian
"Venuses": one carved from the root of a horse's tooth, found
at Mas d'Azil in Ariège; another, known as *Vénus impudique*, is
of ivory. Both are fairly coarse, though more slender in outline
than their Aurignacian counterparts. There are a few very good
animal sculptures—a marvelous little horse head carved in rein-

deer antler from the cave of Mas d'Azil, and a reindeer carved of ivory from Bruniquel. Many implements were also embellished with engravings. But the most celebrated works of art of that period are the cave paintings and engravings.

The centers of Paleolithic cave art in Europe are France and Spain, although some sites have been found in Italy and Austria. Some of the more important caves in France are those of Niaux, Pech-Merle, Portel, Montespan, Tuc d'Audoubert, Trois Frères, Font-de-Gaume, and Marsoulas.

One striking feature of French cave art is the overwhelming preoccupation with animals, which constitute 80 per cent of all depicted images. Almost without exception the animals are those most prized by the hunter: cows and oxen, horses, goats, deer, reindeer, mammoths, elephants, and sometimes fish. Many are masterpieces of artistic technique and reflect careful observation of the animal and its movements.

The animal images form a sharp contrast to the human images which are sometimes depicted. Most of the latter are of the stick figure type, as if they were quite unimportant to the artists.

The drawings and paintings also include a number of figures whose significance is not immediately apparent. They have been classified as tectiform (hut-shaped), scutiform (shield-shaped), or pectiniform (comb-shaped). Where the scutiforms and pectiniforms have defied explanation, much attention has been given to the tectiforms. Breuil (1910), among others, was quite certain that they represent the first evidence of man-made shelters; others saw them as shrines, "soul houses" for the dead, or as traps or pitfalls. Although no one can be certain of their meaning, the idea that they may be traps fits well with the interpretation of cave art as a form of hunting magic.

The animal images are frequently superimposed upon one another. At Font-de-Gaume, to give but one example, the head of a rhinoceros in red outline is covered by a black outlined ox, and on top of this is a slightly polychrome bison. This custom of superimposition has been very useful for relative dating, since the paintings on top are necessarily later than those beneath.

Many animals in the drawings are pierced with painted arrows; some are obviously wounded or dying. In the cavern of Niaux, a large drawing shows a bison with four spears and arrowheads embedded in its flank. Many of the female animals are pregnant. The few scenes that are depicted usually include no more than two animals. One example, found at Font-de-Gaume, shows a kneeling female reindeer with a stag bending toward her.

Many cave paintings were executed deep in the interior caves where daylight could not penetrate. Even within these inaccessible places the most difficult spots were sometimes selected, so that the artist must have stood on the shoulders of a companion in order to reach his stone "canvas." Some very fine engravings and paintings are to be found at the very end of the cave of Font-de-Gaume, but they can be seen only by penetrating some distance into a narrow crevice at the end of the main cave site, and looking upward.

Some of the few well-executed human figures are found in the cave of the Trois Frères, which is reached through a very narrow passage leading from the end of a small cave called Enlène. First there is a kind of alcove where an engraving of a lion may be seen; the tool that made it is still lying in the notch of a rock, apparently carelessly forgotten by the artist. This alcove leads into a chamber, the lower walls of which are completely covered with drawings of animals of all kinds. At the end of this chamber is a tunnel, also engraved, leading upward to an aperture about twelve feet above ground level. The opening, just large enough for a man to stand in, provides a commanding view of the cave chamber. On the wall of this natural pulpit is an engraved and painted figure about thirty inches tall, commonly known as "the sorcerer" (see Figure 6). It is a masked human figure with a long beard, the antlers and face of a stag, the tail of a horse, and human feet. It is not actually known if this figure indeed represents a sorcerer or a shaman, although this is the most common interpretation. The mixture of human and animal features would represent the various animals aiding the shaman on his spirit flight. However this may be, the total setting seems to indicate that some ritual was carried out here.

The same conclusion can be reached from the inspection of one of the Tuc d'Audoubert caves. Here a long and narrow passage opens into a damp gallery with a clay floor. A number of bear teeth are placed in a niche in a wall, and at the end stand two clay-modeled bisons, a male and a female, each about two feet long. On the right is a semicircular depression forming

Figure 6. "Sorcerer" at the Trois Frères Cave, France.

a sort of amphitheatre, and on its clay surface there are marks as if people had danced on their heels around a tiny rise in the center. At least at one spot the impress of a naked human foot is clearly visible. Again, it appears that the site had been used for some ritual purpose (Burkitt, 1963:219–20).

As might be expected, there is considerable controversy over the meaning of Upper Paleolithic cave art. Some scholars believe that the paintings and engravings were merely expressions of the artistic talents which Magdalenian man discovered in himself. Others argue that the art was motivated less by the desire for self-expression than by the love of beauty, which caused Magdalenian man to embellish his utensils and walls. Still others maintain that the paintings and drawings were made to celebrate or commemorate hunting successes. The most common anthropological explanation—which does not disqualify the others—is that the cave art was a form of sympathetic magic designed to insure the success of the hunt and thus the continuance of the food supply.

Although artistic or decorative motives may have played a role in cave art, the fact that some paintings were made in the darkest, most inaccessible recesses of the caves, and that some were superimposed upon others, demands a different explanation. Also, if these artists worked exclusively from the point of view of artistic expression, why did only useful animals inspire them? Why not human beings, or butterflies, or flowers? And why the arrows, the dying animals, and the pregnant females? The superimposition of the drawings cannot be explained by lack of space, for blank walls are often found adjacent to the palimpsests. If the paintings were designed to commemorate a successful hunt, it is strange that there are no human figures and that many paintings were executed in dark and inaccessible areas of the cave sites.

Whether or not the artists of the Magdalenian period had shamans, it appears that the cave art had magical and religious implications. This theory is made plausible by the preoccupation with economically important animals, palimpsests, use of inaccessible places, absence of human figures, absence of scenes, and the presence of arrows and wounded, dying, or pregnant animals. It becomes difficult to deny the magical implications of these elements, and to maintain that the cave paintings were produced on the principle of art for art's sake.

The cave paintings found in Spain tend to reinforce the explanation that magic and ritual inspired this art form. In northern Spain, the style of the paintings is similar to that of the paintings found in southern France—and significant parallels between the polychrome paintings of Altamira and those of Lascaux and Niaux can be drawn. Farther south, the style becomes quite different, and human figures and scenes are more frequent. Thus, in the cave of La Vieja at Alpéra, male and female figures carrying arrows dance around stags and goats. Apparently they are led by a larger male figure who stands above both people and animals.

At Cogul, a group of nine women wearing skirts and possibly also hats dance around a small male figure and a doe (see Figure 7). Although some interpreters have felt that this scene gives evidence of a prehistoric phallic cult, Burkitt points out that the male figure

Figure 7. Ritual scene at Cogul, Spain.

is very much smaller than the surrounding women, more like a
boy than a man, and furthermore that his penis is not in erection (1963:233). Burkitt believes it to be more likely that the
scene depicts some initiation rite.

Hunting scenes are, however, more customary. In the rock-
shelter of La Vieja at Alpéra a complex scene comprises some
thirty antelopes, twenty-six stags, as well as cows, deer, ibex,
moose, wild horses, wolves, and birds, together with more than
seventy human beings, most of them males. Many of the men
are shown aiming drawn bows at the animals, while others
carry arrows. A number of animals are wounded and have arrows
embedded in their backs.

These scenes are somewhat harder to interpret than the single
animals depicted in France. One difficulty is that often they were
not painted all at once, but were added to by successive generations. Certainly these paintings were not mere decorations, for
many of them were found in uninhabitable caves.

The possible foreshadowing of magic in Lower Paleolithic remains highly conjectural, and there are certainly no indications
of any institutionalized form of religion. Neanderthal man (who,
as far as is known, did not leave any form of pictorial art) paid
attention to the dead, and this implies a possible belief in an
afterlife. With the beginning of Upper Paleolithic, Aurignacian

man shifted his attention from death to birth and procreation. The "Venuses" were probably fertility symbols, designed perhaps to facilitate or increase human births or to increase life in general. Magdalenian man seems to have developed a magico-religious cult which has as its primary aim the increase and control of the food supply.

THE MESOLITHIC PERIOD

Mesolithic is a transitional period in more than one sense. The climate had drastically changed. The ice masses had retreated far to the north, and man had to adapt himself to a warmer environment with a changed flora and fauna.

Mesolithic also foreshadowed some of the major inventions and innovations of the Neolithic Period. There are indications of pottery making, and the dog became the first domesticated animal. The carriers of the Mesolithic culture probably came from the south, but in general this era marked great migrations in all directions. When reindeer withdrew into northern Europe, the men who hunted them followed their trail, and many groups settled in northern Germany and Scandinavia.

Among northern lake dwellers we find a curious practice: the drowning of reindeer. Rust, who excavated Mesolithic sites on the lake shores in the neighborhood of Hamburg, found twelve whole reindeer which had been submerged in the lake, weighted down by stones (1937, 1943). The same layer—muddy and no longer a lake—yielded other animal bones and skulls, and Rust estimated that forty-five animals had thus been submerged. He concluded that they had been sacrificed to the gods. Indeed, it is difficult to think of any other reason why people should dispose of animals which were useful to them for food and clothing, except to placate angry gods or spirits, or to induce them to return tenfold what was sacrificed to them.

Many traits of Paleolithic burial cults persisted, although some significant additions were introduced. A remarkable burial site was discovered at Ofnet, near Nördlingen in Bavaria. The deposits of this cave comprised several Paleolithic layers, with a top layer dated as Mesolithic. Two shallow pits contained a large number of human skulls embedded in red ochre. In the larger pit, twenty-seven skulls were placed together; in the smaller one, six. Twenty of these were children, nine were women and only four were adult males. The children wore ornaments of small shells, the women had necklaces of deer teeth, and three of the four men had stone implements next to them. The skulls in the center were closely packed together and partly crushed. Many of the skulls bore the marks of blows, and on some the cervical vertebrae were still attached—hence the supposition that these individuals were beheaded. Speculations have been made that the skulls were headhunters' trophies or battle spoils. It has been suggested that most of the men escaped during a raid, leaving the women and children behind. This hardly accounts for the ornamentation of the skulls, the provision of implements, and the presence of red ochre.

A most significant feature of these burials is that the skulls all face toward the west. This cannot be attributed to accident, nor is it a unique phenomenon. The Semang of the Malay Peninsula bury their dead facing west; the Crow Indians place corpses upon a burial scaffold with the heads turned toward the setting sun; the Hopi seat their dead in a circular pit, all facing the east. It may thus be inferred that some Mesolithic groups not only had a conception of life after death but also a definite idea of where the realm of the dead was located (R. R. Schmidt, 1912).

Tévièc, a granite island off the coast of Brittany, also yielded some interesting examples of Mesolithic burial practices. Ten grave sites were found, each containing from one to six skeletons of men, women and children. All bodies were found in a flexed position and they were sprinkled with red ochre, but there was no fixed orientation. The bodies were accompanied by various ornaments and implements of stone or bone, and many of them had worn shell necklaces and bracelets. Other objects which are probably cloak fasteners were also found, and they made it seem likely that the bodies were clothed when buried. In one case, a male skull was surrounded by antlers of the red deer. Stone slabs covered many of these graves, and small cairns were erected over them (Péquart, 1937).

The presence of antlers is difficult to interpret. It has been conjectured that they were a tribute to a very able hunter, or that they were a tribal symbol, or that they were believed to impart the strength of the animal to the dead and so aid him in the difficult journey to the next world. None of these theories, however, can be substantiated. But it can be stated with certainty that this site represents one of the earliest cemeteries, with markers indicating the graves. In parts of Denmark, several skeletons have been found which had no red ochre, no grave goods, and no ornamentation, but their graves were surrounded by a few large stones—foreshadowings of the later megalithic burial types.

THE NEOLITHIC PERIOD

The New Stone Age has been traditionally defined by its technology. A new method of polishing and grinding tools had been invented, producing stone tools of a much higher quality. But other changes were of far greater consequence for the human species, for in this period man began to control nature. He domesticated many animals and cultivated edible plants, and thus learned to regulate his food supplies. The effects of these inventions were so momentous that Childe speaks of a "Neolithic revolution" (1951).

The first traces of food production appeared about 6000 B.C., somewhere in the area extending from Palestine to Mesopotamia. The practice soon spread by diffusion to Egypt, Syria, Persia, and the Indus region (Braidwood, 1952:5). In the pre-Neolithic hunting-and-gathering era, people lived as nomads, shifting their habitation many times in the course of a year to follow the movements of the food-providing animals. Agriculture made sedentary living possible, and the improved economy, with its storable food supply, made possible the storage of surplus, true division of labor, and rapid increases in population. Neolithic skeletons in Europe alone are several hundred times more numerous than all the Paleolithic skeletons found anywhere.

The increase in population made the disposal of the dead a problem, and cemeteries now became a regular feature. In fact, the finds are so rich that their complete description would demand many volumes. Neolithic burials were certainly not uniform, indicating that there were many different groups living side by side, each with its own culture and traditions.

One of the earliest Neolithic sites is found in Palestine, near

Jericho. Kenyon, a well known archaeologist, discovered at the lowest levels of this site seven skulls, placed together in a nest similar to the one found at Ofnet (1957). But these skulls were notably different from any others yet discovered. The skulls were filled with earth and their faces were modeled in clay. The eyes were inlaid with shell in such a way as to suggest even the pupils. The features and expressions are so natural that they suggest portraits, foreshadowing the funerary masks of Pharaonic Egypt.

Other modeled skulls were discovered at later excavations, and most have been dated by the Carbon 14 method at about 6000 B.C. At the same site in a later phase, the skulls are often arranged in a specific manner, either all in a circle facing the center, or in rows facing the same direction. There is also some evidence of possible child sacrifice: beside one infant skeleton were several skulls of very small children. The upper cervical vertebrae were attached, indicating decapitation at the time of burial. Most of these grave sites were outside the regular settlements, but a number of skeletons were found directly beneath the floors of houses.

In predynastic Egypt, graves were regularly dug near the dwelling sites. Many contained entire skeletons, but here also the skull was sometimes separated from the rest of the body and showed evidence of special attention. The later Pyramid texts make reference to this practice. In the *Book of the Dead* we read: "I am a Prince . . . whose head is restored to him after it was cut off." The heads were sometimes partially filled with spices and unguents to help preserve them.

Somewhat later, but still in the predynastic era, the use of coffins made its appearance, and the graves themselves are sometimes plastered with mud or lined with brick. A contracted burial position and orientation to the west are dominant features, and food is a most common accompaniment. Even the simplest peasant graves contain at least one or two pottery vessels that once held food.

Social stratification is now clearly marked by the considerable differences in the quantity and quality of the grave goods. Some graves contain only the barest necessities—food bowls, a few stone tools for the men, and a slate palette for eye makeup for the women. The wealthier burial sites contain glazed beads, perforated shells, ivory spoons and hair combs, female statuettes, and a great number of cooking pots, storage bowls, and food items. The bodies of the wealthy were often elaborately dressed. Since valuable goods were known to be buried with wealthy people, grave robbery became a problem, and to counteract it, at one side of the burial pits a separate and deeper storage room was sometimes cut and connected to the grave itself.

In Mesopotamia (present-day Iraq), one of the earliest known Neolithic sites is at Jarmo. The excavators found several subfloor burials here, bare of grave goods. In the Neolithic sites of Sumer, the dead were buried with very few grave goods. The bodies were dressed in what was obviously their every day clothing, arranged in flexed positions, wrapped in mats or linen strips, and placed in pottery or wicker coffins. Only a water bowl and a few personal belongings were placed in the graves. These examples show clearly that cultures had become strongly individualized, each having its own burial tradition, and possibly also its own beliefs and religious practices.

At Neolithic sites in Europe, the most notable development in connection with the treatment of the dead consists of the raising of monumental megaliths. Early megalithic tombs were known from certain parts of Palestine, Syria, Kurdistan, and Armenia, some dating back to the fifth and sixth millennia B.C. (Albright, 1957:136). Perhaps stimulated also by the idea of chamber tombs, by this time important in the developing centers of Greece and the eastern Mediterranean, the building of these monuments seems to have spread from the western Mediterranean up the Atlantic coast of Europe, with particular impact upon France, England, and Scandinavia.

Chronologically, most megalithic monuments belong to the Neolithic Period, although some megalithic grave chambers in southern Iberia have yielded metal objects. Metal work signifies the end of Neolithic, and it must be noted that the introduction of metal occurred much later in Europe than in the Near East, so that the Near East was already post-Neolithic when parts of Europe had just entered the period.

Megaliths are monuments of huge, rough stones erected over burial chambers or forming part of them. The simplest form of megalithic monuments are called *menhirs* (or monoliths)—single upright stones, sometimes of great size. Because so many of the megalithic structures are found in Brittany, their names come from the Breton language: *men* means *stone,* and *hir* means *long.* When menhirs are placed in a circle, they are called *cromlech* (*crom* = circle, *lech* = *place*). When two or more upright stones are covered by a flat, horizontal slab, the structure is called a *dolmen,* (*dol* = *table, men* = *stone*). Menhirs placed in long rows are known as *alignments.* Usually, but not always, the dolmen was covered with an earth mound called a *tumulus,* while a dolmen and a tumulus together constitute a *barrow.* Some types of dolmens have long narrow passages, leading into the burial chambers: these are known as *passage graves.* Later, these passages were constructed without the dolmen, and are then called *hallcists.* Eventually these passages were made smaller, to hold but one individual, and such burial places are called *cists.*

Perhaps the most astonishing megaliths are the alignments in the department of Morbihan, in southern Brittany. The Carnac alignment, for instance, covers an area of 12,000 feet long, and consists of 2935 menhirs. To the west of Carnac are the alignments of Menéc, 3795 feet long, in which 1169 menhirs have been counted (seventy of them forming a cromlech, the other 1099 arranged in eleven rows). East of Menéc are the alignments of Kermaria, 3540 feet long and numbering 1029 menhirs. To the northeast is the alignment of Kerleesan, which has 555 menhirs in thirteen rows. Burial places are found around them, sometimes indicated by semicircular cromlechs. Parts of these megalithic sites appear to belong to the early metal ages, but even so, the amount of labor expended on the transportation and erection of these thousands of dolmens must have been stupendous. The significance they had for the builders is not clear, but it must have been great. Grave goods are relatively meager in these megalithic tombs, but include a few ornaments and tools and some pottery.

Numerous megalithic tombs have been found in other parts of France as well as in Portugal, Spain, the Netherlands, England, Scotland, Ireland, northern Germany, and the Scandinavian countries. In Los Millares, in the Almería province of southern Spain, one site held about one-hundred passage graves. The passages are divided into a number of sections by stone slabs, and most are covered by huge mounds. The walls are lined with stone slabs; they are plastered, and show traces of paintings. In the Paris basin, megalithic tombs took the form of

PREHISTORIC RELIGION

long,· narrow galleries entered from a shallow antechamber through a porthole cut into a slab.

A particular feature here is that most of the skulls were trepanned—perhaps as a magical precaution against the unwarranted return of the spirits.

The most famous megalithic monument in Europe is Stonehenge, on Salisbury Plain in England (see Figures 8 and 9). The

Figure 8. View of Stonehenge.

leading excavator, R. J. C. Atkinson, has shown that this imposing structure was not the product of a single period or of a single civilization (1960). He distinguishes three building phases, Stonehenge I, II, and III; Stonehenge III is divided into three substages (*ibid.:* 69).

Stonehenge I, dating from about 1800 B.C., consisted of a circular ditch and an inner rampart or bank, with a wide entrance to the northeast marked by a monolith, the Heel Stone. Along the inside of the rampart there were fifty-six ritual pits, the so-called Aubrey holes. Stonehenge II, consisted of a double circle of eighty-two bluestones, dated from about 1650 B.C. Stonehenge III began a century later, and includes a circle of upright sarsen stones. This famous cromlech was covered with lintels, which at one time formed a continuous circle. The builders of Stonehenge III were not merely adding to the already existing structures, but envisaged a whole new plan, rearranging the bluestones and removing some of them. (*ibid.*:77–80)

The total structure is an arrangement of concentric circles: outermost is the circle of earth, next the circle of sarsen stones, the circle of bluestones is more central (partially destroyed in the reconstruction work of the last phase, so that it now resembles a horseshoe). In the very center are five sarsen dolmens, each consisting of uprights and a covering slab, usually called *trilithons*.

The Aubrey holes are burial pits of some sort. Those that have been excavated held human bones and partially or totally cremated human remains. An unusually large number of Neolithic graves in the shape of long, earthen barrows were found just outside the embankment.

There have been many interpretations of the meaning and function of Stonehenge, some by sensationalistic nonspecialists who saw it as a Druidic temple and a center of human sacrifice. Atkinson points out that the historical records of Druidism go back only a few centuries B.C., but he does not rule out the

Figure 9. Aerial view of Stonehenge (British Crown Copyright).

possibility that human sacrifice occasionally might have been offered, perhaps as part of some propitiatory ritual. In the center of a neighboring sanctuary at Woodhenge, an infant child with a cleft skull was buried, indicating that human sacrifice was not unknown at that time (*ibid.:* 172–73).

The one point of general agreement is that Stonehenge was a place of ritual and worship, where man established contact with the supernatural powers in which he believed. This does not exclude the possibility that it was sometimes used for secular activities as well, such as the holding of political councils or the dispensing of justice.

Atkinson believes that the successive phases of Stonehenge may well correspond with different religious beliefs held by the various colonist groups arriving from the continent. He suggests that in the earlier phases the rites conducted there were in some way connected with the dead, thus possibly indicating the existence of a belief in spirits or ancestor souls who resided in the earth. In Stonehenge II, the entrance of the circle faces the midsummer sunrise, and may indicate a new form of religious belief, the supernatural now residing in the sky and symbolized by the sun (*ibid.:*174). Stonehenge III perpetuated the former alignment on the midsummer sunrise. Rituals were performed within the circles, as is indicated by the buried surfaces compacted by the rhythmic pounding of feet (*ibid.:*174). The shapes of the stones too may have had some symbolic significance: the tall pillars and broad, flat stones may represent male and female, respectively, thus pointing to the possibility of a fertility motive.

Although the orientation of the entrance toward the midsummer sunrise can hardly be accidental, the astronomical implications of Stonehenge have been overemphasized by those scholars who believe that it may have served as a kind of calendar. They base their arguments on the fact that there are thirty linteled sarsen blocks, roughly the number of days it takes the moon to revolve around the earth. After twelve revolutions it would be time for the summer solstice, and great crowds would gather to celebrate the occasion. The Heel Stone at the entrance would mark the point of sunrise on Midsummer day for an observer stationed at the center of Stonehenge. Atkinson shows that, at present, the midsummer sun passes over the Heel Stone in its eastward climb, but only some time after the true sunrise.

Moreover, when Stonehenge was built, the point of midsummer sunrise was farther west, so that by the time it had climbed to a position directly over the Heel Stone it stood clear of the horizon by a space equal to half its apparent diameter (*ibid.*:30).

One thing is certain: an architectural structure of such proportions would not have been undertaken had it not possessed great significance for the builders. The bluestones, weighing up to seven tons, were hauled from a distance of at least 150 miles. The sarsen stones came from quarries not more than twenty to twenty-five miles to the north, but they were taller and much heavier than the bluestones, some weighing as much as fifty tons. It is still not known how they were transported without wheels, beasts of burden, or rope (other than rawhide). Atkinson calculates that the minimum requirements for the transportation of the eighty-one sarsen stones alone would be 1500 men working for ten years (*ibid.*:121)—if they employed sledges over hardwood rollers (which seems likely but is not certain).

There are other English "henge monuments" similar to Stonehenge I. Among others, there are those at Woodhenge, Avebury, Arminghall, Arbor Low, and Dorchester-on-Thames. These are embanked, circular closures with associated ditches on the inside, normally broken by one or two entrances. Some apparently had interior structures of wood rather than stone, while in a number of sites there is no trace of any internal structure at all. Many have ceremonial pits with evidence of cremated burials, and these are nearly always associated with fields of barrow graves.

The influence of the megalith builders spread through northern Europe, but the imitators could not match the elaborateness of Stonehenge. Stonehenge was primarily a temple structure while the megaliths in northern Europe were grave sites, usually for mass burials. In Drenthe, a northeastern province of the Netherlands, fifty-four boulder graves can be counted, locally known as *hunebedden*. Varying in size, the smallest is about twenty feet long and is built of only twelve boulders; the largest is 130 feet long. Stone implements, decorated pottery, and ornaments of amber and jet have been found here. Some of the vessels showed signs of having contained food, and a few metal objects signified the closing of the Neolithic Period. Huge graves erected from massive stones can also be seen in Scandinavia and northern Germany, but on the Jutland peninsula the inhabitants continued to bury their dead in simple individual graves.

Many of the northern megalithic grave sites show signs of cremation, a custom that became quite widespread in the later European Bronze Age, but shortly afterward declined again. It has been noted that crematory practices involve a special kind of belief in the condition of life after death. The evidence of Paleolithic and Neolithic burials, particularly the presence of red ochre, appears to indicate that the idea of a future life was concrete, and that it included the continued physical existence of the dead. Cremation, coupled with the belief in a continued existence after death, must involve the idea of a "soul," a spiritual entity separable from the body itself. Connected to this might have been a concept that the soul could be at peace only if nothing remained of its ties to earth. Cremation would serve this end, and it would also mitigate the survivor's fear of the unwanted return of the dead spirit.

Religious Art Forms

Sculpture appeared early in Upper Paleolithic in the form of the Aurignacian "Venuses," but it virtually disappeared in the subsequent periods. Only in middle Neolithic cultures do female statuettes reappear, showing many of the same features of their predecessors. Available evidence speaks against a historical connection between these two developments: there was a long time gap between them, and the Aurignacian statuettes have been found in only a few parts of Europe. Female statuettes reappear in the Near Eastern region, far from the sites of the original "Venuses," and the new sculptures are collectively known under the somewhat misleading name *mother goddesses*. Their distribution was very widespread, reaching from India to the farthest corners of Europe. They persist well into historic times, and a number of interpreters (James, 1962:153–71; *see also* Graves, 1948) have seen them as the prototype of later great goddesses including the Great Minoan Mother Goddess, Astarte, Aphrodite, Isis, Hathor, Pallas Athena, and the Hindu world mother, Devi. Although certain connections between the mother goddesses and the later true female goddesses may well exist, it is clearly an oversimplification to state that the latter "developed from" the former. The creation of Devi, to give but one example, certainly involves many other cultural developments in India, including the growth of philosophy, economy, and political structure.

The Neolithic mother goddesses, like the "Venuses," appear to be fertility charms or symbols. They usually have oversize breasts, abdomens and sexual organs, while their heads, arms, and legs receive cursory treatment or are absent altogether. In the Neolithic sites of Mesopotamia, some statuettes were headless and in squatting position, suggesting childbirth, and in Palestine a group of statuettes displayed such strong protrusion of the vulvae that it is likely that they were depicted as giving birth. The earliest statuettes in Ur were slender and their bodies well modeled, but many of them hold a child at the breast.

In many instances the figurines became completely stylized, and it would have been hard to interpret their meaning without the presence of the more naturalistic images. In Mesopotamia, some were mere cones with breasts; others (known as *fiddle-shaped goddesses*) resemble violins much more than females (see Figure 10).

From the Near East, female figurines spread both east and west. In the Indus region, terracotta statuettes were discovered in the post-Neolithic sites of Harappa and Mohenjo-Daro—both urban centers resembling that at Sumer. The statuettes are partially stained by smoke and ash, and may have been used as lamps or incense burners. In the Danubian and Balkan regions of Europe as well as in Spain, the statuettes become so numerous that they must have been part of the equipment of every household. Many were modeled in clay, often quite crudely; others were carved in bone, stone, or marble. Some have small holes in the upper parts, so that they might have been worn as amulets. Although also found in France and England, they become less frequent in the northern regions of Europe.

It is clearly impossible to describe here the many shapes and forms in which these statuettes appeared, and it is equally impossible to assign a single meaning to all of them. Diffusion plays a major role in the distribution of material objects, but different usages and different meanings are often attached to them in the process of transmission. This is particularly true if material objects have predominantly symbolic meanings. Yet it appears that the mother goddesses were most often associated with an underlying concept of fertility. This is evidenced first of all, by the

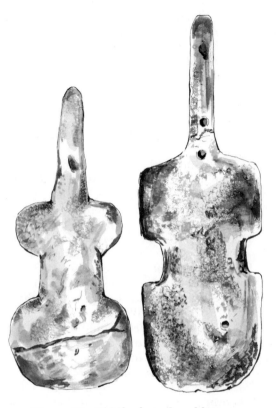

Figure 10. Fiddle-shaped goddesses.

relative absence of statues symbolizing the male principle, and
secondly by the infrequency of their use as grave goods.

   Phallic emblems are occasionally found, particularly in the Indus region where the *linga* is still important in the Shiva cult. In
Mohenjo-Daro and Harappo, many phallic reproductions (*linga*)
were found together with *yoni* (reproductions of vulvae). Some
phalli carved in chalk or engraved in stone monuments were found
in Europe also, but these are far outnumbered by female images. It
has been suggested that the role of the male in the generative
process was still unknown, as it is said to be unknown to some
nonliterate tribes of Australia, to the Trobriand Islanders, and

to the Andaman Islanders. It is more likely that women have more visible aspects of fertility than men, since it is in their bodies that new life originates and develops, and from their breasts that the new infants receive their first nourishment. Women and their maternal attributes are thus life-giving principles *par excellence*.

THE NEW WORLD

This discussion has focused attention upon Old World evidence rather than upon that of the New World. Man came to the Americas at a relatively late date, perhaps 30,000 years ago. Although the New World shared in the general evolution of man's culture, it followed its own path of development. Although there are New World counterparts to the Paleolithic and Neolithic periods in Europe, so far no human skeletal remains have been found that can be positively associated with the many discoveries of Paleolithic stone tools. Either the New World population at this time was much smaller than that of the Old World, or perhaps the New World people did not bury their dead. If the dead were merely left behind or exposed, the chances of finding well-preserved skeletons are very slim.

Nothing has been found in the New World comparable to the engravings, cave paintings, or carved bone tools of Europe, and since no Paleolithic graves have been found either, next to nothing is known about the religious life of these ancient Indians. But archaeologists are ingenious and have made inferences of possible magical beliefs through observation of the tools alone. At the so-called Lehner site in southeastern Arizona, one of the oldest tool types, Clovis points, were found. They are commonly made of flint, but at this site three very small Clovis points were made out of crystal-clear quartz. Transparent crystals of this type are known to have magical significance for many contemporary Indians, and objects made of this material are believed to have special powers. The three small quartz Clovis points may have been some kind of "magic bullets," valued for their supernatural power rather than their physical power (Meighan, 1966:155).

With the beginning of the Neolithic Period, evidence of religious practice becomes abundant. There is, however, so much cultural variance that it becomes impossible to do more than present a few typical examples of burial practices from different culture areas. Many resemble those already encountered in Europe, and their implications for religious beliefs may be drawn along similar lines.

The Basket-Maker Indians, the ancestors of the modern Pueblo, occupied parts of Arizona and New Mexico from about A.D. 100–500. As far as is known, all Basket-Maker burials were in caves, either in suitable crevices or in old storage pits. The bodies were flexed, wrapped in fur blankets, and accompanied by pipes, baskets, beads, sandals, aprons, food, and weapons (Martin, Quimby, and Collier, 1947:110). They were not oriented in a specific direction. In later periods the dead were often buried in refuse mounds, located in the open. The grave goods remained the same.

The Hohokam Indians, who occupied central and southern Arizona from about 300 B.C.–A.D. 500, practiced cremation. The bodies of the dead, along with offerings of stone and bone ornaments and intentionally broken pots, were placed in pits and burned. The ashes and other remains were transferred to a special trench or pit (ibid.:173–74). Much later, about A.D. 1100, the remains of burned bones and ashes were placed in small pottery jars, which were then buried (ibid.:188).

The Frontenac Indians occupied the central part of New York State, roughly from A.D. 300–500. The deceased were buried in pits dug into the village midden. The bodies were in flexed, semi-seated, or extended positions. Grave offerings were common. In many cases the dead were covered with powdered red ochre; in some, with stones. Dogs were sometimes interred with human bodies, sometimes given separate graves (ibid.:242–43).

The most elaborate burial practices were found in the Ohio Hopewell culture of about A.D. 900–1300. The deceased were dressed in their finest clothing and placed in log tombs or on burial platforms. The graves were sometimes lined with large sheets of mica or woven mats. The burial platforms were sometimes covered with mosaics of mineral paints, and linear or conical mounds were placed above them. Cremation was also practiced. Grave goods were rich (ibid.:274, 276).

CONCLUSION

The difficulties of studying religious phenomena and developments increase as one goes further back in time. There is more
to religion than burial practices and the use of ceremonial
objects; and reconstructions of prehistoric religions must thus of
necessity remain fragmentary. It is easier to explain the presence
of tools than it is to interpret less functional items such as
statuettes or cave paintings. The less useful an object appears
to be, the more interpretations are possible. In spite of these and
many other difficulties, archeologists have provided many insights
into religions that have disappeared. Without their efforts,
nothing would be known about these religions.

Although the possible religious meanings of objects, paintings,
and burial practices are discernible only indirectly, some historical conclusions can be drawn with certainty. Among those, the
proven antiquity of religion is of particular importance because
it testifies to the universality and the importance of religion as a
cultural trait. Moreover, archeologists have provided a broad
chronological framework of the development of religious ideas.
Archeology has thus supplied an awareness and appreciation of
the past, and it has shown that all cultures since Neanderthal
man have had a concern with death and with a continuation of
life after death.

6

Religious Beliefs

ALL RELIGIOUS SYSTEMS HAVE IN COMMON THE EMBODIMENT OF SA-
cred beliefs. R. R. Marett's famous aphorism, "Primitive religion
is danced out, not thought out," expressed his sentiment that nonliterate peoples felt the meaning of their religion intuitively
without being able to formulate its principles. Such a situation
has never been found to exist. In every society, however simple
its technology, investigators have encountered individuals who
are able and willing to discuss the contents and meaning of
their religious principles. Marett's assertion neglects not only the
cognitive aspects of religion, but its social values as well. Statements of belief express and sustain a people's worldview, their
style of life, and their order of existence. Religion provides explanations and assigns values to otherwise inexplicable phenomena. Without an ordered system of beliefs, religious behavior
would be irrational and unmotivated.

Beliefs find verbal expression in myth and in direct cognitive
statements. Although the two are not always clearly separable,
myth is generally the more symbolic and indirect. The word
dogma will be used in this discussion to indicate a set of propositions or cognitions about the universe which include the supernatural. The beliefs in any such body of cognitions are validated
by myth (a discussion of which follows in Chap. 7).

Dogma, as the term is defined here, centers on three major
topics: the nature of the supernatural, the nature of the physical
world, and the nature of man and his society. In this chapter

these three forms of cognition will be examined in terms of their nature, their variety, and their social significance.

THE NATURE OF THE SUPERNATURAL

Culturally held cognitions about the nature of the supernatural are basic to any religious system and significantly affect social and religious behavior patterns. Thus, supernatural entities form part of every religious system, but they appear in many different forms and quantities. It would be impossible to compile a complete inventory of all supernatural beings in all cultures. It will be more fruitful to consider culturally held beliefs about the supernatural under headings which are neither mutually exclusive nor all-embracing, but which will illustrate some major types of belief and their possible social consequence.

Impersonal Supernatural Powers

For a long time, students of religion assumed that supernatural powers were everywhere conceived as personalized powers, resembling human beings in shape or character or both. Toward the end of the nineteenth century, R. H. Codrington, as missionary in Melanesia from 1883 to 1887, attracted a great deal of scholarly attention by his published observations about a Melanesian belief in an impersonal supernatural power called *mana*. According to his description, mana was neither spirit nor deity, but an all-pervasive neutral force outside the common processes of nature, working automatically and manifesting itself in objects and people. Ghosts and spirits also possessed this power. According to Codrington:

> A man comes by chance upon a stone which takes his fancy; its shape is singular, it is like something, it is certainly not a common stone, there must be mana in it . . . he lays it at the root of a tree to the fruit of which it has certain resemblance . . . an abundant crop on the tree shows that he is right, the stone is mana. . . . If a man has been successful in fighting, it has not been his natural strength of arm, quickness of eye, or readiness of resources that has won success; he has cer-

tainly got the mana of a spirit or of some deceased warrior to empower him. . . . If a man's pigs multiply and his gardens are productive, it is not because he is industrious and looks after his property, but because of the stones full of mana for pigs and yams that he possesses. Of course, a yam naturally grows when planted, that is well known, but it will not be very large unless mana comes into play . . . (1891:118–20).

Mana was not, then, an inherent property, but a quality that could come and go. A person or object could participate in greater or lesser quantities of it, or possess none at all. Conspicuous success or unusual performance was proof of its presence.

Codrington deserves credit for his initial observations, but his characterization of mana as a purely impersonal power presents certain difficulties, for personified supernatural powers *also* are credited with its possession: "All spirits have it, ghosts generally" (*ibid.*:119). The question arises: Is mana an independent power, moving by itself, but regularly attaching itself to spirits, or is it the power of the spirits themselves? Codrington's own descriptions show that the Melanesians did look upon their spirits as actual beings rather than as mere concentrations of power.

The difficulties became compounded when ethnographers discovered parallel ideas in many parts of the world. Disregarding the problem of translation, they equated the Melanesian mana with the *mana* concept in Polynesia, the Sioux *wakan,* the Iroquois *orenda,* the Algonquian *manitou,* the Crow Indian *maxpe,* the African Ekoi *njomm,* the Nkundu *elima,* and the West Indian *zemi.* Hutton Webster (1948), listing many other examples, included evidence from literate societies as well, and likened mana to the Hebrew *el,* the Latin *numen,* the Greek *dynamis,* and the Indian *brahma.* In every mentioned instance the concepts play an entirely different role, and their facile equation with the Melanesian concept of mana serves no useful purpose but, rather, beclouds their cultural meaning.

It is important to note, however, that the concept of mana or its presumed parallels is always accompanied by beliefs in personified supernaturals. There is little or no indication of existing beliefs in a truly neutral force empowering the personified supernaturals. In other words, it is not mana that gives the gods and spirits their power; rather, power is axiomatic to all that is super-natural. In a number of cultures, however, it is believed that the power of the supernatural can charge other things or persons, and once this happens the deities lose control over it or are no longer concerned with it. The power is not impersonal but, rather, depersonalized; it is no longer influenced by its personal supernatural sources, exists independently, and functions auto-matically. Mana and its possible equivalents thus appear to have a double nature: personal, when possessed by personified spirits or deities; impersonal, when imparted to material objects or human beings.

The question itself is of more than academic interest because the different concepts give rise to different religious attitudes and social behavior patterns. A personified supernatural power is aware, or can be made aware, of people's actions, and therefore can be moved by human behavior—supplication, sacrifice, and so on. Religious activities will then be designed to establish rap-port with these supernatural powers. Impersonal forces, by their very nature, do not perceive human activities. Man need not alter his behavior, but he will direct his efforts to acquiring these powers if he considers them useful, or to avoiding them if he considers them dangerous.

In many Melanesian islands it is desirable to collect mana, and many human activities are directed toward this goal. In Poly-nesia, however, mana has more dangerous qualities and could have dire consequences, particularly when less endowed persons come in contact with a strong source of mana. Many Polynesian island societies have an elaborate class system, and the rulers, nobles, and high priests possessed the greatest amounts of the sacred power. It was considered dangerous for a commoner, who by virtue of his status had little mana, to approach his rulers. Persons and objects with strong mana were considered taboo; contact with them should be avoided, and they could be ap-proached only in a ritual manner and with the greatest precau-tions, if at all. Mana was highly contagious; some rulers were so strongly endowed that everything they touched became contami-nated. In these cultures, taboo was essentially a series of prohibi-tions against contact between those with more mana and those with less, and thus between the higher and the lower social classes. Thus the concept of mana in Polynesia helped to maintain the aristocratic hierarchy.

In most American Indian societies the supernatural power imparted by spirits to men was not considered to have such dangerous qualities. The Plains Indians attempted to gain such power through fasting or self-torture. A vision was the sign that a man had received such power. Such a man could sell some of his power to another one who had been less successful in his effort.

Personified Supernatural Powers

Although the belief in impersonal supernatural powers is not universal, the belief in personified supernatural powers is. Everywhere man has created gods in his own image, as was noted by the pre-Socratic philosopher Xenophanes (*c.* 570 B.C.–*c.* 470 B.C.):

> Yea, and if oxen and horses and lions had hands, and could paint with their hands, and provide works of art, as men do, horses would paint the forms of gods like horses, and oxen like oxen, and make their bodies in the image of their several kinds. (Fragment 13)

And later he says:

> The Ethiopians make their gods black and mule-nosed; the Thracians say theirs have blue eyes and red hair. (Fragment 16)

The term *anthropomorphism* is applied when supernatural powers resemble men in their physical appearance, while *theriomorphism* or *zoomorphism* means that the supernatural powers resemble animals. Deities are not everywhere depicted in human or animal shape, but they always possess some human qualities. Goode has described gods as *anthroposocial,* meaning that these personified supernatural powers are intellectually aware of the values of the society, and generally endorse them (1951:43–44). Moreover, supernatural powers are also *anthropopsychic—i.e.,* they have been assigned many traits of human mentality (Goode, 1951:50–51). The last two traits have great social consequences. Anthroposociality implies that supernatural powers are interested in the social welfare of the group, and it thus establishes a social relationship between gods and men. Because supernatural entities are anthropopsychic, human activities can influence them. Like human beings, deities can be moved by pity, flattered by praise or gifts, or tricked by subterfuge. Like human beings, they may be proud, vain, petulant, moody, wise, loving, concerned, or generous. Such conceptions about the nature of the supernatural are expressed by the religious activities of the people. Ritual represents the major link between the supernatural and the social world: if men make sacrifices, then their gods demand them; if men sing and dance in rituals, their gods must enjoy them. Religious activities reflect, to a significant degree, the qualities people have attributed to the supernatural.

Supernatural beings are sometimes anthroposocial in a different sense: the heavenly social organization often reflects that on earth. Many gods are married, and have offspring. Zeus and Hera in the Greek tradition, and Odin and Trigga of Norse mythology, are two well known divine couples. The Kotas of the Nilgiri Hills in southern India have an Elder Father god, a Younger Father god, and a Mother goddess. The junior male god shares the wife of his elder brother. The Kota men themselves have fraternal rights over the wives of their brothers, so that the marriage patterns of the deities project those of the society (Mandelbaum, 1938:576). In Japan, the household spirits of the deceased retain the family status they held in life, and among the South African Thonga, the status of the spirits depends, in part, upon that of their relatives. Political hierarchy also may be projected into the supernatural world: the hierarchical stratification of the Polynesian Tonga gods, for example, closely resembles that of Tonga society.

The social structure of the supernatural world, however, is never totally identical with the earthly one. Bachofen (1815–87), for instance, tried to reconstruct ancient social organization on the basis of ancient beliefs, reasoning that whatever is true of the organization of the gods must, at one time, have been true of human society. Because there was evidence that many ancient beliefs dealt with powerful female deities, he posited an early evolutionary stage of matriarchy (1861). Present-day anthropologists doubt that such a stage ever existed, and no data have been discovered to substantiate such a theory. Moreover, in societies where the most powerful deities are female, there is no correlation between this sacred power and political power. The human social world cannot be extrapolated from the supernatural world, or vice versa. Both forms of organization must be carefully described before comparisons can be made.

Personification of supernatural beings means that man conceptualizes them in his own physical, social, and psychological image. Given the existing varieties of human personality and appearance, it is not surprising that the concepts of the supernatural show a great deal of cultural variation. In Barton's study of the Ifugaos, some five thousand different deities were identified for him by family priests (1946). They were all named, and could be divided into at least forty categories. This example from only one nonliterate society demonstrates that it is impossible to render the many culturally posited categories of supernatural beings in English. The English vocabulary of the supernatural is quite limited in comparison with that of many other languages. In addition, the available terms do not accurately translate the connotations of supernatural entities in other religious systems. It is not that different religious beliefs are mutually unintelligible, but that the supernatural terms are differently distributed. As a result, great discrepancies can be found in ethnographic literature in the use of such terms as *god, spirit, ancestor, soul, ghost,* and so on. The following discussion of supernatural beings is not an attempt to explain all the complexities of their various meanings and functions, but an effort to show how English terminology can be meaningfully applied to cover a significant portion of cross-cultural supernatural beliefs.

THE ORIGIN OF THE SUPERNATURAL

It is possible to distinguish two major categories of supernatural powers: those which are believed to have a human origin; and those which are not believed to have such an origin. There are, however, several instances in which the origins are not explicitly stated, and thus ambiguous.

Supernatural Beings of Nonhuman Origin

Many supernatural powers to which the generic term *god* is applied are believed to be self-created—if their origin and existence is questioned at all. Gods are individually known, named, and personalized; they are recognizable by their given attributes.

Their numbers within any given religious system may be large or small; occasionally there is only one. The term *pantheon* may be used to speak about the gods collectively, and often implies the existence of a divine hierarchy. The term *high god* or *supreme god* is usually applied to the deity that outranks all others; the same terms are used in monotheism, when there is only one god.

Frequently, gods are called by several names, each referring to a different aspect of their power. The African Ashanti believe in a supreme god whom they call *Onyankopon* (*the Great One*); *Tweaduampon* (*the Dependable One*); *Bore-Bore* (*the First, the Creator*); *Odomankoma* (*the Eternal One*); *Ananse Kokroko* (*the Great Spider: i.e., the Wise One*) (Busia, 1954:192). Different names may also indicate a fusion of one or more older gods with a later one. The Mende of Sierra Leone call their god both *Ngewo* and *Leve*. It appears that Leve is the older deity.

The character traits of gods are as varied as those of human beings. However, although gods are partially anthropopsychic, they also possess superhuman powers. Yet relatively few gods are considered omnipotent and omniscient, and not all are directly concerned with human welfare. The latter are the so-called *otiose* gods, who created the world and then withdrew from it. They are considered either too distant to be approached, or too powerful to be in need of human worship. Otiose, transcendent gods receive very little ritual attention, and have neither cults, nor priests, nor houses of worship. In these cases lesser gods, or spirits, or ancestor souls play more important social roles. Pettazzoni stated that an otiose god is often a symbol of the world order, and is generally not approached by man because it would be dangerous to upset the once-established order of the universe (1922:239). Indeed, otiose gods are addressed only in very extraordinary circumstances, when only a divine act of "recreation" can set the world right again. The high god of the Nigerian Igbo is known by several names, but he is withdrawn and has neither shrine nor priest dedicated to his service. The Igbo call on him only in great distress, and usually feel that their appeals evoke no response (Uchendu, 1965:94–95). The already mentioned high god of the Mende has little immediate contact with the affairs of men, and, therefore, most ritual observances are directed toward ancestral spirits (Little, 1954:114–15).

Creation is, of course, but one possible attribute of godhood, and one that usually does not loom very large in the minds of believers. Creator gods receive greater social consideration and ritual attention when they are also believed to be interested in assisting man to attain his worldly goals. Gods active in human affairs have shrines or houses of worship, priests or other religious specialists will attend to them, and often are depicted in images.

Many religions do not contain any beliefs about creation. The Cheyennes, for instance, do not view their gods as creators. The attributes of the gods rest in their knowledge of how to make the universe work properly. Religious activities are thus directed toward making the gods share their knowledge with man, so that the world will produce what man needs. In ritual, the Cheyennes demonstrate what they have learned, and thus uphold what the gods have taught them (Hoebel, 1960:83).

Supernatural beings, like humans, usually have a division of labor. The Maori of New Zealand call upon the god of the sea for help in fishing and ocean voyages, the god of the forest for help in bird-snaring and canoe-building, and the god of agriculture for help in planting and harvesting (Firth, 1956:179). The Tonga even have a special god assisting thieves in their trade. The ancient Romans carried this divine specialization to an unusually high degree. Since the fields were plowed three times, there were three gods of the plow: Vervecator, Reparator, and Imporcitor. The god Insitor watched over the sowing of the seeds; Sarritor, over the weeding; Messor, over the reaping; Conditor, over stored grain; Sterculinius, over the manuring, and so on. Such narrowly specialized deities have been called *attribute gods*. Only a few of the most important ones had special cults and rituals among the Romans; the others served to create an awareness of divine governance in all aspects of life. They were invoked only in the context of the specific tasks over which they presided, and although they occasionally received small offerings, no priesthoods were attached to them.

The departmentalization of gods is largely a function of economic and social stratification in human society. The favorite or chief deity may correspond to the most influential group of the society. The religion of pre-Columbian Mexico, for instance, reflected the dominance of the Aztec military organization: the gods of war received much greater ritual attention than the agricultural gods (Vaillant, 1966:183). Although divine specialization usually takes place when social structure becomes more complex, there is no one-to-one correlation, as the monotheism of Christianity, Islam, and Judaism clearly indicates.

Gods may change in a number of ways. They may become more or less important, acquire different attributes and functions, or disappear altogether. Important social and historical changes are usually reflected in the history of the rise and fall of divine popularity and importance. In pre-Columbian Mexico, where religious and social systems competed for the domination of the valley, successful invasions brought about numerous changes in religious ideas. The gods of the conquerors gained supremacy or merged with older deities, until newer invaders overtook them in turn. At the time of Spanish contact, many different gods were fitted into a calendar, with special ceremonies assigned to each.

While the term *god* is best applied to those supernatural powers of nonhuman origin that are individualized and personally known, the term *spirits* would refer to those that appear collectively. The spirit population is too numerous to be counted, and, as a consequence, spirits are not usually named individually but referred to by category. Some cultures have many different categories; others recognize only a few, or one, or none at all. The Gururumba of New Guinea, for instance, recognize two groups of spirits: the *nokondisi,* who live in the upland forest area; and the *gwomai,* who inhabit the riverbanks of the lowlands (Newman, 1965:62–63). The Javanese recognize many more categories: *memedis (frightening spirits), lelembuts (possessing spirits), tujuls (familiar spirits), demits (place spirits),* and *danjangs (guardian spirits)* are some of the better known ones (Geertz, 1960:16–29).

Spirits are usually below gods in rank. When gods and spirits coexist in one religious system, as is often the case, the gods are the creators, the upholders of the universal order. Spirits are usually created by the gods. However, the power of creation is of less social importance than the power to intervene in everyday human affairs: the growing of the crops, health, and other matters directly concerning human welfare. When spirits are believed to be responsible for common aspects of daily life, they loom larger in man's consciousness, and rituals in their honor are more frequent.

Although spirits appear as multitudes, and often act in concert, individual members of their group may operate on their own as well. Guardian spirits, for instance, have their individual tasks as protectors of human beings; shamans or other religious practitioners often single out a few spirits as their helpers. Spirits may also detach themselves from their group and take up temporary or permanent abode in specific objects and places, or in human beings. The nature of the spirits determines whether this will be desirable or not. Gururumba men build small garden shrines to attract a spirit which will protect the fields against theft. Family rituals are held in front of the shrine, and offerings of food are regularly made (Newman, 1965:63).

If thus singled out, spirits may receive temporary names. But as long as they are considered as members of a multitude, they remain spirits rather than deities. In time their individuality may increase, so that they are no longer seen as components of a homogeneous crowd. In such instances, spirits have become gods. It is not always possible to determine precisely at which state of development a spirit might be, and a number of ambiguous cases will regularly be encountered. Yet with the given criteria that gods are *individualized* and spirits are *collective* supernatural entities, much confusion in terminology can be avoided.

The social functions of spirits overlap with those of the gods. Spirits may aid or punish, be favorably or unfavorably inclined toward mankind, demand offerings and sacrifices, and be worshipped and invoked. Some spirit categories seem to serve merely as *post hoc* explanations of events that are otherwise inexplicable: unexpected bits of good or bad luck, small mishaps, noises heard in the night, and so on. The Polynesian Tonga, among others, believed in such spirits of the hobgoblin type, who took delight in mischief, but were never invoked or otherwise manipulated. It is doubtful that they can be considered "sacred," although they were unquestionably supernatural.

Supernatural Beings of Human Origin

Beliefs in the continued existence of the human soul after death are quite widespread, but the nature of this existence is variously conceived. The already complex situation is made even more complicated by the not uncommon idea that man has not one, but a number of surviving souls, each with its own ultimate destiny.

The dead may become like gods or spirits, but often they retain their old individuality and personality, forming a separate category of the supernatural. Sometimes they are quite powerful in their own right, or have great influence upon gods and spirits.

In some societies, including most Western ones, the condition of the soul after death is closely related to the behavior of the individual during his lifetime. When this is the case, religious beliefs have ethical implications of a personal nature. In such religious systems, the survivors have relatively little influence upon the situation, and rituals for the dead tend to be commemorative rather than manipulative. But probably in most nonliterate societies, the position of the departed souls is powerfully affected by the behavior of the survivors.

Alternatively, the type of afterlife may depend on the social status of the person and his family. The souls of kings and nobles, for example, automatically may go to a more desirable place than those of common people. Rituals tend to reinforce the social hierarchy of both the living and the dead, reflecting the status differences.

VIEWS OF THE AFTERLIFE

No matter what these beliefs may be, two major attitudes toward the dead can be recognized and contrasted: the departed are considered to have left the society; or the dead are regarded as active members of the group. Each attitude gives rise to different types of supernatural beings with human origins, and will have widely different social and ritual consequences.

The Separation of the Dead from Society

In cultures where the dead are believed to take no part in the regular activities of the community, survivors attempt to adjust themselves to the loss and to establish a new equilibrium. The return of the dead is not desired, for the departed ones would only interfere with the social order and the business of the living. In these cultures, the dead are usually greatly feared. Sometimes the survivors spend time, money, and effort to keep the souls of the deceased as happy as possible in their otherworldly existence, so that they will have no desire to return to earth. Other cultures do everything in their power to obliterate the memory of the dead as soon as possible so that the community will be able to function in its accustomed manner.

Such conceptions have different ritual and social consequences. When it is felt that the dead must be kept comfortable in their new existence, it follows that the type of postexistence relies heavily upon the ritual behavior of the survivors. The set of religious actions carried out primarily to keep the dead separated from the living is called a *cult of the dead*. Cults of the dead naturally do not exist in societies where the dead remain part of the community.

At the time of the death and the funeral, ritual action is directed toward assisting the soul in its readjustment to a new type of existence, in its journey to another world, and in its acceptance there after arrival. Later rites are meant to insure the soul's peace and comfort, or aid its advance to higher status in his world, often by means of regular sacrifices and offerings. The frequency of these rituals usually diminishes with time. The recently dead are held to be more dangerous than the long dead. From psychological and social viewpoints, we may observe that the memory of the dead gradually fades away, and their absence in the community is no longer strongly felt. The cult of the dead, therefore, aids the bereaved toward gradual adjustment. Moreover, the rituals insure continued interaction between members of the kin group and the community, often accompanied by extensive economic exchange.

In societies geared toward the obliteration of the memory of the dead, there are no such cults. Burial rites emphasize that return to the world of the living is undesirable, and elaborate precautions are taken to prevent the return of the souls. The Yuma Indians burned the house of the deceased and all his important possessions; his horses were either killed or given away, and his fields were left untilled for a season (Castetter, 1951:232–33). The Blackfoot Indians abandoned or tore down a house in which a person had died, so that the deceased would not return looking for it (Wissler, 1912:30–31). Some Australian aboriginal tribes broke up whole settlements after the death of a member, rebuilding them at different locations (Elkin, 1964:302).

Taboos against uttering the name of the deceased frequently accompany these practices, and are intended to keep the dead away. The Yuma avoided the names of the dead, while among the Salish Indians of northwestern Canada a name taboo was kept for one year after the funeral. After the death of a prominent adult, not only his name became taboo, but a word in the language that bore a phonetic resemblance to it was obliterated as well. Thus in the 1860's a chief died whose name was Xatwas, and the word *xatxat,* meaning *mallard duck* was changed to *hohobsed* (*red foot*). In 1940 only a few older persons recognized *xatxat* as a Salish word (Elmendorf, 1951:205–8).

Such ritual actions are ostensibly directed toward the dead, but they also hasten the fading of their memory by making final the separation between the dead and the living, and by indicating to the survivors that the deceased are no longer of social account.

In spite of all precautions, the dead sometimes do return as ghosts and in dreams, or as fireflies (on Guadalcanal), as twirling dust clouds (Washo Indians), or other animal and nature forms. Usually this is believed to be an indication that the souls have been neglected. Even when no direct manifestation of their presence is observed, they may signify their dissatisfaction by bringing disease or other misfortunes. Ritual actions will be renewed or intensified in order to appease them, and to send them back to their own realm.

The Dead as Members of the Society

Quite different are the attitudes of peoples who feel that the dead remain members of their group. Although here, also, the dead are sometimes feared, ritual activities tend to promote interaction between the living and the dead, rather than keeping them away. Funeral rites are acts of reincorporation, readmitting the deceased to the community in their newly achieved status. They surrender one set of rights and duties, and assume another. These beliefs do not give rise to a cult of the dead, but develop into ancestor cults. In cults of the dead, burials stress the separation between the realm of the dead and that of the living, and further ritual activities tend to minimize their relationship. Ancestor cults, on the other hand, ritually bring the spirit of the deceased back into the community and tend to reaffirm or reinforce the connections between the dead and the survivors.

Linton reports that a Tanala clan has two sections which are equally real to its members: the living, and the dead (1936:121–22). The latter remain an integral part of the group, and take constant interest in the activities of their descendents.

The degree of interaction between the dead and the living varies from culture to culture. In parts of rural Japan and China there was regular and intimate contact between the living and the ancestors. The ancestral shrine, built in the home, was the center of family life, and contained wooden tablets inscribed with the names of the dead. Food sacrifices were offered daily, and important family affairs were conducted in front of the shrine. Marriage plans were presented for the approval of the ancestors, and their blessing was invoked when a journey or any important business transaction was undertaken. Daily rituals often included the reading or reciting of recent events, so that the ancestors might be fully informed, and the reading of the biographies of the ancestors themselves, so that they remained familiar to their descendants (Noss, 1963:330–40).

Elsewhere, however, the ancestor souls are consulted only on special solemn occasions. Among the South African Swazi, each family propitiates its own ancestors at births, marriages, deaths, and the building of new huts. The dead are not otherwise addressed, except when calamities befall the family (Kuper, 1963:60).

The social position of the ancestor souls is often derived from their status during lifetime. If their roles were not very strong outside their own family, they become family ancestors; lineage heads become lineage ancestors; clan leaders sometimes come to be considered the supernatural protectors of the whole group. According to Herskovits, the ancestral cult was the focal point of social organization of the African Dahomey. New settlements were established by the installation of ancestral shrines, and it was the prime duty of the various family heads to carry out the necessary rituals and sacrifices (Herskovits, 1938:Chap. 11). Chinese villages typically have an ancestral hall for the entire community, several smaller ones for lineages and moieties, and cubicles in every homestead.

SEMI-DIVINE
SUPERNATURAL BEINGS

Culturally held beliefs about the nature of the supernatural powers usually specify or imply their human or nonhuman derivations, but the origins of some supernatural powers are left ambiguous.

Murdock, writing on social organization and structure, has made an important distinction between lineages and sibs: lineages are unilineal kin groups in which the members can actually trace their relationships; sibs acknowledge a kinship bond but cannot trace the genealogy (1949:46–47). This distinction may be carried over into the realm of the supernatural: lineages have supernatural ancestors with a known human origin, while sib ancestors may well be mythological. Myths may, in fact, recount that these ancestors were semi-divine—direct descendants of the gods, or specially created by the gods to establish the sib. Such group ancestors are usually the chief protectors and the focus of communal worship.

Often, but not always, these ancestral deities are also culture heroes, which means that they taught people the tasks and practices on which the continuance of the group depends. Those deeds are also recounted in myths. The Tenetehara of Brazil believe that they received their staple food, manioc, from their culture hero, Maira. Before that time they were hunters and gatherers, living on wild fruit. At first, the manioc miraculously planted itself, matured in one day, and was harvested without labor. But Maira's second wife refused even to collect the manioc, and caused him to decree in anger that henceforth it would take the entire winter for the manioc to grow, and that it would have to be planted and harvested (Wagley and Galvao, 1949:132). Maira also introduced cotton and taught the Tenetehara how to make hammocks. He stole fire from the vultures and taught his people how to roast meat (*ibid.*:101).

Trickster gods are somewhat related to culture heroes, but they are usually not considered ancestral. They, too, are semi-divine, but Boas pointed out that they are typically unconcerned with human welfare, so that their acts are only accidentally beneficial to mankind (1940:395). The famous American Indian

Coyote (*Prairie Wolf*) is a trickster: he stole the sun, the moon, and the stars from the spirits who had held them before, but he did not know what to do with them, so he placed them in the sky. He carried out this theft for his own pleasure, and not, like Prometheus, because he pitied mankind. Similarly, Coyote stole fresh water from the spirits because he was thirsty, and clumsily spilled it all over the world when he tried to escape, thus creating lakes and rivers.

On the Carolina Islands, Iolofath is the son of the god Lugei-lang, who had a tryst with a woman on earth; she subsequently gave birth to the trickster. Iolofath is thus semi-divine, or half-mortal: in the stories he is sometimes killed, but always brought back to life by his divine father (Lessa, 1966:57). Iolofath is no culture hero, and no creator, but sometimes mediates between the celestial and terrestrial realms (*ibid.*:58).

A number of supernatural creatures do not easily fall into our categories. Dwarfs, elves, pixies, and so on—at least in the Western tradition—belong to the literary realm rather than that of the sacred supernatural. Other supernaturals partake of the characteristics of more than one category: ancestor souls may become deities, gods may become spirits, and so on. Yet, the given terminology covers and identifies a great many supernatural beings, whose characteristics may be summarized as follows:

1. *Gods:* personified, named, individually known supernaturals of nonhuman origin.

2. *Spirits:* collectivized, usually not individually named supernaturals of nonhuman origin.

3. *Souls of the dead:* supernaturals of human origin, at first individually remembered, later tending to merge in an unnamed group like the spirits.

4. *Ghosts:* souls of the dead which, in spite of precautions, return to the living, usually to disturb them.

5. *Ancestor gods:* supernatural beings of human origin, related to the group, and raised to the status of gods.

6. *Ancestor souls (or ancestor spirits):* supernatural beings of human origin, related to members of a group, and considered actual and active members of that group.

7. *Culture heroes:* supernatural beings of semi-divine origin who gave important culture traits to the group.

8. *Tricksters:* supernatural beings of semi-divine origin who may accidentally give important culture traits to the group, but are not basically concerned with human welfare.

COSMOLOGY

The second major area of religious beliefs deals with explanations of the origin and general structure of the universe. The term *cosmogony* is sometimes applied to such theories if they specifically deal with creation. When these theories involve sacred supernatural principles, they form part of religious dogma. Explanations of this kind cannot be scientifically verified, but religious cosmology is more than a mere explanatory device. It defines the power of the supernatural, guides human behavior, provides a system of norms with ethical implications, and upholds and sanctifies the values of society. The degree to which cosmological values are integrated with social values is not uniform; it depends on the coherence and stability of cultural patterns and norms. Unfortunately, the comparative study of religious cosmologies is a relatively unexplored field, but its importance is now beginning to be recognized.

Religious views of the world are as diversified as culturally held conceptions of the supernatural. Sometimes all-embracing and complex systems deal not only with the immediate surroundings of man, but also with the heavens and the earth and all they contain. Particularly in highly organized cultures, where economic surplus makes possible the establishment of priestly classes, it is likely that complex cosmologies and cosmogonies will be developed, often attempting to account not only for the universe, but also for abstract concepts of justice, power, good and evil, beauty, and change. The elaborate Dahomean system did all that, and also explained the division into countries and nations, the constitution of clans, and the founding of families (Mercier, 1954:210–34). The highly stratified Polynesian island cultures developed intricate theories of the creation of the universe and its evolution.

New Zealand Maori priests told how the original state of the universe was one of chaos and nothingness, containing only some unrealized creative powers. In this naught grew a yearning, and a vague possibility of becoming gave rise to immeasurable darkness. The darkness was empty and uninformed, but carried within itself the essence of all life. Thoughts began to grow, slowly turning into energy, and energy produced life, first lower plants, then animals, and finally also men. Light dawns, sun, moon and stars appear; the gods are born with light (Linton, 1926:177ff).

Australian aborigines, on the other hand, take the existence of the world as given, and their cosmology concentrates on their immediate environment. Water holes, rivers, hills, and rocks—each has its own creation story; thus the landscape is filled with sacred spots inhabited by spirits and ancestor souls. In cultures where cosmological explanations are particular rather than universal, items of social or religious importance will usually be selected for elaboration. Eskimo myths deal primarily with the origin of seals and sea mammals which form an important part of the Eskimo's subsistence; among many American Indian tribes corn has a sacred origin; and rice receives similar explanations in Asiatic countries.

Although cosmology frequently deals with creation of the universe, in a number of cultures it is its maintenance or function that demands explanation. The Lovedu of the Transvaal, for instance, do not speculate about first beginnings or final causes; although they have a vague myth that the god Khuzwane created the world, it carries little social interest and no ritual consequence. The Lovedu are less interested in the origin of the world than in its order—an order which, although upheld by supernatural powers, is controllable by man. Only those aspects of nature that are of immediate usefulness and can be manipulated to serve human purposes receive cosmological treatment (Krige and Krige, 1954:59ff). The Cheyenne Indians, too, are much more interested in the functioning of the world than in its beginnings. In their view, the world order is a system of interrelated parts, each of those governed by a supernatural being who knows how to operate and uphold its domain. Cheyenne ritual action is directed to learning these operations (Hoebel, 1960:83).

When the social order is considered to be sanctioned by the cosmic order, religious conceptions about the world order include normative elements. In these instances, the order of society is a more or less accurate reflection of the order of the world or the universe. The closer human society approaches the model of the sacred order, the better will be its functioning. The African Dogon possess such a world view. This idea permeates family organization, marriage rules, and extends to many other interpersonal relationships; even the layout of the cultivated fields is organized in accordance with the principle that the world developed in the form of a spiral (Griaule and Dieterlen, 1954:83–110).

Among the Trobriand Islanders, as well as in a number of other agricultural societies, the world order is seen in terms of the changing seasons. Garden rituals are held not only to insure fertility and success, but also to mark the various sacred phases of nature. Kwakiutl Indians cannot begin their salmon-catching season until their priests have marked its beginning by ritual, ceremonially catching the first salmon and offering it to the gods.

The Pueblo Indians generally hold a world view that man and the universe are interrelated and in equilibrium—an equilibrium that man can disturb. This is an example of the ethical implications of cosmology. Misfortunes and illness are not seen as direct punishments by the gods, but as results of man's behavior. Man may upset the harmony of the universe by demonstrating greed, hostility, or lack of either hospitality or generosity. Such misbehavior brings misfortunes not only to the individual or his family, but to the whole community (Dozier, 1966:81–82).

A few religious cosmologies deal with the future of the world. In millenarian cults the future of the world plays an important role, and usually involves a cataclysmic event which ushers in a different and better world. Elsewhere, cyclical theories play a certain role: the Dahomey believe in a series of worlds and a series of creators (Mercier, 1954:217).

Durkheim was much impressed by the fact that cosmological statements seem to be universally present in religious systems, and he concluded that all philosophical and scientific thoughts about the cosmos arise from religious speculations (1961:165ff, 476ff). Malinowski rebuffed this idea by pointing out that secular and religious world views exist side by side, and evolutionary development from religion to science is neither demonstrable nor logical.

THE NATURE OF MAN

The last of the three major themes expressed in religious dogma centers on the nature of man and his society. It includes ideas about origin and creation, the order of human life, human existence and purpose, and—most important—human destiny.

With respect to human origins there are two major modes of explanation: one holds that man has his beginnings on earth; the other, that he is a descendant of the gods. The Bible relates how Adam was "formed from the dust of the ground" (Gen. 2:7). The Koran teaches that Allah created man from clots of blood (Sura XCVI). The same motif is found in many nonliterate societies. The Yuma Indians believe that their creator god made the first human beings out of mud (Forde, 1931:176). The African Dogon believe that the first human couple sprang from two balls of clay, kneaded by the god Amma (Griaule, 1960:367–68). The Thonga hold that the first people came out of the reeds (Junod, 1913:I, 348–50). The Tullishi tribe of the African Nuba group believe that their god planted a gourd on earth; as the gourd grew, it ripened and split open, and a man and a woman emerged from it (Nadel, 1947:323). Sometimes human origins are not initiated by a divine act at all. An example of a nonreligious and non-scientific theory comes from the Andaman Islands, where it is believed that the first man emerged from a tree, and that when he became lonely, he fashioned a wife from clay taken from a nest of ants (Radcliffe-Brown, 1964:191–94).

These and similar explanations tend to stress man's mortality and his separation from the divine. Quite different are situations in which man believes himself to be descended from the gods. The first human offspring of the gods are the sacred ancestors, founders of the clan, sib, or lineage. Such beliefs not only influence man's view of his own person, but, more important, they validate and sanctify kinship among members of the group. Consequently, these views are most often found in small, homogeneous, kinship-based societies. However tenuous the claim of blood relationship may actually be, a postulated common descent from common gods and ancestors acts as a powerful impetus toward group integration, the more so because rituals are communal, directed to the common ancestral supernaturals.

When such societies become too large or too complex to operate as a single unit, social stratification begins to develop. Explanations arise to account for social differences that both explain and sanctify the hierarchy.

One strong expression of man's relationship to the divine was made by the Japanese Shinto theologian Airata Atsutane:

> We [*i.e.*, the Japanese] who have been brought into existence through the creative spirit of Kami, are, each and everyone, in spontaneous possession of the Way of the Gods. We are one with our ancestors, and a part of divine nature (quoted by Holtom, 1943:16).

THE CONCEPT OF THE SOUL

The most conspicuous aspect of man's religious self-image is his concept of the soul. All known cultures make some distinction between man's body and at least one other element with qualities different from those of the body, although intimately associated with it. This element, the soul, is believed to survive the body, but it often plays a significant role during life as well.

Single Souls and Multiple Souls

In many cultures it is believed that man has not one soul, but many. The languages of such cultures have a separate term for each of these, while English has only one word, *soul*. Thus the translation of some native conceptions about nonphysical human properties into the term *soul* has been inaccurate. Some of these ideas seem to correspond more closely with our concepts of *personality, vitality,* or *subconsciousness*. For instance, a number of Athapascan tribes possess a dualistic concept of "soul": one is the *ne-tsen* (the *free soul*), which can wander outside the body and leaves permanently at death; the other is the *nazael* (the *body soul* or *human heat*), the function of which is to give warmth to the body, and which dies when the body dies (Hultkranz, 1953:63). The *nazael* is therefore not really *soul,* but closer to our idea of *vitality*. The Coast Salish of British Columbia, too, believe in the existence of two souls. One resides in the head, maintains rational behavior; when it leaves, people behave foolishly. The other soul resides in the heart; its loss brings physical illness and death (Barnett, 1955:211). The "soul" in the head is in no way comparable to a religious concept of soul; it appears to be a secular explanation for brainless behavior, similar to our expression, "I must have been out of my mind," which is used to account for unreasonable acts.

But true multiple-soul concepts do appear, and often have significant consequences for socioreligious behavior patterns. The Jivaro head hunters of southern Brazil recognize three souls: the *nekas,* the *aruntam,* and the *muisak.* The *nekas* is born with the body, and leaves it after death, remaining in or near the house in which the deceased was born. It is, to the Jivaro, the least important of the souls, for it does little to help the individual to survive in his insecure society. Instead, the *aruntam* ranks first. It is not inborn, but acquired. A young boy goes with his father to the sacred waterfall of his neighborhood, and together they fast until his *aruntam* arrives in a vision. The *aruntam* of an unknown Jivaro ancestor enters the body of the boy, and endows him with intelligence, power, and immunity from death through violence or sorcery. Once a man has acquired one *aruntam* soul, he may join the war parties, and after killing an enemy, he will add the enemy's *aruntam* to his own, thus increasing his power and immunity. But the *muisak,* residing in the head, will attempt to take revenge by killing the murderer. The head of a slain enemy is taken, shrunk, and ritually treated so that the *muisak* will not be able to fulfill its function (Harner, 1962:258–72).

The Dahomey believe that human beings possess more than one soul: women and children have three; adult males, four. Every person inherits one soul from an ancestor; during his lifetime it acts as a guardian spirit, and after death it acts a counsel for the deceased. The second soul is the personal soul, shaped like a human being, but surviving him. The third is described as "the bit of Mawn which is placed in every person's body." Mawn, one of the most important creator gods, put a part of himself into every Dahomey in order to give divine guidance. After death, the second soul comes before Mawn to tell what the person has made out of his life, and the third soul is witness to the truth of this account. The last soul, possessed by adult males only, is associated with the concept of purpose and destiny—not only that of the individual in which it resides, but also that of the household of which the men become heads and leaders (Herskovits, 1938: 233–35).

Multiple-soul concepts may also correlate with aspects of kinship organization. In a number of societies, notably in Africa, an individual is related to both his mother's and his father's lineage, but in different ways, and for different purposes; such a system is known as *double descent*. Children derive their paternal souls from their fathers, and maternal souls from their mothers.

In societies in which man believes that he has only one soul, the most common function of that soul is to guard the body's health and maintain its normal physical functioning. Consequently, illness is often explained as the temporary loss of the soul, and curing entails bringing back the soul. Permanent loss of soul results in death.

Location of the Soul

The location of the soul in the body is frequently associated with the breath, but the Menomini Indians say that it resides in the head, the Yuma Indians place it in the heart, while others believe that it is connected with the liver, the genitals, the stomach, the nape of the neck, or the shadow. The part of the body serving as the soul's point of entry or exit is often culturally defined. When the soul is associated with the breath, the nostrils or mouth are the obvious points of departure. The Javanese say that the soul comes and goes through the feet, and this is one reason why small children, whose souls are less permanent, are not allowed to touch the earth until they are about eighteen months old. At that time, the first contact of the feet with the earth is made under specific ritual conditions. Other points of departure include the whorl of the hair, the back of the neck, the genitals, the big toe, and many more. Such ideas may be connected with culturally held ideas of body images, but these relationships have not yet been studied in any systematic way.

The Destiny of the Soul

Religious views about man's existence after death are invariably connected with the idea that the soul survives the body, but it is not always considered immortal. Beliefs relating to the afterlife often have significant social consequences. In Christianity, Judaism, and Islam, the afterlife depends largely upon the behavior of the individual during his life on earth. Culturally approved behavior will be rewarded after death; disapproved behavior will be punished.

Such beliefs are relatively rare in the religions of nonliterate peoples, and when they are found, missionary influence can often be discovered. Yet, they do occasionally appear in indigenous religions. The Cubeo Indians of the northwestern Amazon region say that souls of people who have committed adultery, broken bonds of ritual friendship, committed incest, or eaten a taboo fish assume an animal form after death (Goldman, 1963:259). Other examples can undoubtedly be found, but the idea of individuals working toward their own salvation by ethical and moral behavior is not predominant in nonliterate societies.

The absence of this concept does not indicate the absence of an ethical system, although world religions with concepts of personal salvation are frequently referred to as *the ethical religions,* with the implication that tribal forms of religion cannot be so described. Max Weber, for one, contrasted the ethics of world religions with nonethical "systems of magic." Yet many such systems include the belief that supernatural punishments and rewards are meted out to the individual during his lifetime rather than after death, and that a man's family, sib, or lineage may, through correct behavior, determine the ultimate destiny of his soul. In both cases the ethical implications are obvious.

Not all beliefs relating to the destiny of the soul have moral or ethical implications. In rigidly stratified societies, the individual's social or occupational status may determine the fate of his soul after death. In Polynesia, where commoners are forbidden to mingle with kings and nobles, the latter retain their lofty isolation even in the hereafter. The heavenly abode of the nobility is comfortable and luxurious, while that of the commoners is much more modestly furnished.

The Yao of Malawi did not think that the souls of important members of their group went to a separate realm, but they did believe that social positions were retained in the hereafter: chiefs remained chiefs, the wealthy remained wealthy, and the poor remained poor (Stannus, 1922:311). The Yao may well be motivated by these beliefs to seek higher rank in their society, not only because of the advantages and privileges in this world, but also because of those in the next. A somewhat related concept is found among the Chagga of East Africa, who believe that they can improve their lot in the afterlife by sacrificing animals. A Chagga who offered many head of cattle during his lifetime can claim them after death, and will thus be well off in the supernatural realm (Dundas, 1924:125). The Tonga of Zambia believe that a person leaves two spirits after death: the "ghost," originating at the person's death, and the *muzimu,* which is given to him at birth. When the person matures and takes a position of responsibility within his matrilineal group, his *muzimu* becomes eligible to turn into an ancestral spirit when death comes. Since his *muzimu* would represent the position he held in the community, only those who have achieved a certain status can become ancestral spirits after death (Colson, 1960:376–82).

Occupational status may determine the future position of the soul. Shamans, often set apart from others during lifetime by distinctive dress and behavior patterns, may maintain this social distance after death. Aztec warriors were rewarded for bravery by being assigned to their own supernatural realm, one more fitting to their interests and accustomed modes of life. The manner of death may also be influential: the Ainu believed that those struck by lightning had been singled out by the gods for special powers and positions in the supernatural realm.

Many cultural beliefs specify that the dead go to the same realm, regardless of their social behavior during their lives. They become restless and angry, however, when their relatives break the accepted norms of behavior, or fail to carry out the mortuary rituals which they have the right to expect. Punishment, in the form of misfortunes or illness, is the result of such neglect.

CONCLUSION

This account of some types of social beliefs relating to the supernatural shows how these beliefs may influence social behavior and contribute to the maintenance of social order. The sum total of a people's religious beliefs about the gods, the world, and their own nature are guideposts to systems of life. These beliefs can be studied in terms of their social functions and purposes, but they also have symbolic meanings. These meanings are usually appropriate within the total system, and have an underlying rationale which is not always easy to discover. In one sense, people always know the meaning of their own symbols, but find it difficult to formulate it clearly. The relevance of religious systems of belief can be assessed only by studying these systems in action—*i.e.*, how they are expressed in ritual and myth, and how they relate to values and social institutions.

7

Myth and Ritual

MYTH AND RITUAL HAVE ENGENDERED WIDE SCHOLARLY INTEREST.
Some students consider them entirely separate subjects; others
maintain they are closely correlated. Some of these theoretical
approaches will be explained and analyzed, particularly those
which have exercized influence upon anthropological thinking.

MYTH

Nearly every branch of humanistic scholarship has attempted
to explain the existence and meaning of myth. One of the major
disagreements centers on the proper definition of myth. But
definitions may legitimately vary. If the concept under consideration is very complex, there can be many definitions, none of
which need contradict another. Each definition tends to stress
that aspect which is of the greatest professional interest to the
person making the definition.

Myth consists of language; it appears in the form of a narrative
with a plot; it has style and, often, beauty; it has a history and
cross-cultural distribution; it is a cultural institution and, as
such, possesses psychological, social, and religious functions and
meanings. Thus, a linguist will analyze the language of myth, the
folklorist is interested in its motifs and plots, the literary critic

172

focuses on its style and aesthetic value, the psychologist searches for its emotional content, the theologian examines its relationship to religious truths, and the social scientist concentrates on its social meanings and functions.

The Linguistic Approach

The linguistic approach is exemplified by Max Müller's attempts to trace the origin and meanings of myth through nineteenth-century methods of comparative linguistics and etymology. Müller defined myth as a story dealing with the gods, and he believed that all folk tales and fairy tales were originally myths whose meanings had been obscured by changes in language. Accordingly, he saw no need to separate myth from other tales, except for the fact that myths were much older.

Although Müller's theories have been discarded by modern scholars, his equation of myth with folk tale is adhered to by all who concentrate upon the analysis of myth as a linguistic or literary phenomenon. Folklorists generally have no need to distinguish myth from any other traditional type of story. Stith Thompson defines myths as "stories about the gods and their activities in general," pointing out that though the definition may not be accurate, it is useful for the classification of tales by subject matter (1958:104, 106).

The major occupation of folklorists is, indeed, the collection of all kinds of traditional folk beliefs and stories. Because the material so patiently accumulated is extensive, its cataloguing and classification become a major task. Classification is based upon specific narrative elements, called *motifs,* which may be thought of as "the smallest divisible narrative unit of a tale" (Clarke and Clarke, 1963:27). Thompson's *Motif-Index of Folk-Literature* (1955–58), a monumental reference work, sets forth the basic elements of folk narratives of all kinds, including myths. Such cataloguing is a necessary prerequisite to any systematic study of folklore, and gives important and fascinating insights into the distribution and variations of these tales.

As long as folklorists concentrate upon the content of tales, they are fully justified in defining myth as a narrative dealing with gods. Yet, there is a certain uneasiness among folklorists about their equation of myth and folk tale. Some have sought a way out by speaking of "serious myths" or "veritable myths" when dealing with narratives with strong religious implications (Murray, 1962:27). Others rationalize their lack of distinction by reverting to the erroneous nineteenth-century argument that native storytellers themselves would not know how to distinguish between myth and secular tales (Thompson 1946:303). This is certainly not always the case. Malinowski showed that the Trobriand people made both conceptual and linguistic distinctions between sacred myths and secular stories (1954:106–7). In some cultures, even finer distinctions exist, and several different types of sacred narratives are recognized.

Nineteenth-century anthropologists approached their study of myth with the conviction of their own cultural superiority. Unable to account for the presence of myth in their midst, they placed all responsibility for its creation upon prehistoric man. Myth was considered the product of the prelogical mind (Lévy-Bruhl), a disease of language and thought of mythopoetic man (Müller), or a faltering attempt by early man to be scientific (Tylor, Frazer).

When these views became discredited, but alternate explanations were not at hand, anthropologists turned to collecting, as the extensive volumes of Boas show (1894, 1902, 1905, and so on). Eager to preserve ethnographic evidence before the Indian cultures vanished, Boas collected many narrative texts and published them with interlinear translations. But these collections were accompanied by a minimum of theory: Boas merely observed that the Indian tales mirror the traits of material culture. He also traced the paths of diffusion of the tales from tribe to tribe (Boas, 1940:437–45). But Boas did not distinguish myths from other types of stories; he merely followed the conventional folklore categories of his time.

The Psychoanalytic Approach

These approaches to myth consider only its external appearance and see it as a linguistic phenomenon or a narrative. The conclusions to which they led tended to neglect the carriers of these traditions. All this changed when the psychoanalysts turned their attention to myth. Psychoanalysts showed that myth was not to be found and analyzed only in nonliterate societies and cultures of the past, but that it exists and has meaning in all cultures and in all periods of history, including the present.

The key to Freudian myth analysis rests in the equation of myth with dream. In *The Interpretation of Dreams,* Freud presented his thesis that dreams, by distorting reality, symbolically express unconscious wishes (1900, reprinted in 1938:181–552). Later, he became convinced that all irrational stories represented such wishes: "The prosecution of dream-symbology led to the very heart of mythology, folklore, and religious abstraction" (1938a:954). Unconscious wishes, moreover, were predominantly of a sexual nature, according to Freud, for "humanity as a whole is oppressed by its sexual needs" *(ibid.:*970). Consequently, myths deal with sexual hunger and guilt, manifested in fantasies of incest, castration, physical destruction, masturbation, penis envy, or homosexuality. These fantasies are not overt, but symbolic. The psychoanalytic method can discover the hidden meanings by learning the vocabulary of the "forgotten language."

Freud's followers applied themselves to this task with enthusiasm and imagination. Any object resembling the male genital in form or function became a phallic symbol; anything fluid or sticky or white came to symbolize semen. The female genital was represented by objects resembling containers, buildings, or openings; sexual intercourse was signified by any verb indicating movement. With this basic vocabulary, which can be extended at will, the interpretation of myth and folklore was no longer difficult. The story is fragmented into its linguistic components; the key words ("symbols") are replaced by the appropriate sexual terms; and a new story emerges bearing the "real" meaning of the original myth. A sample analysis of the European version of the "Little Red Riding Hood" story: Little Red-Cap is a maiden who has become sexually mature (red=menstruation), but she has had no sexual experience (she carries an unbroken bottle of wine to grandmother=virginity). She meets a wolf (man) in the forest (trees=phalli). The wolf eventually eats her (aggressive intercourse), and, later on, he is punished by Red-Cap, who put stones (sterility) in his belly. He dies. The story symbolizes "the triumph of man-hating women, ending with their victory" (Fromm, 1951:240–41).

Jung and his followers rejected most of the sexual symbolism, but they, too, equated myth, dream, and neurotic fantasies. These fantasies were explained by Jung through his concept of a "collective unconscious." Myths and dreams reveal this "unconscious"; they arise from the experiences of the psyche. Many of these experiences are of a biological nature and, consequently, are universal, which explains the cross-cultural similarities in myth and dream motifs. One such recurring dream motif, according to Jung, is the *anima,* appearing as an old woman and representing man's unconscious self. She appears as a woman because she is also "the psychic representation of the minority of female genes in a male body" (Jung, 1938:33). This is biological nonsense but, even so, one wonders how biological factors, certainly not known to most people, entered their "preconscious psyche."

Another of Jung's examples involves the number four, which frequently appears in myth and religion. According to Jung, it appears there because it stems from the biological experience of the four-cell stage (*i.e.,* the second cell division of the zygote, the fertilized ovum) (Jung and Kerényi, 1963:17). But he does not explain the odd numbers, which often are given sacred connotations. It can be seen, therefore, that psychoanalytic methods of interpretation are often more irrational than the stories they attempt to analyze.

Many modern psychologists have rejected their predecessors' findings. But there is still a general insistence upon the universality of symbols, both in appearance and in meaning. Common sense observations belie this notion: Jewish men cover their heads as a symbol of their respect for the sacred; Christians uncover theirs for precisely the same reason. Anthropologists have found ample ethnographic evidence that symbols are not universal. The bat, according to Freudians, universally represents the vulva, but Shimkin showed that, among the Wind River Shoshone Indians, it symbolizes male sexual prowess (1947). The snake, the most celebrated Freudian phallic symbol, is a symbol of female jealousy in Japan (Opler, 1945). (Psychoanalysts would be quick to answer that this is a case of penis envy but, even so, penis envy is not the same as the phallus.)

The best testimony to the nonuniversality of symbols comes from the psychoanalysts themselves. Freud saw the Oedipus myth as a symbol of the universal wish of man to possess his mother and to kill his father; Fromm finds in the same myth a conflict between matriarchy and patriarchy; Jung sees it as an ethical conflict between laziness and duty; Ferenczi believes that Oedipus himself is a phallic symbol because his name literally means *swell-foot* (foot=penis, swelling=erection). In the story of "The Frog King," Max Müller stoutly identified the frog as the sun because he sometimes squatted on the water; Ernest Jones saw in it the penis, and interprets the fairy tale as a symbolic description of how women gradually overcome their aversion to sex, (1951:II, 244–46); Campbell said that the frog was a miniature dragon-serpent summoning forth the child to independence and maturity (1956:49–53). If interpreters from similar cultural backgrounds cannot agree upon the meanings of symbols, how different must be the symbolic meanings assigned by people with different cultural experience!

The Anthropological Approach

Cultural anthropologists, although keenly aware of the errors of the older psychoanalysts, have not rejected the idea that myth and folk tale often express unconscious workings of the mind, but they are wary of any sort of generalized interpretations. They observed that Freud himself found it necessary to acquire additional information from the individuals whose dreams he interpreted. When contexts are important for understanding the meanings of individual symbols, they are even more necessary for the interpretation of cultural symbols.

The anthropological approach with psychological implications is exemplified by Kluckhohn's analysis of Navaho myths. Kluckhohn found, upon analysis, that these myths displayed very little sexual anxiety, but a predominant concern with health and life. Checking with the Indian Medical Service Board, he discovered that there was a much higher proportion of sickness among the Navaho than in neighboring non-Indian communities. But even this empirical basis could not sufficiently explain their anxiety. The Pueblo Indians, with a comparable rate of illness, center their myths, not on health, but on rain and the fertility of the land.

Kluckhohn now turned for an explanation to economic and social factors. The Pueblos, he noted, were largely agricultural and had a reserve store of corn which was their staple food. Lack of rain would threaten their main source of food, so that the preoccupation with rain became a basic anxiety. The Navaho, on the other hand, had until recently depended upon hunting and gathering. They had no food reserve except that which nature provided, and ill health would have prevented them from going out and finding their food. The prospect of illness was more threatening to them than the lack of rain. A reinforcing factor was found in the fact that the social organization of the Navaho was based on small-group extended families. Kluckhohn found it conceivable that this "emotional inbreeding," as he called it, increased interpersonal tensions, which, in turn, may have been related to the frequencies of disorders and the anxieties connected with them.

Kluckhohn's analysis is not conclusive, but his interpretations are based upon a solid knowledge of Navaho culture. He also shows how myth, as part of a religious system, expresses supernatural dangers: illness, among the Navaho, represents supernatural punishment. But myths and rituals also provide systematic protection against these dangers: "It is only through the myth-ritual system that Navahos can make a socially supported, unified response to all of these disintegrating threats" (1965:157).

Psychoanalytic interpretations of myth and folk tale, however faulty, attracted many investigators because they endowed the stories—no matter how irrational—with both individual and cultural meanings. Nineteenth-century scholars had tried to explain the irrationality of myths by tracing their origins to ancient times, when people themselves were believed to be somewhat irrational. The question of why these stories had survived and flourished in literate and nonliterate societies alike remained unanswerable. All this changed when Freudian interpretations were applied. Yet, many anthropologists were dissatisfied with the reduction of religion to psychological states of tension, frustration, and delusion.

An alternate explanation, put forward by the functionalists, provided a much more powerful rationale for the existence of myth: myth was a force that helped to maintain society itself. Myth, and thus religion as a whole, continues to play an important part in social life. It became then the task of the function-oriented anthropologist to show what that part is and to demonstrate how, in different types of societies, different myths both shape and are shaped by other social institutions. Although a number of scholars (*i.e.*, Robinson Smith, Durkheim, Radcliffe-Brown) wrote on the social functions of myth, the clearest exposition of the functional interpretation of myth is found in Malinowski's "Myth in Primitive Psychology" (1954:93–140):

> Studied alive, myth, as we shall see, is not symbolic, but a direct expression of its subject matter; it is not an explanation in satisfaction of a scientific interest, but a narrative resurrection of a primeval reality, told in satisfaction of deep religious wants, moral cravings, social submissions, assertions, even practical requirements. Myth fulfills in primitive culture an indispensable function; it expresses, enhances, and codifies belief; it safeguards and enforces morality; it vouches for the efficiency of ritual and contains practical rules for the guidance of man. Myth is thus a vital ingredient of human civilization; it is not an idle tale, but a hard-worked active force; it is not an intellectual explanation or an artistic imagery, but a pragmatic charter of primitive faith and moral wisdom (1954:101).

In a posthumously published article on the same topic, the allusions to "primitive" culture and faith are omitted, and the general tone indicates that Malinowski had extended his views to include all forms of myth and religion (1962:245–55).

Of the various examples which Malinowski gives in order to show the role of myth within its cultural framework, the following is quite representative:

> There are a number of special spots—grottoes, clumps of trees, stone heaps, coral outcrops, springs, heads of creeks—called *holes* or *houses* by the natives. From such "holes" the first couples (a sister as the head of the family and the brother as her guardian) came and took possession of the

lands, and gave the totemic, industrial, magical, and sociological character to the communities thus begun.

The problem of rank, which plays a great role in their
sociology, was settled by the emergence from one special
hole, called Obukula, near the village of Laba'i. This event
was notable in that, contrary to the usual course (which is:
one original "hole," one lineage), from this hole of Laba'i
there emerged representatives of the four main clans one
after the other. Their arrival, moreover, was followed by an
apparently trivial but, in mythical reality, a most important
event. First there came the *Kaylavasi* (iguana), the animal
of the Lukulabuta clan, which scratched its way through the
earth as iguanas do, then climbed a tree, and remained there
as a mere onlooker, following subsequent events. Soon there
came out the Dog, totem of the Lukuba clan, who originally
had the highest rank. As a third came the Pig, representative of the Malasi clan, which now holds the highest rank.
Last came the Lukwasisiga totem, represented in some versions by the Crocodile, in others by the Snake, in others by
the Opossum, and sometimes completely ignored. The Dog
and Pig ran round, and the Dog, seeing the fruit of the *noku*
plant, nosed it, then ate it. Said the Pig: "Thou eatest
noku, thou eatest dirt; thou art a low-bred, a commoner;
the chief, the *guya'u,* shall be I." And ever since, the highest
subclan of the Malasi clan, the Tabalu, have been the real
chiefs (1954:112).

This myth, according to Malinowski, maintains the relationships between the rival clans by referring to the sacred institu-
tionalization of the superiority of the Malasi clan from which
the chiefs are chosen. The myth was, in fact, often cited when
quarrels over land and fishing rights arose. When visitors arrived
who might not know the local differences in rank, the myth
would serve as a means of enlightening them. Other myths, relating how the sacred ancestors had brought the arts and industry to the village, served to make the stranger aware of local
economic monopolies.

Most functionalists look upon myth in much the same manner
as Malinowski, seeing it both as a sanction and a "charter" of

social reality, upholding and reflecting established society. In this view, it is unnecessary to postulate that myth is "indispensable," if this term is taken to mean that the social structure cannot otherwise be upheld. The myth described by Malinowski deals with power relations between the subclans, and thus with the political and social inequalities that prevail among them. But it is clear that such inequalities are, in other cultures, sometimes maintained or enforced by secular forces—by the numerical superiority of the dominant group, its more advanced technology, its military power, and so on. It is logical to conclude that in cultures in which secular means of maintaining the power of a subgroup are relatively weak, myth will have a stronger function than it would otherwise have. Malinowski has been accused of holding the "postulate of indispensability" without allowing for functional alternatives (Merton, 1957:32–33), but his functional myth analysis, objectively considered, merely demonstrates that myth, as it appears in a specific culture, can be explained in terms of some other existing cultural condition. Thus, if the relationship between subclans is a functional requirement of a particular society, and myth is one of the institutions that helps to maintain that requirement, myth is "indispensable" at that time and in that society. If social circumstances change, the function of myth will change too, and other powers come to absorb some or all the functions of myth.

Another flaw in the theory of a generalized indispensability of myth is the fact that myth does not reflect the totality of social structure; it is always selective. Some cultures stress political institutions in their mythology, others concentrate more on economic pursuits, family structure, incest taboos, marriage rules, role changes of adolescents, or other institutionalized cultural concerns. It is likely that the specific points of mythical elaboration represent real or potential areas of conflict, but not all conflict situations find expression in myth.

Although Malinowski's statement can thus be revised to read that myth *can* be a charter of *selective features* of social reality, this should not lead to the conclusion that myth is, by definition, an integrative force. It may be divisive as well. Leach, in his analysis of political structures in highland Burma (1954), showed how the Kachin people possessed many rival versions of the same myth, each tending to uphold the vested interests of different families. Each version of the myth will unite and integrate one family, for it claims for that family a specific relationship to the supernatural and thus validates its rights and privileges. But this also means that the myth invalidates the claims of other families, thereby setting up an antagonistic situation between them. Thus integration of a society or of a segment of a society carries with it a separation from another society or divisions within the society.

Quite a different type of myth analysis comes from the French anthropologist Lévi-Strauss, which he calls the "structural" study of myth (1963b:206–31). Lévi-Strauss repudiates both the functionalistic and the psychological approaches. As he expresses it:

> If a given mythology confers prominence on a certain figure, let us say an evil grandmother, it will be claimed that in such a society grandmothers are actually evil and that mythology reflects the social structure and the social relations; but should the actual data be conflicting, it would be as readily claimed that the purpose of mythology is to provide an outlet for repressed feelings. Whatever the situation, a clever dialectic will always find a way to pretend that a meaning has been found (*ibid.:* 207–8).

He begins to explain his own method by making the common-sense observation that the narratives of myth, taken at face value, express neither logic nor continuity. Yet, there is an astounding similarity between myths in widely different regions. Lévi-Strauss builds up his explanation in analogy with linguistic analysis, where the same or similar sounds are present in various languages, but the combinations, which give the sounds their meaning, are different. In myth, the basic elements are not sounds or words, but short sentences, the "constituent units." An investigator who wants to apply Lévi-Strauss' method must collect all versions of a myth, break them up into their constituent units, write these short sentences on index cards, and place the similar units in each version in vertical columns. An abbreviated example, given by Lévi-Strauss, deals with certain units of the Oedipus myth. A partial arrangement of the units looks as follows (*ibid.:* 214):

Cadmos seeks his sister Europa ravished by Zeus		Cadmos kills the dragon	
	The Spartoi kill one another		
			Laddacos (Laios' father) = *lame* (?)
	Oedipus kills his father, Laios		
			Laios (Oedipus' father) = *left-sided* (?)
		Oedipus kills the Sphinx	
Oedipus marries his mother, Jocasta			
	Eteocles kills his brother Polynices		Oedipus = *swollen-foot* (?)
Antigone buries her brother Polynices despite prohibition			

If we were to *tell* the myth, we would read from left to right, but, if we want to understand it, we should read also from top to bottom. In Column 1, all the elements deal with blood relations which are subject to more intimate treatment than they should be. This can be summed up as the overrating of blood relations. Column 2 inverts this picture; it displays the underrating of blood relations. Column 3 refers to monsters, the dragon and the sphinx, who are unwilling to let man live, but are slain by man. Monsters are chthonic—*i.e.*, they stem from the underworld—and the fact that they are killed by men indicates that man is not autochthonous, not born of the earth. The last column shows that man is, after all, born of the earth: all names have a meaning that indicates difficulty in walking. Pueblo Indian myths often tell how men originally emerged from the earth, in which they had pre-existed in an incomplete form. When they came to the surface, they were still unable to walk or could do so only clumsily.

Lévi-Strauss notes that Column 1 stands in direct opposition to Column 2, while Column 3 opposes Column 4. This implies a kind of mathematical equation: $1:2 = 3:4$, which can now be read as "the overrating of blood relations is to its underrating as the attempt to escape autochthony is to the impossibility to exceed in it" (*ibid.*:216). In other words, experience (man born from man) contradicts cosmology (man born from nature); but also in social life (underrating and overrating of relations), similar contradictions do exist, and the one does not negate the other. Thus, both views may be true.

In Lévi-Strauss' view, then, the purpose of myth is to provide a logical model capable of overcoming contradictions between religious world views and secular experience. The kind of logic used by mythical thought is "as religious as that of modern science." It organizes available cultural information while searching for relationships between inexplicable contradictions. The patterning of this information can be detected by applying Lévi-Strauss' method. Indeed, several newer branches of anthropology study patterning of other cultural phenomena in a similar manner, focusing on the logical techniques underlying native terminologies for kinship (Conant, 1961), plants (Conklin, 1954), color (Conklin, 1955), disease (Frake, 1961), and so on.

Whatever may be the ultimate value of Lévi-Strauss' method, it is interesting to note that myths often display a binary structure. Zuni myth, according to Lévi-Strauss, reveals the opposition between life and death (1963b:220–21). Leach, applying this method to the Book of Genesis, finds a dyadic relation of singularity and plurality: "Unitary categories such as man alone, life alone, one river, occur only in ideal Paradise; in the real world things are multiple and divided; man needs a partner, woman; life has a partner, death" (1965:395). He comes to the challenging conclusion that the binary structure in myth is not accidental; it reflects oppositions intrinsic to the process of human thought (*ibid*.:387).

The various possibilities of this method are challenging and provocative, but many difficulties still have to be resolved. The isolation and arrangement of the "shortest possible sentences" appears to be based upon subjective criteria, and different investigators may well reach conflicting conclusions. The problem of diffusion is overlooked, for although Lévi-Strauss includes all versions of a myth, he ignores the fact that their meanings may change when they are borrowed. Also, the use of Pueblo myth to explain aspects of Greek mythology is of questionable validity.

Some scholars may profit from the insights provided by this method, and be stimulated to clarify some of the problems which Lévi-Strauss himself acknowledges. A beginning has already been made by Colby (1966:793–98). He, too, begins with the observation that myths and folktales are linguistically structured, but he concentrates upon their semantic patterns. He demonstrates that these patterns reveal, or are related to, more basic cultural patterns. In order to find these patterns, Colby begins by classifying words into different semantic domains, such as *time, space, affection, observation, assistance, competition,* and so on. Using computers, he processed large numbers of narrative texts, counting the number of words belonging to each of these concepts.

Comparing Eskimo and Japanese texts, Colby made a number of interesting discoveries. The Eskimo narratives displayed a high frequency of words pertaining to the concepts of *search* and *observation of landmarks,* but this frequency diminished as the tale proceeded. In Japanese tales, words belonging to these two concepts were less rigidly patterned, but this frequency tended to increase as the story progressed. Colby's interpretation is that Eskimos most often tell hunting stories, and their emphasis upon search and observation reflects the cultural interest in skill and hunting ability. The decrease in frequency reflects the success of the ideal hunter, for once he has caught the animal, the search is over and the observation of landmarks is no longer necessary. The Japanese pattern, on the other hand, reflects an interest in strategies of deception and secrecy, and a concern with external, usually social, situations.

Myth can be analyzed by a number of different methods, and the results need not contradict one another as long as they are

based upon empirical observation rather than upon untested assumptions. The examples provided here do not exhaust all possibilities. Componential analysis, as Fischer has shown, can be
meaningfully applied (1963:254–55); historical studies have uncovered much important data; and philosophy has given many
insights into the deeper meanings of myth. What is needed is a
holistic and integrative approach that relates the synchronic to
the diachronic, the individual to the cultural, and the psychological to the social function and meaning of myth.

For linguists, folklorists, and anthropological collectors, myth
need not be defined within its religious framework. But, if the
specific functions of myth within a given society are to be understood, myth must be set apart from all other narratives. It must
be defined as that which deals with the *sacred* supernatural, and
is the counterpart of both dogma and ritual.

The criterion of the supernatural alone is obviously insufficient. The story of "Sleeping Beauty" presents seven supernatural creatures, as well as a mirror of truth, and a raising from
death. But, clearly, the dwarfs are not sacred, the mirror is not
holy, and the awakening of the beautiful maiden does not elevate
her to the status of deity. Fairy tales deal with all kinds of supernatural beings, good or evil ones, but such tales are not sacred
because they are not believed to be "true" by adults. It is the
aspect of belief that gives myth its power. Without belief, myth
cannot function as a "charter of social reality," nor can it uphold moral values or motivate human behavior. Belief makes
myth sacred and relates it directly to dogma. Dogma appeals to
myth to explain and sanctify its truths, and all stories which are
not rooted in dogma are not myths.

Myth, however, is not merely a symbolic description of dogma,
nor are all items of belief expressed in mythical form. But myth
is defined by its reference to belief systems, in which lies its cultural meanings and its ability to justify dominant social institutions. Folktales often have a moral, but they do not establish the
value principles of society, although they may reflect them.

It is not always easy or even possible to distinguish myth from
nonmyth. Folklore studies have revealed the persistence of mythological motifs, and the readiness with which they may diffuse
from one culture to another. Myths thus often remain part of a
culture long after their sacred connotations have faded. In such

cases, myths change into folktales or legends. It is during this
period of transition that they are most difficult to define. This
transition is very significant, for it reflects important changes in
other parts of the religious and social system.

The relative ease of diffusion means that the myth of one culture may well be the folktale of another. The mythological heritage of Greek antiquity has survived in Western culture. It was
handed down from generation to generation long after it had
lost all religious meaning. In the process of transmission, it
nourished European art and literature, and continued to serve
all functions except the sacred (Seznec, 1961).

RITUAL

When the relationship between myth and dogma is neglected,
the connections between myth and ritual are often described in
absolute terms. Many nineteenth-century theorists studied myth
as an isolated phenomenon, but the writings of W. Robertson
Smith (1889) and, later, those of Jane Harrison (1903, 1912)
sounded a different note. They placed myth squarely in the religious domain, but assigned it a position subordinate to ritual.

Robertson Smith described myths as verbal explanations of
ritual, forming no essential part of religion. Early religions, he
explained, originally consisted entirely of institutions and practices, and myths arose mainly to excite the fancy and sustain the
interest of the worshippers. Ritual was the core of religion, fixed
and sacred, obligatory and meritorious; myths were variable, and
man's belief or disbelief was not significant (1956:17–18). Harrison, in a similar vein, insisted that myth was the verbalized
counterpart of ritual action, of "things done" (1912:328), thus
confirming Robertson Smith's thesis of the primacy of ritual.

A number of scholars took the opposite position. Notable
among them was D. Brinton, who claimed that "every rite is
originally based upon a myth" (1897:173). But Robertson Smith's
and Harrison's views attained greater prominence. Early psychoanalysts, including Freud and Reik, tended to agree that myth
was a description of ritual. Boas gave priority to ritual when he
noted that it is often accompanied by a variety of explanatory
myths, and concluded that the different versions must have arisen

from the desire to account for ritual acts (1940:382). He remained skeptical of generalizations, however, and although he conceded that ritual might be older than myth in certain instances, he maintained that neither can be postulated as "primary" in an evolutionary sense.

The "Ritual View" of Myth

Vigorous champions of the "ritual view" of myth are Hyman (1958:84–94) and Raglan (1958:76–83). Following Harrison, they observe that rituals often fade away while myths survive. Hyman suggests that all folktales, superstitions, ballads, and certain forms of modern literature are devaluated myths of ritual origin. Raglan argues along the same lines.

Present-day anthropologists take issue with such dogmatic views, for they believe that the absolute origins of myth and ritual are lost, probably forever. Kluckhohn (1965:147) called the question of the primacy of one over the other as meaningless as the "chicken or egg" question. He disputed the view of Hyman and Raglan that *all* folktales were once sacred myths. Many folktales are purely literary creations devised for entertainment; these never possessed ritual counterparts. Nevertheless, it is true that myths generally do have a longer life span than the rituals with which some were once associated, for myths often have an appeal apart from their sacred implications. They can be told by anyone who remembers them, and can be enjoyed for their beauty or their plots. Rituals, however, once they have lost their religious connotations, are no longer acted out, and if they are not written down they disappear completely.

The Relationship Between Myth and Ritual

The controversies over the relationship between myth and ritual neglect the importance of dogma. Myth and ritual are related not because they sometimes complement or reinforce each other, but because both are based on dogma. Spiro emphasized this important fact when he showed how ritual and myth become inexplicable and meaningless without the basic cognitive assumptions of a religious system, and he stated that dogma is "logically and psychologically, if not chronologically, prior to its ritual aspects" (1964:103). Ritual is instrumental, and the performance of ritual is predicated on the belief that it is efficacious in achieving a certain end. Dogma expresses man's relation to the supernatural, and includes reference to what man must do in order to maintain this relationship and to profit by it. Myth mediates between dogma and ritual for it explains the motives behind both.

The Zuni Indians, for instance, believe that their Kachina gods will bring rain if they are properly received by the villagers at the onset of the agricultural cycle; this is Zuni dogma. Their elaborate mythology explains how the Kachinas became rain gods and why they demand specific forms of ritual action. The rituals carry out these demands, and are socially purposive, for they are expected to bring about the desired results.

In a number of instances, myth appears without ritual, and ritual without myth—but neither one exists without dogma. The Toda seem to have an extensive system of ritual and a relatively small body of myths, while the Bushmen are said to have many myths and few rituals. It is likely that the Bushmen tales are not true myths, but nonsacred stories of the supernatural. In general, ritual and myth appear together.

Types of Ritual

Rituals are designed both to express belief and to bring about specific ends. Ritual behavior is motivated by the desire to gain some form of satisfaction and is expected to be effective. The effects desired are diverse. Although they often deal with such human concerns as health, fertility, and general welfare, the categories are vague and overlapping. Moreover, the purposes may vary with the participants. Nor is a strict classification of rites into individual and communal procedures very practical, for the point of reference easily shifts from the individual to the social. Perhaps the most constructive division is that between periodic and nonperiodic rituals. This distinction is useful because the two types of ritual often carry different social implications, and it is often explicitly recognized by the members of a religious group. Nadel observed that the Nupe have regular, fixed rituals as well as others which, as the Nupe say, "have no month," and the performance of which depends upon the needs of the moment (1954:68). Junod notes that the southeast African Thonga make a similar distinction between "regular offerings" and "those made in special circumstances" (Junod, 1913:II, 362).

Periodic rituals tend to have communal impact. They serve to mark the start of the agricultural cycle, the end of the harvest, the founding of the community, and so on. Occasional rites are most often associated with critical events in the life of an individual. As such, they usually mark domestic events—birth, the attainment of adult status, marriage, or death. The extent of community involvement usually corresponds to the social importance of the individual and his immediate family.

In small, homogeneous societies, almost everyone is useful and socially important, and the birth of a new member, or the loss of another through death, is of great concern to the whole group, so that the rites marking such an event will be communal. In larger, more complex societies, participation is selective. Rituals marking personal events tend to become more domestic.

By and large, anthropologists have shown more interest in the analysis of occasional rituals.

Ritual Motifs

Arnold van Gennep (1908, translated 1960) was one of the first scholars to recognize the social importance of nonperiodic rituals. He noted that they frequently accompanied what he called *life crises,* such as birth, betrothal, marriage, or death. He interpreted these events as a transition from one social status to another, and he termed the rituals performed on these occasions *rites of passage.* Every change of status involves a shifting of roles: at births, married people become parents; at death, relatives become orphans, widows, or widowers, and so on.

Rites of passage, then, mark the important events in the life of a person, and van Gennep insists that these social changes are more important than biological ones. Social maturity only rarely converges with physiological puberty; more often it precedes or follows puberty by a significant number of years (1960:66). Van Gennep believes that the crisis rites facilitate change, helping individuals through the difficulties of transition and preparing the society to accept their new roles. Rituals of this nature are composed of three elements: separation, transition, and reintegration. The element of separation disengages the individual from his former status; that of transition gradually removes the barriers to the new status; and that of reintegration marks his acceptance into everyday life in his newly acquired status.

Pregnant women are often "separated" from their community by dietary prohibitions, sexual prohibitions, and so on. Or they may be separated literally, by having to live in a special hut outside the village boundaries. The Todas of India and the Aranda of Australia build special huts where pregnant women must live until their confinement; the Tungus of Siberia erect a small tent near the home of a pregnant woman, and in that she must give birth. The Buka women of the Solomon Islands mark their condition by wearing a belt of special leaves instead of the usual loin cloth. Reintegration takes place after the birth of the child, and may consist of ritual washings, or other acts of purification, and communal meals, often introducing both the new mother and the new child together. Because the status of parents does not significantly alter once they have a child, subsequent births are usually attended by less elaborate rituals.

Periods of separation, transition, and reintegration are often more clearly discernible in rituals marking the admission of adolescents into adulthood. The separation from childhood is sometimes dramatized by a simulation of death. Transition often consists of a long-term seclusion during which the novice is instructed in tribal law, myth, or other adult knowledge. Motifs of rebirth follow the ritual death. The initiates must pretend that they do not know how to walk, talk, or eat, acting as if they were indeed newly born. The reintegration rite is often accompanied by bodily alteration: circumcision, subincision, the removal of one or more teeth, scarification, or tattooing—all of which serve to make the individual identical to the adult members of the group.

The elements of separation, transition, and reintegration are also seen in funeral ceremonies. The surviving close relatives are separated by specific dress, are "in mourning" for prescribed periods, at the end of which they are reincorporated into the society.

Van Gennep is fully aware that the three ritual elements are not developed to the same extent by all peoples or in every ceremonial pattern (1960:11). Neither does he overlook the existence of the more manifest functions of these rites; he points out, for instance, how the separation of pregnant women is intended to protect her from evil powers, and, thus, to insure her good health. He also applied his system of analysis to some periodic

rituals, and sees New Year ceremonies, for instance, as rites marking the "separation" of winter and "incorporation" of spring.
Moreover, he does not lose sight of the religious characteristics
of these rituals, and he holds that initiates are considered "sacred," particularly during the transitional periods (1960:18).

Elaborations on van Gennep's theory have been made by,
among others, Chapple and Coon (1942, Chaps. 20–21). They,
too, note the existence of two types of crisis rites, but use a
slightly different terminology: *rites of passage,* that center on the
individual and his change of status; and *rites of intensification,*
that affect the group as a whole as a result of environmental
changes, (*e.g.,* the phases of the moon, the change of seasons).
Although the authors do not supply much evidence about the
ritual importance of the "environmental changes," they do explain why the occasions around which rites of passage and intensification revolve are correctly termed *life crises.* Referring to
so-called interaction theory (*ibid.:*36–42), they view culture as a
system of interaction in equilibrium—an equilibrium which is
disrupted by changes in status, in numbers, or in environment.
Changes are, in this view, threatening and upsetting, and thus
"critical." The accompanying rites are designed to restore the
social equilibrium, to establish a new balance based upon the
changed conditions.

Later writers have generally accepted van Gennep's interpretation of crisis rites as a form of social transition, but they have
used different methods. Audrey Richards relates specific details
of the rites to specific features of social structure (1956). Young,
applying modern methods of statistics and cross-cultural testing,
describes initiation ceremonies as "status dramatization" (1962
and 1965). Goffman does not deal with crisis rites *per se,* but he
significantly extends such ritual dramatizations by seeing them as
"performances" that must be continuously renewed and revised
in order to maintain expressive control and thus, also, the social
definition of individual statuses (1959).

These writers, and many others, emphasized the social changes
signified by the rites of passage. But Eliade was disturbed by the
idea that these rituals were mere mechanical social devices designed to usher in new status positions (1965). If they were that,
and nothing else, why should they occur in a religious framework? Eliade answers his own rhetorical question by expressing

the view that initiation not only marks the birth or rebirth of an individual, but also brings the initiated youth to a higher and more sacred level of existence. In his view, the rituals produce ontological transformations in the lives of the initiates, and thus constitute fundamental existential experiences (1965:3). These changes are accomplished by confronting the novices with the sacred elements and the sacred history of their culture. During the transitional periods, sacred articles of material culture are seen, sacred actions are carried out, and sacred knowledge is learned. All these items are symbolic; they refer not only to the adult social world, but also to the realms of religion and of history. Socially, they symbolize the adult responsibilities of the individual; religiously, they represent the responsibilities of every man for the maintenance of sacred traditions; historically, they repeat, and thus reaffirm, the sacred origin and foundation of the group.

Ritual is, in Eliade's view, primarily a re-enactment of sacred prototypes, the repetition of the actions of divine beings or mythical ancestors. Ritual recalls these past events, preserving and transmitting the foundations of society. Participants in the ritual become identified with the sacred past and thus perpetuate tradition as they re-establish the principles by which the group lives and functions. The motif of death and rebirth is both a ritual transformation of the individual and a re-enactment of the birth of the group. By his own rebirth, the individual also gives new life to the group. Existentially, the rites confront the novice with the image of himself and his world, and his acceptance of this image constitutes a spiritual rebirth on a different level of existence.

Eliade's interpretation stresses the sacred meaning and symbolic aspects of initiation rituals. Most anthropologists would agree that these are highly significant features of any ritual, but few have attempted to define or to elucidate such sacred meanings except in psychological terms. Eliade's statement that the initiation experience existentially transforms man is, however, not supported by his descriptive material or by other data on nonliterate societies. It is possible that initiation rites may have the meanings and functions he assigns them, but as long as data are lacking this theory remains speculative. Eliade, moreover, extends his theories to include all nonliterate societies. In doing so, he ignores ethnographic reality. Not all initiation rites display death and rebirth motifs, reveal mysteries, or teach sacred lore. Very few re-enact sacred origin myths. Some societies hold initiation rites for both sexes; others hold them only for girls or only for boys; still others hold none at all. Since no two societies have identical initiation rites, any attempt at generalization must take these differences into account.

Anthropologists have accounted for some of these differences in historical and in cultural terms. Mead, noting the absence of female initiation among the Samoans, showed how in this culture the tasks of young girls blend into adult responsibilities without abrupt change (1949). Young girls of six or seven are already given the task of caring for younger children. As soon as these girls are able to carry heavier loads, they make long journeys to collect hibiscus bark. They will also dig taro, catch fish, and learn the skilled techniques of their group: the weaving of baskets, the pleating of mats, the preparation of food, and all other adult duties. The learning process is a gradual one; initiation rites are not necessary because there is no change in attitude, no marked difference in role, and no specific point of entry into adulthood. Young correlates initiation rites with social solidarity, and shows that status transitions tend to be more intensively dramatized in societies with strong internal cohesion (1965:1).

Rituals may also be viewed as an expression of social conflict rather than social cohesion. However, Gluckman holds that such "rites of rebellion," as he calls them, exist only in stable societies, in which the social order is basically unchallenged (1954). Rites of rebellion are not spontaneous outbreaks, but institutionalized rituals. They serve to burlesque or reverse regular customs, ridicule or threaten rulers, and flout social norms and conventions. Initiation ceremonies may express resentment against the adult sex role or antagonism against the opposite sex.

Gluckman sees these phenomena as ritual re-enactments of social tensions, the regulated expression of which provides a form of catharsis that will preclude the outbreak of actual social conflicts. These rituals can take place only in basically stable societies, for weaker ones could not control such open expressions of antagonism.

However different the interpretations of initiation rituals may be in emphasis and method, all recognize their importance as markers of change in status. Beyond that, their functional significance and symbolic meaning are as varied as their formal expression.

CONCLUSION

Myth and ritual are essentially expressive and symbolic in character. Implicitly or explicitly, they nearly always contain evaluations of what is culturally deemed important. Myths also tend to sustain systems of authority, such as that of the father, the priest, or the political leader. Moreover, myths supply answers to questions about life, creations, misfortune, illness, death, or man's place in the universe. Myths are not mere folk tales, but symbolic statements about social reality and human existence. Ritual is more directly instrumental than myth. Its actions tend to include a symbolic pursuit of a desired result. People participating in ritual usually believe that this will help bring about a wanted state of affairs or prevent an unwanted one. But ritual expresses more than man's dependence on the natural world, and it signifies more than the reinforcement of social solidarity. Ritual is a social act in which the participants re-enact their relationship to sacred objects and beliefs. Both ritual and myth are thus not only founded in dogma, but they make sacred beliefs intelligible by rendering them in terms of human action and human language.

8

Religious Communication

COMMUNICATION IS THE TRANSMISSION OF INFORMATION FROM ONE place or person to another place or person. Human beings have evolved many different systems of communication, both verbal and nonverbal. Human communication generally anticipates that the receiver will react to the messages. The most common expectations are that the receiver will alter his behavior, his plans, his judgment, or his opinion, or that he will give other bits of information in return.

Communication among human beings is essentially a social affair. It may also serve to establish or reaffirm social bonds. Messages conveyed in speech do not always have direct relevance to overt meanings of words. When we greet another person by saying "How are you?" we do not usually mean to inquire into his state of health, but merely to acknowledge our social relationship to him. Malinowski (1943:315) called this form of communication *phatic communion.*

Religious communication, like human communication, is designed to pass on information—in this case, to supernatural receivers. Prayer is the major form of verbal communication with the supernatural, while ritual behavior is the major form of nonverbal communication. In reality, prayer is usually attended by ritual or ritualized gestures, while ritual is rarely, if ever, carried out in complete silence.

Prayer and ritual are designed to engage the supernatural in the lives of human beings while simultaneously acknowledging human belief in the power and existence of the gods. The specific messages convey to the gods man's knowledge, feelings, needs, emotions, moods, and desires. But the communication may also be "phatic"—*i.e.*, directed toward acknowledging or re-establishing man's relationships to his gods.

As in most forms of human communication, man anticipates that the supernatural receivers will react to the information conveyed to them, and will change their behavior, plans, judgments, or opinions, or give other bits of information in return. In the last case, the form of religious communication is divinatory—an attempt to elicit divine guidance or judgments. Divination, accompanied by ritual forms and verbal expression, attempts to coerce the supernatural into giving direct answers to specific questions. This discussion will focus on these three major forms of religious communication: prayer, ritual, and divination.

VERBAL COMMUNICATION: PRAYER

Prayer appears to be a nearly universal feature of religion. It is true that Confucius discouraged prayer, and that Buddha and his early disciples repudiated the notion of seeking guidance through verbal communication with the supernatural, but as Buddhism developed prayer became again quite important.

The purpose and content of prayer vary with the culture and the occasion, but certain attitudes and functions prevail.

A distinction is often made between compulsive and noncompulsive forms of prayer. Earlier scholars saw in this distinction the basic criterion for differentiation between magic and religion. Tylor, for instance, called compulsive prayers *spells,* and found a general evolution from spell to prayer. He believed that spells are directed to selfish ends, an attempt to coerce the supernatural powers into bowing to men's wishes, while prayer is merely a request for the gods' aid and blessings. Neither the evolutionary scheme nor the distinction are presently accepted. Even in technologically simple nonliterate societies there is never an exclusive reliance on "spells." Nevertheless some forms of prayer are highly formalized, and some are accompanied by the belief that they must be letter-perfect in order to be acceptable to the gods. In a classic study, Gladys Reichard characterizes Navaho prayer as "the compulsive word" (1944). She shows that many prayer-chants are formalized not only in verbal content, but also in melody, beat, rhythm, and tone. Ideally, not one word or tone should be altered or omitted, lest the prayer lose its power. But perfection does not assure effectiveness. The Navaho seem to feel that imperfect prayers *cannot* be effective, while perfect ones *may* be. Kluckhohn noted that the Navaho attitude toward prayer is not that they express belief but, rather, that they categorize events with some degree of precision (1964:111). Navaho religious communication expresses delight in sharply defined categories of behavior. Indeed, the formal structure of the Navaho language itself introduces elaborate classifications (*ibid.:* 95). The "compulsion" of the Navaho, then, rests in their own attitudes toward exact courses of behavior rather than in a posited belief that their prayers will have automatic results. Reichard herself grouped Navaho divinities in eight categories as follows (1950 Chapt. 5):

1. Persuadable deities,
2. Undependable deities,
3. Helpers of deity and man,
4. Intermediaries between man and deity,
5. Unpersuadable deities,
6. Dangers conceived as deities,
7. Beings between good and evil,
8. Order of monsters, dangers, and beings-in-between.

These categories clearly indicate that the Navaho do not believe that their prayers and rituals are automatically effective: the gods are persuadable rather than coercible. The distinction between spell and prayer cannot be clearly drawn. Most forms of verbal communication with the supernatural deal with those areas of uncertainty in which supernatural help is wanted and perhaps even expected, but there is little evidence that man expects always positive results.

TYPES OF PRAYER

Highly structured and formalized prayers, if predominant in a given culture, may well express a more formalized attitude toward the supernatural. Zuni prayers are as rigid as those found

in Navaho chants, and they, too, must be letter-perfect. Moreover, among the Zuni, prayer may take place only at designated
times of the year. If any Zuni, even a priest, is found praying at
an hour or a season not prescribed by tradition, he is suspected
of witchcraft (Benedict, 1946:88–89). Prayer, like most other important Zuni activities, is strongly communal. Individual initiative, religious and mundane, is discouraged in this culture. The
discouragement of individual initiative will lead to formalized
and tightly structured religious behavior and language. Benedict
observes that Zuni prayer is not a spontaneous outpouring of
religious emotion, but mild and ceremonious (*ibid.*:57). It does
not follow that prayer is "magical" or coercive; it reflects the
Zuni ethos, which prescribes that communal harmony arises from
correct and inoffensive forms of behavior. Therefore the Zuni
emphasize the correctness of their relationships to the supernatural by their efforts at faultless communication. The gods are
not constrained by this behavior, but more likely to react in a
beneficial way.

The Plains Indians emphasize individual rather than communal experiences. They express this cultural ethos in their religious behavior patterns as well. Every man receives his power
from personal confrontation and contact with the supernatural.
He learns the prayers and sacred songs when he reaches adult
status. He then goes out alone, praying to the supernatural
powers in his own words that a spirit may appear to him in a
dream or vision. Often these young adults fast in solitude for a
number of days, supplicating the spirits to take pity on them. On
these occasions, Crow Indians often cut off a finger joint of the
left hand. Lowie reported that during his visits to the Crow
(between 1907 and 1916) he saw few older men with their left
hands intact (1952:4). When the revelation finally takes place, a
spirit adopts the young man, teaches him his own individual
songs and prayers, and instructs him in the behavior that will
make him a successful warrior or medicine man.

In this culture, as among the Zuni, prayer is not always successful. A Crow who does not succeed in obtaining a personal
vision can sometimes persuade a successful man to sell him some
of his power. This would give an already successful Crow even
more power, for he adopts the less fortunate tribesman as his
supernatural patron adopted him, and teaches him some of the

sacred prayers and songs learned in his own vision (Lowie, 1963:170–75).

In prayer men reveal their attitudes to the supernatural, and thus also the culturally learned ways of dealing with these higher powers. Although these vary widely, the major categories of religious behavior in prayer are petition, adoration, atonement, and gratitude.

Petitionary prayers ask for something—health, rain, "our daily bread," peace, military success, or unspecified blessings. Although usually pronounced in a spirit of humility, the requests may also be arrogant, brazen, or even threatening, depending upon the culturally perceived distance between men and their deities. The Manus are quite familiar with their ancestor spirit "Sir Ghost," whose skull—that of an actual human ancestor—is kept in the very house in which they live. Sir Ghost is not omniscient, but he observes only what is happening in the household over which he has supernatural jurisdiction. His task consists of watching over the moral behavior of household members, and assuring their prosperity. Sir Ghost's continuous presence seems to make him familiar enough to be scolded and threatened if he does not live up to expectations. In such instances the Manus may address Sir Ghost as follows:

> You will be washed away by all rains, scorched by all suns, be homeless and forgotten! You will then be made to understand! You will have no house to rest in, you will be cast out, and you will be miserable! (Fortune, 1935:215–16).

The Tahiti islanders, too, are reported to reject the special god of the family after prolonged and serious illness or misfortunes:

> There is a casting off, I am casting thee off! Do not come to possess me again! ... Go and seek some other medium for thyself in another home. ... I am wearied of thee—I am terrified with thee! I am expelling thee. Go even to the River-in-Darkness into the presence of Ta'aroa, the father of all gods. Return not again to me. Behold the family, they are stricken with sickness, thou art taking them, thou art a terrible man-devouring god! (Lowie, 1952:326–27).

Such attitudes are not common. Western readers are better acquainted with the more humble type of prayer:

I am thankful, O thou great Spirit, that we have been spared
to live unto now to purify with cedar smoke this our house,
because that has always been the rule in the ancient world
since the beginning of creation. When anyone thinks of his
children, how fortunate it is to see them enjoy good health!
And this is the cause of a feeling of happiness, when we
consider how greatly we are blessed by the benevolence of
our father, the Great Spirit. And we can also feel the
strength of him, our Grandfather. First, to whom we give
pleasure when we purify him and take care of him, and
we feed him with this cedar. All of this we offer in esteem
to him, our Grandfather, because he has compassion, when
he sees how pitifully we behave when we are pleading with
all the spirits above, as they were created, and with all those
here on earth. Give us everything, our father, that we ask
of you, Great Spirit, even the Creator (Speck, 1931:II, 75).

In this prayer of the Lenape Delaware Indians, petition comes
only at the very end, after the expression of adoration and gratitude. Adoration or worship deals with the supernatural by acknowledging their higher powers. In a mood of adoration, man
pays homage to the gods, praising and honoring them, and
expressing his devotion and dependence. In expiatory prayers
man acknowledges not only the greatness of the supernatural
powers, but his own shortcomings as well.

Prayers also reflect the culturally conceived nature of the
supernatural. The African Abaluyia of Kavirondo believe that
their creator god made everything perfect, and their prayers im-
plore him to maintain this order, "to let things take their normal
course," "to let the sun rise and shine as usual," and "to spit
his medicine upon the people so that they may walk in peace"
(Wagner, 1954:43). When the creator god is viewed as otiose,
prayers to him will be rare. The Mende of Sierra Leone do not
pray to their high god Ngewo, but frequently use expressions
such as *Ngewo jahu,* corresponding approximately to our *God
willing* (Little, 1954:114). In this same culture, the ancestor
spirits are closely concerned with man's behavior, and they punish misdeeds. Prayers are directed to them and accompanied by
offerings in an attempt to expiate these shortcomings. A father
prayed on behalf of his ailing son:

Ah, grandfathers, I have come to you: Momo is the one who is ill. The soothsayer informs me that you are angry with him because he has not "fed" you for a long time. Do you, grandfathers, kindly pardon him. He is a small boy; he has no senses yet. I have come now to beg you. My heart is now clear. The sky above is also satisfied, and the earth below is also satisfied. Every day that passes, we ask that you people should always be our leaders and should not leave us unprotected (*ibid.:*117).

The role of the ancestors in Mende society is based on their closeness to Ngewo, and they constitute a link between the people and their high god. The ancestors are invoked directly, but the prayers offered to them are also intended for transmission to Ngewo. This reflects mundane political lines of communication, for a Mende who seeks favors from his chief will not go to him directly but will seek the intercession of a lower government official.

Individual and Communal Prayers

Prayers can be individual and communal. Individual prayers, being less accessible to observation, have remained relatively unstudied, and the most that can be said about them is that cultures differ in their emphasis on private prayer. In a number of cultures, frequency of prayer is deemed important. In societies with a well-developed numerical system, devices for counting prayers are sometimes used. Buddhist rosaries have 108 beads, and are used to record the number of times any prayer has been uttered. Tibetan Buddhists use rosaries almost continually, and they also developed the "prayer mill" or "prayer wheel." This may be described as a crank-handled barrel revolving on an axis and containing written prayers and sacred formulae. When the crank is turned, the prayers are tossed about. Miniature prayer mills are carried about on the person. Temples have big prayer wheels, placed in a long line near their entrances. The use of the prayer wheel is based upon two value systems—one assigns special significance to the process of revolving anything revolvable, and the other credits the written word itself with high power (Ekvall, 1964:120).

Pueblo Indians use prayersticks; these do not serve as mechanical aids to prayer but, rather, as their visual representations. Varying between two and twelve inches in length, they are cut from branches or twigs, carved, painted, and decked with feathers (see Figure 11). They are planted in the ground whenever a prayer has been offered, and serve both as visual reminders and as gifts to the gods. They vary greatly in color and carving, the type of wood used, and the number and type of feathers attached. The Hopi often tie small packets of corn meal to the feathered sticks to make the gift even more attractive to the supernatural recipients.

Figure 11. Prayerstick.

LINGUISTIC ASPECTS OF RELIGIOUS COMMUNICATION

Often, but not always, verbal communication with the supernatural is carried out in ritual language. The differences between sacred and secular language range from minor modifications of the voice to the use of a completely different language which cannot be spoken or understood without special training.

In general, religion has exercised great influence upon language. Many ancient written languages are known to us only because they have been preserved in religious documents. The Akkadian cuneiform and the Egyptian hieroglyphics are overwhelmingly concerned with sacred things. The very word *hieroglyph* means *sacred carving*. The Veda scriptures of Hinduism are classics of Sanskrit literature. The oldest, the Rig-Veda, contains some one thousand sacred hymns; the Sama-Veda is basically a rearrangement of the hymns of the Rig-Veda, while the Yafur-Veda includes prose formulations. The Uguvine tablets are the most important surviving documents of the ancient Umbrian tongue, and they contain detailed descriptions of ritual procedures.

Ritual Language

When prayers and ritual language are highly formalized, and letter-perfect recitations are demanded, ritual speech patterns will be less subject to linguistic change than the common language is. In time, the more archaic forms will develop an aura of special sanctity. Tradition will add more hallowing touches, and in this manner obsolete grammatical forms and archaic words will be preserved in religious language. In literate societies, this retention will be further assisted by the existence of written documents. The King James version of the Bible, at the time of its appearance very instrumental in fixing the standards of modern literary English, contains many now archaic forms: old plurals (*kine* for *cows*), old verb endings (*saith* for *says*), and old personal pronouns (*thou* for *you*) are but some of many examples. The Koran similarly preserves earlier forms of Arabic. Both the Koran and the King James Bible can be read and understood by literate speakers of Arabic and English, respectively. But in other instances, sacred languages have become alien to laymen. The Latin of Roman Catholicism, the Old Church Slavic of the Eastern Orthodox Churches, the Sanskrit and Pali of Hinduism and Buddhism, the Avestan of Zoroastrianism were all once common speech, but are now no longer used except in ritual contexts.

Special linguistic modes of addressing the supernatural are frequently found in nonliterate societies as well. Here, too, the differences between the sacred and the nonsacred varies. When the difference is slight, every member of the community will know the proper religious terms and have equal access to the sacred powers (unless other restrictions impede). Extensive differences between sacred language and everyday speech usually implies that religious language has to be learned, and will thus point to privileged forms of religious communication. Knowledge of the sacred language may then function to protect religious officeholders from competition and unwanted imitation. A shaman's special skill consists of his effective personal contact with the supernatural, and his ability to make that contact may well depend on his knowledge of the correct linguistic modes of communication.

The Zuni Indians emphasize equality of status. Older people have great prestige, but there are no significant status differences based upon wealth or occupation. It is thus to be expected that no great linguistic differences will occur. The Zuni recognize three language levels, which differ somewhat in vocabulary but are not incomprehensible to anyone. These three levels are slang, neutral discourse, and sacred language. Slang is used mostly by young people. Like slang everywhere, it contains a number of unique forms of expression, is determined by fashion, and is therefore subject to rapid change. To the native speaker of Zuni, slang is a low-value type of behavior. Sacred language, however, carries overtones of dignity and prestige. It is used in prayers, myths, songs, and ritual. Sacred terms also replace common conversations between members of priestly societies. Because religion itself carries high value in Zuni culture, the words habitually employed in sacred contexts acquire high status. Moreover, the sacred vocabulary is best known by older people, the most prestigious age group. Sacred language, among the Zuni, serves to express respect for religious activities, for the sacred gods and ancestors, and for the older people who have the most thorough knowledge of the religious vocabulary and its special meanings (Newman, 1964:397–406).

In general, when a given language does possess different levels of status or prestige, the highest of these levels will be used to address the gods. The Javanese language, for instance, has a great many different status levels. The one used to address nobility and rulers is also used to communicate with the sacred ancestors.

In some cultures, however, the knowledge of sacred forms of language is reserved for specialists or initiates. Diviners among the Bayaka of the Southwest Congo must learn a new language as part of their professional training. The diviner's language is called *Ki-ngombu;* the regular language is *Ki-yaka.* The word roots of the two languages may or may not be similar, as the following samples show (Huber, 1965:46–48):

English	Ki-ngombu	Ki-yaka
father	*kipfuila*	*tata*
mother	*malambo*	*mama*
child	*kindende*	*mwana*
sister	*khete*	*pangi*
fire	*mulemo*	*mbau*
water	*madibu*	*mamba*
house	*zambisina*	*nzo*
to dance	*kukini sina*	*kukina*

A different linguistic technique is the artificial creation of forms of language similar to our own "Pig Latin." Sounds are substituted for other sounds, or certain sound clusters are added to syllables. In Bunyoro, diviners substitute a double *d* sound for other consonants, which makes their speech sound very different. Beattie reports how a diviner whom he visited spoke in an assumed voice, supposed to be that of the spirit Irungu, and used such substitutions (1967:59). The diviner, or rather Irungu, turned to a woman and said: *"Muddana wandde, ibadda ddyawe niddyo ddiha"* ("My girl, what is your name?"). In normal Bunyoro this would be: *"Muhara wange, ibara lyawe niryo liha."* The liberal scattering of double *d*'s alters the sound of the language considerably.

Shamanistic trances are sometimes accompanied by nonverbal vocalizations. Incoherent mumbling, groaning, sobbing, or wheezing may announce the beginning of a trance. These sounds do not signify communication with the supernatural, but they indicate to the audience that the necessary preliminaries are taking place. When the concept of spirit flight is part of the trance situation, vocalizations imitating sounds occurring in nature will indicate the stages of the shaman's journey to the supernatural realm. The imitation of howling winds or thunder and rain signify his flight through the air; a sound like the lapping of water will mean that he has reached the sea; animal cries will bear witness to his first encounter with evil animal spirits, or will betoken his conversation with the spirit helpers. Lombard called these vocalizations *phonations frustes* (1910:25). After reaching the supernatural realm, he will begin his conversations with the supernatural powers. These may be carried out in an artificial tongue or pseudolanguage, such as the one used by the Nyoro diviner. Rasmussen, although he does not give linguistic examples, writes that the Hudson Bay Eskimo shamans also used such techniques (1930:24–39). Bogoras notes their existence in the shamanistic regions of Chuckchee and Koryak.

When communication with the supernatural is carried out in a language not known to the audience, interpretation is necessary. Sometimes the shaman himself, after returning to normal consciousness, will report the outcome of his conversations with the spirits. Alternatively, when the subject does not remember what has happened, other persons translate or interpret the conversations, an art known as *ermeneglossia*. The subject is a medium who may also be a shaman. According to W. Park, shamans among the Paviotso Indians speak rapidly and in broken sentences during curing rituals, while their assistants interpret what they say (1938:50). In Japan, a woman diviner puts her client into a trance, and interprets his utterances in order to diagnose his disease or misfortune (May, 1956:87). Roscoe reports that, in the African Bakitara tribe, if a divine message was desired, the priest might either act as a medium himself or employ an interpreter (1911:26). If the priest acted as medium, the audience had to interpret the message as well as it could; if another medium was employed, the priest himself would act as interpreter.

Foreign speech patterns uttered in trance or ecstasy have been called *glossolalia*. One specific form, known as *xenoglossia*, is the ability to speak in an existing foreign language which the subject does not understand when conscious. Swanton writes that Haida shamans spoke the language of the country from which the spirit came (1905:38). Often the spirit came from the neighboring Tlinkit country, and the shaman spoke Tlinkit during his trance, although otherwise he claimed no such ability. Glossolalia, including xenoglossia, are by no means unknown in Christianity, and have their reputed beginnings in the Pentecost. The Apostles, filled with the Holy Spirit, spoke some fourteen different tongues, including Arabic, Phrygian, Cretan, and Egyptian, so that every foreigner present heard his own language (Acts 2). St. Paul himself was a glossolalist: "I thank my God, I speak with tongues more than ye all" (1 Cor. 15:18); but he warned against the excessive use of glossolalia. Throughout the history of the Western world, glossolalic phenomena regularly attended revivalist movements; it was found among the early Quakers, the Methodists, the Huguenots, and, of course, in Pentecostal churches. At present, glossolalia is practiced by hundreds of members of well-established Protestant denominations usually occurring as pseudolanguage (Sadler, 1964:84–90). Sample utterance: *Dyoso ki-i-yeno mayashi yekatona masi yamo ma yenda ya kotano masiki* (*Time,* May 17, 1963). Although the words are unfamiliar, the sound patterns are not. The consonant-vowel combinations are those of the English language, of which the glossolalist was a native speaker. Deep trance is not reported in these instances, but states of ecstasy are regularly present.

NONVERBAL RELIGIOUS COMMUNICATION: SACRIFICE

Nonverbal communication takes place both on symbolic and on nonsymbolic levels. Symbolic nonverbal communication is culturally learned. Gestures, postures, facial expressions differ in form or in meaning from culture to culture. The Japanese smile is not necessarily a spontaneous expression of pleasure or amusement, but a law of etiquette. A Maori says "yes" by raising his head and chin; a Sicilian says "no" in exactly the same manner (Klineberg, 1935:282). When such cultural differences can be found to exist on a relatively simple level, it becomes clear that ritual behavior patterns have to be approached and interpreted with great care. Dancing, for instance, does not always imply joy: the Todas dance at funerals; the Bushmen dance to cure the sick.

Of the many different events taking place in ritual settings, sacrifice is one of the most important. It occurs in one form or another in most religious systems, and has received much more attention in the literature than prayer has. Moreover, it is a particularly good example of a form of nonverbal communication, for it involves an exchange of goods and services which, according to Lévi-Strauss, is one of the three most basic levels of communication operative in every society—the other two being the exchange of verbal messages and the exchange of women (1953:536).

The words *sacrifice* and *offering* may be used synonymously, although the former usually denotes the slaughter of animals and human beings, while the latter denotes the presentation of food or material objects. However, the appearance of sacrificial objects is of less importance to the understanding of the nature of sacrifice than are the intentions and motivations behind them.

The communication model used for prayer is applicable to sacrifice. Here, too, a "sender" and a "receiver" must be present, but, instead of words, the sacrificial items are now the symbolic medium of communication. The meaning of the sacrifice and the expected reactions depend upon cultural symbolism and the given circumstances of the ritual. Ritual sacrifice is, therefore, a form of exchange between man and the supernatural and is, in this respect, similar to verbal communication. The human actor presents goods; the divine receiver reacts. Once the sacrifice has been made, subsequent events are interpreted, positive or negative, as the supernatural reaction.

The formulation of sacrifice as a form of exchange has been most bothersome to some Western interpreters who were unwilling to define man's relationship to his gods in such a seemingly utilitarian manner. Plato denounced this principle, adding that the gods certainly could not be bribed (*Euthyphro* 14, *Laws* 716–17). Instead, Plato viewed sacrifice as a part of the cult which, if carried out correctly, is "most conducive to a happy life" (*Laws* 717). Plato's formulation remained representative of most later discussions up to and including those of the nineteenth century. Plato failed to make a distinction between *exchange* and *barter* or *bribe*—while, in fact, the latter are only two of the many possible modes of exchange. Exchange, moreover, does not imply equal reciprocity. Goods may be offered, both in the secular and religious spheres, in order to express gratitude, to celebrate specific events, to pay homage or tribute, to expiate wrongs, to establish good relationships. Almost any human motivation can be served by the communication of goods, including the expectation of "a happy life."

Origins of Sacrifice

With the increase of knowledge about the religions of nonliterate peoples, it became convenient to believe that *do ut des* ("I give in order that you will give") forms of sacrifice were typical of "paganism," while the higher religions had made sacrifice a symbolic act of gratitude and adoration without any utilitarian overtones. When evolutionary principles became superimposed upon this idea, the despised *do ut des* form was automatically assigned to the lowest level of development. Tylor constructed three such stages: gift-giving, homage, and abnegation (1958:II, 461–62). In the gift-giving stage, man offered goods to the gods as if they were people, expecting immediate and appropriate returns in kind. When societies became stratified, gifts were presented to chiefs and kings as homage or tribute in order to gain their good will or protection, or in expiation of offenses. Sacrifice now entered the homage stage, and man expressed his gratitude and respect to the gods, and expected supernatural protection and forgiveness in return. Tylor sees this as a higher form of sacrifice because it involves the return of more abstract forms of welfare. All utilitarian motives are absent in the abnegation stage, which express only man's self-denial. In his attempts to remove the stigma of *do ut des* from higher forms of religion, Tylor also deprives sacrifice of human value and function. Indeed, Tylor himself submits that this last form of sacrifice is "practically unreasonable" (*ibid.*:482).

Robertson Smith, like Tylor, analyzed sacrifice in a broad evolutionary setting. But, unlike Tylor, Robertson Smith clearly saw the social significance of this ritual element. In typical nineteenth-century fashion, he derived the origin of sacrifice from totemism, considered at that time to be the earliest form of religion. Ordinarily protected from destruction by taboo, the totemic animal was ritually consumed at specific solemn occasions, during which the participants assimilated a particle of the sacred to themselves. Sacrifice, in the form of a sacred meal, thus established a *communio,* an interrelation between man and the supernatural, and strengthened the social community through common participation in the sacred meal and the common consumption of the sacred totem. Later sacrificial rituals, according to Robertson Smith, vary in form but not in function. They serve to strengthen or re-establish a covenant between gods and men, and thus also among men. They may stress expiation, adoration, or gratitude, but their final aim is the correction of man's relationship to the supernatural, and thus the correction of interpersonal human relationships as well.

There is no evidence that totemism was the earliest form of religion, and in the vast literature on the subject only a few Australian tribes have been reported to eat their totems ceremonially. But in spite of these errors, Robertson Smith contributed to the understanding of sacrifice by replacing the model of trade and profit with that of the *communio,* a form of communication between man and his gods, resulting also in a communication between man and man.

Sacrifice as Communication

Max Weber agreed with Tylor in that he believed that sacrifice had its origins in "primitive magic," designed to coerce the gods (1964:26). In later developments, the magical motives fade. The change arises from the growing recognition of the god's power. The gifts brought to him become forms of entreaty rather than efforts at compulsion. But Weber does not attempt to divest higher forms of religion of their rational intentions. In all instances, Weber maintains, the central theme of sacrifice remains *do ut des (ibid.:27).* Whether sacrifice is offered as barter, bribe, homage, or tribute, man expects some results—material or immaterial, direct or indirect, in this world or hereafter. Weber also saw the great social importance of sacrifice, the effecting of a *communio* among the sacrificers. To Weber, then, sacrifice is always rational, integrative, and purposeful.

Hubert and Mauss, in their classic study of sacrifice, defined it as "a means of communication between the sacred and the profane worlds through the mediation of a victim" (1964:97). They noted that, as a form of communication, sacrifice can fulfill the most varied functions, but that these are always social functions. All sacrificial systems form a unity—not because they have common origins, arise from common motives, or serve common purposes, but because they are all "social facts" and can be analyzed as such.

Although most early writers on the subject stressed animal sacrifices, Frazer has drawn attention to agrarian forms of sacrifice. He showed how, in agricultural societies, corn, grains, rice, and fruit are offered in the same manner and for the same purposes as animal sacrifice. In his theory, the sacrificial ceremonies served to rejuvenate the "spirits of corn," thus promoting the fertility of the fields. This is, in fact, the basic theme of *The Golden Bough*. In his evolutionary scheme of development, Frazer concentrates on the objects of sacrifice, because he felt that its functions remain constant. In its earliest forms, human beings (more specifically, priests) were sacrificed because they were the closest representatives of the gods (1959:437). In a later stage, they were replaced by animals (*ibid.:*445ff), and still later, —in agricultural societies—by agricultural products (*ibid.:*455). Although Frazer gives only vague reasons for these changes in types of sacrificial items, he seems to hint at a possible correlation between methods of subsistence and types of sacrifice.

This interesting problem, which would lend itself to a statistical approach, has been taken up by Jensen but in a rather impressionistic manner (1963:162–90). His correlations may be summed up as follows:

1. Hunting-and-gathering societies sacrifice neither animals nor human beings.

2. Post-Neolithic pastoral and cattle-breeding societies sacrifice domesticated animals, never wild ones.

3. Archaic root-crop cultivators do not make bloody sacrifices.

4. Developed root-crop cultures carry out both human and animal sacrifices.

Although it is difficult to follow Jensen's subsequent "explanations," he appears to state that in hunting-and-gathering societies the killing of animals was a professional act, dictated by the need for survival. When people resort to frequent slaughter of animals for a livelihood, they will attempt to negate rather than to glorify these acts. Pastoral and cattle-breeding societies, on the other hand, propagate animal life rather than taking it away, and the killing of animals, no longer professional, can thus become a sacred act. Early Neolithic cultivators, evolving directly from hunting societies, left the religious systems intact, except that they developed myths in which the gods were slain. Later cultivators then acted out what the myths proclaimed, and because human beings and animals became identified with deities, they also became the sacrificial objects: "The slaying of the deity became a proposition of a mythic verity" (*ibid.*:181).

The Purpose of Sacrifice

Although such reasoning is subjective rather than scientific and Jensen's conclusions remain unproven, he touches upon a question of significance. Robertson Smith observed that the sacrifice of wild animals is relatively rare. This indicates that sacrifices have some economic value to those who make the offerings. Firth, without denying the religious importance of sacrifice, showed how the frequency, the size, and the quality of sacrifices in a given society are largely determined by its economic resources (1963b:15). Firth gives a number of examples to show that this might be so. Among many cattle-breeding African peoples—*e.g.,* the Dinka, the Nuer, and the Lugbara— cows are ostensibly not killed for food, but for sacrifice. Although the victims are dedicated to the gods, they are subsequently eaten by the people. Firth shows that it is easy enough to find reasons and social occasions for sacrifice, but the frequency of such rituals must necessarily depend upon the size of the herds. Prudent handling of relatively rare resources is, then, a test of the relative importance of values. When cattle is plentiful, sacrifice will be more frequent. It becomes useful to investigate on which occasions the Nuer and the Dinka do offer sacrifices, and when they postpone them.

Although sacrifice is determined by the availability of resources, there are many occasions when sacrifice is obligatory— for example, to cure illness, to avert calamities, to install a new chief, or to expiate wrongdoing. But even when sacrifice cannot be postponed, economic factors must be considered. Goode notes that the anticipation of funeral and ancestor sacrifice among the Dahomey causes a decrease in immediate consumption (1951: 92ff). Among the Navaho, borrowing from relatives for purposes of ritual and sacrifice is a common procedure. In some societies, sacrifice may be determined by ability, the wealthy giving more and the poor less. In some cases, the size of sacrifices is decided by the issue at stake—the less important the issue, the less valuable the sacrifice (Evans-Pritchard, 1940:26). Sacrifices may also be postponed or replaced by a vow; or they may involve a less valuable object than the one offered. Thus the Nuer sometimes sacrifice a wild cucumber instead of an ox (Evans-Pritchard, 1956:146, 184). The substitution may or may not be temporary. Substitution may well be a reflection of the availability of oxen; if there are not enough, the Nuer has a choice between not sacrificing at all, or using a substitute.

Apart from its economic implications, sacrifice also interrelates with other social institutions. Oberg, for instance, described how in the native kingdom of Ankole in Uganda, people make regular sacrifices in a shrine which is located in the royal enclosure (1940:121–62). In this shrine there are two drums: the larger one represents the god Bagyendawa; the smaller one, his female consort. Although there are indications that human sacrifices were once offered, now the drum requires cattle, milk, meat, millet, and beer in order to remain strong. It is not accidental that this shrine is in the royal enclosure, for the drum symbolizes not only the supernatural power of Bagyendawa, but also the worldly power of the king. Bagyendawa's power is greater and stronger than that of the king. Kings die, but the drum is immortal. The drum therefore represents not the specific incumbent of the office, but the office itself, safeguarding the continuity of political structure.

It has other functions as well. In the Ankole kingdom, a number of tribes of different origins lived together under the same political rule: the Bahima pastoralists, the Bairu agriculturalists, and a slave class of uncertain status. Slaves were not permitted to sacrifice to Bagyendawa; they had no legal status and were therefore set apart from the other groups. The drum and the right to sacrifice to it contributed to the maintenance of the political organization and the status hierarchy. Because no other tribes possessed a cult of Bagyendawa, it also constituted a common core for otherwise divergent beliefs in the Ankola kingdom, overriding the many sectional practices and differentiating the Banyankole from neighboring tribes (*ibid.*:155).

A final example of modern anthropological analysis of sacrifice is Frake's study of the Mindanao society of the Subanum (1964: 111–29). He compares and contrasts religious rituals with complementary types of secular behavior, showing how sacrificial rituals are patterned upon human social relationships. Sacrifice is carried out by the Subanum in the belief that one can accomplish a task by inducing others to act on one's behalf. The supernatural powers are influenced by devices that have proven effective in human relationships—offerings of food and drink, verbal appeals, and so on. Sacrifice results in a network of relationships linking each Subanum to the supernatural by ritual obligations. Ritual action takes place during actual or potential crises. Periodic sacrificial rites are designed to prevent calamities, while occasional rites are held to cope with emergencies, to put events back in their proper course. In secular action the Subanum rely on their own skill, but religion is designed to deal with areas of uncertainty, in which human skills are insufficient.

DIVINATION

Divination is a form of religious communication in which supernatural powers give, or are coerced into giving, direct information. In nondivinatory prayer and ritual, subsequent events are generally interpreted as supernatural answers or reactions, but these reactions may well be delayed or postponed. In divination, supernatural answers are more immediate. Moreover, divination differs significantly from other forms of religious communication in that it does not generally attempt to alter the behavior or judgment of the supernatural powers, but merely to discover their opinions. It tries to discover the will and intention of the gods, and thereby to foretell the future, or explain past events. Once supernatural plans and intentions have been discovered, divination may well be followed by prayer or sacrifice in an attempt to alter them.

Divinatory practices play a significant role in diagnosing illness, in deciding the guilt or innocence of an individual, in finding the best places and times for hunting, warring, trading, or building a new settlement, or in corroborating important social decisions such as a marriage choice or royal succession. Divination thus generally operates in those areas of life where decisions are not lightly taken.

Considered as a form of communication, three major types of divination may be distinguished. One is based upon the idea that the supernatural powers initiate the communication process, and are the senders of messages. In the second type, man takes the initiative by asking specific questions; he performs some kind of experiment, the outcome of which is interpreted as the supernatural answer. The third type involves the idea of verbal communication; man speaks directly to the gods in a face-to-face relationship, and the gods answer in words and sentences. This usually takes place in trance or in dreams. The spirits themselves may be believed to take the initiative and speak to man in dreams or, entering his body, speak through his mouth.

Divination Without Human Experiment

Spontaneously given supernatural messages are, ideally, independent of the diviner. The skill of the specialist in these instances consists of correctly observing and interpreting the phenomena. The cultural context determines which phenomena are to be considered divine messages. This type of divination takes one of four forms: augury, astrology, somatomancy, and dream interpretation.

Augury was well known in the ancient civilizations of Greece and Rome. Augurs were priests who could read the will of the gods in omens. Animals were the favored vehicles of communication and, among them, birds prevailed in importance. The very word *omen* is derived from the Greek *oionos,* the name of a hawk-like bird that was particularly important as a divine messenger. *Ornithomancy,* prophesy through the observation of birds, is a subdivision of augury. The officially appointed priests watched the birds and interpreted the direction of their flights, their formations, their numbers, and their position relative to the observer; they also derived meanings from the birds' cries—the time, the frequency, and the volume.

There were a number of other techniques. *Geomancy* interprets the cracks that appear in dried mud; *pyromancy,* the shapes discovered in flames; *lithomancy,* the formation of rocks and stones; *hydromancy,* the flow of water or the form of waves. Unusual natural phenomena were considered to be of great importance. Eclipses, comets, and earthquakes usually expressed the anger of the gods and foretold social upheaval or war. In Rome, freaks of nature were considered very ominous: animals with two heads or five feet or human hermaphrodites were looked upon with great horror, and the unfortunate creatures were generally expelled or killed.

Diviners often wielded a significant amount of political power. Their advice was eagerly sought by rulers and military leaders in matters of national importance. The rules of augury were secret, and the signs were usually vague enough to allow alternate interpretations in order to please the rulers in power and to dispose of others. Socrates, reflecting on the practices current during his lifetime, declared: "The augur should be under the authority of the general, and not the general under the authority of the augur" (*Laches,* 198).

Much less is known about these types of divination in non-literate societies, but there, too, they appear to have political implications. The *orkoiyot,* the observer and interpreter of omens among the East African Nandi, was also the most important figure in the political structure (Hollis, 1909). In some societies, observation of omens is incidental, and more of the nature of unsystematic superstition rather than that of sacred knowledge. The Samoans are reported to observe birds before setting out on a war party; if an owl, a heron, or a kingfisher flies ahead it signifies victory, but if any of these birds flies in the opposite direction the planned attack is postponed.

Astrology is one form of divination that is still popular. In the third millennium B.C., Sumerian priests observed that some stars and planets move across the sky in regular paths. Later, particularly in Babylonia, the notion developed that the movements and conjunctions of the stars were divine messages with significant effects on earth. Complex systems of prediction became ever more elaborate, and were often wedded to numerology. Astrology entered Greece in the fifth century B.C., or perhaps even earlier. It was well suited to Greek religious ideas, which considered the stars and planets to be divine entities, perfect and incorruptible. Although Babylonian and Egyptian priest-astrologers had limited their predictions largely to matters of national and public interest, in Greece astrology attained individual significance and the casting of personal horoscopes became a profitable profession.

Systematic astrology is not found in nonliterate societies, for they lack the complex mathematical concepts that make it possible to calculate the movements of the heavenly bodies. The position of the stars may sometimes be used as a guide. The New Zealand Maori, for instance, are said to believe that it is not good to start a warring party if Venus appears over the moon. But this cannot be called astrology.

The Aztecs, on the other hand, were quite sophisticated in this art. They had extensive mathematical knowledge and had also developed a form of writing. Their astrological calendar was based upon the observed movements of the stars. Months lasted twenty days, and were divided into four five-day weeks. Every day was identified by a number and a sign: the numbers were from one to thirteen; the twenty signs were *alligator, wind, house, lizard, snake, death, deer, rabbit, water, dog, monkey, grass, reed, ocelot, eagle, vulture, motion, flint, rain,* and *flower.* The astrological year thus had 260 days. A civil year of 365 days was also recognized; it was divided into eighteen twenty-day months, plus five unnumbered (and unlucky) days. A different deity ruled the calendar each year. Thirteen "lords of the day" and nine "lords of the night" governed the days in rotation. Separate deities presided over each of the five-day weeks; others, over the twenty-day months; and still others, over specified longer periods. It is clear that an almost infinite number of combinations of supernatural influences became possible, and the learned astrologers, who had priestly status, could calculate these and make predictions accordingly.

Astrology was not unknown in ancient China, but there the stars were not equated with divinities. Their orderly course emphasized the principle of harmony existing in the universe. The relationship between man and the heavenly bodies was mutual: the stars ruled men, but man's behavior also influenced the course of the stars.

Somatomancy is basically a European development, and shows how divination may become completely secularized. It may or may not be connected with astrology, as Lessa has shown (1965:

352–63); he calls the two types "astral" and "natural" somatomancy, respectively. The basic idea is that every human being bears signs which reveal his temperament, his character, and his destiny. *Neomancy* interprets moles on the body; *phrenology,* cranial protuberances; *ophthalmoscopy,* the eyes; *palmistry,* the hands. *Astral body divination* correlates body parts with the position of the stars: *metoscopy* maps the forehead into regions correlated with the planets; *chiromancy* relates the palm of the hand to the planets; *physiognomy* relates all parts of the body to the signs of the zodiac.

Divination Involving Human Experiment

When it is important to know the will of the gods, it is sometimes impractical to wait for them to speak first. More immediate answers can be found when an experiment of some kind is carried out which forces the supernatural to reveal its plans or judgments. Such experiments are called *oracles.* When it is designed to elicit an answer concerning a human being's guilt or innocence, the term *ordeal* is often substituted, referring to a form of divination in which the accused risks bodily injuries or unpleasant physical reactions.

Animals are as important in oracles as they are in omens. One form of oracular experiment is *haruspicy*—divination through inspection of the shape or the condition of the animal's entrails or other internal organs. In some instances, this practice is connected with sacrifice.

Among the Babylonians, the liver was singled out as the most significant organ, and *hepatoscopy*—divination by inspection of the liver—became an elaborate art. Schools were established to instruct novices, and archeologists have found thousands of little clay models of the liver and its various lobes, each part inscribed with the significance that may be attributed to its appearance.

These forms of divination do not, in fact, constitute a true experiment, except that the animal had to be killed. Scapulimancy, the interpretation of shoulder blades, is different in this respect. The bone is boiled, wiped clean, and hung up to dry; then it is held over hot coals or a fire so that cracks and burnt spots appear, which form a pattern that can be "read." The practice seems to have developed in ancient China. In the Shang Dynasty, before 1000 B.C., tortoise shells were used in the same manner. In

Japan, deer shoulder blades replaced the costly tortoise shells, and among present-day Siberian tribes, such as the Chuckchee and the Koryak, seal and reindeer scapula are used. Also Athabascan and Algonquian-speaking American Indian tribes divine in this manner, most often for the purpose of locating the best hunting grounds. They used shoulder blades of reindeer, otter, elk, and moose, according to which animal was sought in the hunt. Scapulimancy was not known in the ancient Near Eastern cultures, but a modified form of this type of divination diffused to Europe and Africa. Scorching of the bone was omitted, and it was merely inspected for thickness, shape, or natural veining (Kroeber, 1948:476–78). Our own use of the "wishbone" (a united pair of clavicles) appears to be a playful survival. Among the Naskapi, the caribou hunters of the Labrador Peninsula, scapulimancy was combined with divinatory dreaming. The diviner induced dreaming by taking sweatbaths and drumming before going to sleep. If he saw game during the dream, it meant that animals were available somewhere in the neighborhood; scapulimancy then indicated the direction in which they might be found (Speck, 1935:150).

Animal bones are also used in another form of divination, the casting of lots. The small carpal and tarsal bones are most suitable for this purpose, and the Romans particularly favored the four-sided ankle bones, which were marked on each side with special inscriptions. The scientific Latin name of one of these bones is still *astragalus,* indicating its former use as a bone which, like the stars, was used for purposes of prediction. Other small objects are used elsewhere: pebbles, shells, seeds, nuts, beans, leaves, twigs, and almost anything else that is small and readily available. The usual method is to throw them like dice, and to interpret the resulting patterns.

In some cultures animals, rather than human beings, were used to manipulate the lots, thus assuring a greater measure of objectivity. Herskovits reports that, in one small region of the Cameroons, palm-leaf lots with special markings are placed at the hole of a trained tarantula so that it will scatter them (1952: 371). Gebauer describes how, in the same general region, the Kaka make a pack of "cards" out of stiff, trimmed leaves decorated with symbols. A bottomless clay pot is used to enclose the entrance of a spider's burrow. The cards are placed inside this pot, together with a bait to attract the spider, and the enclosure is covered with plantain leaves. Later, the disturbance of the marked leaves caused by the spider's actions is interpreted by a diviner (1964). The Azande, whose many different forms of divination have been described by Evans-Pritchard, place two branches of different trees in a termite mound, and determine the answers from the supernatural according to which of the two twigs has been gnawed by the termites (1937:352).

Ordeals typically involve experiments with human beings. Generally employed to determine guilt, they tend to give yes-or-no answers—if the test is passed, the accused is innocent; if not, he is guilty. In severe cases, the failure *is* the punishment. The Ekoi of Southern Nigeria give an accused sorcerer a potion made from poisonous wild beans. If he is innocent, he will recover; if he is guilty, he dies. More often ordeals result in some physical discomfort rather than death. The African Dahomey had many such ordeals: placing a red-hot machete on the tongue of the accused to see if he would blister, taking a seed from a pot of boiling oil to see whether the oil would burn the hand, placing a pepper under the eyelid to determine whether the eyes would tear, and so on (Goode, 1951:142). The Chewa of Northern Rhodesia sometimes administered poison to whole village populations at a time when the death of an important person or a series of deaths led them to believe that witches or sorcerers were active. Those who vomited—and thereby expelled the poison from their system—were innocent: those who did not, became ill. Those who became ill were judged guilty and were usually executed (Marwick, 1963:45).

Variations in the Forms of Divination

Within the major forms of divination, innumerable cultural variations exist. In some form or another, divination seems to occur in most—if not all—religious systems. Among the ancients, the Etruscans probably had the strongest penchant for divination. Coming from Asia Minor to Italy about 800 B.C., they brought with them the divinatory practices of the region. Once settled, they elaborated these arts to a degree unequalled by any other people since. The Etruscans established several schools of instruction with separate departments and specialized instructional literature. There were the books of haruspicy, of fulgerales (lightning), of ritual, and of the ostentaria or "marvels." Much of our knowledge about them derives from Greek and Roman commentators, particularly Cicero's *De divinatione*. Although divination was used for many purposes, it was especially important in the political sphere (*cf.* Thulin, 1906–09, 3 vols.). This tendency prevailed in Rome, too, where many of the Etruscan practices were taken over (cf. Bouché-Leqlerq, 1879–82, 4 vols.).

Divination is also extremely common in Africa. In few African societies is divination a more central concern than among the Azande, and detailed descriptions of its various forms have been provided by Evans-Pritchard (1937). One of the major forms of divination involves the use of a "rubbing board." Generally between ten and twelve inches long, this implement is made of wood and consists of two table-like parts. One, the "female," is supported by one or two legs and its "tail"; the other, the "male," is an inverted little table, the leg now serving as a handle. The flat side of the "male" fits the surface of the "female" (see Figure 12). The diviner pours certain fruit juices upon the flat surface of the "female," steadies it by holding his foot on the "tail," and rubs the "male" over it. If it moves smoothly, the answer is "yes"; if it sticks to the board quite firmly, the answer is "no" (*ibid.*:362–64).

Of even greater importance to the Azande is the "poison oracle," which involves the use of chickens. The poison is a red powder made from a forest creeper, which is mixed with water to form a paste. The characteristic quality of this poison is that it kills some chickens, but leaves others unaffected. The behavior of the fowls under this ordeal, especially their death or survival, gives "yes" or "no" answers to questions asked beforehand.

Both practices are carried out within the framework of Azande religion. The rubbing board is considered inferior to the poison oracle, but its use is hedged by many religious taboos and precautions. The manufacturer of a rubbing board must abstain for two days from sexual intercourse and certain foods. When the board is ready, it is anointed with a mixture of juices and oil, boiled in a pot, and then wrapped in bark cloth and buried for two days. Although the owner of a rubbing board is supposed to observe sexual and dietary prohibitions before consulting it, this rule is not adhered to when the need for consultation is urgent

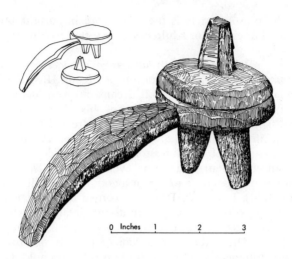

0 Inches 1 2 3

Figure 12. Azande rubbing-board oracle.

and arises suddenly (*ibid.*:370). The use of the rubbing board is restricted to adult males.

The taboos and prohibitions governing the consultation of the poison oracle are kept much more strictly. Resort to the oracle, like the use of the rubbing board, is restricted to adult males; young boys are rarely allowed to attend the sessions. One man administers the poison to the chicken while another one, seated opposite, questions it. The fowl is considered only the medium, it is the *benge* or poison which is the supernatural substance. Before the poison is squeezed into the chicken's mouth, the questions are addressed to *benge* in such a way that they can be answered "yes" or "no." The question ends with a command: "If this is true, poison oracle, spare the fowl" (*ibid.*:296–97). Two tests are usually made: the second either confirms the verdict or contradicts it, making it invalid (*ibid.*:300).

The rubbing board and the termite oracle are generally used to decide on everyday affairs. Matters of health are a prominent concern, and minor ailments are diagnosed by the rubbing board. Questions about where to plant a crop, where to hunt, if and when to go on a journey are generally placed before the rubbing board. The poison oracle is used for more important purposes, dealing with questions of adultery or suspected witchcraft.

Divination in Dreams or in Trances

Oneiromancy is the interpretation of dreams. Because dreaming is relatively frequent, not all dreams are considered divine. Homer indicated that the Greeks of his time distinguished between significant and nonsignificant dreams. Later Greek writers classified significant dreams in three types: the symbolic dream, which cannot be understood without interpretation; the *horama,* an enactment of a future event; and the *chrematismos,* a revelation by a parent, a priest, or a god of what will or will not happen (Dodds, 1957:107). Dreams recorded in Assyrian, Hittite, and ancient Egyptian literature are divine dreams in which gods appeared and communicated with men. The dreamers were usually kings. Often they had a staff of priestly oneiromancers, who were permanently attached to the royal household. Common people, whose dreams were secular, could seek their meanings in dream books.

In the middle of the fourth century B.C., Hippocrates rationalized dreams by relating them to the physiological state of the dreamer. He anticipates Freud by more than two millennia in his recognition that many dreams are disguised wish fulfilments.

Malinowski observed that the Trobriand Islanders made a distinction between dreams very similar to that made by Homer. (1955:88–97). There are "free" dreams and "official" dreams. The former are of no interest, but official dreams are those given to secular or religious leaders, and are of divinatory nature. Leaders of fishing expeditions will dream about the weather, about the place where shoals may appear, or about the best day for the expedition, and they give their orders and instructions accordingly. Those in charge of the Kula trading expeditions will dream about the success of their undertaking (*ibid.*:90). In parts of Australia, the supernatural reveals in dreams the names of newborn children, thereby indicating the ancestor of which the child is a reincarnation.

Communication with the supernatural in trance or ecstasy may all or not be divinatory. The Eskimo shaman going on a spirit flight to find the lost animals will simultaneously induce the sea goddess to release them; thus he attempts to alter the behavior of the supernatural rather than merely observing it. Clear-cut examples of divination in trance come from Bali, where diviners may enter a trance themselves or use a medium. Belo reports that, when two sacred images were stolen from a Balinese shrine, a female diviner was asked to identify the thief (1960:231–38). She prayed, rubbed oil on the thumb nails of a small boy, and made him concentrate so that he fell into a light trance. Encouraged by the diviner, he saw the theft enacted on the shiny surface of his nails. He saw not one but two people entering the sacred shrine, coming out again, and running away in a specified direction. But the images were so small that he could not distinguish their faces, and the boy could not positively identify the thieves.

The Nyoro of East Africa diagnose illness by means of divination in trance. The shaman induces the disease-causing spirit to enter his own body. When he is successful, the spirit will identify itself and, speaking through the shaman's mouth, will tell why it was offended and what should be done to appease it (Beattie, 1960:77–78).

CONCLUSION

Divinatory practices must be analyzed within their social context. Their functions and meanings differ from place to place. Wilson relates the reliance upon divination in ancient Egypt to the social and political insecurity of certain periods (1949:130). But among the Ibo of southern Nigeria, divination served to strengthen the internal organization of the group (Ottenberg, 1958:295–317). At the time of study, the Ibo population was organized in more than two hundred independent patrilineal clans. About six of those possessed oracles whose powers were recognized by all others. Diviners, priests, and other adult males often traveled considerable distances outside of their own community, acting as representatives or "agents" of the oracle. Interested persons would be led by the agent to the oracle. They were assured of relatively safe travel, for it was believed that the oracle would kill or make ill those who harmed the agents and their clients. During their stay in other communities, or during the trip itself, the agents obtained information about the case, often casually. They undoubtedly related this useful information to the diviners of the oracle, because the interpretations generally corresponded with local opinions and feelings. The oracle conferred high prestige to the clans who owned it, and the prestige gave rise to both political and economic supremacy. Through the oracle, these clans decided such important matters as land disputes, property or inheritance disagreements, or accusations of witchcraft, sorcery, murder, and theft. The oracle-possessing clans also held powerful trading positions. Their agents were protected in their travels by the supernatural power of the oracle and they often carried out trading activities as well as religious and political functions.

Divination may also be an important principle of social control in societies that lack an effective central political authority. Dole describes such a pattern among the Kuikuru, a Carib-speaking tribe in central Brazil (1966:73–87). Although the Kuikuru recognize one of their members as headman, he exerts no political or economic control. There is no formal mechanism for punishing infractions of Kuikuro social norms, and divination is one of the most important alternatives to political authority, insuring a relatively peaceful coexistence and a considerable amount of internal cohesion and cooperation. Divination is carried out by a shaman, who assesses guilt after a crime has been committed. The shaman has the power to accuse, but he does not possess the political power to punish. Through divination, however, the identity of the criminal becomes known throughout the community, and the suspect may well decide to leave the group to live with another tribe in which he has relatives. When the accusation is very serious, some individual members of the group may take it upon themselves to kill the criminal identified by the shaman. In every case recorded by Dole, the suspects were people who were generally disliked in the community, so that divination also served to eliminate anti-social individuals.

The economic implications of divination have been largely neglected. It is significant that the economic value of animal victims of divination is generally much smaller than that of animals used in sacrifice. Snakes, rabbits, mice, mantis, spiders, and wild birds have been mentioned as media of divination. Nondomesticated animals are rarely used in sacrifice. The use of chickens for divinatory purposes is very common, but they are not to be compared in value with sacrificial cattle. Eduard Hahn suggested that chickens were domesticated by man purely for their use in divination, and that the consumption of their meat and eggs was a much later development (1896).

Some modern interpreters have considered the problem of the effectiveness of divination. Moore, observing that the Naskapi Indians use scapulimancy largely to insure success in hunting, asks whether it would not be better if they used their heads instead of shoulder bones (1957:69–74). Moore finds that this is not the case. Without scapulimancy, the Naskapi would be likely to return to those areas where they had been successful on previous occasions. But such habits may lead to depletion of the game supply. The randomness, dictated by the cracks appearing in scorched shoulder blades, thus has the useful effect of avoiding regular hunting patterns and produces positive long-range results.

But divination is not always as impersonal and uncontrolled as it appears to be among the Naskapi. Diviners are often shrewd judges of human nature, with a wide knowledge of local affairs. Their interpretations generally confirm the suspicions of their clients or coincide with their opinions. Diviners may thus well be official supporters of law and authority.

Religious communication has been treated here as the attempt of man to convey messages to the supernatural. These attempts have important social implications. Prayer, ritual, and divination unite the participants by the expression of common concerns. As such, religious communication contributes greatly to the internal cohesion of the group.

Divination is of special importance because it is carried out in situations where decisions or plans of action are not lightly taken. Indecision is thus eliminated, and the tasks at hand can be carried out without delay and further distraction. But more than that, divination stamps the decisions thus taken with a mark of special legitimacy. In doing so, it establishes an effective consensus upon the project to be undertaken, be it the determination of guilt and subsequent punishment of the offender, the selection of a house site or of hunting grounds, or the choice of a marriage partner. Divination has, therefore, as its regular consequence the elimination of important sources of social disorder, as G. K. Park has pointed out (1963:195).

9

Religious Specialists

A RELIGIOUS SPECIALIST IS SOMEONE WHO IS MORE SKILLED IN THE performance of certain religious tasks than other members of his community. Specialization is related to division of labor, so that the degree of specialization in a society is a function of its technological development. In simple societies division of labor is usually determined by age and sex only. Such a "natural" division of labor is found in every known society, even if the specific tasks assigned to each age or sex group differ from culture to culture.

THE RISE OF RELIGIOUS SPECIALIZATION

With the development of agriculture and animal domestication, sedentary living replaced nomadism. Societies became so organized that some individuals with special skills or abilities could devote all their time to particular occupations not necessarily involved with food production. Some made pottery, built canoes, or worked metal, exchanging their products for food or other necessities of life. This "true" division of labor involves the idea of a learned skill. Some true specialists devote only part of their time to their specialty, while others make their living by practicing those skills full-time.

In many societies, full-time and part-time specialists exist side by side, but simple hunting-and-gathering societies have part-time specialists only. Even the religious practitioners in those societies carry out their tasks on a part-time basis, devoting most of their working hours to hunting, fishing, collecting, and other forms of food production, much as other members of their group do. With technological development and the concomitant increase in social complexities, full-time religious specialists began to emerge. By definition, such specialists are not actively involved in food production, and must be supported by the labor of others.

SHAMANS AND PRIESTS

Although anthropologists recognize that religious specialists have many different types of duties and functions, depending upon the cultural expectations and the religious frameworks of their society, they have nevertheless attempted to classify such specialists in two broad types: *shamans* and *priests*. It has been found that specialists of the shamanistic type appear more frequently in technologically simple societies, where food production is an arduous task, while priesthoods are developed only on a more complex social level. This discussion will focus on the major criteria which have been advanced to distinguish shamans from priests.

Personal Powers and Ritual Duties

Perhaps the most basic distinction is that recognized by Lowie, who wrote that a shaman is a person who receives his powers directly from the gods and spirits, and acquires his status through personal communication with the supernatural, while a priest is a ceremonial practitioner who is trained in the competent performance of rituals (1963:175–76). This does not mean that shamanistic performances are not ritualized. Ritual is a form of religious communication, and shamanistic performances are ritualistic in that they attempt to communicate with the spirits and in that they are culturally standardized. The shaman, however, does not rely on ritual exclusively, or even primarily. His claim to professional status is not determined by his knowledge of ritual, but by his personal ability to contact the supernatural—with or without the benefit of ritual. In order to become a successful shaman, the candidate must secure "spirit helpers," and without them all ritual knowledge would be futile.

The training of shamans—the acquisition of knowledge about ritual requirements—is regularly preceded by, and predicated upon, the acquisition of spirit helpers. Among the Salish Indians, those who desire to become religious specialists set out on four full years of seclusion, self-denial, prolonged fasts, and strenuous exercise. This regimen usually produces dreams and visions in which the seeker meets with spirits, some of whom promise to become his helpers, and endow him with special powers. Only then does he go into training with an older specialist, to be educated in the ritualistic aspects and techniques of the profession (Hill-Tout, 1907:173–75).

Priests do not have spirit helpers, and their relationship to the supernatural powers depends upon, and is mediated by, ritual. To them, ritual knowledge is of the essence—the established and major mode of contacting and influencing the supernatural.

Requirements for Entrance to the Profession

The idea that a shaman receives his powers directly from the supernatural also involves the concept that prospective shamans are regularly singled out for their tasks by the spirits. In more anthropological terms, this means that there are certain culturally recognized criteria of aptitude which indicate to the individual, as well as to other members of his society, that he has the prerequisites for the religious occupation. The criteria themselves are determined by the manner in which the shaman is expected to carry out his religious tasks. In many Eskimo groups, drumming is the accepted way of contacting the spirits, and an early fascination with drums will generally be interpreted as a "divine call" and as an implicit indication of professional aptitude. When trance is the expected mode of shamanistic behavior—as it often is—the ability to enter into this state will be regarded as an indication of the supernatural selection. Among the Chuckchee of Siberia, anyone who spontaneously entered a trance was obliged to become a shaman; anyone who ignored the call would be supernaturally punished by illness or death. Among the Tapirapé Indians of Central Brazil frequent dreaming foreshadows future shamanistic powers. Young people who sleep restlessly, tossing and talking in their sleep, give indications of becoming powerful shamans later on, because spirits are believed frequently to reveal their messages in dreams (Wagley, 1959:420–21). Recovery from serious illness, survival of an accident, or other miraculous escapes from death are also frequently taken as indications of supernatural favor, and thus as a prognostication of future success in dealing with these powers.

Although these and many other possible signs were culturally interpreted as divine callings, there is a great deal of ethnographic evidence that the individuals themselves had some choice in the matter. Tapirapé youths who aspired to shamanism, whether they dreamed frequently or not at all, would gather in the central plaza of their village during the days of the dry season to seek dreams. An older established shaman would pass around his pipe and the young men were instructed to swallow the smoke. This induced violent vomiting and the neophytes would fall down, fainting or ill, during which states they often dreamed. If not, they would go home, and their uncomfortable physical feelings, together with the expectation that they would now dream, often brought about the desired results (ibid.: 421).

Lantis reports that an Ammassalik Eskimo boy sought to become a shaman, always thought of the power he wanted to possess, and anxiously awaited some great event that would give it to him (1965:311–12). But he did more than just wait. Every summer for three or four years he went to a solitary spot, rubbing a small stone on a larger rock for days on end, until he entered a state of semi-consciousness in which he had visions. In this manner, he acquired several spirit helpers which had first shown themselves in his visions but which he later could call at will.

On the other hand, spontaneously occurring indications of divine call to religious office are not always held desirable by the individuals who receive them, and they may attempt to suppress or ignore the symptoms. The degree to which people welcome or attempt to escape religious callings is itself a measure of the power and prestige that a society affords to the specialization. Lantis also tells how an Eskimo boy started "dreaming" but was ordered by his father not to tell anyone (ibid.:313). According to Lantis, shamans in this particular group were not generally wealthy and were targets of suspicion. It is not surprising, therefore, that the profession was not always eagerly sought.

Priests may also enter their profession because they feel that they have received a divine call. These indications may appear in dreams, in visions, or in states of trance or ecstasy. These indications, however, only beckon the priests to office; they do not necessarily reflect professional aptitude. Rather, they seem to provide a rationalization of the desire to enter the priesthood, or may serve as a justification for attaining priestly status if the position is a privileged one. A priest may receive a revalation in trance, but, unlike a shaman, he does not usually employ trance in his ritual activities. The priestly call is, therefore, more subjective.

Individual competence in contacting the supernatural is, for priests, of lesser significance than the ability to memorize rituals. Memorization can be a very difficult and demanding task which requires qualifications other than those necessary for shamans.

Zuni priests often enter their profession after they have been successfully treated for an illness by a priestly curing society. This is, in a way, a form of "divine call," indicating that the supernatural beings associated with the curing society look with some favor upon the individual, for they have cured him. At the same time, this is his justification for membership in that priestly society, which is considered honorable and desirable. Within this curing society there are, however, different levels of office, and the new member will have to learn the long and complex rituals, the prayers and the sacred songs. If thus he demonstrates the personality characteristics valued by the Zuni, such as lack of social aggressiveness, modesty, sobriety, and piety, he may rise through the various levels and eventually become the high priest and leader of rituals. His status and prestige, therefore, derive from his membership in the curing society, his ability to learn the rituals, and his personality—but not from his personal relationship to the supernatural powers.

Weber has expressed these differences between shamans and priests by applying the term *charisma* to considerations of the types of power accruing from religious occupations. The term is derived from New Testament Greek (*charisma = gift of grace*), and Weber distinguishes between personal charisma and charisma of office (1964:46). The shaman bases his authority as religious specialist mainly upon personal charisma, which gives him both the assurance that he can deal successfully with the supernatural powers and the confidence to communicate this authority to his fellow men. Priests, on the other hand, depend much less on personal success; the priestly office gives them prestige and authority. They deal with the supernatural not by the strength of their personal confidence, but by learning the culturally prescribed methods of communication.

Succession of Office

Although divine calls are less important for priests than for shamans, there must be a number of other ways by which a person qualifies for entrance in this profession. Heredity is one of those, and in a number of societies priestly occupations are regulated by descent. Occasionally, a shaman may train his own son to become his successor, but he can do so only if the son shows the personal abilities necessary for the profession. When religious occupations carry power and prestige, there will be a tendency to keep them in the family, if possible. Thus, among the Coast Salish Indians of British Columbia, a shaman will try to pass on his powers to his son or grandson. He does so by singing over the sleeping boy, and he also blows his powers over the boy's chest, rubbing them in with his hands. However, the boy must also receive his special powers through personal communication with the spirits (Barnett, 1955:149–50). The Tlingit shamans, too, are eager to pass on their profession to sons or grandsons, particularly because the inheritance includes expensive regalia: masks, drums, and costumes. But the inheritance can be made valid only if the son is willing to go through a period of spirit search, and succeeds in finding spirit helpers (Krause, 1956:195).

A different attempt to keep shamanistic powers within the family is found in some African Nuba tribes. Nadel reports that the call to the profession is initiated by any spirit that decides to enter a human being (1946:28). The spirit is usually identified by older men who recognize its specific manifestations and behavior patterns; if these are unfamiliar, the experts will diagnose a new and different spirit that has not been incarnated before. Although this is a clear example of a "divine call," it so happens that the spirits tend to remain within one family, and the shamanistic offices thus tend to become hereditary. The spirits may even try out several persons in order to find the most suitable one, incarnating themselves in one individual and abandoning him after a while. Only when the manifestations become regular are they taken to be a sign that the spirit has decided to stay, and the person may then be initiated as a shaman. Because this is an exalted and prestigious position, every Nuba man would wish to have a spirit and enjoy the benefits of the profession. The unsuccessful attempts of the spirits are, in our terms, the unsuccessful attempts of human beings to acquire the wanted position.

In societies in which priesthood begins to emerge, heredity of office is not immediately in full force. When several different positions exist side by side, those which are the highest and most prestigious are the first to become regulated by descent. Among the Cheyenne, only the positions of the "Keeper of the Sacred Arrows" and the "Keeper of the Sacred Buffalo Hat" traditionally remained within one family, unless the priests appointed a different successor before their deaths. All other religious occupations, less prestigious, were nonhereditary (Berthrong, 1963: 57–59). In the more highly stratified societies of Polynesia, priesthood became regulated by descent in a different sense—the position and status of a member of the priesthood depended upon the status of his class position. In Hawaii, the status of a priest was determined by his inherited rank (Sahlins, 1958:14). In the Society Islands, a priest's status was the same as his inherited secular status (*ibid.:*38), and the same was true in Mangareva (*ibid.:*49). In the Easter Islands, however, the paramount religious leader, as well as his priests, came from one lineage only. Other well-known examples of a priestly lineage are the Levites of the Old Testament and the Brahmans of Hinduism.

But priestly occupations are not always regulated by hereditary descent patterns. In many societies the offices are, in principle, open to everyone. This is particularly true in societies with a very elaborate and complex priesthood, where many religious specialists are needed to maintain the temples. This occurs only in societies which are technologically advanced and populous. In such situations, the motivations to become a priest will be complex. Some will seek security; others, material rewards. Still others may be personally attracted to such occupations. Although individual choice appears to play an important role, there will always be a number of influential cultural circumstances. In complex agricultural societies, scarcity of land may be a decisive factor. In rural Europe, for instance, when a farmer has more sons than can be supported by the farmland, it is not unusual that at least one of those becomes a priest or a monk.

Part-time and Full-time Specialists

Another possible difference between priests and shamans is that shamans usually devote only part of their working hours to religious tasks, while priests usually commit all of theirs.

In simple hunting-and-gathering societies, where food production is a continuous and time-consuming task, the labor of every able-bodied person is needed. Full-time religious specialization would be economically wasteful in such societies. Part-time specialists make their living like other members of the group and do not depend upon material support from others. Because part-time specialists are no great economic burden for the group, any individual may, in principle, claim to be a shaman and to have received supernatural powers. His reward will be prestige rather than material goods—but prestige will only come if he is effective.

It is generally accepted that religion gave rise to the first true part-time specialists. This idea receives considerable support from observations made in existing hunting-and-gathering societies, which usually have at least one part-time shaman even if there is no other kind of specialization.

The early appearance and near universality of religious specialization point to the social importance of religious functionaries. In the eyes of his fellow men, the shaman contributed significantly to the two most basic areas of life: health and food supply.

The situation is quite different in technologically advanced societies that begin to develop full-time religious specialization. By definition, such specialists are not actively involved in food production, and they must therefore be supported by others in exchange for their services. Different societies handle this matter in different ways. Often, full-time religious occupations are made a prerogative of old age. This is an economically sound procedure, because older people are usually less actively involved in food production, so that their removal from these activities is less of a strain upon the economy. Although in most such instances the older specialists are men, a few societies favor older women. Among the Kalinga of the Philippines, for instance, shamanism is almost exclusively in the hands of older women whose souls have "married" the supernatural spirits. A few men are shamans, but they are concerned with officiating at head-hunting rites rather than with treating illness (Barton, 1949).

Alternatively, particularly in those societies where ritual demands and elaborate and extensive, there may be few, if any, full-time specialists. Instead, nearly every adult male is a part-time specialist. This is the case among the Hopi Indians, where all men become members of at least one priestly society, attend the gatherings in the *kiva*, learn the songs and rituals, and officiate in the ceremonies controlled by these societies. Although this procedure is economically expensive in terms of manpower, the disadvantages are compensated for by a reliance upon the participation of women in agricultural work, and by the absence of material remunerations for ceremonial duties.

Full-time religious specialization may also be combined with the assignment of certain secular duties—a saving, from one point of view, in terms of manpower. The Yakö, who are primarily subsistence cultivators, call upon their priests to settle disputes. Because there are only two priests in every village, one from the patriclan and one from a matriclan, their selection is undoubtedly influenced by personal characteristics, such as wisdom and the capability to make unbiased decisions.

With technological development and increased social complexity, more full-time religious specialists can be maintained.

Yet, in most instances, access to full-time religious office has to be restricted, because no society can maintain itself if everyone withdraws from the food-production process. Sometimes this is accomplished by making training hard, lengthy, and expensive, so that many will be deterred from trying to enter the profession. These forces of selection operate both on the shamanistic and on the priestly levels. But the harshness of shamanistic training is usually geared toward the establishment of his personal qualifications, while the obstacles to priestly apprenticeships are more often economic. For the Navaho, to become a Singer is highly prestigious and economically rewarding, but the training is both lengthy and expensive. The established Singer who teaches a novice has to be paid a regular fee over many years, and a prodigious memory is demanded of the pupil. Kluckhohn and Leighton wrote:

> The Singer who knows one nine-night chant must learn at
> least as much as a man who sets out to memorize the whole

of a Wagnerian opera: orchestral score, every vocal part, all the details of the settings, stage business, and each requirement of costume. Some Singers know three or more long chants, as well as various minor rites (1962:229–30).

Religious Functions

Although the duties of a shaman can be directed toward many different goals, they usually include the treatment of illness and attempts to safeguard or increase the food supply. But it cannot be said that these tasks are unique to shamans; for religious therapy and animal or crop fertility rites form a part of many priestly religions as well.

The difference between priests and shamans lies not in their goals but in their methods. Shamans conduct their curing rituals as individual healers who know how to contact supernatural powers. Priests, when treating illness, conduct rituals designed to pacify the disease-causing supernatural powers, but their success depends upon the ritual itself and upon its reception by the supernatural. When a shaman fails to cure, it is to some measure his own failing. Although he may advance alternate explanations, a shaman who is persistently unsuccessful will no longer be consulted. Priests are not individual healers. Of course, they will be afforded greater prestige when their ritual activities are successful, but failure will not deprive them of their jobs. One explanation given for the lack of success is that the ritual itself was not carried out correctly. In such cases, the ritual is usually repeated, indicating that the action is more important than the officiant.

It is also true that shamans are more often considered capable of doing both good and evil, while priests are supposedly less capable of using their powers adversely or less inclined to do so. A shaman is believed capable of prompting the spirits by his powers of persuasion, adjuration, and inducement; he can ask the spirits what he wishes to ask. Priests can theoretically bring about undesired results only by willfully distorting the rituals.

Secular Powers

Another distinction is that shamans do not regularly possess secular powers, while priests often exercise considerable political influence.

First, it may be noted that simple homogeneous societies, in which the shaman typically appears, have not developed offices of genuine political power. At most there will be some temporary leaders, those directing communal hunting activities or deciding when to break camp and where to go next. Such leaders attain their position because of their proven ability; the most experienced or the most successful hunter will be a leader, but he has no legal power to enforce his decisions. People will follow his directions when they go on an expedition or a hunting party because his previous instructions have yielded good results. Such a leader will be followed as long as he is successful. Lantis writes about the Nunivak Eskimos:

> If one, besides being a shaman, were a strong, industrious, and effective worker and hunter, he certainly would be able to dominate the community. But some shamans were cripples or sickly people or others who for some reasons could not be outstanding hunters (1953:99).

Priests, as they appear in more stratified societies, often have a measure of secular political power, and are called upon to settle disputes, or to mete out punishments. In simple stratified societies, priestly office is sometimes combined with that of headman. In Ontong-Java, priest-chiefs had the power to punish those who stole reserve foods; this was, according to Hogbin, the only organized sanction on this Polynesian island (1934:211). Also, at the major annual communal ritual, the priest-chiefs presided over the redistribution of food taken from reserve lands (*ibid.*:187). Among the African Bemba, priests possessed much greater political power. The ruler was assisted by a group of hereditary priests who were in charge of rituals and sacred shrines. They alone could purify the ruler so that he could perform his ritual duties. These priests also acted as regents at the death of a chief, taking temporary possession of the sacred heirlooms which were the symbols of royal office. The priests did not themselves select the successor to the throne, but if they did not approve of him, they would refuse to give him the heirlooms or to install him (Richards, 1940:109).

In these attempts to contrast and compare shamans and priests, we have set up ideal types only. In reality, the criteria overlap. Yet, if we take the distinction made by Lowie and consider the shaman as a religious specialist who acquires his powers through his face-to-face encounters with the spirits, and the priest as one trained in the competent performance of rituals, we will find that a number of typical characteristics emerge (1963:175–76).

First of all, a shaman is usually a part-time specialist, while priests are part-time specialists only in those societies in which almost every adult man has priestly functions.

The position of the shaman is usually nonhereditary, and rarely the prerogative of a single lineage, caste, or class. Priesthood is more often hereditary, except in those societies in which almost every adult male is a priest or in which an almost unlimited number of people is needed to maintain the temples, to conduct the rituals and to serve the gods. In some societies priesthood is determined by age and sex; in others, priestly vows of celibacy naturally preclude heredity. In societies in which priesthood is regulated by descent, it often becomes a prerogative of a particular lineage, class, or caste.

Personal charisma and individual ability are important for the establishment of a shaman, and he must enjoy conspicuous success if he is to keep his position. For priests the charisma of office tends to overshadow personal characteristics and to excuse personal failures.

Entrance into the shamanistic profession is usually validated by divine call. Although this call may be spontaneous, many prospective shamans consciously attempt to seek visions or to receive other indications of divine favor. Priestly office is less often initiated by divine call. When the positions are hereditary, divine calls become of lesser significance; when the positions are open and abundant, validation by divine call becomes unnecessary.

The functions of shamans are usually directed toward practical ends, those relating to man's control over nature. Priests often have similar functions, but their practices tend to be of a ceremonial nature—attempting to maintain or to re-establish the correct relationship between man and the supernatural.

Shamanistic rites usually take place on the request of an individual or a group, after a crisis, or when a calamity seems impending. Shamanistic rituals, therefore, are not scheduled or calendrical. Priestly ceremonies tend to be more regular. Often associated with the agricultural cycle, they may also be of a commemorative nature. There are always some unscheduled rituals as well, notably after the death of a king or ruler.

As a result of the tendency of shamans to conduct their services on request, the relationship between a shaman and other members of the community is usually that of a professional-client type. The relationship between priests and other members of his group is more that of a leader with a following; it is sometimes called a shepherd-flock relationship. Nor do shamans regularly carry out their rituals and practices in permanent houses of worship. A developed priesthood, on the other hand, is nearly always associated with permanent, sometimes elaborate, religious shrines.

The office of shaman is not usually attended by political influence or other forms of secular power, although the shaman may attain a position of temporary leadership. Priests, on the other hand, frequently do possess a certain amount of secular power. This may be because shamans are often considered capable of doing both good and evil, while priestly functions are generally considered beneficial for the whole society.

Within this range of the shaman-priest continuum, many variations appear, so that it may become impossible to say if such or such a specialist is closer to the shamanistic or to the priestly end of the scale. Further difficulties arise from the inconsistent usage of the terms *shaman* and *priest* in ethnographic writings. In part, this confusion arises from the problem of translating native terms. Some societies do make linguistic distinctions between types of religious specialists which roughly correlate with our shaman-priest distinction. But often there are many different types of religious specialists in one society, and the native terminology cannot be easily rendered in English.

OTHER TYPES OF RELIGIOUS SPECIALISTS

Attempts have been made to overcome these difficulties by employing a number of other terms to denote certain types of religious specialists or practitioners. Some of these may be briefly discussed.

Diviners

A diviner is a religious specialist whose major function is to discover the will and intentions of the supernatural or to ask for divine judgment. Astrologers and haruspices were priestly classes in the civilizations of the Babylonians, the Etruscans, the Greeks, and the Romans. Their prestige was high, and they were relatively powerful. However, their religious authority was generally not as great as that of religious practitioners who perform rituals without attempting to pry into the supernatural mind. Almost invariably, when the two types appear within one religious system, diviners will be ranked the lower.

Shamanistic practices are often divinatory, but shamans read the mind of the supernatural by direct contact. Diagnosis of illness, if carried out within a religious framework, usually takes the form of divination, for the shaman or priest tries to find out what has angered the supernatural powers or which particular evil spirit has entered the body of the sufferer. Diviners are sometimes divided into diagnosticians and curers. The Navaho "hand trembler" merely finds the causes of illness; the priests carry out the healing ceremonies.

The diviner is fundamentally a technician. His interpretations are not based upon individual religious expressions but upon the traditions of his profession. These traditions, in turn, reflect the systems of belief and values within his culture.

Seers

A seer is a diviner who is able to discover the will and intention of the gods not through the interpretation of specific phenomena but through intuition. As such, he is a more marginal type of specialist. There are no schools for seers; they are not organized as classes or groups within a priestly hierarchy. Often, a seer is burdened by what he knows and reveals his insights to people only when he believes that they may avoid a catastrophe. Although seers do not have a well-defined status in any social hierarchy, they may be held in great honor and respect. Occasionally, a person may become attracted by the powers and way of life of a seer, and become his disciple. The social relationship between a seer and his disciples is unlike that of a shaman and his apprentice. The shaman teaches the practical skills of his profession to his pupils; the seer has no traditional techniques to impart—he can only introduce his followers into his world and way of life.

Prophets

Prophets also receive divine revelations, usually by means of visions and dreams. These revelations are neither actively sought nor induced by artificial or mechanical means; the gods take the initiative. The prophet is distinguished from the diviner in that he receives direct and usually explicit messages. Often, the gods include the command that their messages be extended to all men.

The functions of the prophet are not directed to practical matters—rather, he has a mission. What is revealed to him most often is the anger of the gods, and what these supernatural powers demand of the prophet is that he convince the people to change their ways. In other words, prophets are potential agents of change. Consciously or not, they are dissatisfied with the present; they either demand a return to the old ways of life, or they want to break with the established norms and introduce new ones. It is thus not accidental that in times of upheaval and change, when social identification becomes difficult, hundreds of prophet cults arise.

Prophets and priests are antagonists almost by definition: prophets endanger the priestly positions by their attempts to change the principles upon which the power of the priests is based. The Old Testament provides us with many revealing examples of this antagonism.

A prophet, if he wants a following, must have personal charisma. However, as Max Weber pointed out, a prophet also needs charismatic authentication, which, in practice, means a demonstration of his powers (1964:47). Hence, prophets would often also practice divination, produce miracles, or show other proof of their claims of divine revelation.

The so-called prophetical mandate, the order issued by the gods to inform the people of their messages, means that the prophet will "preach," thereby subjecting his ideas to public opinion. Sometimes, he will have only a limited number of disciples, and he may train a "band" of prophets who will then receive similar revelations. Examples of such bands of prophets are found in the early stages of Judaism, Islam, and Buddhism. Or a prophet might succeed in establishing his authority over a larger section of the population and found a new cult which, under favorable social circumstances, may become a full-fledged religion.

Weber extends the term *prophet* to include what he calls *the exemplary prophet*. His function, unlike that of the "ethical prophet," is not to preach a change in the way of life, but merely to show, by personal example, the way to religious salvation (*ibid.:*55). Weber feels that this type of prophet is particularly characteristic of India and also occurs in China and the Near East.

Founders of Religion

Founders of religion are, basically, successful prophets. The term, therefore, does not denote any intrinsic quality of personality or type of revelation but refers to historical facts. It is interesting to note that Jesus, Mohammed, Buddha, Zoroaster, and Luther were "reformers" with strong personal charisma and prophetic qualities, but that they referred to old traditions rather than attempting to establish a radically new faith. Each was concerned, in his own way, with acting out his convictions, which were different from, and usually critical of, certain aspects of the religious practices of his times.

Curers and Medicine Men

Religious curers are specialists whose primary task is the healing of the sick by supernatural means. Religious therapy is worldwide, and it is scarcely an exaggeration to state that all types of religious specialists are, to a greater or lesser extent, involved in these practices. (In Chapter 10, the various principles and techniques are discussed in greater detail.)

The term *medicine man* can serve as a synonym for curer, although it is commonly used to refer to American Indian religious specialists. Curing was often one of their most important functions, but the term obtained currency because many Indian concepts of supernatural power were translated into English as *medicine* regardless of whether these powers were used for curing, for rainmaking, or for other religious techniques (Norbeck, 1961:103).

Witches

Witches are persons who are believed to use supernatural power for evil purposes, but who perform no rites, utter no spells, and possess no medicines. Witches use psychic powers to attain their ends. They are not religious leaders; they do not have a following; and their art is secret. People may consult witches if they want to harm others, but they cannot learn witchcraft from them. Generally speaking, witches are low in status, and accusations of witchcraft result in the most serious consequences.

Sorcerers

Sorcerers, like witches, are generally evil-minded, but, rather than depending upon their psychic powers, they perform mechanical acts to harm others. The art of sorcery, unlike that of witchcraft, can be learned. Sorcerers are, therefore, not quite as innately evil as witches, and they may also use their techniques to counteract evil wrought by other sorcerers.

Witch Doctors

The term *witch doctor* is usually employed by the layman rather than by anthropologists. If it is to be used at all, it should be applied to religious specialists whose main function lies in the control of witchcraft and sorcery and in the curing of illness caused by witches and sorcerers.

Magicians

A magician is a person who uses magic, and this definition is both so obvious and so vague that it is not very useful. The term is not generally used by professionals, unless they employ it to refer to what we have called *shamans* (Wach, 1944:353–56; Weber, 1964:20–31). Anthropological convention avoids the term *magician* as an indication of a specific type of religious specialist. The common English meaning of *magician* now refers to the clever entertainers who amuse us at parties or on the stage. They are well-established professionals, and they do not claim supernatural powers.

Teachers

Well-developed religious systems often include persons whose specific task is the transmission of sacred knowledge. Such teachers are erudite persons steeped in the wisdom of religious tradition, dogma, and sacred history. They transmit acquired, not revealed, knowledge, and are thus very different from prophets. They tend to safeguard tradition and the proliferation of dogma, while prophets seek to announce a new order.

Teaching takes a variety of forms and may be directed to the laity as a whole, to disciples, or to novices. In this sense, teaching is not confined to literate societies with a priesthood. The shaman who instructs a younger one is also a teacher; he, too, transmits the knowledge and traditions of his profession to others, even if the relationship is less rigid and less institutionalized than in situations in which religious teaching has become a separate occupation. The most completely institutionalized religious teacher-pupil relationship is found in Hinduism. Every young man of good Hindu family was formerly required to devote himself for a number of years to the instruction and direction of a *guru*. The bond between master and disciple was uncommonly strong, and regulated in an authoritarian fashion. The *guru* had absolute power over his charges, and their loyalty to him took precedence over the loyalty to family (Weber, 1964:52).

CONCLUSION

The universality of religious specialization indicates that all societies recognize religious authority. This authority, however, can be of very different types. In simple societies it is most often derived from personal endowments and skills. Experience, shrewdness, resourcefulness, power of observation, good memory, and ability to inspire trust and confidence are of greater importance than the ability to go in trance or to practice legerdemain. In more complex societies, the authority of religious office will tend to diminish the necessity of specified personal qualifications, but these qualities are not necessarily absent altogether. From what is known about the religions of the Maya, Aztecs, Egyptians, Babylonians, Etruscans, Phoenicians, Chinese, and Japanese, it becomes evident that priests were often highly gifted individuals. They laid the foundations of medicine, law, irrigation agriculture, astronomy, mathematics, and calendrical time reckoning. Religious specialists are also guardians of tradition. They transmit to future generations the sacred knowledge upon which the religious organization of a given society is dependent. As such, they are often instrumental in the creation or the fostering of the arts: sacred music, song, dance, sculpture, painting, and architecture. History bears witness to the far-reaching influence of religious leadership in both religious and secular spheres.

10

Religious Healing

THE SERVICES OF RELIGIOUS SPECIALISTS CAN BE DIRECTED AT ALMOST any human need or goal, but the treatment of illness is very prominent. A great many religious specialists, in all societies, attempt healing of some sort, although the degree of supernatural assistance that is sought may vary. This discussion will focus on religious healing as one important example of how religious professionals may carry out their social tasks.

THE CONCERN FOR HEALTH

Health is of universal interest and concern. The oldest existing written records show a highly developed mythology explaining phenomena of disease and suggesting possible cures. All known nonliterate societies have developed theories about the causes of illness and possess methods of treatment. Naturalistic methods seek explanations of illness without invoking supernatural causation, and usually attempt to cure it without supernatural aid. Religious healing is based upon the premise that health is supernaturally given and maintained, and that disease is supernaturally caused.

Nonliterate peoples do not avoid naturalistic explanations, but they often combine them with supernatural ones. Every known society applies naturalistic treatments, even if these may consist merely of removing thorns from fingers or extracting ailing teeth.

But most are much more sophisticated in their medicinal knowledge, and even societies on a very low level of technological development possess a surprisingly elaborate pharmacopoeia. Some know the techniques of setting bones, lancing, massage, cauterization, heat and water therapy, blood-letting, and so on. Ackerknecht estimates that 25–50 per cent of the herbs used for curing in nonliterate societies are objectively active in producing the desired results (1965:399). Hoebel writes that the Cheyenne Indians have knowledge of some fifty wild plants used for the cure or relief of one illness or another, and he says: "Some of them are very effective, indeed; all of them are effective to some degree" (1960:88). Paiute and Shoshone Indians used approximately three hundred species of plants for curing purposes (Train, *et al.*, 1941). The Hanunóo of Mindoro can name over 1600 distinct plant types of their local flora, outnumbering by about four hundred the taxonomic species recognized by systematic botanists. Many of these are further classified as medicinal herbs, are grown in houseyards, and used with good effect (Conklin, 1957: 44, 92). Many other examples could be given to show that practical and naturalistic types of treatment of illness are not unknown among nonliterate peoples, and that they often use practices which are effective. But supernatural treatment is also successful, or appears to be so. Many illnesses cure themselves, but if some treatment has been applied and the person subsequently recovers, the treatment is naturally thought of as effective. Moreover, the psychological effects of supernatural treatment should not be overlooked. Illness causes anxiety, and the idea that something is done about it will tend to remove fear and create hope.

A number of nonliterate societies make clear-cut distinctions between supernatural and natural causes of illness. The Black Carib of Honduras consult a religious healer in case of any affliction, but he will attempt to deal with it only when he is convinced of its supernatural origin; he refers other cases to local curers (Taylor, 1951:111). Paiute Indians believe that most illness results from sorcery or from attacks by ghosts, but that some diseases result from a deterioration of the blood. Older people often become ill in this way: their blood has aged, and hardened in the body. Blood-letting is the traditional treatment (B. Whiting, 1950:37). The Cheyenne Indians use herbal remedies or surgery when illness or injury is believed to spring from natural causes, but they attempt magical cures when supernatural origins are suspected (Hoebel, 1960:88).

CAUSES OF ILLNESS

There are three major culturally perceived ultimate causes of illness involving the supernatural:

1. Illness is brought about through the behavior of the individual or his relatives.
2. Illness is brought about by other human beings.
3. Illness is brought about by evil supernatural powers.

These theories may well exist side by side, but each involves a different mechanism of projection.

The Behavior of the Individual

Illness brought about by the sufferer's own behavior is punishment, signifying personal guilt. The patient has offended the supernatural powers by neglecting his ritual duties, by breaking taboos, or by exhibiting antisocial behavior. In cultures in which this type of explanation prevails, illness may indeed be brought about through transgression of social or religious norms. When a person commits an act culturally defined as wrong or evil, and he feels sufficiently guilty about it, his self-condemnation may well make him physically indisposed.

Curing will, in these instances, be directed toward removing the person's guilt and propitiating the angered supernatural powers. Confessions accomplish the first; sacrifice or other expiatory rituals, the second.

The Behavior of Other Human Beings

Occasionally, other human beings are believed to be the instigators of disease through the arts of witchcraft and sorcery. Guilt is significantly lessened (although it need not be absent) and is replaced by suspicion. This explanation of illness generally reflects a strain in social relationships, and the direction in which the suspicions are cast tend to indicate the sources of interpersonal antagonisms. The African Bunyoro, for instance, experience the strongest social tensions between co-wives and also

between brothers, and accusations of sorcery occur most frequently within these groups (Beattie, 1960:75–76).

Counterwitchcraft is the indicated cure. The first task of the
religious healer is usually to locate the human source of evil—to
identify the witch or sorcerer. Divination plays an important
role, but the local curer usually also knows which people are at
odds with one another. Confessions on the part of the suspected
sorcerer, and withdrawal of the evil influence, may have the desired results.

The Behavior of the Supernatural

Finally, it may be believed that supernatural powers suddenly
attack a person without provocation and make him ill. Guilt and
suspicion are here virtually absent; the blame falls on the supernatural powers alone. Curing will take the form of exorcism, or
pacification by forms of sacrifice or other material concessions.

These three general theories attempt to locate the efficient
causes of illness, but every known society brings forward additional explanations as to how the bringers of disease technically
make the body infirm or indisposed. Of these, the three major
explanations are loss of soul, intrusion, and possession.

Loss of the Soul

Loss of soul looms high on the list of culturally conceived
dangers to health. Witches may steal the soul, sorcerers may dis-
place it, evil spirits may capture it, deities may take it away as
a punishment. The soul itself, leaving the body at night, may
fail to find its way back. More detailed conceptualizations will
depend on how the soul itself is culturally depicted and where it
is supposedly located in the body. Some Australian tribes identify
the soul with kidney fat, and a minor loss of this substance will
subsequently result in minor indispositions, while continuous
leaks are more dangerous. High infant mortality is often explained by the idea that a child's soul is not yet firmly settled
in its body, so that it can be stolen or lost quite easily. The
Angmasilik Eskimos of East Greenland believe in multiple souls,
each one of which resides in a specific part of the body; that part
of the body which has lost its soul becomes ill (Hultkranz,
1953:55). The Tarahumara of northern Mexico say that the soul
sometimes leaves its house in the heart, and during its wander-

ings it becomes frightened and lost, or is eaten by malevolent whirlpool spirits. Not all of the soul travels at one time, or death would result immediately. But a partial soul cannot permanently sustain life, and the lost parts must be retrieved or replaced (Bennett and Zingg, 1935:259). The idea that the soul leaves the body after death is found all over the world.

Intrusion

Intrusion is the theory that illness ensues when a foreign object or substance enters the body. Sometimes immaterial, this substance is usually believed to be real—insects, worms, bugs, stones, thorns, splinters of wood, seeds, twigs, or almost any other small object will do. Although gods and spirits may occasionally inflict disease in this manner, it is usually believed to be the work of sorcerers who magically transmit the disease-causing substance from a distance, or bring it into actual contact with their victims. Ethnographic reports of the practice are not numerous. Secrecy usually surrounds evil intentions; moreover, accusations of witchcraft and sorcery generally outnumber the actual attempts to practice it. In some instances, sorcery is the socially accepted form of punishment. Such seems to be the case in the Australian practice of "bone-pointing." The deadly instrument is ideally a bone taken from a dead man's body, but a kangaroo bone or a ritually prepared pointed stick can serve as suitable substitutes. The supernatural powers are invoked to make the bone effective. When two persons work together, as often is the case, they adopt a prescribed ritual attitude. One man kneels on the ground, supporting himself with his hands, while the actual pointer leans over him, chants certain traditional songs, and jerks the bone or stick into the direction of the distant victim. It is believed that the power of this bone travels invisibly and unerringly toward its destined victim. The victim will fall ill and die, unless the bone is magically removed by a curer (Elkin, 1964:286–88).

Although intrusion is frequently related to witchcraft and sorcery, possession is usually considered a direct supernatural act, although the possibility that a witch or sorcerer has persuaded a spirit to inhabit someone's body is by no means excluded. Possession is related to intrusion in that both involve the

entrance of a foreign object into the body. In the case of possession, the "foreign object" is an anthropomorphized spirit.

The theory that spirits can enter the human body is not always related to illness. Trance, for example, is another form of
spirit intrusion and one that is deliberately sought and deemed
desirable for given ritual purposes. Shamans induce spirits to
descend into their bodies temporarily; Balinese trance dancers attract the spirits by their performances; when the ritual is finished
and the trance lifted, the spirits disappear and the person suffers
no ill effects. In other words, spirit intrusion in trance is voluntary, as Oesterreich pointed out long ago (1930).

Possession

Possession, on the other hand, is involuntary and usually undesirable. It may cause the person to behave immorally or anti-
socially, but most often it makes him physically ill. In Western
tradition, possession was generally linked to epilepsy or to mental disturbances, but data on mental illness in nonliterate societies are incomplete and difficult to interpret. Undoubtedly,
mental illness occurs everywhere, and some field reports indicate
that in nonliterate cultures it is explained by possession. Data on
possession as the cause of physical illness are less ambiguous. The
Javanese of Surinam, for instance, feel that young children are
particularly subject to spirit intrusion, and possession is evidenced by such physical symptoms as lack of appetite, vomiting,
general listlessness, and crying without tears (de Waal Malefijt,
1963:135).

One of the earliest medical documents in existence, the Assyrian Tablets, dating from about 2500 B.C., contain incantations
to evil demons to depart from their victims. Hippocrates, in the
fifth century B.C., wrote that epileptic disorders had physiological
and environmental causes rather than demonic ones (*On the
Sacred Disease,* reprinted in Ehrenwald, 1956:200–13). But the
theory that illness, epilepsy, and insanity was caused by devils,
and that curing could be effected by driving them out, remained
current in Europe until well in the nineteenth century. The
concept was reinforced by Biblical accounts of the driving out of
demons from the bodies of the afflicted.

Apart from the major ideas of soul-loss, intrusion, and possession, other supernatural explanations of illness are sometimes

brought forward. Among the Australian Murngin, bad dreams
are believed to cause illness (Warner, 1964:199). Planets and
stars may make a person ill, as was believed by the ancient
Etruscans and Romans.

DIAGNOSIS

Diagnosis of the cause of illness is an important first step
toward subsequent therapy. Nearly all known societies recognize
that illness may have a variety of causes. Even when all forms
of illness are attributed to witchcraft, as appears to be the case
among the Azande, it is deemed important to search out the
identity of the witch and to discover which particular magical
means he used.

Diagnosis and healing are often carried out by the same specialist, but in some cultures the two skills are kept separate. The
diagnostician will then attempt to identify the disease and its
causes, but he will not apply any therapeutic practices. Instead
he will suggest a specific curing ritual to be conducted by priests
or medicine societies, or he refers the patient to a healer who
is, in his opinion, most qualified to treat the diagnosed illness.

The Navaho hand-trembler is such a diagnostician. His technique consists of applying corn pollen to the body of the patient, and he also daubs this substance on his own arm and four
fingers (four is the Navaho's sacred number). He then prays to
the Black, Blue, Yellow, and White supernatural Gila Monsters,
offering them beads in their appropriate colors. Then he must
sing four sacred songs, during which his arm and hand begin
to tremble. He claims to have no control over the movements,
but he can interpret the type of movement and the direction it
seems to take, and thus provide information about the location
and the cause of the trouble (Kluckhohn and Leighton, 1962:211).

More traditional forms of divinatory diagnosis include the
throwing of bones, as practiced by the African Lovedu. The resulting patterns reveal both the nature and the cause of the disorder (Krige and Krige, 1943:228). The Nyoro possess a number
of such methods. They scatter cowry shells or small squares of
leather, sprinkle ashes of burned leaves upon water and interpret
the pattern, use a rubbing board, and inspect the entrails of

animals; they also make diagnoses while in a trance state. The rubbing board is a variant of that used by the Azande. It consists of a short wooden stick, which is dipped in goat blood. The fingers of the diviner will stick to it at certain points when he is handling it, and from these clues he can supposedly learn how the illness came about (Beattie, 1960:71–73).

The Black Carib diviners place a mirror between two candles in an otherwise dark room, telling the patient to look in the mirror until the face of the sorcerer appears (Taylor, 1951:136). Both the Balinese and the Manus consult a medium to determine the source of maladies (Belo, 1960:228ff; Mead, 1953:67).

Dreams are sometimes believed to have diagnostic value, both by Freudian psychoanalysts and by nonliterate healers. Among the Navaho it is the patient who dreams and the diviner who interprets, while among the Jie of Uganda it is the diviner himself who does the dreaming (Gulliver, 1965:88).

The Dobu take it for granted that illness is brought about by witchcraft and sorcery, but it is important to them to find the culprit. To this end they practice water-gazing and crystal-gazing. Fortune describes it as follows:

> In the former case [*i.e.*, water-gazing], water is put into a wooden bowl and hibiscus flowers thrown on the water. The diviner charms: "the water is water no longer." He cuts the water-in-changed-nature open. At the bottom of the cut he sees the spirit of the witch who has abstracted the spirit of his patient and who now has it concealed, or the spirit of the sorcerer who has the *sumwana,* body leavings of the patient, and now has them concealed. Volcanic crystals may be used instead of water. Spirit abstraction by a *gelaboi* may be indicated by the patient making delirious or semi-delirious statements about canoes at sea, canoes used by these spiritual *gelaboi.* Great attention is paid to the patient's ravings if there are any.
>
> If the patient runs about in a delirium, then again his *sumwana* has been taken by a sorcerer. The sorcerer in such case has bound up the *sumwana,* winding it about in some receptacle with bush creeper. This winding is compared to the way in which the tree oppossum, Cuscus, winds its tail around branches and darts around apparently aimlessly. The

sorcerer's winding of *sumwana* has made the patient run about like the oppossum.

The diviner may bend forward the middle finger of the patient, grasping it tightly at the first joint. If the tip of the finger does not flush, then spirit abstraction by a witch has occurred. If it does flush, then the patient's *sumwana* has been taken by a sorcerer.

Again, the diviner may tell by the body odor of the patient the sex of the person responsible. None could define how this was done.

These measures of noting the symptoms of delirium, or of trying the finger-bending or the smelling tests, precede the water- or crystal-gazing which finally determines the exact identity of the person responsible for the illness. The attention paid to delirium narrows down the circle of people within which the diviner's judgment may operate, but the other two tests leave him free by their nebulousness. Flushing or no flushing in the finger bent is rarely so obvious as to rule out subjective appraisal of the results, a subjective factor that is even more obvious in the smelling test (Fortune, 1963:154).

This passage gives a good insight into the possible complexity of the methods used. Divination is definitely a learned skill. Moreover, this example shows how diviners and diagnosticians do not merely rely upon the supernatural for their answers. Often they accompany their magical techniques by shrewd questioning, or by taking their cues from the patient's own suspicions. In the "delirious ravings" of the Dobu, their suspicions will come out, and when the Black Carib are directed to stare in a mirror, they will undoubtedly "see" the shape of the person most suspected of sorcery. In small communities, where not many things remain hidden, the diviner will usually be quite familiar with the personal circumstances of his patients as well as with local antagonisms. This knowledge will assist him in reaching conclusions which are satisfying to the sufferer and acceptable to the community.

Diagnosis of illness sometimes takes place after the patient has died. On Guadalcanal, the diviner holds an acra nut loosely in one hand and persuades the soul of the dead man to enter it. Once this is accomplished, the diviner addresses the soul, posing a series of questions that can be answered by a simple "yes" or "no." The nut moves if the answer is affirmative; otherwise, it remains still. The questioning continues until the guilty party has been located. The family of the deceased will then seek compensation from the offender, or will take steps to avenge his death. (Hogbin, 1964:58–59). The social implications of diagnosis are quite apparent here.

Diagnosis is often as valued as curing. Regardless of the methods used, it has important psychological connotations. The identification of the source of the ailment makes it possible for the patient and his family to understand the suffering, which will tend to reduce anxiety, and the suggestion of proper cures gives further relief as well as reassurance and hope.

HEALING

Supernatural healing methods, like all other forms of therapy, attempt to remove the causes of disorders and to relieve their symptoms. When illness is considered to arise from the anger of the gods, curing methods involve propitiation of the higher powers. When human agents are involved, counterwitchcraft is an obvious method. In cases of intrusion, the disease-causing spirits or objects need to be rendered harmless. Spirit possession is regularly treated by exorcism, and the logical cure for soul loss is to restore it to its proper place.

As may be expected, there are many specific methods of achieving these aims, and many different curing systems usually exist within one society. Indeed, it is not uncommon to find medical specialization even in fairly small communities, each specialist treating only those diseases in which he claims competence. The Sia Indians, for instance, have separate healers to treat snake-bite, burns, wounds obtained in warfare, and sterility (White, 1962:285). Several types of treatment are often combined within one curing ritual. The Northern Athabaskans believe in soul loss and in intrusion, and their healing methods are simultaneously directed toward finding the soul and removing the disease-causing objects (Lowie, 1952:177). For this reason, it is not possible to discuss curing methods in clear-cut categories, and the practices often tend to overlap.

Retrieving the Soul

When illness has been diagnosed as arising from partial or total loss of the soul, attempts to restore it may be direct or indirect. The most direct method is for the shaman to go on a spirit flight, engaging himself in a face-to-face combat with the supernatural powers who hold the soul in custody.

According to one observer, the shaman of a Carib Indian group works himself into a trance by chanting, smoking, and drinking tobacco juice, until his own soul leaves his body (Koch-Grünberg, 1916–28). By means of a ladder, he ascends to the realm of the spirits, and the first struggle takes place. The hostile powers try to destroy the ladder to prevent the shaman's soul from climbing it, or to cut off its return. They are usually beaten off with the aid of the shaman's spirit helpers. When the shaman reaches the supernatural realm, he seeks out the specific spirit who has stolen the soul. The encounter usually begins with mutual boasting, each showing the other his powerful magical weapons. Then they engage in a duel, which involves all kinds of fearful transformations on the part of both adversaries, but in the end the shaman usually manages to abduct the lost soul and bring it back to earth. The shaman in trance reproduces the voices of all the spirits and the animals participating in the combat. The whole procedure is thus vividly experienced by the patient and all other onlookers.

Haeberlin described a similar ritual for the Coast Salish Indians, who attribute illness to loss of the guardian spirit (1918: 249–57). Not one but eight curers undertake the mystical journey. They line up in two rows of four, representing the crew of a burial canoe, paddling to the land beyond. Their journey, too, is beset by dangers—they cross dangerous rapids, transfer from one stream to another over slippery logs, and finally encounter the demon who holds the guardian spirit in confinement. After a fierce battle, they wrest the soul from its captor, place it in the canoe, and paddle homeward. Once returned, they sing and dance, and the patient, hearing the specific song of his guardian spirit, is supposed to get up and join in. If he cannot, the shamans have brought back the wrong guardian spirit.

Eskimo shamans, too, go on spirit flights for curing purposes, but rather than assailing the supernatural powers, they ask the reasons for which the soul is held in bondage. Illness, among the Eskimo, implies not only loss of soul, but also supernatural punishment for human offense. In the curing rites, the answers come not only from the spirits, but also from the confession of the victim himself. Rasmussen described such a ritual for the Iglulik Eskimos (1930:133–41). The shaman, after making contact with the spirits and summoning his spirit helpers, asks leading questions "prompted" by the spirits but based upon his own knowledge of the situation. His questions evoke responses from the patient and from the audience. The shaman begins by asking the spirits who is at fault for the sickness—the shaman himself? his wife? The patient, in this case a woman, immediately answers that she herself has been at fault: "My thoughts have been bad and my actions evil." The shaman then "sees" something that gleams white; it looks like the edge of a pipe. Some people in the audience answer that she has smoked a pipe which she ought not to have smoked, adding that it is a small thing, for which she certainly should be forgiven. Subsequently, the suffering woman confesses a great number of broken taboos—she ate a piece of caribou meat at a forbidden time; she touched a dead body without later purifying herself; she slept with a man at a time when she was unclean; and so on. After every confession, the audience asked that the offense would be removed, and at the end of the session the shaman and the listeners went home, believing that the confession of sins and offenses had taken the sting out of her illness, and that she would now soon be well again. The public confessions led to forgiveness not only on the part of the spirits, but, more important, also on the part of the human community. Should she not recover, the effects of the ritual remain positive, for her soul has been cleansed and will be better off in the place beyond.

In a number of societies the loss of the soul is formulated, in seemingly more naturalistic terms, as the loss of some vital function of the body, or of a specific organ. The Paiute Indians believe that one of the major causes of illness is loss of breath, and "breath" is more or less equated with the soul. The soul-breath is usually stolen by an evil spirit, and the healer's first task is to identify the thief. As long as the symptoms are not very serious, the curer will simply attempt to drive away the scheming spirit by sprinkling ashes around the house, or putting bunches of wild roses near the door. If the patient worsens, it means that the spirit has already captured the breath, and the curer must now pursue the spirit. The curer first dances until he himself is "out of breath," and his own breath then goes up to the Milky Way to search for the lost breath of his client (B. Whiting, 1950:41–42).

Among the Sia of New Mexico, one of the causes of illness is "loss of heart." The heart can be restored only by means of the proper heart songs. One such a song, in free translation, follows:

> You, Arrow Youth, why is it that you are going about, throwing your heart away?
> Come back, whole, and sit down in front of the altar where the *iarako* [corn fetishes] are sitting (White, 1962:296).

But the Sia curers may also go out to battle with the witches who have stolen the heart. They put bear's paws on their left arm, don a necklace of bear's claws, and set out. On returning, they carry the "heart," in the shape of a ball of rags wrapped around a kernel of corn. This kernel is examined closely. If it is blemished, the prognosis is bad; if not, the patient will recover promptly. In either case the sufferer must swallow the kernel, and the heart-soul is thus "replaced" in his body (*ibid.*:297–98).

Removal of Disease-causing Objects

The theory of intrusion of disease-causing foreign objects is found in many parts of the world, but is particularly widespread among American Indians. Occasionally, the objects are invisible. Some Carib and Arawak tribes believe that illness may be caused by intangible magical arrows. But the intrusive items are usually believed to be real, and healing will concentrate upon their physical removal. The specific techniques consist of manipulating the body, kneading, rubbing, brushing, or blowing smoke over the affected parts, or passing an object (often an egg) over the sore spots. Using sleight-of-hand methods, the healer will finally produce the offending object and display it to the patient and his family. In other cases, he may apply his mouth to the body of the sufferer, either directly or using a hollow tube, shell, pipe, or reed, and then sucking out the intrusive object (which the curer held hidden under his tongue).

These healing procedures are regularly carried out in a ritual setting. There are no known instances in which the healer simply visits the patient, "removes" the object, and declares him cured. The Sia Pueblo Indians provide an example of the complexity of such a ritual (White, 1962:296–98). Here the curers usually belong to a medicine society. When a patient or his family request a cure, the members of the medicine society spend four days preparing the ceremonial rooms in which the curing will take place. During that time the curers, the patient, and the patient's close relatives observe sexual continence, and further purify themselves every morning by drinking a herb brew which causes vomiting. On the fourth day the healers prepare a sand painting, and toward evening the sufferer and his family are brought to the ceremonial enclosure. The ritual opens with chants and songs that invite the animal spirits which possess supernatural healing power to enter the room, and to settle upon their symbolic images represented in the sand painting. Next, the sacred medicine is prepared: six dippers of water—one for each of the six directions—are blended with herbs in a ceremonial bowl. The healers then go to the fireplace, rub ashes over their heads, and begin to look for the illness by feeling all over the patient's body. Whenever they find something, they suck it out, and the thorns, sticks, pebbles and rags thus produced are held up to the audience, and then deposited in a pottery bowl. Afterward, all participants drink some of the medicine, and the patient is brought home. His mother and other female relatives bring in food, and a communal meal closes the ritual.

Exorcism

When a spirit is believed to have entered a person and caused illness by its presence, healing procedures will naturally attempt to drive away the intruder. The evil spirit may be lured out by spells, bribery, coaxing; or he may be induced to leave by making the body of the patient a very unpleasant place of residence. Other attempts to flush out the evil power involve blood-letting, emetics, or purgatives.

Kapauku Papuan exorcistic rituals combine a number of these techniques. Evil spirits are associated with particular plants which are used in curing as a lure. The *ti* plant is considered particularly powerful. The curing shaman starts the procedure by invoking the Sun and Moon Creator, as well as the shaman's own guardian spirits. He then carries the plants around the patient, shaking them furiously, and touching the head and other parts of the patient's body with them. He also uses many spells, spits on and around the sick man, and splashes water over his body. Simultaneously, the spirits are bribed to leave the body by glowing embers, augmented by the sacrifice of small birds, rats, or the intestines of some larger animals. These offerings are later hung on a pole, or thrown behind the shaman into the bush. The ritual is often combined with sleight-of-hand removal of intruding evil objects. Sometimes the healer tries to recapture the soul on the end of a *ti* plant bundle, and he then returns it to the body to which it belongs. At the end of the ceremony, the healer prescribes some special procedures (often food taboos) to be carried out as a continuation of the cure (Pospisil, 1963: 80–81).

In some parts of Africa, disease-causing spirits are lured outside the body by music and dancing, in which they will want to participate. Once the spirit has joined in, it is coaxed by gifts, sacrifices, and songs, and asked to identify itself. When the spirit finally complies and reveals its name, its power is broken and it will be unable to re-enter the body. The healer draws a picture of its face, or makes a small clay image, which is subsequently thrown into the river or buried under a breadfruit tree (Dammann, 1963:113–15).

In India, certain "spirit repellents" are used both as remedies and as preventatives. The simplest one, a kind of household remedy, is made from a mixture of burned cow dung and urine, ritually prepared, and kept in the most sacred area of the house. A sufficient quantity will usually be made at one time to last a household for about five years (Harper, 1964:186). Attacks from spirits may also be prevented or repelled by wearing a small sheet of metal upon which sacred inscriptions have been drawn (*ibid.*:187). On Ceylon, exorcism typically takes the form of dancing, accompanied by the presentation of impure offerings (Ames, 1964:33).

A very spectacular method which possibly relates to exorcism is trephining, or trepanning. This form of skull surgery was practiced both in the Old World and in the New World in

Neolithic times. By means of a flint knife or a scraper, a circular —or, more rarely, a square—hole was made in the skull. While the alleviation of pressure on the brain caused by skull fracture was the most frequent reason for the operation in Peru and Melanesia, the evidence of skull fracture of trephined skulls in Europe is less frequent (T. D. Steward, 1957:481). Probably, then, the operation must have been undertaken for other reasons, and it is believed that the openings were sometimes made to let out harmful intruding spirits who had taken up residence in the head. When it is remembered that these operations were performed with stone tools, without anesthetics, and without sterilization, it is remarkable that they were often successful—or, in any case, that the patients survived. That not all operations were fatal is proven by the fact that many skulls show complete healing. Steward, examining 214 trephined skulls from Peru, noted that 55.6 per cent showed complete healing; 16.4 per cent, beginning healing; and 28 per cent, no healing (*ibid.*:486). The most remarkable of all is a skull from Cuzco, Peru, with no less than seven circular healed trephine openings. Moodie writes:

> I believe it to be correct to state that no primitive or ancient race of people anywhere had developed such a field of surgical knowledge as had the pre-Columbiam Peruvians. Their surgical attempts were truly amazing, and include amputations, excisions, trephining, bandaging, bone transplants, cauterizations, and other less evident procedures (1927:278).

Although the rate of healing in Neolithic Europe was nowhere as high as in Peru, Piggott says:

> The proportion of survivals from this operation ... is extremely high, as is evidenced by skulls showing the healthy growth of new bone around the edges of the opening; nor is it unusual for one skull to exhibit evidence of two or more openings all with healed edges (1940:122).

Further evidence of the supernatural implications of trephination lies in the discovery that the round pieces of bone cut from the skull were used as amulets. These "rondelles," as they are usually called, were highly polished and sometimes perforated so that they could be suspended and worn as pendants. Although the meaning of trephanation in Neolithic times is not clear, surviving medieval records indicate that such surgical measures were undertaken in cases of dementia and epilepsy, and these disorders were, in the Middle Ages, generally believed to arise from spirit possession.

Confession and Sacrifice

When illness is believed to be caused by human offense against supernatural powers, confession and sacrifice are usually integral parts of the healing ritual. Confession will also help the healer to diagnose the illness because it will indicate the nature of the offense, and thus suggest a cure. Sacrifice is directed toward the removal of divine wrath. It may be noted that such confessions are frequently public, and so is repentance and sacrifice. Recovery reflects divine forgiveness, and the cured individual can re-enter the community, redeemed and exonerated.

PREVENTION OF ILLNESS

Every society with a causal theory of disease will also subscribe to certain means of prevention. If witchcraft or sorcery is believed to be the major causes of illness, prevention may well consist of the attempt not to arouse anyone's anger or enmity. The fear of witchcraft and sorcery can, therefore, be a positive factor in that it may tend to foster harmony in interpersonal relationships. When illness is believed to arise from the anger of supernatural powers, prevention will take the form of endeavoring to remain on good terms with the gods and spirits. Because the rules of these relationships coincide with the value system of the group, this belief will contribute to upholding the norms of the society.

Prevention may also take more direct and more material forms. Items considered therapeutic are often also considered preventative. Carrying them around on the person, or keeping them in the house, will protect owner or household from illness or misfortune. Such protection may work either by attracting good supernatural powers, or by repelling evil ones. Those items attracting supernatural guardianship are usually called *charms* or *talismans*, while those that work defensively are called *amulets*. The differences between them are not always clear-cut.

It should be noted that prevention of illness is more rarely of a religious nature than healing is. By definition, prevention is the attempt to ward off something that has not yet occurred, and anticipatory measures are less urgent than those designed to resolve an actual emergency. Prevention, then, takes the form of superstition or of home medicine; it rarely involves ritual action or religious healers. Superstitious practices are based upon vaguely determined supernatural beliefs and are characterized by an absence of ritual. Home medicine is nonprofessional prevention or cure by means of remedies known to everyone in the society. The use of amulets among the Copper Eskimo appears to be superstitious rather than religious. Thus, the skin of a red-throated diver, a bird which hangs on to life quite tenaciously, gives health and long life when carried about on the person. Although supernatural powers are ascribed to this amulet, it is not sacred, nor is it ritually treated. One simply has to find it and wear it. Similarly, small snail shells are hung around the necks of dogs for their protection. But anyone can find these objects and use them in this manner. By contrast, the Ashanti make protective amulets out of their old household brooms—but the formerly secular objects are rendered protective by a ritual of transformation. This ritual can be performed only by a priest or medicine man, who reads spells and prayers over it and brings it into contact with many sacred objects. Even clearer is the case of the Pueblo Indians, who regularly feed their amulets with cornmeal in order to keep them sacred and powerful.

Of a clearly religious nature are the communal rituals sometimes held to purify a village, to drive away all evil spirits and witches, and to treat all sickness that may be found. Among the Sia, the head of political and religious organizations orders such a ritual for the entire pueblo toward the end of each winter. The major medicine societies participate, and the preparations are similar to those for the curing of individual patients. The pueblo leader, although usually in good health, plays the role of the patient. As the representative of the community, he is symbolically "cured" by the regular methods, including the sucking out of a large number of disease-causing objects (White, 1962:299).

A related concept is that of the scapegoat. A representative of a group, be it animal or human, symbolically gathers upon himself the accumulated ills and sins of the community, and is then expelled or sacrificed. Such communal rituals regularly include fasting, ablutions, extinguishing of fires and ritually rekindling, and similar symbolic actions which are believed to have a wholesome effect upon the whole community.

EFFECTIVENESS OF SUPERNATURAL HEALING

Can supernatural healing techniques really cure a person? Religious healers themselves would undoubtedly answer this question affirmatively, and back their statements by giving many examples of people who came to them for treatment and went away fully cured. How can we explain this in terms of Western medicine?

In the first place, it is well known that many illnesses cure themselves. Most people recover in spite of the treatment they receive, not because of it. Furthermore, almost every ritual treatment includes some prescriptions or practices of a nonsupernatural nature: administration of drugs and herbal medicines, massage, blood-letting, sweat baths, and similar cures not unrelated to those of Western medicine. Some are effective, others are probably therapeutically neutral or decidedly harmful.

Illness also often arises from the fear of becoming ill. It is not for us to decide if such disorders are organic or not; the important thing is that people actually feel ill and seek treatment. This phenomenon is by no means confined to nonliterate peoples and societies, as any Western doctor knows. In cultures in which illness is conceived of as divine punishment, a person who has committed a punishable act will expect illness, and his body may eventually react. In these situations, confession and subsequent forgiveness will have great effect. Even when no punishment was expected, a disorder may well be explained in this manner once it has occurred. To err is human—everyone sometimes breaks a taboo or neglects his ritual duties at one time or another. The subsequent explanation then is often fixed upon past shortcomings. Here, again, confession and expiation may have wholesome effects.

Illness caused by witchcraft or sorcery generally points to a break in interpersonal social relations, and in these instances the patient may remember with whom he has quarreled, or whom he has offended. The mending of these social relationships, often in a ritual manner, may have the desired physical results.

In a much-quoted article, Cannon described in physiological terms how fear may cause illness and eventually can result even in death (1942:169–81). Fear and rage, he states, have similar effects on the human organism, bringing the sympathetic nervous system into special action. Under normal circumstances, this system regulates the action of internal organs and blood vessels, but when the body is stimulated by great fear, the sympathetic nervous system accelerates the heart and other organs under its control. The blood vessels contract, the liver releases great quantities of blood sugar, and the adrenal glands send a large amount of adrenaline into the system. If this condition prevails over a period of time, the blood pressure may fall very low, and the patient dies. Persons thus knowing or fearing that they have been the victims of sorcery or supernatural punishment may well die from a true state of shock induced by prolonged and intense emotion.

Warner (1964:230–33) described how the social circumstances surrounding a victim of black magic among the Murngin in Australia help to explain its potency and unusual effectiveness. When the supposed theft of a man's soul becomes known, all his kinfolk withdraw their support so that his whole social life collapses. No longer a member of the group, he is already "half dead." His social isolation increases his fear, and his physical condition worsens. Meanwhile, the group moves with all complexities of its organization to emphasize the atmosphere of doom. The ceremonial leader and his followers, who specialize in rituals of death and mourning, gather around and force the sick man to participate in his own mortuary rites. He cannot refuse, for he would thereby endanger his future position in the totemic hierarchy in the sacred realm of the dead. Nothing is done, even by his closest relatives, to undo the evil magic; on the contrary, everyone seems bent on making it more effective. This most harmful form of sorcery is adopted only when a member of the group has acted in a flagrantly antisocial way—as, for instance, in the breaking of incest taboos. The group withdraws its support, ostensibly because the case is hopeless, but also because it subconsciously realizes that the punishment is socially just.

This makes it possible to understand how supernatural treatments may also cure. Psychologists have demonstrated the close interrelationship between physical illness and the patient's state of mind. Anything that can be done to alleviate his anxieties will have a wholesome effect upon the course of the illness. Thus when the tribal healer removes fear and creates faith, and the patient is sustained by the conviction of his relatives and his community, seemingly miraculous cures may be effected.

THE RELIGIOUS THERAPIST

Are religious healers frauds, or do they believe in their own powers? No other practices arouse so much suspicion in the Western mind as the shaman's "sucking out" or otherwise "removing" disease-causing objects from the bodies of their patients. Clearly, these practices are examples of sleight-of-hand. Some shamans have admitted this, but simultaneously they proudly enumerate the cases in which their methods brought positive results.

A number of earlier interpreters, notably Frazer, felt that shamans were deliberate deceivers. But Frazer never saw a shaman in action. Field workers such as Boas, Rivers, and Lowie have repeatedly vouched for the subjective honesty and sincerity of shamans they had interviewed. Even Lévy-Bruhl, the stout defender of prelogical mentality, wrote that the curer's intention was the expulsion of evil influence in his patients, and that the object he "removed" was a symbol of that influence. Norbeck finds it difficult to imagine that a medicine man could achieve lasting professional status on the basis of legerdemain alone (1961:116). Moreover, as Ackerknecht points out, the legerdemain itself is often common knowledge (1965:398). Dakota Indian shamans use the same stone in every therapeutic ritual, and it is unlikely that the patient and other onlookers would never realize this. Yet they continue to believe in its power, and in the power of the healer—because many people do benefit from such treatment.

It must be remembered that the shaman is a religious curer rather than a scientist. As such, he will claim that his healing powers come from the supernatural. He is a curer only because he has successfully learned how to contact the spirits, and he follows their directions.

Successful curers are often highly respected members of their society. Pospisil describes a Papuan shaman, whom he met during his field work, as a healthy middle-aged man, and prosperous, a superb speaker and performer who was credited with many cures (1963:80). In addition to his wealth, he held great political power, and was believed to possess twelve helping spirits as well as five souls. Many similar reports about powerful and wealthy shamans have come from other observers.

Medicine Societies

In small and relatively simple societies, the shaman is usually in charge of all religious activities. If there happen to be two or more shamans within the same community, they are likely to be competitors rather than cooperators.

In larger and more complex societies, ritual activities are often restricted to special "societies," each of which has its own area of specialization. Those specializing in the treatment of illness are called *medicine societies*. These medicine societies are sometimes further subdivided, with each member group specializing in a particular type of ailment. For example, the Sia have a Snake Society (whose members specialize in the cure of snake bite), a Fire Society (whose members treat burns), a Shima Society (whose members treat illness caused by ants), and at least six other medicine societies (White, 1962:140).

The members of such societies are not necessarily skilled healers, but often former patients who had been cured through the services of one of the societies. Membership in a medicine society is generally prestigious, and often restricted by economic factors, for entrance and initiation may be quite costly. Among the Zuni, membership is, in principle, compulsory after recovery, but initiation is so expensive that several years may pass before the former patient can afford it. Occasionally, membership claims are relinquished through the payment of a fixed sum of money to the society, after which the patient is "given back" to his family (Goode, 1951:78). Curing rituals are often equally expensive, and therefore carried out only in very serious cases after private cures and home remedies had failed.

Each medicine society possesses its own origin myth, which serves to validate its power and existence. Here is the myth of the Seneca Little Water Society, which specializes in the healing of wounds:

Once upon a time there was a fine young chief who not only was popular with his people, but was also a great hunter who always observed the necessary proprieties when killing animals. For this reason, when the young chief was sorely wounded and left for dead on the field of battle, his friends the animals (for they are the great medicine people) gathered around him. After a council, they agreed that a wonderful medicine should be made to cure their friend. All of the good animals helped in one way or another to brew this potion, some even giving up their lives so that their friend might live. As the young chief regained consciousness, he not only recognized his friends but also understood the charm song which the animals were singing, and this song they taught him, as well as the dance that went with it. But the young chief could not be told the various ingredients of the medicine, for he was married, and the secret could be given only to a virgin youth. Sometime after this, when the chief had returned to his people, an occasion for another war party arose. Before the conflict, the group heard a mysterious voice singing and the chief recognized this as the medicine song of the animals who saved him. So he sent a number of youths to find the singer and learn the secret of the medicine. They located the mysterious voice as coming from a magic corn stalk whose roots spread in four directions. After a ceremony, the youths were given the composition of the medicine and taught the song which makes the medicine strong and preserves it. This medicine was used when the raid was over, and was found to cure all wounds (Corlett, 1935:137–38).

DISEASE AND SOCIAL ORDER

Concepts of disease and therapeutic practices are interrelated with the social aspects of the cultures in which they appear. The supposed supernatural origin of many disorders and the fact that illness is always undesirable work together to foster the maintenance of the rules and values of a society, particularly because illness threatens every individual. Examination of the specific acts which are culturally believed to cause illness will afford important insights into the value system of the society.

In the Philippine community of Sibulan in the southern Bisayan islands, for example, the religious system includes a belief in *ingkantos*, spirits which can attain human form (Lieban, 1962: 306–12). Encounters with such beings are dangerous, as the following case shows: A young man met a beautiful girl who was really an *ingkanto*. She was wearing a shiny dress that looked as if it were made of gold, and a gold wristwatch much superior to his own. The girl offered to trade watches, but when he refused she disappeared. Later, the young man fell seriously ill. He was treated by the local healer, and only gradually recovered his strength (*ibid.:*308). In similar reported instances, sexual motifs were often expressed in relationships which people have with *ingkantos*, but these motifs are usually associated with economic factors. The enticing maidens are not only physically attractive but very rich; they live in luxurious palaces and own watches, automobiles, and other luxury items. *Ingkantos* tempt people with wealth and with power—but encounters with them, even when the attractive items are refused, are inevitably followed by illness.

The relationship between certain forms of illness and social control in Sibulan rests in the fact that the *ingkantos* offer a power and a wealth inaccessible to members of the community. These temptations are considered dangerous, and lead to illness or death. The belief in *ingkantos* supports the social equilibrium by dramatizing and reinforcing the danger of coveting wealth and power unattainable within the community as well as the value of accepting the limitations of life in the barrio.

The belief stresses the danger of foreign influences in Sibulan and reflects the actual experiences of those members of the community who have gone to Manila or other cities to find work. Attracted by the idea of money and what can be bought with it, most migrants return home disappointed and disenchanted. Wealth is difficult to come by, and the cities offer less security, less personal contact than Sibulan. Illness attributed to *ingkantos* will help to reconcile the individual to social reality by demonstrating that it is a mistake to overindulge in personal desires.

Another example comes from a study of the Fiji Islands (Spencer, 1941). The relationships between illness and social aspects of Fijian life are revealed by the fact that in many cases illness is believed to result from failure to fulfill one's obligations to his fellow men. Fiji society is organized in exogamous, patrilineal clans; the members of each clan consider themselves related by common descent from one supernatural ancestor. The founding ancestor spirits also set down the rules of marriage: clan exogamy, and the right of the girl's male relatives to choose her mate. Once the decision is made, the relatives of the prospective groom carry out betrothal ceremonies, which are considered binding. Should the girl refuse to abide by this contract, she would not only be insulting the groom but causing a real economic loss for his clansmen, for they have presented betrothal gifts to the members of the girl's clan and received none in return, and these gifts are not given back if the girl refuses her consent to the match. At one time, such a situation frequently led to warfare between the clans, but now girls are generally restrained from upsetting the social balance by the threat of illness. One girl who refused a man after the betrothal ceremony and later married a man of a different clan was soon afflicted with a serious disease (*ibid.:*29). The social rules are believed to be divinely instituted, and any transgression is supernaturally punished.

CONCLUSION

Although most of the examples given in this chapter illustrate the positive effects of supernaturally based healing practices, it cannot be denied that they may have harmful effects as well. Clements, writing about concepts of disease in nonliterate societies, gives some gruesome examples of very sick people treated by bleeding, violent rubbing, beating, or shaking, mostly for reasons of exorcism (1932). The majority of such examples come from older sources, from a period thus when ethnographers were more interested in demonstrating the shortcomings of nonliterate peoples. The truth lies in the middle, for curing systems in nonliterate societies are neither completely beneficial nor totally destructive. The same may also be said about more scientific methods of therapy.

11

Witchcraft and Sorcery

WITCHCRAFT AND SORCERY GENERALLY REFER TO MALIGN ACTIVITIES attributed to human beings who use supernatural powers to harm others. To modern eyes, these are perhaps the most illogical and despised practices involving the supernatural. Their persistence in many societies seems to contradict the functionalist's conviction that "no cultural forms survive unless they constitute responses that are adjustive or adaptive, in some sense, for the members of the society or for the society" (Kluckhohn, 1967:79). This discussion will examine some of the social concomitants of witchcraft and sorcery, and will show that, in all known instances, they possess at least some positive features.

SIMILARITIES
AND DIFFERENCES

Witches and sorcerers represent sources of danger recognized by other members of the society. Some societies have only one category of harmful magic; others have many more. The translation of native terminology is attended by the difficulties adhering to all other attempts to render foreign concepts into English. In older ethnographic writings, the terms *sorcery* and *witchcraft* are used interchangeably to refer to any act of harmful magic. It was found, however, that many peoples made a conceptual and linguistic distinction between the two. According to Evans-Pritchard,

. . . [The Azande] believe that some people are witches and can injure others in virtue of an inherent quality. A witch performs no rite, utters no spell, and possesses no medicines. An act of witchcraft is a psychic act. They believe also that sorcerers may do them ill by performing magic rites with bad medicines (1937:21).

A similar distinction is made by the Barotse of Northern Rhodesia (Reynolds, 1963:14), by the Lunda-Luvale of South Africa (C. M. N. White, 1948:83), by the Cebuanos of the Philippines (Lieban, 1967:65–66), and many others. This distinction has guided modern anthropological investigations of harmful magic.

WITCHCRAFT

In its most typical form, witchcraft implies the ability to injure others. A witch usually acquires his power through an inherent physical factor or through the power of another witch.

The first idea is particularly widespread in Africa. The Azande, for instance, believe that a witch possesses a special organ called *mangu,* located somewhere behind the sternum or attached to the liver. It is oval, and variously described as reddish, blackish, or hairy (Evans-Pritchard, 1937:21–22). This condition is hereditary; according to the Azande, sons inherit *mangu* from their fathers, while mothers transmit it to their daughters.

One may also become a witch through the influence of, or contact with, another witch. Lieban describes several such instances among the Cebuanos (1967:72–75). A girl encountered an older man who was known as a powerful witch. He asked her who she was, and after she had identified her parents the old man said: "So Pedro has a big child and a beautiful one." These seemingly innocent words made her feel ill; when she recovered, she possessed the power of witchcraft.

When it is culturally accepted that one usually becomes a witch involuntarily, the individuals so designated may be viewed with some degree of pity and tolerance by others. These witches do not intend to do harm; they are as much the victims of witchcraft as those upon whom they practice it. The Cebuano girl just mentioned found out that she was a witch only several months after her encounter with the old man. She became very careful in her dealings with people, and although her status in the community was a delicate one, she stressed her good relations with her neighbors and emphasized that she had no grievances against those whom she involuntarily bewitched (*ibid.*:74–75). Even when witches are quite malevolent, their desires to kill or to cause illness may be thought to be beyond their own control, as appears to be the case among the Barotse (Reynolds, 1963:16).

The belief in witchcraft is perhaps basically an explanatory device, fixing the causes of illness, death, and misfortune experienced by a person or a group when no other explanations can be found. Witchcraft beliefs among the Azande provide them with a kind of natural philosophy that ultimately explains all unfortunate events. This belief does not replace concepts of natural causation. When an old granary collapsed, everyone knew that termites had undermined its wooden supports. But some people happened to be sitting under that granary when it fell down, and they were hurt. This could only be explained by witchcraft, for why else would these particular people be sitting there at that precise moment? A boy knocked his foot against a stump of wood, and received a cut. The cut itself was naturally caused, but a witch was believed to have placed the woodstump in his way. When the wound began to fester, it was further proof of witchcraft, for most cuts heal rather quickly (Evans-Pritchard, 1937:63–83).

Although witches are not always to be blamed for their actions, they are nevertheless considered to be real sources of danger. If witches persistently create injury and calamity, they must be punished—usually by death, sometimes by exile. No other method can effectively rid the society of the disturbing factor, for imprisonment would not restrain the witch's power, and any other punishment sparing their lives would make them more vindictive than before.

When calamities attributed to witchcraft have befallen people, the obvious first step is to identify the witch. This is often done by divination, which sometimes takes the form of ordeals. Confessions of guilt are usually obtained. These confessions are sometimes genuine: the confessed witch may well believe that his thought-processes have the power to harm others. Most human beings will, at one time or another, wish bad luck on another; if something bad subsequently befalls that person, the ill-wisher may well become convinced that he is responsible. Undoubtedly there are some instances in which the self-confessed witch is neurotic and obsessed with guilt feelings (Field, 1960). Witches may also be forced into admission of guilt by torture, fear, or the hope for lighter punishment, as Honigmann has shown (1947: 222–43).

Many societies, although they ostensibly wish to do away with witches, simultaneously possess some beliefs that serve as protective mechanisms for the suspects. It may be thought, for instance, that witches cannot be killed by human beings, and must await supernatural punishment. Or, it may be believed that the witch alone can undo the harm he has perpetrated, so that killing him would preclude all possibility of the victims' recovery.

Although the techniques of witchcraft vary from culture to culture, there are some remarkably persistent common features that cannot be explained by diffusion. Most witches work by night, are capable of covering long distances very rapidly, and have the ability to fly. During these wanderings, the body of the witch usually remains behind, but its other self travels invisibly, or temporarily assumes an animal form. Witches are generally thought to be very fond of eating human flesh. They make their victims ill, and wait for them to die in order to consume their bodies after burial. For this reason, they often gather at cemeteries. They also consort with demons, meeting at night in a sort of coven. The Navaho believe that the witches' coven is socially structured: there are higher and lower witches, head witches, and workers.

SORCERY

Sorcery differs from witchcraft in that its methods are not psychic but real. A sorcerer is someone who intentionally tries to harm his enemies, or who uses his powers on behalf of others upon their request and for a fee. A sorcerer's trade is learned. He may use words, gestures, spells, rites, formulae, objects, or various concoctions to achieve his ends.

On the one hand, sorcerers are socially more contemptible than witches, for they deliberately cause others to suffer. On the other hand, witchcraft is always antisocial and illegitimate, while sorcery need not be. Sorcerers may be consulted and asked to harm those who need punishment. Their services are particularly necessary to those afflicted by sorcery or witchcraft. A sorcerer is therefore often a healer as well.

The actions of witches are usually fairly random. They may attack their own kinsmen or strangers, their friends or their enemies. Sorcerers act because they or their clients are provoked —they are angry, insulted, or envious of someone else's success. Belief in sorcery is therefore more persistently associated with social conflict. Societies which count both witches and sorcerers among their members may take stronger measures against the former although feeling greater hostility against the latter. The witch may be tolerated as long as he attempts to control his powers to do evil, but the sorcerer will be maintained as long as he is considered to have some useful function. Not all scholars have found it useful to distinguish between witchcraft and sorcery, and in some cultures, the two practices merge.

THE USE OF WITCHCRAFT AND SORCERY

The Melanesian Dobu

The Dobu have acquired a certain notoriety because of their practice of witchcraft and sorcery. Benedict calls the Dobu "lawless and treacherous," and adds that they are living out "man's worst nightmares of the ill will of the universe" (1946:121,159). Benedict never visited these islands; her descriptions are based upon those of Fortune, who stayed six months among the Dobu (1932, reprinted 1963). Although his language is more sober and restrained than Benedict's, he notes that the suspicion of witchcraft and sorcery runs so high that the men of Dobu feel safer in the neighboring Trobriand Islands, among a people whose language they do not speak, than they do in their own homes (1963: 151). Nevertheless, Fortune clearly shows that positive functions of sorcery and witchcraft exist side by side with disruptive ones.

Dobuan distinctions between witchcraft and sorcery differ from those made by the Azande: sorcery is considered the prerogative of men; witchcraft, that of women. Men have the monopoly of causing sickness by casting spells on the personal leavings of intended victims: scraps of food, excreta, footprints, or body dirt. Women also have disease-causing or lethal powers, but they do their work in spirit form by night, while their bodies sleep. The women are not unconscious of their powers, and their witchcraft is a voluntary act; in order to send their souls on a nightly mission of evil, they cast spells while fully awake (*ibid.:* 150–51).

Every individual, male or female, is believed by the Dobu to have the ability to harm others by supernatural means. The Dobu have no concept of accident; misfortune, illness, and death are always attributed to witchcraft or sorcery (*ibid.:*150). Successful gardeners are accused of sorcery—they are believed to have stolen, by supernatural means, the yams from the fields of those who have a less plentiful crop.

Individual supernatural powers are jealously guarded and passed on along matrilineal lines. Because the matrilineage is exogamous, husbands and wives each have different spells, and a man does not know the secret powers of his own wife, nor does she know his. Even within the nuclear family, competition and mutual suspicion are the rule.

The Dobu are matrilineal and bilocal—married couples live for alternate years in the husband's village and the wife's. Each year one of the partners is a tolerated alien, suspected of sorcery, and in turn suspicious of the villagers. The divorce rate is exceedingly high, for Dobuan husbands and wives cannot trust one another (*ibid.:*155).

The descriptions of Dobuan antagonisms, expressed by belief in witchcraft and sorcery, are such that some anthropologists have doubted their accuracy. The whole social structure appears to be geared toward conflict rather than unity. In any society people must cooperate in order to survive, but the Dobu appear to thrive on discord. Had Fortune misunderstood the Dobu? He lived on the island only six months, did not speak the native language when he arrived, and did not gain the natives' confidence until after six weeks had passed. Chowning, who has worked on the neighboring islands, feels that Fortune's accounts are not exaggerated (1964:455–57). Apart from this ethnographic evidence, Fortune's own functional analysis demonstrates why the seemingly disruptive beliefs persist among the Dobu: witch-craft and sorcery take the place of legal systems, enforcing, among other things, economic obligations.

Alo's second wife of the Brown Eagle village died. Alo per-formed the mourning observances for a year, and shortly after his mourning was done and he returned to his own Green Parrot village, he fell seriously ill.

Bwai of the place Bwaioa, two days' journey away, was summoned, as diviner. Bwai duly performed the water-gazing divinatory rite, and saw at the bottom of the wooden dish Alo's recently deceased wife's mother. He pointed out that Alo had failed to give her her due of bananas (in an obliga-tory gift to his mother-in-law incumbent on the widower a year after the death of his wife). Bwai had probably made discreet inquiries before doing his divining, as the sequel proved. A summons went out to the Brown Eagle people. They filed past Alo one by one, each protesting innocence. When Alo's late wife's mother came, she was given no time to protest. Bwai accused her of witchcraft from the evidence of his water-divining, and asked her if Alo had not a bad debt with her which he had been obdurate in paying. She admitted that Alo had declined to pay her her just due, and she admitted anger and witchcraft against him. She assured Alo that he would not die, at least by her witch-craft, if the bananas were paid her at once. She would restore his spirit to him the moment the bananas were received by her. He would not die while she lived. But if she herself died, he would also be likely to die at the same time (with a veiled threat and a shrewd warning against his under-taking future sorcery reprisals against her) (Fortune, 1963: 156).

As long as witchcraft and sorcery have at least some important positive functions, they constitute adaptive responses. The Dobu have not been studied again recently, but it may be predicted that when the legal or other positive functions of witchcraft and sorcery become institutionalized in different ways, the beliefs in these powers will lose their efficacy, and will either alter or decline.

Azande

Among the Azande, the belief in witchcraft functions to explain the intersection of two events—the collapse of a building, and the fact that it fell on certain people and hurt them. The second important way in which the belief in witchcraft functions among the Azande is that it aids to uphold the moral codes of their society. The Azande, like all other peoples, distinguish between good and bad behavior. When they say that a certain action is bad, they mean that it is socially deplorable and condemned by public opinion, but it is also deplorable because it may lead to witchcraft. Jealousy and adultery are socially disapproved not only for their own sake, but because a person may be tempted to carry out witchcraft or sorcery to attain his ends. An adulterer may carry out sorcery on his wife in order to have more freedom; a jealous man may attempt to victimize the objects of his suspicion. It is significant that belief in witchcraft and sorcery works most strongly in those instances which are beyond the control of Azande secular laws. This is also the case among the Dobu, and the beliefs thus work primarily as law-enforcing mechanisms in cases where civic laws have no jurisdiction.

The Navaho

The Navaho afford an example of a society in which many different categories of harmful supernatural powers are recognized. Kluckhohn, struggling with the problem of translating Navaho terms into English, glossed the four main categories as witchery, sorcery, wizardry, and frenzy witchcraft (1967:22).

Witchery supposedly makes use of evil substances to harm others. These are said to contain the skin and ground-up bones of human corpses. The "corpse poison," ground into powder, looks like pollen, and may be thrown into houses of enemies, buried in fields, or surreptitiously placed on the victim. Illness, often fatal, is inevitable.

Sorcery employs contagious magic. A sorcerer does not need to have direct contact with his victims; he must only obtain something that has been in contact with the victim—hair, nail parings, urine, or a bit of clothing. These are rubbed together with human flesh or with "corpse poison," and buried in or near a grave. Spells or songs are then recited over the spot. Sorcery is carried out against animals and crops, as well as against persons (*ibid.*:31–33).

Wizardry supernaturally shoots poison into the victim's body, always from a distance. Bits of bone or teeth from a corpse are favored materials, but slivers of glass or poisonous beans may do the trick as well. Frenzy witchcraft involves the use of a narcotic plant, and is primarily employed for love magic, or to acquire success in gambling or trading (*ibid.*:36).

The various methods result in illness which resists all regular treatment. Fainting, seizures, sudden onset of pain, bumps in a localized area of the body are warning signals. Conversely, when an illness appears to be incurable, or if death occurs, witchcraft is usually believed to be the cause, although disease may also result from the violation of taboos.

Witchcraft is to the Navaho one of the most repulsive of crimes. Only incest can vie with it for disapprobation. The beliefs in witchcraft play important roles in social and individual life. Nearly every household has antiwitchcraft medicine on hand, and many charms and spells are known. When Kluckhohn asked about the most effective counter-methods, good songs and prayers and stories were most often mentioned. Divination, or community agreement that a certain person acted in highly suspicious ways, lead to specific accusations. The accused is publicly questioned, sometimes also tortured, until he confesses. Confession is said to have a twofold effect—the victim will recover, and the poison used by the witch or sorcerer will be turned back on him so that he will die within a year. The stigma of accusation is so strong that confessed witches often leave the community and live in exile.

Kluckhohn offers an extensive analysis of the functions of witchcraft and sorcery among the Navaho (Kluckhohn, 1967; Kluckhohn and Leighton, 1962). He is not unaware of their dysfunctional aspects; they increase fear, give rise to occasional violence, and subject guiltless individuals to accusation. But these beliefs have many more positive functions than negative ones, both in the realm of social control and on the psychological level.

In the social sphere, the beliefs help to maintain a system of checks and balances and tend to counteract socially disruptive forces. Social balance is strengthened because witchcraft and

sorcery act as economic levelers. Rich people are generally suspected to have acquired their wealth by secret supernatural techniques. Gossip about them can only be quelled by generosity.
Wealthy Navaho are therefore under social pressure to be liberal
in giving gifts to needy relatives and neighbors, and to sponsor
expensive curing ceremonies for ailing family members. Stingi-
ness and avarice are definite signs of involvement in witchcraft.
These beliefs thus work to lessen economic differences and
prevent the wealthy Navaho from attaining too much power. In
this manner, the belief in witchcraft helps to maintain the coherence of Navaho social life and to preserve its continuity
(Kluckhohn and Leighton, 1962:247).

Witchcraft beliefs also assist in enforcing social cooperation. It
is thought by the Navaho that old people will turn into witches
if they are not well cared for. The death of close relatives, particularly that of siblings, carries with it the possible suspicion
that a survivor is learning witchcraft. The effectiveness of leaders
is sometimes increased by the fear that they are witches and
may use their supernatural powers against the disobedient. Even
the fear of going about at night has social value, for sexual
jealousy is one of the main sources of friction among the Navaho.
Nocturnal fear of witches may help to deter extramarital relations (Kluckhohn, 1967:113). In general, the fear of being accused
of witchcraft helps to check those individuals who might disrupt
the smooth functioning of society.

In the psychological sphere, the belief in witchcraft and sorcery supplies many outlets for hostile impulses. Harmony in
human relationships is a highly desired goal, but the Navaho,
like anyone else, sometimes feels frustrated by his relatives, his
neighbors, or life. By projecting his anger onto witches rather
than onto relatives, the hostile impulses are directed into oblique
channels where they are less disruptive socially. Significantly,
witchcraft accusations are frequently directed to distant witches,
less often to members of the community. Witches thus serve as
scapegoats, and the displaced aggression is not punished as open
hostility against close relatives or in-laws would be.

Furthermore, beliefs and practices related to witchcraft provide
a means of defining anxiety in a socially understandable manner
which will usually evoke responses from others. Many of the
individuals who suddenly show symptoms of illness supposedly

caused by witchcraft are those who are somewhat neglected or of a low social status. These attacks, moreover, often happen to occur at large gatherings (Kluckhohn, 1967:83–84). The curing ceremonies focus attention on the victims, and affirm to them that they are supported by the members of their group, particularly by their relatives.

These and other functions indicate that the belief in witchcraft and sorcery serves an important purpose in Navaho society. Kluckhohn's analysis is strengthened by the observation that suspicions of witchcraft, and actual trials of accused witches, increase in times of social upheaval and disequilibrium. This was the case in the period following the Navaho's imprisonment in Fort Sumner, and again in more recent years, after the government lifestock reduction program began to affect the Navaho. Apart from the fact that many suspected witches were killed during that time, there were several attempts to bewitch government officials concerned with stock reduction (Kluckhohn, 1967:114–15).

The Paiute

The interpretations discussed so far demonstrated the contributions that witchcraft and sorcery may make to the maintenance of a society. Other investigators have attempted to discover specific correlations between witchcraft and sorcery and other social institutions. B. Whiting undertook a cross-cultural analysis in order to ascertain whether such correlations are regular and, therefore, predictable (1950). She had done field work among the Paiute, and used them as her type case. The Paiute, according to her descriptions, do not distinguish between witchcraft and sorcery. A Paiute who possesses supernatural power to harm others can do so by thinking evil thoughts, by using contagious magic, or by dreaming. Whiting elects to call all such practices *sorcery*.

Among the Paiute, sorcery is used almost exclusively to cause illness or death. Although other causes of illness are also recognized, those supposedly resulting from sorcery are the most dreaded. Accusations of sorcery are equally perilous. Individuals who tried to deviate from socially approved norms are apt to be accused of being sorcerers; if convicted, they are persecuted or killed. The belief in sorcery functions, therefore, as a regulatory mechanism, because the fear of accusation motivates the Paiute to adhere to regular patterns of behavior. Whiting feels that the social controls resulting from belief in sorcery are particularly important in Paiute society because there is no centralized government, no political power and authority to settle disputes and punish offenses. These functions are, in part, taken over by the extended family, which avenges wrongs done to its members, often through direct violence. Whiting calls this form of social control *coordinate control,* as distinguished from the *superordinate control* of a political authority *(ibid.:82).*

In Paiute society, sorcery and coordinate control appear to be functionally related. According to Whiting's hypothesis, the two should occur together in other societies, too. An analysis of fifty societies, based on data from the Cross-Cultural Survey Files, showed that twenty-five had coordinate control and twenty-five had superordinate control. All but two practiced sorcery in one way or another. Next, Whiting considered the relative importance of sorcery, because it played a much greater role in some societies than in others. She defined sorcery as important when it was culturally conceived as a source of illness. Now correlations were sought between the importance or unimportance of sorcery as an explanation of illness and the absence or presence of coordinate control. The result was as follows *(ibid.:85):*

	Coordinate Control	Superordinate Control
Important sorcery	24 societies	11 societies
Unimportant sorcery	1 society	14 societies

Of the fifty societies examined, 48 per cent showed the expected correlations between disease-causing sorcery and absence of central government. But a significant number, 22 per cent, had important sorcery and a central government. The correlations were by no means conclusive. Narrowing down the criteria still further, Whiting made a distinction between control and punishment, and investigated a possible correlation between the importance of sorcery and the absence of superordinate *punishment.* The findings are *(ibid.:87):*

	Absence of Superordinate Punishment	Presence of Superordinate Punishment
Important sorcery	30 societies	5 societies
Unimportant sorcery	3 societies	12 societies

Although this correlation is more positive than previous ones, the original hypothesis has been significantly modified. It is clear, however, that there is a significant correlation between the belief in illness-producing sorcery and the absence of superordinate punishment. In Whiting's own words: "In the selected sample there is less than one chance in a hundred that the correlation between sorcery as an important explanation for sickness and coordinate control is due to chance" (*ibid.*:86–87).

Several criticisms have been leveled against Whiting's methods and findings. Pilling, for one, feels that Whiting had inadequate command of the data (1962:1057–59). He believes that several societies which were counted as having no superordinate justice, in fact, did. But the problems adhering to statistical analysis of anthropological data go beyond errors of counting. The major difficulty is that the diagnostic features are, by necessity, taken out of their total cultural context and treated as equivalents when, in fact, they have different connotations and denotations. It appears true enough that the connection between sorcery or witchcraft and social control is generally important. Swanson, for example, found statistical evidence that the presence of beliefs and practices of this nature generally suggests a lack of legitimate means of social control (1964:146). However, it does not follow that witchcraft and sorcery will be absent in those societies which do have adequate secular means of superordinate punishment. Sorcery and witchcraft may be maintained to bolster secular control, or to serve important functions of a different social or psychological nature.

The Nupe and the Gwari
Several other investigators employed the comparative method on a much more modest scale. Nadel, for one, examined four African communities with which he was intimately acquainted through field work (1952). The small-scale results have less

predictive value, but are much more realistic. The variables are better known, and their meanings and roles can be evaluated within the societies under consideration.

The Nupe and the Gwari, two of the communities studied, have many similarities. Living in the same physical environment, their subsistence patterns, social organization, marriage rules, and religious systems also show great affinities. Both believe in the existence of witches who cause illness and death by eating the souls of their victims. But among the Gwari, witches can be either male or female, while among the Nupe they are always women. Nupe witches are sometimes assisted by men in carrying out their evil purposes, but only under specific circumstances and the men are not censored for their roles in witchcraft.

Because the tribes are similar in many respects, Nadel searches for other differences which might account for the difference in the sex of witches. Interpersonal relationships between the sexes offers itself as a fruitful area of investigation. Wife-husband relationships among the Gwari were relatively tension free, but Nupe marriage is full of stress. Nupe men are frustrated by the behavior of their women because the latter have become traders, and have thereby acquired a greater measure of independence. Women threaten to usurp the male's leadership of the family. Moreover, the market activities give the women many opportunities to be unfaithful toward their husbands. The identification of witches with women thus appears to be related to the tension between the sexes, more specifically to the frustration of men by the behavior of women. Nadel describes the Nupe conception of a witch:

> She is the enemy of man and male authority; she seeks to dominate men; her evilness is somehow bound up with the married state and occasionally old age, that is, age beyond child-bearing, and her evilness is often directed against a husband and kin (1954:174).

The Korongo and the Mesakin

Honigmann generalized these observations, stating that witchcraft accusations are leveled against people whose behavior generates frustration (1959:78). His own examples come from comparison between the Korongo and the Mesakin, two neighboring communities in East Africa that display many similarities. The Korongo, however, have no witchcraft beliefs, while the Mesakin live in constant fear of witches. The accusations are usually directed toward relatives, and most often occur between mother's brother and sister's son. The relationship between these relatives is frustrating because it is connected to the socially standardized concept of aging. Neither the Korongo nor the Mesakin like the idea of old age, but the Korongo accept it as inevitable, while the Mesakin regard aging as much more frustrating. Among the Mesakin, old men are assigned to carry out many unpleasant ceremonial duties. In both communities men inherit from their mother's brothers. Demands that the inheritance be paid represents a sign that the owner of the property is growing old. These demands are highly resented, because they involve the relinquishment of power and property, a recognition of aging, and the assignment of onerous new duties. Older people try to hold on to their property as long as they can: this, in turn, frustrates the sister's son, who wants the property. The two men will seek an outlet for their frustration in mutual accusations of witchcraft (*ibid.*:79–80).

The Cebuano

The Cebuano distinguish between witchcraft and sorcery. A witch in this society does not necessarily have evil intentions, and the belief in witchcraft does not bear a strong relationship to social conflict. Rather, a witch is "a carrier of the blight of envy" (Lieban, 1967:79). Anxiety about envy is characteristic of Cebuano society. Sorcery, on the other hand, is pre-eminently associated with social conflict. In rural areas, twelve of twenty-two sorcery cases involved disputes over land ownership. In Cebu City, twenty-one of thirty-four sorcery cases revolved around difficulties with courtship and marriage (*ibid.*:132). In the latter instance, recourse to sorcery occurred more often among women than among men, and it is convincingly shown that these patterns are consistent with the double standard of control among the Cebuano. Although women are expected to be virtuous and stable, men are not subject to the same pressures, and the laws deal less stringently with the infidelity of husbands than with that of wives. For the Cebuano wife with an errant husband legal action is not feasible, for a courtsuit involves scandal and expense, and infidelity is difficult to prove (*ibid.*:133–36).

Of particular interest is Lieban's observation that sorcery is not necessarily more frequent in rural areas than in the city. The highest incidence of these practices is found in communities that are in a state of transition and have not yet found a new equilibrium (*ibid.*:150).

WITCHCRAFT IN LITERATE SOCIETIES

Belief in witchcraft and sorcery is by no means confined to nonliterate peoples. The ancient Greeks acknowledged a special goddess of witchcraft, Hecate. Although she had other functions as well, her popularity testifies to the fact that the practice of witchcraft, or the belief in it, was not uncommon (Nilsson, 1961: 91). Greek writers give further evidence that this was so. Plato proposed punishment for those "who can do injury by sorcery, incarnations, and magic knots; for those who place waxen images at people's doors, or at places where three roads meet, or on the sepulchers of their parents" (*Laws* XI:993). He suggests that officially recognized religious specialists (prophets and diviners) who try to harm people by supernatural means should be put to death, while witches should be brought before a court, which would decide "what witches ought to pay or suffer."

Western history provides excellent documentation of the belief in witchcraft in literate society. Such beliefs attended the development of Christianity from its inception. Saint Justin, in the second century A.D., explained that witches were the offspring of evil angels who had come down to earth and had had sinful intercourse with women. Saint Augustine (354–430) in *The City of God*, condemned "those human creatures whom we call witches, who are bound to the observations of false filthy devils instead of angels." Nearly every important writer of the early Middle Ages has something to say about witchcraft. The earliest known document dealing with the illegality of witchcraft dates from the eighth century. Known as *The Law of the Northumbrian Priests*, it reads, in part: "If then anyone be found that shall henceforth practice any heathenship . . . or in any way love witchcraft . . . let him pay ten half-marks; half to Christ, half to the King." Records of actual witch trials, however, are not available until the fourteenth century.

Before that time, the Church had taken the official position that witches did not exist. But the famous bull of Pope Innocent VII (*Summis desiderantes affectibus,* December 1484) showed clearly that the Church had changed its position, and that the belief in witches was quite prevalent:

> It has come to our ears that members of both sexes do not avoid to have intercourse with demons, incubi and succubi, and that by their sorceries, and by their incantations, charms, and conjurations, they suffocate, extinguish, and cause to perish the births of women, the increase of animals, the grain of the earth, the grapes of the vineyard, and the fruit of the trees, as well as men, women, flocks, herds, and other various kinds of animals, vines, and apple trees, grass, corn, and other fruits of the earth; making that men and women, flocks and herds suffer both from within and without . . . over and above this they renounce the Faith which is theirs by the Sacrament of Baptism, and at the instigation of the Enemy of Mankind do not shrink from committing and perpetrating the foulest abominations and the filthiest excesses . . ." (quoted in Davies, 1947:5)

It has often been said that this bull marked the beginning of the persecutions of witches in Europe. This may be so—but Innocent VIII was certainly not the first Pope to denounce the evil practices. Numerous other bulls, dealing with witchcraft in no uncertain terms, were published before 1484—the first of them, by Pope Alexander IV in 1258.

Nevertheless, Innocent VIII is important in the history of European witchcraft, because he appointed Henry Kramer and James Sprenger to write an exhaustive report on the subject. Both men were erudite scholars, professors of theology at the University of Cologne, distinguished and undoubtedly sincere ecclesiastics. They set themselves to their task with great energy. The result of their labors was published in Rome and in Cologne in 1489 under the title *Malleus Maleficarum* ("Hammer of Witches").

One of the most terrifying documents in existence, it defies all concepts of human dignity, human rights, and human justice. Through meticulous scholarship, the examination of many ancient and contemporary sources, and the support of quotations from the Bible and the Church Fathers, the authors "conclusively proved" that witches exist and must die. Accused witches were allowed virtually no defense, for their guilt was presumed *a priori* and torture was advocated as a means of extracting their confessions. The book suggested numerous ways in which to confuse and trap the suspect. In the words of one commentator, it was "a complete guide, theoretical as well as practical, for the discovery, examination, torture, trial, and execution of witches" (Davies, 1947:6).

In the years following its publication, thousands of suspect people were tortured, tried, and executed. The Inquisition, originally established to deal with heresy, was later charged to turn its attention to witches as well. Local bishops and priests and secular authorities were also permitted to pronounce judgments and to order execution. Although the Reformation arose, in part, as a protest against the Inquisition, many Protestants continued the witch hunts with zeal and conviction. Luther was never personally involved in witch trials, but he stated nevertheless: "I would have no pity on them, I would burn them all." Calvin furnished testimony against accused witches in his native city, Geneva. King James I of England, under whose reign the King James Version of the Bible was produced, wrote a case book on witchcraft, *Daemonologie* (published in 1597, six years before he ascended the Throne). In the first Bill of his first Parliament, King James introduced legislation against witches far more severe than had existed in England before—witchcraft became punishable by death on first conviction. In 1647, witch hunting spread to New England, and culminated in the Salem witch trials of 1692. In the seventeenth century the persecution of witches declined. Holland abolished it in 1610; Geneva, in 1632; England, in 1682. The last known burning was in Scotland, in 1722. Unofficial ordeals continued much longer, and as late as 1768 John Wesley, founder of Methodism, proclaimed that "the giving up of witchcraft is in effect the giving up of the Bible." (Presumably, he meant the giving up of the persecution of witches.)

Anthropologists have only rarely applied their methods to the analysis of witchcraft in Europe and in the United States. When they have done so, they have found certain functional parallels between Western and non-Western forms of witchcraft. Bohannan explains the logic and function of witchcraft beliefs in Geneva in much the same way as Evans-Pritchard did for the Azande (1963:340–50). At the time of the Geneva trials, this city was besieged by epidemics of disease and pestilence. Because there was no scientific knowledge of the causes of these outbreaks, they were attributed to witchcraft. The confessions of the accused confirmed these beliefs. On January 22, 1545, one Bernard Dallinges of Geneva confessed to having joined with other people in a plot to put ointment on the foot of a man who had been hanged, and then to smear this powerful unguent on the doors of houses in the city for the express purpose of spreading the plague. The plague actually spread through the power of Satan, but Satan needed human agents to do his work (Bohannan, 1963: 348).

CONCLUSION

Although many aspects of the witchhunts in Western history have remained unexplained, it may be posited that some of their functions overlap with those of similar activities found elsewhere. Witchcraft and sorcery have many cultural dimensions. They may contribute to social continuity by pointing out socially disapproved actions; they may express and strengthen group affiliations by accusing outsiders; and they affirm cultural values and norms by working against certain types of social deviants.

Witchcraft and sorcery also have psychological dimensions, for they provide outlets for aggression, anxiety, and hostility. Witchcraft and sorcery arise as a symbolic means of handling otherwise unresolvable situations.

These functions explain, in part, the persistence of witchcraft and sorcery in many cultures. They also explain why witchcraft practices tend to increase in times of social stress and tension.

12

Functions of Religion

RELIGION CANNOT BE FULLY UNDERSTOOD IN ISOLATION FROM SO-
ciety. Any study of religion must begin by observing and
describing belief systems and behavior patterns, but these data
will become significant only when they are related to their
social meanings and functions.

The study of functions in the social sciences is the study of
the social consequences of an institution. The function of religion is, in this sense, the relationship it bears to family patterns,
political and economic organization, social values, and the social
structure as a whole. Social conditions affect the forms and
values of religion, and these, in turn, influence social organization and social institutions. The strength of these interrelationships is not always equal. Religion is much more pervasive in
some cultures than in others; and within a given cultural system
religion may have greater bearing on some institutions than on
others.

Although religion always relates to other social institutions
and values, in no society is the totality of social life manifestly
governed by religion. Several nineteenth-century scholars imagined that this was the case in early or nonliterate societies, that
the mentality of "primitive men" was such that they gave to all
activities, experiences, and observations a supernatural interpretation. Modern anthropologists have found, however, that all
societies have secular areas that are not considered to be under
supernatural jurisdiction.

It is true that religion has a structural interrelationship with all social institutions. Because culture can be viewed as a more or less integrated system of principles, religion—as one system of principles—will tend to strain toward the consistency of the whole. This is what traditional functionalists noted when they stated that the function of religion (or that of any other social institution) is its contribution toward the maintenance of the total social life (Radcliffe-Brown, 1952:181). This type of function is universal. This discussion, however, will stress the particular instances of the function of religion, and select examples where the interpenetrations are particular rather than general.

If the study of functions is defined as the study of social consequences, it is important to keep in mind that consequences may be either positive or negative. Most often they will be both. This means simply that few, if any, social institutions are always beneficial for every member of a society. Belief in witchcraft may well relieve some tensions and cause others; divination will benefit some people and harm others. The same is true on a structural level. Religion is group-integrative, but strong internal group cohesion has as its social corollary the exclusion of outsiders, often leading to hostility and strife.

Earlier chapters have already indicated some of the social consequences that religion may bring about. In this discussion, religion will be more specifically related to other social institutions, with specific emphasis on the family, law, and political and economic organization.

RELIGION AND FAMILY ORGANIZATION

In societies in which religious worship is basically a family affair, strong interrelationships between family organization and religious structure may be expected to exist. In these societies, the household religion is generally of the nature of ancestor worship. Ancestral deities are lineage gods. When a person dies, he does not lose contact with the lineage, but remains an important link between the living and the older lineage ancestors. Ancestors are usually considered to require continuous attention; neglect of the ancestors means misfortune for the family. Normally, then, each family will hold rituals for its own ancestors. The material remains of the ancestors are usually buried near the homestead, and the rituals are carried out inside the house. Such frequent family interaction, directed toward common ancestors and common goals, exercises a strong integrating influence upon the family, and many specific features of family organization are functionally interrelated with religious systems of this nature.

The Ancient Greeks and Romans

Fustel de Coulanges, in *The Ancient City* (1864), analyzed the functional interrelationships between religion and social organization among the ancient Greeks and Romans. Although most other writers of his time focused their attention on the state religions, he stressed the religion of the common man.

Family structure, both among the Greeks and among the Romans, was patrilocal and patrilineal. Each child belonged to his father's line, and married sons remained in their parents' household, adding their wives and children to the family unit. Daughters, upon marriage, entered the households of their husbands. Each extended family among the Greeks and Romans consisted of several generations of patrilineally related relatives, including nonmarried daughters, and daughters-in-law.

These family units also constituted units of worship. In the household, the hearth was an altar on which live coals glowed by day and by night. The sacred fire was closely related to the worship of the lineage ancestors who were buried in a tomb near the entrance to the house. These ancestors remained important family members. They presided over family meals, they were prayed to, and they received libations of food and wine. It was the duty of the oldest male to offer regular sacrifices to the ancestors, both on the tomb and by the sacred hearth. Each family had its own lineage ancestors; each also possessed its own rituals, prayers, and hymns, which were different from those of other households (Fustel de Coulanges, 1956:38).

Upon marriage, a daughter had to abandon her childhood allegiance to the hearth and the fire, thus breaking her emotional ties with her own family and lineage. She had to adopt the ancestors of her husband, and learn new rituals, new prayers, and new hymns. The husband, on his part, had to bring a stranger to the sacred hearth, and share with her the ceremonies which were the sacred heritage of his lineage ancestors. Marriage was, therefore, a very serious step for both partners and for their families as well. The wedding ceremony was a sacred ritual, carried out in the house of the groom, in front of the sacred fire. When the partners were thus united by religious, sacred bonds, marriage was not easily dissolved. One of the few legitimate reasons for divorce was sterility, for the absence of offspring— more particularly the lack of sons—would mean the future neglect of the ancestors and the disappearance of the lineage itself.

For the very same reasons celibacy was discouraged. It was considered a severe social stigma not to marry, and in some instances the failure to do so was punishable by law. Once a woman had been accepted by the lineage ancestors, and thus also by the living lineage members, she usually did not leave them again. Even if her husband died, the rule of levirate kept her in the lineage: the deceased man's brother or other close male relative would marry her, particularly when the husband had left no male offspring. Levirate gave rise to some of the few instances of polygyny. Although polygyny was not officially forbidden, it was nevertheless rare, for admission of new members to the household was considered disturbing to the ancestors. A widow was already accepted by them, and thus might as well remain.

The religious structure strengthened the dominant position of the males in these societies. Sons, not daughters, perpetuated the lineage, and only men were allowed to lead the rituals for the ancestors. The laws of adoption reflected religious sentiments; for only those families without sons were allowed to adopt one. Adoption ceremonies took place in front of the hearth, and were therefore binding. Inheritance laws provided that the house and hearth, the agricultural land, the sacred tombs, and all other lineage property were to be passed on to those who participated in the domestic worship. Property was not individually owned, but remained within the lineage from generation to generation. Adopted sons inherited in their adopted households, and could not claim rights to the inheritance of the family in which they were born. True sons could never be disowned unless they renounced the family by leaving it, thus also ceasing their participation in the family worship.

Religion promoted family stability by discouraging divorce. Only in later years, when cities became powerful, was this stable system disrupted. Families no longer sacrificed to their own lineage gods, but to the city gods. The divorce rates became very high, and very strong laws became necessary to curb excessive divorce and marital infidelity. In Rome, Augustus required the party initiating divorce to give written notice to his mate in the presence of seven witnesses, and divorced persons were obligated to wait eighteen months before remarrying. These and similar rules, which made divorce both difficult and expensive, testify to the changed conditions which attended the changes in the religious structure.

The Dobu

Perhaps no society stands in greater contrast to that of the ancient Greeks and Romans than that of the Dobu. Here, neither husband nor wife give up religious allegiance to their lineage ancestors, and, consequently, neither do they sever ties with their lineage relatives.

Ancestors are as important to the Dobus as they were to the Greeks and Romans. The Dobuan village consists of a circle of huts built around, and facing, the sacred graveyard. The Dobu are matrilineal, and only the relatives of this group may be buried in the ancestral cemetery. The graves contain mothers, mothers' brothers, mothers' mothers and their brothers, but no fathers or fathers' brothers, for these were buried in the village of their own matrilineage. Each marriage partner is required to keep up his relationships to the sacred matrilineal tombs. Because members of the same lineage are not allowed to marry each other, postmarital residence cannot be permanent. One year the couple live in the village of the wife; the next year, in that of the husband. Marriage is not a sacred act; it is not attended by elaborate ritual, and divorce is very frequent indeed.

The rule of alternating residence is quite strictly enforced because protracted neglect of the ancestral graves is believed to result in loss of magical power. Without supernatural power, the crops would fail, illness would strike, and the individual could fall an easy victim to witchcraft. Because each individual obtains his magical powers from his own lineage ancestors, he does not share it with his marriage partner. Each partner also possesses his own yam seeds, saved yearly from those handed down in the lineage. Man and wife also have their separate plots of land, which they each work with the aid of their own magical methods. The yams that are harvested later are as "matrilineal" as people; they are of a strain that was planted before by the matrilineal ancestors.

Among the Dobu, then, each partner clings tenaciously to the ancestral spirits of his childhood. Religious beliefs are not shared —on the contrary, magical formulae, the most powerful items of religious property, are jealously guarded. It is not surprising that there is very little affinal cohesion, for the members of the lineage feel much closer to one another than to their marriage partners. After divorce, father-child relationships are severed, for the children will remain with the mother. After the death of a mother, a father may not again enter the village where his wife is lain to rest; upon the death of a father, a child may no longer enter the father's village. Inheritance of property, including the knowledge of religious formulae, takes place primarily through the female line. A son inherits from his mother or his mother's brother, but not from his father. Although adoption occurs, adopted children are not considered equal heirs.

Roman and Dobuan societies have two common elements: lineage exogamy and lineage religion. But Greek and Roman brides renounced their childhood gods upon marriage, thus bolstering affinal ties, while the Dobuan marriage partners display lifelong adherence to ancestral lineage gods, thus weakening marriage ties, but supporting lineage cohesion. The ritual interactions among the Romans and Greeks solidified the patrilineal households, while among the Dobu such action strengthened the lineage. Fortune writes that the Dobuan relationships hinge upon the conflict between the lineage and the marital groupings in their clash of incompatible solidarities (1963:43). These clashes are both reflected in, and aggravated by, the separation of ritual.

The Yakö

The Yakö of Southeastern Nigeria afford an example of a different type (Forde, 1950:285–332). The religious structure in this society is such that it functions to connect the lineages rather than to separate them, in spite of the fact that each lineage has its own ancestral gods.

The Yakö have a form of kinship organization known as *double descent*. An individual is related both to his father's and his mother's lineage, but not in the same manner and not for the same purposes, as will be seen presently.

The Yakö are polygynous and patrilocal. Each of a man's wives lives in a separate hut with her own children. Because married brothers remain together, several dwelling sites are usually clustered together, forming a compound. This compound will then be occupied by a patrilineage, the wives of adult men, their married sons and daughters-in-law, and their unmarried children of both sexes. Every Yakö settlement contains a number of such compounds, and the various patrilineages tend to be related to one another.

A child grows up in the hut of his mother, in the household of his father, and in the compound of his father and his married brothers. Each patrilineage possesses individual tracts of land, but the patrilineages have communal rights and duties in the whole of the village. Together they own a sacred shrine, dedicated to two or three ancestors of the combined lineages. The shrine contains sacred tusk trumpets and staves, and is guarded by a priest who is the ritual head of the combined patrilineages in the village. He officiates at the shrine rituals in which the members of the patrilineage participate, but he has also some secular powers and duties. Disputes between members of the patrilineages are brought before him, and after hearing all sides he imposes fines upon those judged guilty.

By virtue of their relationships to the patrilineage, sons will inherit the collective rights to village sites and lands, as well as the right to participate in rituals connected with the patrilineal ancestor shrine. They may also bring their grievances to the priest, and expect justice.

In the double descent system of the Yakö, children are also related to their matrilineage. As a result of the rule of patrilocality, matrilineages are scattered all over Yakö territory and they do not form consistent residential units. Because a man may not marry a woman from either of his own lineages, many different matrilineages are represented in each village. Each matrilineage also possesses one sacred shrine and the various shrines are distributed among the villages. Each village, therefore, contains one patrilineal shrine for the combined residential patrilineages in the community, and one matrilineal shrine for one of the existing matrilineages. This means that the members of a matrilineage must usually travel to the village in which their shrine is located in order to attend the matrilineal rituals.

Each matrilineal shrine has its own priests. Apart from religious functions, the matrilineal rituals serve to assemble regularly the members of the matrilineage, who otherwise would have no continuing contact. The social reality of this group, then, is largely maintained through the periodic rituals.

While the spirits of the patrilineal shrine function primarily as peacemakers, those of the matrilineage also promote fertility. Thus they are responsible not only for the matrilineage, but also for the welfare and prosperity of the community in which their shrine is located. Because their powers are considered to be superior to those of the patrilineal supernaturals, the yearly matrilineal ritual is of great importance. It is attended by the scattered members of the matrilineage and the local members of the patrilineage. The matrilineal priests preside; the patrilineal priests assist.

Matrilineal priests also possess secular powers. They settle civil disputes among members of the matrilineage, and serve as a court of appeal when members of the patrilineages feel that their priest has not made a just decision. The authority of matrilineal priests is thus greater both in the secular and in the religious realms.

From his mother, a child inherits the right to participate in the rituals of her matrilineage. Movable property is also transmitted in this manner: a child inherits from his mother's brother such important items as livestock, currency, implements, household goods, and stores of food. When a man dies, his land and village rights go to his own sons; his movable property, to the sons of his sisters.

In Yakö society neither husbands nor wives sever their relationships with the shrines and ancestors of their own lineages. A married man continues to pay homage to the shrines of his patrilineage, and occasionally travels to those of his matrilineage. He also participates in the yearly fertility rituals of the matrilineage in his own village. A married woman usually does not par-

ticipate in the rituals of her husband's patrilineage, but she
attends the yearly rituals of her matrilineage.

Family integration is not exceptionally strong. Men and
women tend to conduct separate economic, ceremonial, and rec-
reational activities. Divorce is, however, not very frequent.
Women are considered definite assets to the household because
they take part in agricultural pursuits; to the lineage, because
they perpetuate it; and to the community at large, because they
reflect the supernatural fertility powers of matrilineal spirits.
Affinals are not hostile outsiders, as they are among the Dobu.
The matrilineage is maintained not by the Dobuan pattern of
alternating residence, but by the fertility rituals at the matrilineal shrines. The resulting network of interrelations and interactions encompasses all members of the Yakö group, connecting
lineage with lineage, and village with village. Within the villages
these relationships correlate with social and ritual patterns: patrilineage and matrilineage have their own functions and powers
which are meaningfully related to one another.

The Manus

The example of the Yakö has shown not only how religion
may function to unite lineages, but also how separate lineage
beliefs may become common concerns of the whole group. Although the Yakö achieved these results by means of ritual patterns, the Manus use different techniques (Fortune, 1935).

Among the Manus, religion is strongly household-centered.
Every house has its own supernatural ancestor, Sir Ghost, whose
skull rests in the family shrine. He protects the family and
watches over the moral behavior of its members, punishing sex
offenses, obscene behavior, neglect of the house, failure to pay
debts, and failure to help relatives.

The particular beliefs about the nature of Sir Ghost and the
resulting behavior patterns help to integrate Manus religion. Sir
Ghost is not considered to be omniscient; he can only observe
what goes on in the household. When he observes violations, his
punishments—most often in the form of illness—are not necessarily inflicted upon the violators, but upon any member of their
household. When a person from another household comes within
the range of his observation, he or his relatives become susceptible to punishment. Consequently, when a person falls ill, it

becomes important to know whose fault it is, and which Sir Ghost has sent the supernatural punishment. Without this knowledge, no cure is possible, and, moreover, everyone would remain suspect. A diviner goes around to all households to question the Sir Ghosts, and usually discovers the culprit. He makes his findings public, and demands public confessions.

Manus religion is, therefore, not merely a contract between individual supernaturals and their households; rather, it tends to uphold the values and morals of the whole group. Manus culture is singularly integrated, and the individual behavior of each member of a household toward his own household spirit is the concern of the whole community, for deviation from established norms endangers the welfare of every Manus.

RELIGION AND THE MAINTENANCE OF SOCIAL ORDER

Manus religion affords one example of how religion may function to uphold the norms of a society, thus contributing to the maintenance of social order. This function of religion is a universal one, but the specific procedures by which it is accomplished differs from culture to culture.

Every human group is governed by a series of rules defining correct or acceptable behavior among individuals and among groups of individuals. Without such rules, written or unwritten, society could neither function nor exist. Adherence to these rules should, therefore, be fairly close, and every society has ways and means of enforcing its rules. Some of these techniques are quite familiar: there are written laws which must be obeyed, and institutionalized authorities have the power to punish offenders. But social order can be maintained in other ways as well. Many rules are unwritten, and offenders are not punishable by law. People continuously judge others by their behavior, and commendations or criticisms are regularly formed about how a man behaves at a job, how he dresses, how he spends his money, and how much he drinks, or about the way a woman keeps her home or treats her children. Such judgments work very strongly to uphold the day-to-day rules of life, and regularly carry with them social rewards or punishments—invitation to, or exclusion from important social gatherings, and so on.

The techniques of rule enforcement are called *sanctions*. Positive sanctions reward, negative ones punish. Legal, institutionalized sanctions are known as *organized sanctions*, while more or less spontaneous community judgments have been called *diffuse sanctions* (Radcliffe-Brown, 1952:205). A further distinction can be made between secular and religious sanctions. The latter are culturally held beliefs that socially approved behavior will be supernaturally rewarded, and serious deviancy supernaturally punished. Such beliefs help to channel human behavior into accepted social avenues. The degree to which religion functions to uphold social norms is markedly different in different cultures. Some religious systems impinge on nearly every important form of social interaction and behavior, others leave punishment of deviant behavior largely to secular institutions.

Ethical Religions

Those religions which have great influence on human behavior and on the social order in general have been called *ethical* or *moral religions*. Nineteenth-century evolutionists generally felt that ethical considerations were absent from religions of nonliterate peoples. Tylor, for instance, wrote: "Savage animism is almost devoid of that ethical element which to the educated modern mind is the very mainspring of religion" (1958:II, 360).

Ethics is commonly defined as "a system of moral standards of conduct." Such standards are not uniform, but in all cultures religious beliefs function to uphold or reinforce at least some of the socially accepted norms of moral behavior. It is thus a false distinction to call some religions *ethical* and others *nonethical*. At most, it can be said that some religious systems are more prescriptive, or function more strongly in secular realms, than others. Moreover, there is no one-to-one correlation between the technological development of a culture and the moral strength of its religion. On the other hand, there have been those who spoke of religion of nonliterate societies as if it were totally identical with the social order. Durkheim, for one, posited that in simple societies codes of social behavior were necessarily religious rules, for the god of the society was, in fact, society itself. The moral constraint of society and its religious system were thus, according to Durkheim, one and the same (1961:236–39). This condition has not been found in any known culture.

The Eskimo

Eskimo religion affords a good example of a system that functions quite selectively in secular realms. Eskimo social organization has no true government, no permanent rulers with political authority. Recognized leaders have such tasks as directing hunting parties, or deciding when to break camp and where to go next, but they have no power to punish deviant behavior. Sanctions were diffuse rather than organized, and rules of behavior are enforced by the threat of ridicule, gossip, insults, or social ostracism. Powerful in any society, these techniques operate even more strongly in smaller groups, where face-to-face encounters are regular and no one can retreat in anonymity. In serious instances, such as murder, the family of a victim seeks revenge or retribution, but a single case of murder is considered a private matter rather than a public wrong. Only when an individual becomes dangerous to the whole community does he become an object of public concern. Boas reported that among the Baffinland Eskimos, a powerful sorcerer had already killed a great many people and was suspected of plotting to kill more. The community talked it over, and the consensus was that he should be eliminated. An older man took it upon himself to stab the sorcerer in the back, and was rewarded with the gratitude of the community.

Neither in cases of murder nor in cases of wife-stealing, adultery, chronic lying, or theft is supernatural punishment expected or involved. Religious sanctions in Eskimo society operate in relation to subsistence patterns. Life depends primarily upon hunting, and in these undertakings man is considered subordinate to the will of the supernatural powers. Religious action is directed toward assuring a continuing supply of game. The Bladder Festival is extremely important among the Behring Sea coast Eskimos, serving to ritually dispatch the soul of seals (contained in their bladder) back to sea, so that they will multiply. It is a social obligation to attend these rituals, for neglect would have dire consequences.

But most religious rules of the Eskimos are formulated as taboos, and pertain to three major areas of life: subsistence, pregnancy, and death. In the first category, perhaps the most important taboo is that forbidding to mix caribous and seals. Caribou hunting is a summer activity; seals are hunted during the winter in a different part of the territory. The meat of these animals cannot be eaten together, and items of clothing made from their skins may not be worn together. Also, seal bones cannot be carved in caribou season, and caribou skins cannot be prepared in seal season. Transgressions of these rules had consequences for the individual and the whole community, for the individual would become ill, and the supernatural powers would withhold the life-sustaining food supply of the group.

The Nuer

The African Nuer, like the Eskimo, lacks true government. Some individuals bear the title *Leopard-skin Chief,* but they do not possess political authority. They are specialists concerned, in a ritual capacity, with various aspects of nature (Evans-Pritchard, 1940:291).

When serious breaks in the social order occur, there are two possible solutions: compensation or vindication. The former is by far the more desirable. The families involved try to agree upon a payment to the wronged party. They may also appeal to the Leopard-skin Chief for mediation, and they usually do in serious cases, notably those involving murder or incest. But the Leopard-skin Chief has no power to summon the parties, nor does he really sit in judgment on the case. His sole task consists of discovering how much the slayer's kin are prepared to pay in compensation, and to persuade the relatives of the dead man to accept this sum. He speaks now with one party, then with the other, in the hope of arriving at an acceptable conclusion. His opinion is not binding, and he has no power to compel acceptance of his decisions. At most he can curse the unwilling or overly demanding family—but this is a face-saving device rather than a demonstration of power (Evans-Pritchard, 1940: 291).

When a settlement cannot be reached, the Leopard-skin Chief withdraws, and feuding inevitably follows. Feuding involves not only the families in question, but whole communities and even larger tribal units. Vengeance is sought by the injured family in attempts to kill one or more relatives of the murderer, which, in turn, evokes countervengeance. Under such conditions, traveling is very dangerous, economic relations are severed, and marriage plans between members of the group may have to be cancelled.

In these circumstances, religious sanctions function toward the encouragement of compensation. More serious crimes, considered highly offensive to the supernatural powers, include murder, incest, and adultery—and these automatically result in supernatural, physical pollution of the wrongdoer and his kinsmen. This great physical danger increases unless the wrong is redressed by compensation, by sacrifice, and by purification. Compensation appeases the injured party; sacrifice is then accepted by the gods, while purification rituals wash away the physical contamination. Feuding cannot accomplish these ends. Feuding families are, therefore, exposed not only to the threat of human vengeance, but also to the danger of supernaturally imposed illness (Evans-Pritchard, 1956:190–92).

The Cheyenne

In contrast to the Eskimo and the Nuer, the Cheyenne Indians possessed a well-instituted system of government. Chiefs and councils of chiefs had the power both to judge and to punish deviant behavior. Horse-stealing, adultery, violence, and civil disobedience were generally punished by the councils. Murder and incest, the most serious of crimes, incurred civil punishment backed by the authority of supernatural powers.

The Cheyennes possessed some sacred objects of great antiquity. Among those, the Medicine Arrow bundle was of singular importance and holiness. It symbolized the unity of the tribe, safeguarding it by sacred supernatural powers. Together with some other ritual objects, the bundle contained several arrow feathers which were to be kept pure and unpolluted, lest they lose their protective powers. Murder and incest, committed by any member of the tribe, polluted the sacred arrows. This created a situation of utmost danger for the whole community. Unless something were done, crops would fail and hunting and warring parties could not hope for any success.

In these instances, the council did not wait for complaints or requests for help. It summoned the guilty man or brought him in by force. He was not killed—this would contaminate the sacred arrows even more—but he was banished from the tribe for a period of five years. He would usually try to take up residence in neighboring tribes, but these would not be eager to accept him. After the criminal's expulsion, the sacred bundle was purified through the ritual of Renewal of Medicine Arrows. Order was thus restored both in the human world and in the supernatural realm (Hoebel, 1954:157–59).

These are but some of the many possible examples of the functional relationships between religion and the maintenance of social order. In general, it may be noted that in societies where divination is prominent, religious sanctions may be expected to function strongly. Divination is the verification of the will and judgment of supernatural powers, who will reveal the guilty persons, and thus justify secular punishment.

A similar positive correlation may be expected in societies practicing ancestor worship, under condition that living parents are the punishing agents of their children. Among the Lovedu of Transvaal, the ancestral gods have no interest in the morality of their descendants (Krige and Krige, 1954:80). Neither do living parents discipline their children: a parent loves his wayward son as much as he loves his virtuous children, and would not ever withhold his protection from him. Among the African Tonga, the situation is reversed (Colson, 1965:437–41). The ancestral *mizimu* ("spirits") are thought to be eager that the social order be kept. They reward its maintenance, and punish deviance. According to Tonga belief, there are different types of *mizimu*. Perhaps the most important among those are the *mizimu* of the matrilineal group. No *muzimu* will watch over all people, and no living Tonga is concerned with all *mizimu;* each individual stresses his relationship with the spirits of former members of his matrilineal group, the basic kinship unit of Tonga society. Interaction between living members of a matrilineage centers on important areas of life. They are obliged to visit each other during illness, mourn the death of each other's families, help to provide bridewealth for the males of their group, and assist in the ritual purification of the spouses of those who die. As a group, they are held jointly responsible by outsiders for each other's actions. It is perhaps not surprising, therefore, that the deceased members of the matrilineage continue to interact with the living and maintain their concern over the social order of this kinship unit and over the actions of its members.

There is no necessary correlation between the status of the gods and their concern with correct social behavior. In the Society Islands two types of supernaturals are formally distinguished: the official high gods who are served by a formalized priesthood, and lower, rather evil-minded spirits who are manipulated by professional magicians. Thieves appeal to the gods for assistance and protection in their trade; robbed persons, on the other hand, appeal to magicians to discover the culprit by divination. The magician pours some water in a coconut shell and invokes the spirits; the thief's likeness then appears on the surface of the water. When it becomes known that the victim of a theft intends to consult a diviner, the thief sometimes returns the stolen goods in order to avoid detection and supernatural wrath. If he does not, the identification of the thief usually leads to his capture. But his guilt is not established until he confesses. The spirits are quite powerful but not totally trustworthy—some are terrible liars. But the religious mechanism is strong enough to be effective in many instances (Williamson, 1936:234ff).

RELIGION AND GOVERNMENT

Religious systems may also function to maintain social order in a more indirect manner—by upholding and endorsing the offices of those whose task it is to regulate and maintain social order. Not all societies possess true government. Simple, homogeneous societies, which do not display sharp divisions of rank and status, maintain social control by communal sanctions. Severe disturbances are dealt with individually by families or lineages, who will seek compensation or revenge when one of their members has been wronged or killed. Leadership, in such societies, is usually of a temporary nature, and does not extend to the control of all social activities.

The majority of societies, however, operate on principles of differential distribution of power, and possess true government. This implies, by definition, that certain office-holders exercise control over the behavior of others, and are in a position to punish deviant behavior and to make decisions binding on the community. Offices of political authority often correspond to differences of birthright or wealth, and leaders come from certain lineages only. Criteria of demonstrated ability are considerably lessened, and other validations of privileged power become necessary. Every stratified society possesses means toward this end. The power of a ruler is upheld by an army, by tradition, by promises of protection, or by secular law. But not infrequently, the differential distribution of power is further upheld by religious techniques. Religious validation of political power takes on many different forms, some of which will now be discussed.

Validation of Political Power by Myth

One of the many possible functions of myth is that it can serve as an explanation of social situations to which people cannot remain indifferent. Differential distribution of power not based upon proven personal ability is clearly one situation for which some form of explanation is in order. Myth often provides such answers, relating how the social and political order came into existence, or explaining why one lineage should always provide the rulers. The political order is then validated because it is "god-given."

The royal dynasty or ruling lineage may be further strengthened by a mythical genealogy, which demonstrates that the rulers are direct descendants of the gods, or of the first divinely installed ruler. Similarly, myth may authenticate the political dominance of a particular group. The Iroquois League of the Five Nations was a complex political structure managed by fifty clan leaders: fourteen Onondaga, ten Cayuga, nine Mohawk, nine Oneida, and eight Seneca. Iroquois myth relates how the League was established by the semi-supernatural heroes, Deganawidah and Hiawatha. Paddling from tribe to tribe in their white canoe, they urged unity for the sake of peace. Atatarho, the powerful Onondaga leader, at first refused to cooperate, but after Hiawatha combed fiery snakes from Atatarho's head, the latter promised support under condition that his tribe should have chairmanship of the League and a majority representation (Underhill, 1953:92).

In the small native kingdom of Ankole in Uganda, the pastoral Bahima were the rulers of the land, while various agricultural tribes were serfs. In the complex cycle of Ankole myths, the political dominance of the Bahima receives supernatural explanation and divine sanction (Oberg, 1940:122ff). And in northern Nigeria the myths of the Kede give strong supernatural backing to the fact that Kede political rule is defined on the basis of locality and not of tribe (Nadel, 1940:189).

The Divine Nature of Rulers

Kings or rulers who trace their descent to gods or divine ancestors are not themselves necessarily considered divine. But in some situations the position of a ruler may be validated by the belief that he is an incarnation of a god. This is a very powerful sanction, found most often in complex political situations. In Egypt, a dynasty which came into power about 2750 B.C. assumed the title *Son of Re* (the sun god) for its ruler. The earthly Pharaoh was believed to be the heir of the powers and qualities of Re, whose functions and attributes were displayed in the ritual and regalia of royal office. After death, he returned to the celestial realm of his divine father to reign with him in the heavens. Re supposedly engendered a new heir to the throne by visiting the queen in her palace. In Babylonia, kings were divine because they were suckled at the breasts of the goddess Ishtar. In Japan, the Emperor gave up his claims to divinity only in 1947 (Williamson, 1936:257–59).

Of course, the divine qualities of rulers not only validate their power and authority but also reflect their obligations. In the Society Islands, the royal chief must be just, but he must temper his justice with mercy, show energy and patience in the discharge of his duties, exercise wisdom and tact in handling public affairs and in selecting counsellors and advisors, and, above all, embody the highest ideals of generosity, honor, and courage. In spite of their sanctity, chiefs can be unseated by priests if they fall seriously short of these ideals, because their failures would prove that their nature was not divine. A myth setting forth the precedent of such a disposal is repeated at solemn occasions to remind the ruler of what might happen if he does not fulfill his duties, and to give divine sanction to his possible disposal by priests (*ibid.:* 258–59).

Privileged Relationships to the Supernatural

Another religious concept which may function to uphold political power is the idea that the king or ruler is not divine, but has privileged access to supernatural powers. In these cases, the ruler is believed capable of manipulating the gods to the benefit of his country and his subjects. This simultaneously symbolizes his concern for the welfare of his people and demonstrates his ability as political leader. Rain production and weather control are among the most notable of his supernatural tasks.

Frazer has called this phenomenon *the magic of kings,* and devoted a long section of *The Golden Bough* to its description. By doing so, Frazer drew scholarly attention to this religious technique of validating political power, but he uncritically generalized his data and made unwarranted conclusions about the origin of kingship. In his view, priests and magicians attained powerful political positions by virtue of their proficiency in magic, and almost everywhere kings had arisen directly from priesthood. Frazer's descriptions of such magician-kings made it appear as if they had no secular political duties at all, but existed primarily in order to control the weather.

Clearly, this cannot be the case. Political power, by definition, involves political responsibilities and duties. In societies in which the king was credited with great supernatural powers, these served as qualifications for his secular duties, both affirming and symbolizing them. It was expected that a king would promote the welfare of the land, and his imputed supernatural powers safeguarded and sanctioned his exalted position and defined his duties. If droughts, crop failures, invasions, wars, or epidemics befell his realm, they were signs that the gods had withdrawn their support from him, so that he was no longer fit to rule. In other words, these beliefs provided a legal device for the disposal of unwanted or incompetent rulers.

The importance of these techniques under given cultural conditions cannot be underestimated. Powerful rulers often realized that consolidation of supernatural power implied consolidation of secular powers. Zulu kings, for instance, often attempted to outlaw private rainmakers and diviners, proclaiming that no one but the king could control the heavens. The king was in charge of, and responsible for, all national magic. He possessed important therapeutic medicines with which he would treat the ailing. Even accused sorcerers could not be executed unless the king's diviners confirmed the verdict (Gluckman, 1940:31).

Where kings were held responsible for the material and physical well-being of their subjects, the failing of their own health could be interpreted as a first sign that supernatural assistance was failing and that their powers were waning. Again, it was Frazer who recognized that this was an important device for disposing of unsuitable rulers. His theory was that many kings were inhabited by nature gods. A king's health and sexual potency were believed to have a direct influence upon the well-being of the country and the fertility of the land. Because the king's body was the temporary dwelling place of the gods, its ailing, aging, or impotence would directly affect its divine residents, and the country would be beset by calamities. In order to prevent these undesirable events, the king was killed as soon as he showed signs of failing strength. His office was then handed over to a vigorous new king and the gods would be transferred to the younger and healthier body.

Although Frazer believed that it was the custom of many non-literate peoples to slay or depose kings in order to forestall the natural infirmity of old age, ethnographic evidence is somewhat ambiguous. Evans-Pritchard, for instance, writes that there are some indications that the rulers of the African Shilluk might have been put to death when they were ailing or aging, but he is by no means certain that regicide did, in fact, occur (1964:202). He suggests that most Shilluk kings might have been assassinated by their enemies. Yet, he also observes that the Shilluk, in any case, *believe* that people might suffer when kings become physically ill, and that under those circumstances the kings *should* be killed in order to save the kingship and the people. There is an alternative Shilluk tradition that any noble pretender to the throne could challenge the ruling monarch to single combat, and, should he prove himself to be the stronger by killing the king, he could claim the throne.

Monica Wilson found the same situation among the Nyakyusa of southern Tanganyika (1959). Here, too, a tradition existed that kings could not be allowed to die naturally, but there was no direct evidence that ritual killing actually took place. But the fact that old Nyakyusa men gave detailed accounts about the process of ritual killing of ailing kings shows clearly that the concept was not unknown. Audry Richards admits the possibility that such killings of Bemba chiefs took place, and records that the Bemba felt that the health of their chief directly affected the prosperity of the fields (1940:98n).

It is quite possible, and indeed likely, that it will never be known for certain whether or not such killings took place. But the belief in the desirability of destroying aging kings did exist, and it served to validate the supernatural and thus also the secular powers of the royal office, and symbolized the king's responsibilities and duties.

In many Polynesian societies, the idea that kings had mana served the same purposes. Moreover, mana could serve as a powerful instrument of government. It could be communicated to objects and people, which would make them dangerous, untouchable, and taboo. In this manner a king could stop traffic on a river, or cause great inconvenience to recalcitrant subjects by tabooing a forest or a tract of land. In New Zealand, a pole with a bunch of leaves was put up to indicate that a site had been declared taboo. Infringement of the taboo was a crime, and also invoked the wrath of the gods, who would strike the offenders or punish them by illness or even death (Lowie, 1947:362–63).

Religious Functionaries

Even in those societies in which kings are considered divine or semi-divine, are acknowledged as skilled rainmakers, or possess healing powers, they are rarely absolute monarchs. They are usually advised and assisted in their tasks by noble viceroys, councils, headmen, lineage representatives, or religious functionaries. The relative influence of these various office-holders varies. Not only is the balance of power different in every political system, but it will also be subject to change. In literate as well as in nonliterate societies, power politics, power clashes, struggles over rights and privileges, and problems of succession cause shifts in the balance of power. Although religious office-holders may well be involved in competitions for power and privileges, they tend to have a stabilizing influence upon the political equilibrium. They sanctify the royal office, assist the king in his ritual duties, and simultaneously check and control his actions, often wielding a considerable amount of political influence.

A good example of such a situation is found in the political organization of the Rhodesian Bemba (Richards, 1940:83–120). There were several positions of leadership in Bemba society, but the most important were those of the paramount chief and the council of priests.

Chieftainship was limited to one royal clan, but because this group was fairly large, succession was not automatic. Upon the death of a ruler, there was usually more than one eligible candidate, and priests had considerable control over the choice of a successor. Priestly offices were strictly hereditary, passed on in matrilineal lines of descent. Claiming divine sanctions for their positions and inheritance patterns, priests could not be removed at will, not even by the paramount chief.

Once in office, a chief was believed to have strong supernatural influence over the productive capacity of his territory. His state of health and his actions, including his sex life, affected the whole group. A chief who broke a sex taboo could bring calamity to his people, and the conduct of purification rituals after sexual contact was one of the most important tasks of the priests, requiring the participation of thirty to forty of these hereditary religious officials. The priests also guarded the sacred person of the chief by preserving the ritual purity of the royal fire, the royal sacred food, and the royal wardrobe. They carried out many rituals to protect the chief from the contagion of illness, death, or sexual defilement (*ibid*.:98–99). These priestly services were of the utmost importance for the chief, for without them his health would be in danger and the well-being of all his subjects would be jeopardized. The priests, therefore, held the strongest check on the powers of the paramount ruler. By refusing, or threatening to refuse, to carry out the rituals which safeguarded the ruler's health and position, they could force him to make certain decisions in their favor or to appoint the leaders and headmen of their choice.

When a chief died, the priests immediately took hold of the sacred relics and symbols of royal office. They then conducted elaborate funeral rituals, which could last as long as two years. The installation of the new ruler was also their responsibility, and was accompanied by complex and elaborate ritual. The heirlooms were handed over to the new chief only after all the rituals were completed. The secrecy and awe surrounding these ceremonies increased the people's reverence for their chiefs. The priests were, therefore, very instrumental in the validation of the royal office. But, while sanctifying the chief by ritual and supernatural means, the priestly council exerted a salutary influence over him by postponing the ritual functions necessary for his installation and for the maintenance of his office. The priests thus not only validated political power, but also restricted it.

RELIGION AND ECONOMIC ORGANIZATION

Economy is a cultural institution centered on the production, distribution, and consumption of goods and services. The functional connections between economy and religion have received a great deal of scholarly attention. One of the great pioneers in this field was Max Weber. In his studies of non-Christian world religions, he discussed and analyzed the functions of those religious systems as independent causal elements influencing attitudes toward labor, commerce, property, money, and usury. Even better known is his *The Protestant Ethic and the Spirit of Capitalism,* in which he argued that the religious principles of Calvinism were conducive to the rise of capitalism. Puritanical Calvinism taught that a man's profession was a God-given task, to be carried out with the utmost devotion. Economic success became both an indication of adherence to God's will and a mark of His acceptance. Luxury was sinful, for it threatened to divert man's attention from his daily tasks and religious duties. Money should not be wasted on "worldly" goods, but was to be invested wisely so that it would multiply. The combination of industry and thrift led to the formation of capital, and thus also to the social ethic or "spirit" of industrial capitalism. When the material insecurities of life diminished, the reference to religion eventually decreased. But the radical reorientation of man's attitudes toward economic activities had been accomplished, and prevailed over the secularization of Western societies.

Weber's challenging thesis caused considerable discussion and controversy about the impact of religion on the economic activities of mankind (*cf.* Sombart, 1913; Tawney, 1926; Robertson, 1933; Fanfani, 1935; Parsons, 1937; Lenski, 1963; Samuelsson, 1964). The common viewpoint of anthropologists is that religion and economy are, indeed, everywhere functionally interrelated, but that the magnitude of these relationships varies. Moreover, most anthropologists have become more cautious about the imputed causal role of religion in economic matters. Economic and religious changes arise from multiple factors, and functions are mutual, so that economic ideas influence and adjust themselves to religious concepts, and vice versa.

Rather than investigate the connections between whole religious systems and whole economic systems, we shall examine how the three traditional subdivisions of economy—production, distribution, and consumption—relate to religious beliefs and actions. Although these three aspects of economy are not strictly separable, this approach will afford some insights into the ways in which religion and economy may interact in different types of societies.

Production

The study of economic production deals with the procedures and conditions under which goods and services needed by human societies are made available. Production includes the making of artifacts and other items of material culture, and the production of food through hunting, fishing, collecting, farming, cattle-breeding, and industry.

Possible evidence about the relation of religion to economic production goes back to the Paleolithic Age. On the walls of caves frequented by these early hunters are found paintings of food-producing animals. Often they were pierced by arrows, and the common interpretation is that this was done to increase the food supply by supernatural means.

Many rituals in contemporary nonliterate societies are directed toward the same goal. Perhaps the majority of Hopi and Zuni rituals are carried out for the explicit purpose of producing rain and thus to insure or to increase agriculture crops. Moreover, the different ceremonies connected with the agricultural cycle tend to systematize and regulate the work. The Hopi ceremonial year begins at the winter solstice, when a ritual is held to insure the return of the sun. After the corn is sown, the next ritual is held to make the seeds germinate and grow. Later, a very important ceremony invokes the ancestors and kachinas, who return with rainclouds and ears of corn. The kachina dances produce rain, and these supernatural beings remain until the first green ears of corn appear. The Hopi Snake dance is held to insure a bountiful harvest, while in the last ceremony of the year the sacred fires are rekindled in order to facilitate the later rebirth of the sun. The various rituals also mark the agricultural stages of sowing, sprouting, ripening, and harvesting.

Malinowski described how gardening rituals regulated the production cycle among the Trobriand Islanders (1961:59). The season is officially opened by a big ceremonial performance which consecrates the garden plots. Rites accompany every stage of the production process—burning the scrub, clearing, planting, weeding, and harvesting. At every important point the religious leader ritually assists the plants in sprouting, budding, bursting into leaf, climbing, forming the foliage, and producing edible yams. The garden magician regulates the whole system and ritually compels people to apply themselves to certain tasks at appointed times. Other economic production processes, such as canoe-building or deep-sea fishing, are also regulated by ritual, and Malinowski feels that "by its influence in ordering, systematizing, and regulating work, magic is economically invaluable for the natives" (ibid.:60).

In the African kingdom of Dahomey, ritual not only structures the agricultural cycle, but also determines the selection of the plots to be cultivated. A Dahomean farmer will take a soil sample from the possible cultivation site to a diviner, who first determines (by throwing palm kernels and interpreting the resulting patterns) whether the gods will permit this plot of land to be used. When the answer is favorable, the farmer returns to the field and molds a human head from the soil, using cowry shells to represent the eyes. After having made offerings of palm oil and chicken blood, he returns to the diviner, who now identifies the guardian spirit of the field. From then on, sacrifices have to be made to the deity at the beginning of every four-day week.

These procedures serve two purposes. The supernatural establishment of correct choice will guarantee ownership of a plot and its legal use, thus forestalling quarrels over land rights. The regularity of the prescribed sacrifices compel the cultivator to be present on the land quite frequently, and the whole process thus becomes a sacred contract between farmers and spirits, each doing their part to make production successful (Herskovits, 1938:I, 31–32).

On the Society Islands, religious observances connected with deep-sea fishing not only function to increase the catch, but also have direct effects on family behavior as well. A fisherman is not supposed to quarrel with his wife or daughters before setting out to sea, for this would anger the gods and endanger his life. The wives, daughters, or sweethearts of the fishermen must observe sexual taboos during their absence or suffer supernatural punishment. Clearly, this prohibition further helped to ease the minds of the absent fishermen, so that they could better concentrate upon their dangerous work (Williamson, 1936:249–51).

In the Marquesas Islands, too, religion was connected with fishing activities. Professional fishermen kept special sacred shrines which women could never enter. Here they kept their fishing gear as well as the sacred images and ritual paraphernalia connected with their trade. Fishing then became a semi-religious occupation, and also a male prerogative.

Distribution

Economic distribution deals with the ways in which goods, once produced, are exchanged or allocated. Society could not function if individuals produced goods exclusively for their own use. The family is a small economic unit: productive adults support not-yet-productive children and no-longer-productive old people. Husbands and wives divide economic tasks between them, each contributing toward the maintenance of the family, and thus also exchanging goods and services.

But exchange patterns are universally extended well beyond family bonds. In all human groups there are specialists of some kind, men or women who have skills which others do not have, and who are regularly called upon to render services. Even in simple hunting-and-gathering societies there are at least one or two religious specialists, shamans or diviners, whose special ability consists of effective communication with supernatural powers. When the struggle for the basic necessities of life is severe, shamans are part-time specialists, otherwise actively involved in the food quest, as everyone else is. Societies of this type can ill afford to support and maintain able-bodied adults who are not spending most of their working time in the actual production of food. Under such conditions, very few surplus goods can be produced, consumption is immediate, and wealth will be rather equally distributed among all people.

Yet, in nearly every known instance the shaman receives some material rewards for his services. These remunerations are often minimal, and in hunting-and-gathering societies they do not give rise to significant differences in the distribution of wealth. Mirsky observes that the Amassalik Eskimo shaman is likely to have a few more possessions obtained as fees for his services, but that his economic position is not basically different from that of others (1961:77).

Cheyenne Indian shamans were skilled leaders of the communal antelope hunt. After an all-night ritual, a shaman would lead people to the spot designated by the supernatural powers. The hunters went on horseback, while the shaman, the women, and the children went on foot. Two virgin girls were given a supernaturally charged "antelope arrow"—a wand with a medicine wheel on one end—and directed to run outward on diverging diagonal courses so that their path described a wide **V**. Two young men chased after them on the fastest horses available, and later the other hunters followed in two long lines. The remaining women and children formed a circle at the foot of the **V**, with the shaman in the center. As the two leading young men passed the virgin girls, they took over the supernatural wands and continued on the diverging line for several miles, until they flanked the antelope herd. The hunters then attempted to surround the herd, driving them in the direction of the shaman, and into the circle of old men, women, and children, who, with waving blankets, closed around them to form a human corral. Using antelope arrows as directional signals, the shaman made the animals rush around and around until they were exhausted and befuddled, and could be killed with clubs. For his supernatural assistance and considerable skill in directing this hunt, the shaman received all the tongues and two antelopes (Hoebel, 1960:65–66).

Where in the described instances the material rewards for part-time religious specialization are relatively small, in well-developed agricultural societies such payments are often much higher. Malinowski (1961:426–27), although he does not specify the amount, states that Trobriand garden magicians received substantial fees. Navaho singers, presiding over important curing rites, received fees ranging from five dollars to five hundred dollars, depending upon their reputation, the distance to be traveled, and the complexity of the ritual. A singer also had the privilege of producing and selling ceremonial equipment, and many of these part-time specialists became well-to-do (Kluckhohn and Leighton, 1962:226). On the other hand, a succession of illnesses may well bring a family to bankruptcy, even if relatives are obliged to share the costs. It has been calculated that the Navaho spent an average of 20 per cent of family income on ceremonial doctors' bills (*ibid.*:227).

Although material compensation of part-time religious specialists may vary, full-time specialists must be fully supported, for they make their living by devoting their working time to religious services. But also in these instances, remunerations vary with the reputation of the practitioner, the relative wealth of the community, the prestige accorded religious office, and the ethics of the religious system itself.

Support and maintenance of full-time religious specialists is accomplished in a variety of ways. When the number of specialists is small and their duties include household services, such as curing or private divination, direct payment by the clients constitutes the major part of their income. But, more often, full-time specialists will also be in charge of shrines or other religious buildings, and have communal ritual duties. They may then be paid regular seasonal fees by every household. This situation exists, for instance, among the Javanese settlers in Surinam (de Waal Malefijt, 1963). The *ka'um,* a full-time specialist, is in charge of a religious building known as the *langgar,* the modest counterpart of a mosque. Here he conducts regular services, and he is also responsible for the maintenance and upkeep of the building. On the last day of Ramadan, household heads go to the *ka'um* and, after reciting the Moslem confession of faith, they pay the *ka'um* a fixed amount of money for every member of their household. In return, the *ka'um* is expected to preside over the *slametans,* the household rituals so important in Javanese life. More often than not, a *ka'um* receives some food or money after leading such a ritual, but payment is not compulsory and a *ka'um* would never ask for it. Generosity is, however, pleasing to the spirits whose blessings are invoked during the *slametan,* and this supernatural reinforcement usually brings about extra payments.

In other societies, sacrifices and offerings to the gods may form a substantial part of priests' income and subsistence. Sacrificial items are not always totally attributed to the gods, but portions are left over which are used by the priests later on. In the ancient Hebrew ritual of *shelamin,* the blood of sacrificial animals was poured out at the foot of the altar, but the flesh was considered to be the divine share of the priests (Lev.8:31–32). Similar, in Roman rites of expiation, the priests ate the flesh of sacrificial animals, and Greek texts reveal that priests took their own portions home with them, and made money from the sale of skins of the victims (Hubert and Mauss, 1964:37). In Hindu sacrifices, too, the priests ate their portions (*ibid.:*43).

Religious specialists may also be partially or totally supported by the state. When kings rely upon priests or diviners to uphold their exalted position by ritual, they generally also support such a priesthood, attaching them to their courts, or giving them other privileges. The king's own wealth comes, in turn, partially from taxation. In at least one known instance the priests themselves gave supernatural assistance to the tax collections upon which their own income ultimately depended. In Hawaii, the royal tax collectors were accompanied by at least one priest who carried with him a large image of the Hawaiian god, Lono. With the aid of this mana-laden idol, the priest declared the area in which the taxes were to be collected taboo for all inhabitants, so that no one could leave his residence to escape payment. The tax collector simply went from house to house and had a much easier task (Hogbin, 1934:266–67).

There are many other techniques for support of religious offices. One, which Weber has called *monastic landlordism,* was found operative on Ceylon (1958:257). Buddhist temples were granted large estates for their maintenance. Both the state and private individuals made bequests to temples, ranging from small buildings or plots to vast areas. Such bequests were considered meritorious, because acts of giving belonged to the most important of Buddhist religious duties. The system of temple estates served several functions. Economically, they sustained the ceremonial life of the temples and their priests, and provided the peasants who lived on the estates as service tenants, and their families, with land, labor, and food. Politically, they bolstered the control of kings over their subjects. The king selected and appointed the chiefs and priests of temples, and the estates thus provided a network of fiefdoms (Ames, 1964:43–44).

Payment of valuables to maintain religious personnel is but one of the many examples of economic exchange and distribution within a religious framework. Religious ritual not only involves offerings to gods and payments to priests, but is frequently accompanied by exchange of goods among the participants. The function of ritual as a convenient setting for exchange is particularly important in nomadic hunting-and-gathering societies. The Blackfoot Indians, like most other societies of this type, were organized in small bands which hunted buffalo and other game animals during the long winter season. In summer, when the food supply was more abundant, the various bands congregated in a central camp. This was the occasion for great ceremonial activity, culminating in the annual Sun Dance ritual. During this period, much trading and redistribution of power took place. With appropriate ritual, "medicine bundles" and the formulae necessary for their effective use were often transferred from one man to another in exchange for horses, hides, robes, tent covers, or other useful items. Ceremonial societies performed their special rituals and dances, and if purchase or transfer of society membership was due, great triple tipis were built for the lengthy rituals of exchange (Forde, 1934:57). The religious setting of these meetings accomplished both the distribution of supernatural power and the exchange of more material valuables among the otherwise isolated bands.

In the sedentary agricultural society of Tikopia, male initiation rites involve extensive and very complex economic exchange patterns. Firth provides a detailed description (1963c:392–433). The relatives of a young man approaching adulthood save and accumulate goods and valuables over a period of one to two years. At the time of initiation, they will have amassed vast quantities of food, pandanus leaf mats, bark cloth, coils of sinnet cord, and other items considered necessary for the ritual exchange. The ceremony lasts several weeks, and is attended by all relatives. The food is partly consumed by participants and guests, partly given away. Material items are exchanged, leaf mats changing hands in return for bark cloth or other valuable items. The handling of food and material goods attendant upon these occasions is so elaborate that it is difficult to decide whether the primary element of the ritual is trading or initiation (*ibid.*:393).

Economic exchange in nonliterate societies, too, is often extended far beyond the confines of tribal boundaries, and such exchanges may well be carried out within a religious framework and accompanied by elaborate ritual. The best known example of such a situation is the famous Kula trade, first described by Malinowski (1961). This trade is carried out among communities on a wide ring of islands which include the Trobriands, the Dobu, the Amphlett Islands, the Wari, the Tubetube, and several others, as well as the coast of New Guinea (see Figure 13). Along this route, two types of objects are formally and ceremonially exchanged: *soulava* (necklaces of red shell discs) and *mwali* (bracelets of white shell). These ornaments are passed on from partner to partner in opposite directions: necklaces move clockwise; bracelets, counterclockwise. They are valued, semi-sacred items, worn

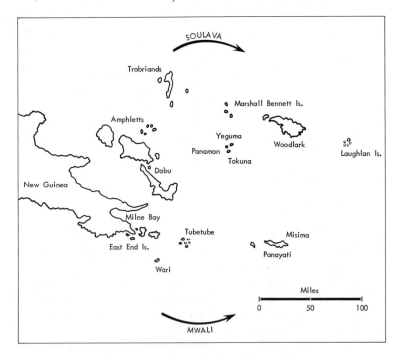

Figure 13. Area of the Kula trade.

on important ritual occasions. No man may hold them permanently; each Kula partner must pass them on after a given period. Every Kula trader thus receives bracelets and necklaces and passes them on at the next trading expedition. The exchanges involve a great deal of ritual activity. Before the voyages, seagoing canoes are built or repaired, and these activities are accompanied by ritual and the keeping of certain taboos. The ceremonial items are not the only ones traded, for the canoes set out with commercial goods and utilities which are often peculiar to, or exclusively produced on, one island and are not available elsewhere except by trading.

It is possible, of course, to trade without religious and ritual trappings. But it has been found that the religious framework of the Kula exercises considerable influence upon the creation of friendly and stable relationships among the islands involved in the Kula ring. Their economic relations have been more enduring and more effective than those among island traders in most other parts of Melanesia, who exchange without the benefits of a religious framework.

There also exists a relationship between religion and markets. Although markets are often thought of as places for buying and selling goods, they also provide convenient occasions and settings for a great many other purposes—meeting friends and acquaintances, exchanging news, establishing new relationships. Religious ends, too, can be served as they, in turn, serve the market.

Apart from the fact that supernatural assistance is often deemed necessary to make trading prosperous, markets need protection. Many different local and tribal groups meet and mingle in the marketplace. Sometimes they are feuding or hostile, but economic exchange cannot flourish in a hostile environment. African Berber tribes, for example, were often at war with one another, and yet were dependent upon each other for trading. Supernatural sanctions protected those who traveled to the markets through enemy territory. The markets themselves were held on different days in different villages, and fighting in the marketplace was not only a crime, but subject to supernatural punishments.

In medieval Europe, rulers and bishops protected merchants on their way to and from markets, and the traders received guarantees that they would not be prosecuted on market days even if they were involved in outstanding litigations.

African markets were often religiously founded, both to insure market peace and to obtain the cooperation and protection of the spirits. In Dahomey, when a new market was to be established, diviners were first consulted to enlist the cooperation of a spirit whose specialty was market protection. They found out if it was permitted to set up a market at a given spot in a given village, but needless to say, this practice also allowed time for the reactions of the people to confirm the desirability of a market at such a spot. When the answer of the spirits (and the people) was positive, a sacred shrine for the supernatural market guardian had to be erected before trading could begin. The shrine took the form of a mound of earth, under which a specimen of every commodity to be sold on the market was to be buried. The mound itself contained soil from seven other established marketplaces (Herskovits, 1938:I, 53).

In other parts of Africa, markets are often founded with religious ceremonials and their peace is kept by the presence of shrines and the supernatural powers they symbolize. Ibo markets and Tiv markets (Bohannan, 1963:243) still use the traditional patterns, and Islamized areas maintained the relationship of religion and market activities. When Hausa villages wish to establish a new market, they direct prayers to Allah, asking him to make the undertaking prosperous. There are several market-opening rituals, led by the village headman and local religious officials. The latter may give special instructions to the headman, telling him to distribute alms or to carry out other meritorious acts to obtain Allah's blessings. Other rites are sometimes independently carried out by those who still belong to the ancient Hausa cult of spirit beliefs. These groups attempt to settle one or more benevolent spirits on the market site, and to erect a shrine for them. The chiefs and Moslem priests dare not forbid traditional rites, even if they are conflicting with their own religious principles. They do not want to alienate the non-Moslems whose support and participation is essential to the success of the market (Smith, 1965:140–41).

In ancient Mexico, popular markets were held in temple squares. The peasants brought their goods to the center of the gods weekly, or in the course of pilgrimages. Permanent markets appear to have existed at Teotihuacan, the central ancient Mexican metropolis. Today, the Indian markets of Middle America are still intimately linked with centers of worship. The Indian peasant comes to town to sell his goods, but he comes also to seek supernatural favors in the temples of his saints (Wolf, 1962: 82–83).

Consumption

Consumption refers not merely to the ways in which goods are used up, but also to the roles which property and wealth play in the lives of their consumers. Everywhere, the use of property takes on meanings beyond the satisfaction of primary biological needs. Comfort, security, prestige, status, power, pride and pleasure are but some of the intangible benefits of ownership and consumption. However, there are great cultural differences in the appreciation of wealth and in the items considered desirable. "Property" may consist of privileged knowledge or rights, including methods of dealing with the supernatural. Such knowledge or rights may well possess trading value. The Blackfoot Indians traded the supernatural powers of their medicine bundles for useful material items, while the Arapesh and Tschambuli tribes of New Guinea traded magical knowledge for material goods (Mead, 1950:19, 153).

Cultural attitudes toward the accumulation of wealth are determined by other aspects of the social structure. In nomadic hunting-and-gathering societies, where mobility is essential, material property is a burden, and only the most useful items are carried about. In sedentary groups, where the problem of transportation is less pressing, the social structure and value system may be organized along lines of status equality. Differential wealth is then undesirable, and the culture provides means for liquidating property that might otherwise upset the economic status balance. Quite frequently, this siphoning off of extra goods takes the form of ritual consumption.

The cultural ethos of the Zuni Indians favored social equality. This value concept permeated all social institutions, including economy. Individual wealth was balanced in lengthy and expensive rituals. Each year eight men—the most affluent—undertook to sponsor and finance the costly annual harvest ceremony. This involved the building of a large new house to receive the sacred ancestors and kachinas. Many people were called to help, and since they were also to be fed, many additional crops had to be planted. This, in turn, meant employing more help. For those who undertook this ritual responsibility, the months from July to December constituted a continuous work party. The last few weeks before the great event were marked by frenzied activity. The ovens were kept going day and night, great bins were erected to hold the bread, and hundreds of sheep were slaughtered and prepared for the feasts. Needless to say, these rituals were very costly. One family who had sponsored this ceremony three times in twenty years estimated that each time it cost about one thousand dollars in sheep and store goods, not counting the field produce. Little prestige was attached to this financing, for it was something that everyone had to do sooner or later. It was a social responsibility to the group and to the supernatural powers from whom all blessings were believed to come. The pattern was most effective for the maintenance of the cultural ideal of equality (Bunzel, 1938:355–56).

Even in societies which are quite status-conscious, the desired status positions may be assigned on considerations other than the possession of property. Status may even ensue from large-scale public destruction of property. Ritual consumption of this nature was carried out in the form of the potlatch in several Indian tribes on the northwest coast of the United States, notably among the Kwakiutl, the Haida, the Bella Bella, and the Bella Coola. Here, nonmaterial property took on much greater cultural value than material possessions. Salmon, cod, halibut, and seals were extremely plentiful and could be caught without great effort and in huge quantities. They provided preservable stores of dried fish and oil. The Kwakiutl also possessed many engraved copper shields, blankets, mats, canoes, and slaves. But such property did not confer prestige or status. This only came from honorific names and nobility titles, and the myths, songs, dances, and crests that went with them. The glory and power of names and titles was attained and increased not by the accumulation of material wealth, but by its public destruction in a potlatch.

A potlatch was a ceremony to which one invited friends, but particularly enemies and competitors, to witness the destruction of goods. Valuable copper items were smashed and the pieces scattered about, blankets were burned by the hundreds in huge bonfires, canoes were destroyed, dishes broken, slaves sacrificed. A carved figure of a man, the "vomiter," was placed upon the roof, and pipelines were so arranged that a steady stream of valuable fish oil poured out from its gaping mouth into a fire below. The greater the destruction, the greater the prestige and rank of the giver of the potlatch, and the higher his rating in society (Benedict, 1946:175–78).

The religious implications of the potlatch are relatively small. A potlatch is not held in honor of supernatural spirits; it serves almost exclusively to further the aggrandizement of the host. The potlatch songs recorded by Boas are hymns of self-glorification and have little or no reference to the gods. There are some indications that the sacred ancestors were believed to be pleased when their lineage names were thus upheld. The origin of the potlatch appears to be grounded in myth.

The religious nature of liquidation of property is much more obvious in the many known instances in which goods are destroyed or considered unfit for further use after the death of their owner. Nearly everywhere at least a few material items of personal property are buried with the dead. Often, but not always, the motivation for these practices is religious. The grave goods are meant to speed the soul on its way, to prevent its return, or to serve the deceased in supernatural realms. When such beliefs are strong, the value of grave goods increases. Among the Eskimo, dogs are among the most basic assets for transportation and hunting, but some Eskimo groups slaughtered a man's huskies at the time of his death. Kazaks buried a man's favorite horse with him, and when a Crow Indian died, his family gave away or destroyed most of their property. After the death of a Witoto chief, his house and everything in it was burned. The most elaborate and costly grave furniture known was that afforded to Egyptian Pharaohs, who often spent their lifetime in building their own grave chambers—the mighty pyramids—and furnishing them with the most expensive goods they could obtain.

Expenditures of this nature often do not end with the funeral. Graves and shrines must be upheld and regular offerings made to insure the continued happiness of the dead. The Dahomey afford a striking example of a society in which the maintenance of the dead was perhaps even more expensive than that of the living. According to Dahomean beliefs, the dead do not immediately attain sacred status; their deification is a slow process which requires considerable assistance from their living relatives. Numerous costly rituals must be carried out to promote the deceased to higher status; when they have reached deification, their position must be upheld by similar rituals. Neglect would deprive the lineage of its power and fertility. The tradition is described in detail by Herskovits (1938), and Goode gives a short and useful summary of the many tasks, contributions, and expenditures involved in these ritual obligations (1951:96–98). He mentions no fewer than twenty-five categories of ritual consumption of this type. The material goods include hundreds of chickens, numerous goats, rams, and ducks, and quantities of palm oil, corn flour, beans and rum, full-sized shelters of bamboo, many lengths of white cloth, as well as pots, drums, and money. Although a number of these items re-enter the redistributive channels, many are simply destroyed.

CONCLUSION

There are many reciprocal relationships between religion and economy. Economic activities are basic to the survival of a group, and it is to be expected that all societies attach great importance to economic undertakings and often reinforce them by religious definitions and sanctions.

Several scholars have questioned the efficiency of these relationships in economic terms. Many have stressed the dysfunctional, antirational, and useless aspects of religiously inspired distribution and consumption patterns. Simoons, dealing primarily with food taboos, decried the fact that religion may lead men to overlook foods that are abundant locally and of high nutritive value:

> Beef, chicken-flesh and eggs, dog meat, and horse and camel flesh comprise such important potential sources of animal protein that their more general use might contribute substantially to reducing the widespread and serious protein deficiency that prevails in large parts of the Old World (1961:3).

In a similar vein, Goode notes that religious restrictions "prevent production at the highest level of efficiency" and that Dahomean funerary practices represent an economic burden on the distributive system of the collectivity (1951:98, 136). Earlier, Linton noted that the elaboration of certain phases of culture is sometimes carried to the point where it becomes actively injurious, and endangers the existence of society (1936:89–90). One of his examples is the Eskimo prohibition against hunting seals during the summer, a taboo kept even when land game hunting fails. A tribe may well starve while there are plenty of seals in sight.

On the one hand, it is certainly true that cultural institutions, including religion, have both functional and dysfunctional aspects. On the other hand, there is good reason to believe that the positive aspects of religion generally outweigh its negative effects. Cultural institutions are established and maintained in order to serve human needs. Sustained failure to meet these needs would lead to institutional and ideological change, or to the extinction of the group.

Harris has shown that positive factors of religiously influenced "ecosystems" are frequently overlooked (1966:51–66). His specific example treats the economic role of bovine cattle in India. The orthodox Hindu doctrine of *ahisma* forbids the taking of life in any form, and the sacredness of cattle is its principal symbol. It has been regularly maintained that this is an important example of religiously inspired resource mismanagement, but Harris shows convincingly that the sacred cows provide milk, traction, fertilizer, fuel, beef, and hides. Although there is a taboo on slaughter, 25 million cattle die each year from natural causes, and may be eaten by some groups, thus contributing to protein resources. Harris suggests that the relationship between human and bovine populations is symbiotic rather than competitive, and that the nonexploitation of cattle resources does not impair the survival and economic well-being of the human population. Although Harris does not deny that more efficient food-energy systems would be possible, he maintains that the Hindu peasant utilizes cows as capital assets which continue to pay material dividends to the end of their lives at low maintenance costs.

Other apparently improvident forms of religiously motivated economic action reveal, on closer analysis, many positive factors. Spiro relates how Burmese peasants allocate a large percentage of their economic resources to religious ends and spend much of their funds on religious displays, lavish feasts for monks, and apparently useless pagodas (1966:1163–73). Western economists would certainly suggest that the Burmese would be much better off by investing their savings rather than "squandering" them on religion. But Spiro shows that the quantity of savings potentially available to the average Burman peasant would, if invested, provide him only with the smallest returns, which would not make much difference in his standard of living. Instead of increasing his capital by saving his earnings, the Burman who wishes to satisfy his desire for material pleasure could increase his merit by spending his earnings on religion. The Buddhist dogma of rebirth teaches that accumulated merits in one life are carried over into the next. Religious spending thus becomes the Burman's soundest long-term financial investment. This type of spending is not only important for his future existence, it is also a crucial means for the acquisition of religious prestige, which is considered highly desirable. And, finally, the consumption patterns provide immediate gratifications as well. The building of a pagoda, contributions to monasteries, and provisions for monks are accompanied by feasts that serve to gratify the desire for physical pleasures—good and abundant food, beautiful costumes, gaiety, and frivolity. For the average Burman, the choice between economic saving and religious spending is a simple one. Religious spending is a highly profitable investment for the future and a source of prestige and pleasure in the present. Economic saving is both risky and relatively unprofitable—and precludes the few enjoyments available in the present. Rather than being wasteful or antirational, religious spending in the Burmese behavioral environment is both profitable and rational.

In every instance, then, analysis of interrelations between economy and religion should not be based upon models of Western economy and its ideals, but upon the framework of the specific sociocultural environment.

13

Religious Change

ANTHROPOLOGISTS AGREE THAT HUMAN CULTURES ARE SUBJECT TO continual change. Anthropologists are not, however, of one mind about the causes and functions of change.

Although it cannot be denied that cultures and their institutions change continuously, the relative rate of change is not always the same in all societies and at all times. The transformations may be so gradual that they are barely noticeable from generation to generation, or they may proceed so rapidly that they are conspicuous from year to year. These rates of change are not random; they are a function of numerous internal and external factors. Internal conditions affecting the rate of change include the relative degree of cultural receptivity to new ideas, the amount of freedom of inquiry and of competition, the degree of cultural elaboration, the population size and density, the presence of innovators and inventors, and—perhaps most important —the degree of harmony between cultural and social values. Among the external conditions affecting culture change, the degree of contact with other groups is the outstanding factor. The relationships between groups may be friendly or hostile, the groups may be unequal in technological development or political strength; the contacts may be voluntary or enforced, sporadic or continuous.

What is true for culture change in general is also valid for religious change. It, too, is universal. It may be slow or rapid, proceed from within or be strongly influenced from without;

furthermore, the nature of contact will strongly affect the process of religious change and the form it will assume. The many different variables impinging upon the many forms of beliefs and practices will naturally produce a great variety of cultural responses. Although no two such reactions are identical, it is nevertheless possible to find similarities. These similarities are found among societies with a somewhat similar historical background, which have been in communication with each other through trade, war, or geographical proximity, and which had, moreover, similar experiences with Western civilizations. It will be convenient, then, to discuss religious change by geographical areas, and to focus on those religious changes which have developed in nonliterate societies exposed to Western civilization.

THE RISE OF NEW RELIGIOUS CULTS AND MOVEMENTS: MILLENARISM

The development of religious cults or movements is a recurrent feature of cultural contact between Western and nonliterate societies, particularly when technological and other cultural differences are great and the impact is strong and sudden. These cults have been called by a variety of names: *nativistic movements, revivalistic movements, messianic movements, millenary movements,* or *prophet cults.* As religious phenomena, they are neither new nor confined to nonliterate societies. Similar movements have arisen in complex modern societies as a result of economic or other social discrepancies between subgroups.

Millenarism flourished in Europe during the Middle Ages and the Renaissance (Cohn, 1961) and in Spain and Italy in the nineteenth and twentieth centuries (Hobsbawm, 1965), and exists in Europe at present (B. Wilson, 1961). The term *millenarism* itself is derived from a very early Christian movement which expected a millennium—a thousand years in which the world would be at peace and its inhabitants perfectly good and perfectly happy.

The various names attached to these movements tend to stress their predominant characteristics, but there is no agreement on their usage. *Nativism* implies that the dogma of the movement emphasizes the value of indigenous cultural elements. In the words of Linton, a nativistic movement is "any conscious, organized attempt on the part of a society's members to revive or perpetuate selected aspects of its culture" (1943:230). The term *revivalism* indicates a tendency to reinstitute former customs and ways of life, and to stir up religious faith among the indifferent. Messianic movements indicate the expectation that a supernatural deliverer or deliverers will bring redemption and salvation, and a state of happiness and well-being. Millenarian movements foretell a future of social and spiritual bliss on earth, not necessarily lasting a thousand years, but arriving in the foreseeable future. Prophet cults are characteristically initiated by a divinely inspired individual who validates his claims to religious leadership by visions, dreams, or other indications of supernatural inspiration. These various religious manifestations and elements do not fall into clear-cut categories, and the phenomena thus described could well be found in one and the same cult.

Wallace suggested the term *revitalization movements* as a label for all cults of this type, arguing that they have in common the "deliberate, conscious, organized efforts by members of a society to create a more satisfying culture" (1956:279). We prefer the term *millenarism,* for it avoids the question of whether or not the attempts are conscious, and we define it as any religious movement that expects a change in social conditions here on earth. Millenarism is thus distinguished from eschatological or salvation religions, which transfer their hopes for a better future to a hereafter. The two concepts are not mutually exclusive: early Christians both expected a Millennium and hoped for eternal salvation. But the emphasis of the expectations is usually one or the other.

Millenarian movements view time as a linear process, as Talmon pointed out (1965:526). In their expectations of a new and better social order, people may envisage the terrestrial paradise as a re-establishment of happier past conditions, or they may anticipate bold innovations of a social nature. If it is true that millenarian movements expect a better future in this world, it follows that dissatisfaction with existing conditions will favor the rise of such movements. This does not mean that every form of social dissatisfaction will find its expression in millenarian cults. The presence of a strong belief in otherworldly salvation may preclude the rise of millenarism, or social discontent may find expression in secular uprisings. Furthermore, specific cultural configurations may well hinder the rise of certain new beliefs.

Melanesia is one area in which movements of this type have been particularly numerous. Melanesia, one of the three main divisions of Pacific Islands, includes New Guinea, the Solomons, New Hebrides, New Caledonia, the Bismarck Archipelago, the Admiralty Islands, and the Fiji Islands. Before the nineteenth century, Western influence was relatively slight. Mission work began early, but became widespread only after colonization. Although some converts were made, Christian dogma did not fit easily into native social structure. Oliver observed that, in many of the matrilineally oriented island societies, God-the-Mother's-Brother would have been a much more meaningful deity than God-the-Father (1952:128). Native interpretations often departed from official Christian dogma, but the influence of missionary teachings was strong enough to survive in many aspects of subsequent native cults. The techniques and methods used by active missionary societies varied widely. Apart from ideological and theological differences, some maintained large European staffs at the outposts, while others only sent a ship at infrequent intervals; some were backed by ample financial and material resources, others were ill-furnished; some trained native clergymen, others relied exclusively upon their own personnel. After 1850, more intensive colonization brought increasing numbers of traders, missionaries, government officials, company agents, and planters. On many islands plantations were established, and native laborers were recruited to work there. Often, when the local labor supply proved inadequate, Asiatics were brought in, thus exposing the native peoples to more foreign cultural models.

These influences, however, were relatively small in comparison with those brought about in World War II. The parapharnalia of modern warfare provided a most drastic change in the outlook of those who, only a few generations ago, did not even know what metal was.

As a result, many island societies were not only in the throes of internal transition, but also in conflict about the acceptance or rejection of the goods and values of the intruding Western culture. Millenarian movements provided ways in which people could consolidate their feelings and take a more or less united stand against the impact of the new conditions. Early movements tended to reject European goods, and to view the Western invasions as wholly undesirable.

The Milne Bay Prophet Cult

One of the first recorded movements in New Guinea occurred in 1893, at Milne Bay. A young native prophet named Tokerau or Tokeriu foretold the approach of a terrifying cataclysm. Volcanic eruptions and a great tidal wave would destroy all existing settlements and kill all those who refused to follow the prophet. Afterward, the winds would suddenly change, and fair weather would cause the fields to produce yams and taro in great abundance. Trees would be laden with fruit, and pigs would multiply rapidly. A huge ship would come, carrying the deceased ancestors, and a new era of happiness would begin (Lanternari, 1965:167; Worsley, 1957:51–54). Because food in plenty was expected, Tokerau and his followers consumed all garden produce normally saved for a longer period, and they slaughtered and ate all their pigs. Tokerau placed a taboo on all European goods and objects. People abandoned their houses, and followed their prophet further inland in order to be safe from the predicted disasters. When there was no tidal wave, but instead a scarcity of pigs and yams, the followers lost faith in Tokerau and threatened to kill him. The government intervened and sentenced him to two years' imprisonment.

In this movement, Tokerau promised a supernatural increase of food supplies after the cataclysm, and the millennium was envisaged as a period without material wants. This theme prevailed in most other movements. But rather than expecting an increase in native supplies, it was often believed that goods would arrive in the form of cargo made up of Western commodities, brought to the islands by Western means of transportation— that is, by steamship or airplane. The generic term *cargo cult*, regularly applied to Pacific millenarian movements, derives from this central and recurrent belief. The general features of these movements can be partially explained in terms of the contrasts between native cultures and the models of Western culture. European ships, airplanes, trade articles, and military equipment appeared not to be man-made, and thus they must have been derived from supernatural sources. Cargo beliefs indicated how native peoples could have access to them through the supernatural ancestors and by following the commands of a prophet. Cargo ritual was any religious activity designed to bring the goods to the cult members. It might include the building of airstrips to facilitate the arrival of the planes, or erecting large storage houses to deposit the new supplies. The prescribed ritual behavior patterns were presumably taught to the leader by ancestors or other supernatural entities in visions or dreams. Other recurring features included the belief that the new order would be inaugurated by a cataclysm, and that the invading whites would leave, be killed, or be reduced to the status of servants and slaves.

The German Wislin Movement

One of the earliest recorded full-fledged cargo cults developed just prior to World War I on the island of Sabai in the Torres Strait. The movement was known as *German Wislin,* a name which demands some comment. *Wislin* was the native pronunciation of *Wesleyan,* thus testifying to the influence of Methodist mission work. The term *German* seemed to have been inspired by the idea that these creatures, whoever they might be, were the enemies of the British, and were trying to oust them. They thus had common cause with the natives.

It is not known who originated the movement, but leadership was soon in the hands of three natives who assumed the title of *general* or *captain.* They promised the arrival of a steamship in the very near future. The ancestors would be aboard, bringing with them money, flour, canned goods, flashlights, knives, and printed cotton. The ancestors would also expel or kill all British invaders. An important meeting was held on Good Friday, 1914. All men of the island were ordered by the Wislin generals to come to the central graveyard, where the most important ancestors were buried. A strong attempt was made to consolidate the movement: failure to attend would be punished both by the spirits of the dead and by God. During that meeting the leaders proclaimed that the time of delivery was near; work was to cease, for the ancestors would provide, and people were to be serious and prayerful during the interval. Rituals were to be held on

Fridays and Sundays, and prayers were to be addressed to the
spirits (asking them to come soon) and to God (asking him for
money and cargo). The millennium was to begin in two weeks.
When it did not arrive the date was postponed—first for another
three weeks, then for an indefinite period. The cult ended in
disappointment; government officials stepped in, exiled the
leaders, and forbade any further cult activities (Worsley, 1957:
94–96).

The Vailala Madness

Cargo cult behavior, however, became well established in the
area and spread to widely divergent cultural units. Soon after
World War I, movements of this nature appeared all over New
Guinea and on adjacent islands. Although the basic tenets of
cargo ideology remained similar, the specific rituals and associated behavior patterns showed considerable variations. The
so-called *Vailala Madness* was a cult of the New Guinea Orokolo
tribes on the Gulf of Papua. It was begun by Evara, a man who
had been in close contact with European activities. He was
subject to trances with convulsions, and prophesied the coming
of a steamship, carrying the spirits of the dead ancestors on board,
and bringing flour, rice, tobacco, and rifles. The visionary shaking fits became contagious, and many followers of the prophet
were subject to them; during these trances, they confirmed the
truth of his revelations and sometimes further elaborated them.
Some had visions of Ihova Kekery ("Jehova's country"), where
such Christian deities as Ihova, Noa, Atamu, Eva, Mari, and
Yesu intermingled with aboriginal deities and ancestors. Food
was abundant there, as it would be on earth, and the supernaturals wore long, flowing white or red garments. Flagstaffs or
similar long wooden poles, designed after the models of Western
telegraph poles or radio towers, were erected in order to facilitate
communication with the supernatural powers. Although the traditional respect for ancestors and spirits remained very important, it is interesting to note that the ancestors, upon their return,
were expected to wear European garments, and their skin color
would have changed to white (Mair, 1948:64).

There were other indications that the movement was forward-
looking and envisaged a break with the past. Ritual parapharnalia, considered sacred in the older religion, were openly

burned. Instead, European-style tables and benches were set up in the center of villages, and offerings to the ancestors were placed upon the wooden tables (Williams, 1934:369–79). Several times the rumor spread that a ship had been sighted, and great excitement ensued. Although repeated disillusionments caused the movement to wane in some places, it spread to many other tribes which had not heard of it before, and which now joyously took it up (Williams, 1940:123–24).

The Vailala Madness was more realistic than the Milne Bay Prophet movement. Tokerau had made no attempt to adjust to the new; he sought a solution in a flight into the past under the mistaken idea that the tide could be turned and the good old days revived. The Vailala Madness accepted the inevitability of change, and its leaders realized that the past was irrevocably gone: even the ancestors now resembled Europeans. Western goods were desirable, and would play a significant role in their future. Selected aspects of Christian dogma and ritual were adapted to the new form of religion, and the destruction of the formerly sacred ritual parapharnalia symbolized the realization that a new social order must also have new forms of religion.

The Taro Cult

There were other movements which did not rely on cargo, but incorporated other ideas which might more actively assist in hastening the arrival of the millennium. The Taro cult emerged in New Guinea in the Bunay Bay area around 1914, promoted by a prophet named Buninia, a native of the village of Taututu. Buninia was visited in a trance by the spirit of his deceased father, who was accompanied by other spirits, all eating the native staple food, taro (Williams, 1928:12ff). The spirit demanded that his son establish a new cult, and gave specific instructions about the planting of taro and other gardening activities which would promote crop fertility. The followers of Buninia also had visions, and were instructed in new ways of cutting taro, cooking, serving, and eating it, and they were also taught taro words, taro greetings, taro songs, taro drumbeats, and taro handshakes. Rituals incorporated this new taro symbolism. Trance was an essential part of the rituals, and new curing methods were also introduced.

Although there was an emphasis on newness, in fact the taro

doctrines focused upon two traditional interests: crop fertility and the curing of illness. The movement was not a cargo cult, and it was millenarian only in the sense that social improvements would come, not after a supernaturally created cataclysm, but through accepting the doctrines of the Taro spirits. But there were other developments of very great importance. The principles of the Taro movement stressed friendliness and cooperation among cult members, even if they belonged to different and formerly hostile tribes and lineages. Intervillage taro feasts and rituals regularly took place. Members, upon meeting, always shook hands, and were forbidden to carry weapons to the communal rituals. Earlier, no one would have dared to enter a hostile village unless heavily armed.

Several offshoots of the Taro movement came into being, each with its own prophetic leaders. Although varying somewhat in symbolism and emphasis, they shared a body of common doctrine. The universal Taro custom of shaking hands was not a mere imitation of Europeans; it became a symbol of changed social relationships among villages and tribes. The doctrines of unity and cooperation reflected not only the breakdown of old barriers between diverse social units, but also the new common interests which these groups had developed vis-à-vis the white invaders. Williams noted that this "elementary tendency toward cohesion" was prevalent in many other movements (1928:19).

The Naked Cult

The so-called Naked Cult, occurring on the island of Espiritu Santo in the New Hebrides, emphasized cooperation and cult solidarity among members, regardless of their other loyalties. This island had received the full impact of Western occupation, and the movements were strongly anti-European. A great many earlier cults had already been suppressed when, in 1923, a new local prophet arose whose name was Ronovuro. He promised, like so many before him, that a ship carrying the dead ancestors and cargo would land on the island; but he also prophesied that the Europeans would attempt to prevent the ship from landing. He urged the natives to stage a revolt, and to kill one European as an initial victim and a warning to the others. Subsequently Clapcott, a plantation owner, was murdered (Raff, 1928:100). Although there was a period of relative quiet after severe government reprisals, new movements were gaining strength by 1937, culminating in the Naked Cult about 1944. The leader of this movement, Tsek, told his followers to destroy all European goods, to stop working for the Europeans, and to await the arrival of Americans, who had replaced the supernatural ancestors in the consciousness of the islanders.

In spite of the fact that European goods were to be destroyed, the movement was forward-looking. Americans would bring goods superior to the European. Many old and sacred traditions and taboos were abolished, clan exogamy and marriage payments were discarded, and the houses burned down and replaced by two communal buildings—one for men and the other for women. Clothing and ornaments were no longer to be worn, and sexual intercourse could take place in public because it was a natural act of which no one needs to be ashamed. Friendliness, cooperation, and harmony among cult members were considered to be as important as their common hatred of the European invaders. Tsek maintained that quarreling and friction were the main causes of illness, and cooperation was promoted by much visiting among cult villages. Status differences were minimized in the stress on unity, and economic differences weakened by the killing off of pigs. Because the movement embraced different dialect groups, attempts were made to develop a new common language to foster intertribal unity.

Both the Taro movement and the Naked Cult, as well as many others that cannot all be described here, had important consequences for the native sociopolitical order, for they helped to overcome tribal cleavages and attempted to create larger regional units. Some movements went much further in their political aspirations.

The Chair-and-Rule and Marching Rule Movements

In the Solomon Islands, notably on Santa Ysabel, a European missionary encouraged the natives to petition the government for participation in the nominated Advisory Councils, and to demand fairer rules. A movement subsequently arose, with a wooden chair and a wooden ruler as its major ritual symbols. Known as the *Chair-and-Rule* movement, its native leaders attempted to stage anti-European revolts. The movement was forcefully suppressed by the colonial government, but not for long. The Masinga (or Marching Rule movement) made its appearance at Malaita, the main island of the Solomons, bearing the same political imprints as the Chair-and-Rule movement. Buildings were erected for the storage of the expected cargo, monetary contributions were demanded from cult members, and the leaders organized and trained people to resist and fight colonial administrators as well as Christian missionaries. Local groups were drilled like soldiers, wooden sticks temporarily replacing the firearms which were expected with the arrival of the cargo.

The Marching Rule symbolically provided many of the functions of which the natives were deprived by government refusal to let them participate in native courts and councils. The leaders were energetic men who had had contact with Western ways. Nori had worked for Europeans most of his life; Vouza had fought with the Allies during the war; Timothy George had been educated in Australia, where his father had been taken as a worker. Malaita, the headquarters of the movement, was divided by native leaders into nine districts, each of which elected a native head chief who was assisted by chiefs in charge of subdistricts. There were line chiefs, leader chiefs, farmer chiefs, and strife chiefs, and native courts were set up. Laws were drawn up, combining rules of customary law with more modern ones about labor wages, tax payments, and government duties. Although these institutions had no real power, the organization was a blueprint of an expected state of affairs. Impatient, huge demonstrations were staged in front of official government buildings, and people demanded higher wages, education, political participation or independence, and removal of missionaries and European officials. Unable to suppress this large movement, the British eventually opened a school to train native students for posts in government positions, and also established native councils.

MILLENARISM AND THE STRUGGLE FOR POLITICAL INDEPENDENCE

Even in situations in which such measures have not yet been taken, it is clear that millenary movements often involve active struggles for greater political participation or independence. The attempts to create larger regional units, as in the Taro and Naked

Cult movements, may well be seen as a necessary first step in the direction of self-government. These observations have led a number of interpreters to the view that millenarism is essentially a prepolitical phenomenon (Worsley, 1957; Hobsbawm 1965; Cohn, 1961; Lawrence, 1964). Lawrence, who made a detailed study of the cargo cults in the Madang District of New Guinea, writes that they gave rise to a form of "embryonic nationalism," a "political structure of indigenous growth which expresses *militant opposition* to European rule, and is designed to hold together a *permanent* combination of hitherto autonomous political groups or equivalent associations by means of centralized authority and an incipient ranking system" (1964:257–58). Lawrence admits that such embryonic nationalism is not an invariable feature of every millenarian movement.

Worsley, on the other hand, holds that millenarism appears mainly in nonliterate stateless societies, those which possess no over-all unity and lack centralized political authority. When these movements occur in modern cultures, they arise among the lower orders of agrarian feudalistic societies as part of the opposition to the official regimes (1957:229–30). Injecting Marxian ideology into his theories, Worsley also feels that the movements will wither away once the political goals have been attained (*ibid.*:225). Hobsbawm and Cohn are in basic agreement, though Cohn believes that millenarism (in Europe) will lead up to, or is in any case closely related to, Nazism and Communism. He characterizes millenarism, Communism, and Nazism as "collective megalomania," paranoid fantasies born out of hatred and irrational fears, inspired by "archaic" fantasies (1961:3). Each of these authors has a fairly negative approach toward these religious phenomena. Lawrence, taking the side of government administration, feels that the cargo cults in New Guinea have a "disruptive influence" (1964:1). Worsley and Hobsbawm see millenarism as a useful tool, unimportant in itself, but serving an important end.

The insight that millenarism may lead to political developments is of great importance. The movements usually demand intense commitment and unconditional faith and loyalty from their followers. The expectations are, most often, tersely stated, and the movements are generally action-oriented. By concerted, communal efforts, people themselves can help to hasten the coming of the millennium. The greater the cooperation, the sooner its arrival. Tribal lines and cultural differences can be easily forgotten or overcome, for the different groups all have the same goals. Communal work and the excitement of the new ideology may well bring about a new awareness and a change in attitudes toward life. When sociocultural conditions are conducive to political possibilities, the future millennium is likely to include expectations of local autonomy and political identity.

It is undoubtedly true that millenary movements are powerful potential agents of social and political change. Their expectations are directed toward social improvements in this world, rather than in an afterworld. Nevertheless, characterizations of millenarian movements as "prepolitical" or as "forerunners of nationalism" are unfortunate, because they imply prediction and, by extension, imply that the movements are directed toward one ultimate purpose—political development. Such a view suffers from the shortcomings common to all deterministic explanations; it is one-sided, for it precludes the operation of all other forces and treats the phenomena under consideration merely as means toward a preordained end.

The adherents of the "prepolitical theory" confuse explanation with prediction. Their theories ably explain certain developments on a microspecific level. But it does not follow that all millenarism is inherently directed toward political aims and purposes. Lawrence showed that many cargo cults in New Guinea were dominated by economic rather than political motivations (1964:273). Cults such as the Milne Bay Prophet movement, stressing return to past conditions, do not reflect any incipient desire toward political freedom or political participation; they aim only at the expulsion of the invaders. Firth, among others, pointed out that the movements have psychological functions, providing an emotional outlet for frustrations (1963c: 113). The communal ritual activities are really imaginative projections of otherwise frustrated desires. Margaret Mead observed that cargo cult behavior has become so well established in New Guinea that it has diffused as a model among island peoples who even lacked direct contact with Europeans (1964:195–96). In the New Guinea Highlands, where people sometimes still cultivated their gardens with Neolithic tools, "radio towers" were constructed for communication with the supernaturals who, in some magical way, would bring them the desired gifts; and airstrips were built by people who had never seen an airplane. Clearly, it would be stretching a point to call such behavior "pre-political."

MILLENARISM IN NORTH AMERICA

North American Indian religious movements have been dealt with most frequently by American anthropologists, who have generally shifted attention from the role and contents of the movements to the social conditions surrounding their inception. Acknowledging the importance of the prepolitical theory for the explanation of specific developments, they have tried to show that millenarism is basically a religion of socially deprived or oppressed groups. Deprivation of some sort regularly attends the rise of religious movements, but this observation needs further scrutiny. There are few—if any—historical situations in which all members of a given society agree that the world is perfect.

In order to make the deprivation theory more meaningful, the term *deprivation* should be defined and further analyzed. Aberle pointed out that deprivation is always relative and defines it as "a negative discrepancy between legitimate expectations and actuality" (1965:537–41). Relative discrepancy may refer to differences between past and present situations, between present and future, or between one man's lot and another's. The deprivation may relate to material goods, to status, to behavior, or to worth, and so on. No one cult fits neatly into any such category; for the deprivation of material goods often goes hand in hand with that of status and worth, and may refer to past, present, and future at once. Nevertheless, this scheme gives important insights into the nature of deprivations which are conducive to the birth of religious cults.

But personal dissatisfactions alone are not sufficient to set such movements into motion. People will follow a prophet only when he strikes responsive chords and promises the alleviation of commonly experienced social deprivations.

There are many cultural conditions which may affect the

appearance of such movements. Stratified societies, in which discrepancies of status, wealth, and worth are sometimes very pronounced, will not produce millenary movements as long as they can reasonably explain and justify the social differences. This may be done by myth, by the concept of social contract, or by guarantees of peace and protection. When the framework of authority is disrupted, however, the disoriented classes will revolt; or, if revolt is not possible, they will follow a prophet who formulates a new and better order.

The Ghost Dance

No myth, no value system can justify future foreign invasions and occupations, although such vindications often appear when a new balance of power has been established and accepted. It becomes understandable, then, that millenarism frequently accompanies invasion and colonizations. In some cases, however, there may be other cultural factors of value and belief that prevent the acceptance of specific new doctrines. The Ghost Dance religion promised the Indians a restoration of old forms of life, the expulsion of the invaders, and the return of the deceased ancestors. The cult found wide acceptance, but it never attained a foothold among the Navaho Indians. Although the Navaho undoubtedly would have accepted the first two prospects, the third was to be avoided at all costs. No greater calamity than the return of the ghosts could be envisaged by the Navaho, because there was nothing they feared more than death, the dead, and everything connected with them (Hill, 1944:523–27).

Indian contact with Europeans has a long history. Many Pacific island groups were rediscovered only in the latter part of the eighteenth century, and did not receive much political attention until the nineteenth century. The Iroquois Indians, however, signed a treaty with the Dutch in 1644, and another with the English in 1664. Missionary activities in the Pacific region remained sporadic for a long time, but by 1711 the Iroquois had been subjected to so many different influences that they could say: "If the English sell goods cheaper than the French, we will have ministers; if the French sell them cheaper than the English, we will have priests" (Parkman, 1892:I,10).

It is possible to distinguish two major phases of development in the religious movements arising in the wake of Western civi-

lization in North America. The first reflects ever-increasing hostility toward the white invaders, coupled with the desire to expel or kill them, and to reinstitute the old culture. The second reflects adaptation to the inevitable, with partial acceptance of Western culture and its possible advantages. The earlier movements emphasize the past, and envisage the millennium as similar to—but also better than—the past; the later movements focus on the hope for gradual change and progress, with the retention of Indian identity.

This situation shows that deprivation itself may be transformed into something more positive. Human societies tend to adapt, to seek adjustment to changed conditions. This means that unrealistic expectations will sooner or later disappear. Movements derived from such motivations cannot be long-lived.

Of the many clearly millenary American Indian cults, the Ghost Dance religion is particularly well documented. Its two major outbreaks have been described by James Mooney, who witnessed the last one. Employed by the Bureau of American Ethnography, Mooney was dispatched to the Sioux and other tribes in 1891 in order to investigate this new religious phenomenon, The research was not motivated by anthropological interest, but by the government's fear that another Indian revolt might be afoot. It is fortunate that Mooney was a sympathetic and careful observer with some ethnological knowledge and insights. He provided a vivid and detailed account of the Ghost Dance (1896, reprinted 1965); and theoretical considerations were not absent from his descriptions.

Although the dates are not precise, the two major outbreaks of the phenomenon are generally known as the Ghost Dance of 1870 and the Ghost Dance of 1890. The originator of the first one was Wodziwob, a tribesman of the Northern Paiute (or Paviotso) Indians, at Walker Lake, Nevada. Visions and dreams had revealed to him that the Great Spirit was on his way back to earth, accompanied by the spirits of the dead. A great cataclysm would shake the world, in the course of which the white men would vanish, although their buildings and goods would remain for the use of the Indians. Afterward, an earthly paradise would commence in which life would be eternal and food plentiful.

Wodziwob's message was basically simple: only the ancestors of those who believed would return to earth, and participation in

a ritual dance would hasten their arrival. The dance pattern was a circle which should not be entirely closed in order that the ancestor ghosts might enter it and watch the proceedings. Supernaturally revealed songs accompanied the relatively simple steps. Before the ritual dance, participants purified themselves by bathing in the lake, and decorated their bodies with black, red, and white paint.

Wodziwob died three or four years after initiating this movement, but the cult had been taken up by other Indian leaders. Wenyuga, also known as Frank Spencer, carried the Ghost Dance religion to the Washo Indians; and later, it spread west among the Modoc, the Klamath, and other Indian groups in southern Oregon and California. In the process of diffusion, a number of adjustments to local conditions were made. The Californian Earth Lodge cult and several other cults were local offshoots of the Ghost Dance. Members of the Earth Lodge cult, who expected the return of the dead after a large-scale natural catastrophe, sought protection in specially built circular underground chambers in which the ritual dances were carried out (Du Bois, 1939: 79–116). This cult diffused back along the same route from which its impetus had come. In Oregon it was known as the Warm House cult. The centers were square instead of round and had a hearth in the center (ibid.:27–31). In some places these cults completely overshadowed the Ghost Dance; in others, the two movements were mixed.

Another derivation, the Bole-Maru cult showed greater evidence of Christian influence. It was not millenarian, did not anticipate a world catastrophe, and expected salvation only in a life after death. The Bole-Maru cult nevertheless maintained a number of modified native dances as part of its ritual, and introduced the use of patterned flags and the wearing of white dresses (ibid.:133). Of all these various cults, the Bole-Maru was the most enduring. It was still active at the outbreak of World War II. All other movements, including the Ghost Dance, waned, partly because they were discouraged by government interference, partly because the predictions did not materialize.

The Ghost Dance of 1890 was more spectacular and dramatic. Like the first, it started among the Paiute Indians. Its prophet was Wovoka, the son of an early convert of Wodziwob (Du Bois, 1939:3). Although this relationship is not entirely clear (cf.

Mooney, 1965:5; Wallace, 1965:viii), it is very likely that Wovoka, who was born in 1856 or 1858, had seen Ghost Dance ceremonies in his youth or had heard its doctrines being discussed. Wovoka was also well acquainted with Western culture and with the teachings of Christianity: after the death of his father, he was taken in by a local farmer who gave Wovoka his American name: Jack Wilson.

In or about 1886, Wovoka had a vision in which he was instructed to reinstate the Ghost Dance. A message of peace was added to the earlier doctrines. People were not to fight, even against white men, nor should they lie, steal, or drink whiskey. The white men would eventually be carried away by high winds, leaving all their possessions to the Indians (Lesser, 1933: 109–15), or else they would change, becoming one with the Indians (Mooney, 1965:27). (The latter version may well have been given in order not to insult or alarm the white investigators.)

The dance itself was reinstated largely in its original form. Purified participants painted their faces and bodies, danced in a circle, and sang divinely revealed songs. They wore white garments, the so-called ghost shirts. These garments were made of cotton, sewn with sinew, and painted with a variety of designs (see Figure 14). They were believed to be bullet-proof.

Figure 14. Ghost shirt, used in Ghost Dance religion.

This movement spread rapidly eastward to other Indian tribes. Mooney estimates that between thirty and thirty-five tribes were affected by the Ghost Dance, notably Shoshoni, Arapaho, Cheyenne, Caddo, Pawnee, and Sioux (*ibid.*:199–200).

Particularly among the Sioux, the movement ended in tragedy. In the process of diffusion, the peaceful message of Wovoka was lost. Sitting Bull, the famous Sioux chief, had fled to Canada after the annihilation of Custer and his army in 1876, and had returned after four years. Now, shorn of his power and influence, he lived in comparative seclusion as a "reservation Indian." When the Ghost Dance reached the Sioux, Sitting Bull saw it as a means of returning to power, and he became its most influential Sioux leader and prophet. The government, dismayed over his renewed power and the new outbreak of the Ghost Dance, decided to arrest Sitting Bull. Fighting broke out, and Sitting Bull, two of his sons, and a number of others died in the battle (*ibid.*:104–5). Two weeks later, on December 28th, 1890, during the Battle of Wounded Knee Creek, some three hundred followers of Sitting Bull were killed, many of them wearing the ghosts shirts that were to make them invincible (*ibid.*:119).

Not everywhere did the Ghost Dance end in such tragedy. Mooney reports that, at the time of publication (1896), the movement was already extinct in some tribes (*ibid.*:200), while in others it was still very active, and "developing new features at every performance" (*ibid.*:xi). Mooney, of course, could not know at that time how the Ghost Dance was further transformed in the process of its perpetuation.

In his interpretations of the Ghost Dance, Mooney may be considered as an early exponent of the deprivation theory. He regarded the movements as responses to the "groaning beneath an alien yoke" (*ibid.*:1). Several times he refers to the Ghost Dance as a "new religion," born of the contingencies of the moment.

Later studies, however, have shown that many of the basic elements of the Ghost Dance were present long before 1870. Spier derives the Ghost Dance from a complex of religious cults among Indians in the Northwest Plateau area, and calls these movements collectively *the Prophet Dance* (1935). The Prophet Dance was based on the belief that shamans could visit the land of the dead and return with messages from them, that the world was worn out and in need of renewal, that this renewal would take place after a cataclysm, that the ancestors would return to earth, and that the happy event could be hastened by dancing in imitation of the dances of the dead. These dances were typically held under the leadership of a supernaturally inspired shaman or prophet who had had dreams and revelations about the future. The similarities to the Ghost Dance are obvious.

Spier felt that the Prophet Dance itself had developed in three historical stages: (1) prior to 1820, without Christian influence; (2) from about 1820 to 1850, when Christian elements entered; and (3) from 1850 onward, when more direct contact with Europeans brought about the idea that not only the world, but also the white invaders, would be destroyed. The last phase then led eventually to the Ghost Dance. A smaller but even more detailed diffusion study showed, furthermore, that among the Coast Salish Indians the Prophet Dance was derived from a similar movement of the Plateau region (Suttles, 1957:352–396). It was adopted before 1840, before intensive contact with Western society. Until 1840, the Coast Salish were visited only sporadically by fur traders, who did not exercise great influence upon the social structure and did not cause any deprivation.

These historical explanations show how deprivation alone cannot account for religious change and millenarism, and that diffusion is a factor that cannot be discounted. The Ghost Dance, like all religious movements, contained aboriginal elements, borrowed and diffused elements, and (in mission areas) Christian elements. These influences merged; the new synthesis expressed the contingencies of the moment and strove to find solutions to unprecedented dilemmas. The Ghost Dance was thus not merely a reaction to direct contact with dominant alien societies, but had many internal and intertribal concomitants.

The Peyote Cult

The second major phase of religious change among American Indians reflected an increasing tendency to adjust to, and accept, the changed cultural situation. There is, of course, no sharp break between the phases, except, perhaps, for the abandonment of the idea of a millennium, of a future in which all non-Indians would disappear. Instead, there was hope for salvation after death, and for emancipation and equal rights on earth.

Of the various religious movements of this nature, the Peyote cult has been the most influential and the most enduring. The Peyote cult centers its rituals on the eating of peyote, a small, spineless cactus with hallucinatory qualities.

The special psychological states thus produced have been variously described by non-Indian users as an "ineffable transcendental experience" (Huxley, 1954), one that gives "increased powers of introspection..., mental telephathy...," (Slotkin, 1965a:515); but we also find the following statement: "Taking peyote is hard. The taste is bitter, the nausea unpleasant, the anxiety and depression overwhelming..." (Aberle, 1966a:9). Clearly, the effects are not uniform, and even one person may experience different reactions on different occasions. Although much has been written about the possible harmful effects of peyote, the Indians believe it has curative powers. However, scientific investigation has not yet determined that peyote has either harmful or beneficial mental or physical effects on American Indian users, and it has not created physical dependence (ibid.:399–400).

The Peyote ritual is typically an all-night ceremony, usually held in a native building—a tipi among the Plains Indians, a hogan among the Navaho. The rite is divided into four periods, and the four most important officiants are the road chief (who leads the meetings), the drum chief (who accompanies the songs), the fire chief (who maintains the ritual fire), and the cedar chief (who sprinkles cedar incense on the fire). The rite has four major ritual elements: praying, singing, peyote eating, and contemplation. The peyote is usually taken around midnight. At dawn the Morning Water Song is chanted and a vessel of water is brought in; everyone drinks, and a Closing Song ends the ceremony, often followed by a communal breakfast.

To the participants, the use of peyote has two major benefits: spiritual knowledge and power, and cure and protection. Peyote may be used as a home remedy for minor disorders; in more serious cases the patient may be brought to the ritual and given larger quantities of peyote, which will generally cause him to vomit. It is believed that vomiting has purifying effects, both physical and spiritual. Peyote also provides the believer with visions in which direct communication with the supernatural is regularly experienced, so that guidance to the solution of problems in daily life may thus be obtained.

Peyotism developed in a period of rising Christian influence. Although few such influences could be discovered in the early Plains rites, the Winnebago Indians have said that the road chief, the drummer, and the cedar man represent the members of the Trinity. The Winnebago also maintain that the Bible contains a reference to peyote: "And they shall eat the flesh in that night, roast with fire, and unleavened bread; and with *bitter herbs* they shall eat it" (Exodus XII:18). Their songs and prayers express such sentiments as "This is the road that Jesus showed us to walk in," or "God, I thank you for all you have done for me in Jesus' name."

Other acculturative influences include the organization of national Peyote cults. In 1906, loose inter-tribal organizations of Peyote groups were in Oklahoma and Nebraska; in 1909 they became the Union Church, and later the Native American Church. Under this name, the religion was officially incorporated in Oklahoma in 1918, and became a national organization in 1944. By 1955, thirteen states and one Canadian province had issued local charters to its Native American Churches. Largely modeled upon the example of other American church organizations, the Native American Church grew out of the necessity to find legal status and security after a number of states had outlawed the use of peyote. In 1962, three Navaho Indians were arrested and given suspended sentences for the religious use of peyote, but they appealed the decision on grounds that their religious freedom had been violated. In 1964, California's Fourth District Court of Appeals confirmed the conviction, ruling that the use of peyote was a threat to public safety. The next appeal brought the case before the Supreme Court of California, which declared that the use of peyote does not violate state narcotic laws (*The New York Times*, August 25, 1964).

Although the Peyote religion has become more structured, and its rituals more standardized, its patterns of belief are not very clearly defined. In part, this is to be explained by the peculiar nature of peyote itself, for it provides individual visions rather than communal encounters with the supernatural. The visions, and their interpretation, are at least partly conditioned by the social experiences and views of the participants. Therefore, the belief patterns are flexible, and open to the accommodation or rejection of acculturative elements.

It becomes understandable, then, that some Peyote cults are apparently much more Christianized than others. Cheyenne, Menomini, and Winnebago Peyote cults have long been known to use more Christian elements than most others. Among the Menomini, the sign of the cross is regularly made, and the ashes are shaped in the form of a dove, the symbol of the Holy Spirit. Nevertheless, it is not always easy to decide what is a Christian element and what is not. Slotkin, himself a member and an officer of the Native American Church, and eager to minimize the differences between Indian religion and Christianity, compared the eating of peyote with the Christian Holy Communion and the taking of the sacramental bread and wine; and he also equates the mana-like power of peyote with the power of the Holy Spirit. He adds: "From the viewpoint of almost all Peyotists, the religion is an Indian version of Christianity." (1965a:513–14). Such comparisons are forced and superficial. Most forms of religion have a concept of supernatural power, and many include a communal meal as part of their ritual. Slotkin would have to admit that all were "versions" of Christianity.

Although there is some disagreement on this point, diffusion studies tend to indicate that peyotism is basically aboriginal, and has received differing degrees of Christian additions and reinterpretations. The current acculturative states of the various Indian groups probably have some bearing upon the degree of acceptance of Christian elements. The possibility that Christian elements may diffuse together with the rite itself cannot be wholly discounted.

RELIGIOUS CHANGE IN AFRICA

Religious movements of all kinds have been particularly numerous on the African continent. For the Bantu region of South Africa alone, Sundkler reports the existence of well over two thousand separatist churches and an equal number of mission churches (1961:374). Millenarism is not unknown, but is by no means as dominant as it is in Melanesia. Although anti-white feelings are often very strong, there are remarkably few cults that predict apocalyptic doom and expulsion of non-Africans.

Missionary policy in Africa tended to be one of self-propagation; native priests and pastors were trained and installed as religious leaders so that European missionaries could be employed elsewhere. Although white missionaries exercised a certain amount of supervision, local interpretations and readjustments were possible.

Christian dogma teaches that all men are brothers, and equal in the sight of God. Nevertheless, it soon became clear that Africans could not enter "white" churches, and were not considered equals to the Europeans who had seized African lands and herded the natives onto reservations or into the cities. The unrelenting segregation policy, particularly in South Africa, was extended to all realms of life, including religion. Not by chance, then, did separatist movements arise and proliferate. Most of these reinterpreted Christian beliefs, some promising independence and reinstatement of rights; others, peaceful coexistence; still others, the expulsion of the hated invaders. But many movements merely attempted to search for a new African identity in a world in which old values seemed no longer acceptable and new ones were unattainable.

Religious change under Christian influence manifested itself in Africa on three different levels: (1) the native mission churches, officially recognized by mission societies as "orthodox," but with varying reinterpretations of Christian dogma and ritual; (2) separatist churches, split from the native churches, with greater departures from Christian dogma; and (3) "new" cults, arising under the leadership of inspired prophets, claiming neither secession from nor identity with Christian churches, but usually displaying a considerable degree of reinterpreted Christian influence together with many traditional patterns.

The results are confusing, to say the least. The names given by African people to their new or separatist movements reflect the entanglements: "Christian Catholic Apostolic Nazareth Church in Zion of South Africa," "The Pentecostal Baptist Apostolic Church of South Africa," and "Sun Light Four Corners Apostolic for Witness of God Jehovah" are but some of the telling examples (Sundkler, 1961: Appendix B).

One can find in these movements almost any form of religious behavior: baptism, communion, confession, testimony, trance, possession, divination, witchcraft and antiwitchcraft, curing, dancing, drumming, singing, shouting, speaking in tongues, revelations, taboos of all kinds, and the use of every piece of ritual paraphernalia ever invented by man, or so it seems. One admittedly extreme example shows that this is hardly an exaggeration. In a number of churches, the use of purgatives plays an important ritual role, and one of these churches was officially named "The African Castor Oil Dead Church." This "medicine" was not only used for ritual purification, but also symbolized the hope for a new and better life where malnutrition, constipation, and indigestion would be absent (*ibid.:* 212).

Most services are patterned after the liturgical order of official Christian churches. The mission churches conform more closely to these patterns than the separatists, and there is less deviation in the cities than in smaller villages. The services are held on Sunday mornings, except by those groups who call themselves "Israelites" and worship on Saturdays.

Sundkler describes as "fairly typical" a Sunday service held in a small village. The prophet "rings the bell," beating a ploughshare, and the service begins. Some thirty people, ten of them children, congregate in a sod hut used as religious meeting house.

Hymn singing is frequent, and the leader opens the ritual by leading the congregation in song. Soon, people begin to sway with the rhythm, and a few women "get the spirit"—they throw themselves about on the ground and speak in tongues. After all are seated again, the confessional part of the service begins. Three or four women rise and confess, telling how they have been cured, and giving testimony of their faith. This testimony is followed by prayer, in which all participate, individually but simultaneously, and as loudly as possible. During the prayers, the prophet and a number of others receive the spirit and speak in tongues until one woman, the drummer, intones the Lord's Prayer. Others now join in the singing of this prayer. More singing follows, until the prophet orders, "Present arms!" A man in a long green coat takes a bundle of wooden crosses from a corner. Placing himself in the middle of the hut, he begins to sing the "Hymn of the Cross." All except the prophet begin to walk around the man, and he hands a cross to each one. After

this, the sermon begins. But even during sermon there is a great
deal of audience participation. People shout "Hallelujah!,"
"Amen!", "Peace in Zion!," or they continue to sing. Then the
most important part of the service begins. The sick and ailing
are carried to the center of the room, while the others walk
around them, singing and praying. The prophet determines the
cause of the ailments, and then expels "snakes" and other disease-
causing demons by seizing the arms of the patients and shaking
them vigorously. Children are treated in a more gentle manner.
The service ends with more singing and finally with a prayer of
thanks to "the God of Shadrach, Meshach and Abednego" (ibid.:
183–87).

Many other cults, particularly those in areas near rivers and
lakes, practice baptism by total immersion. The streams and lakes
are almost invariably called "the New Jordan," and immersion
serves not only to admit new members, but also as a symbolic
repetition of the baptismal ceremony. The leader of these services
first stresses the dangers of the waters before they have been
purified. He proclaims that they are inhabited by snakes, croco-
diles, demons, and water-monsters. Then he proceeds to subdue
these creatures by praying to God and to the Water Angels, simultaneously scattering ashes or leaves over the waters. When
this has been accomplished, the prophet steps into the river and
immerses himself three times or sometimes seven times; his example is then followed by the faithful. The ritual bathing serves
to purify, to protect, and to cure illness.

Although the services vary, they have some common characteristics—singing (accompanied by drums, rattles, or hand-clap-
ping), loud and lengthy sermons interrupted by exclamations
from the audience, testimonies and confessions, baptism and
curing. Although the Christian influence is unmistakable, its
relative strength is uncertain. Some of the elements which appear
to be "typically" Christian were also known in indigenous African
religions. Herskovits (1958:207–60) pointed out that confessions,
in many parts of Africa, were important prerequisites for the
successful curing of illness or for the undoing of witchcraft, while
baptism had its counterparts in the river cults common throughout South and West Africa. Singing, chanting, the religious use
of musical instruments, and praying are traits found in religions
all over the world. When one considers that baptismal immer-
sions and religious healing are not unfamiliar in Christianity,

there are very few traits left that can be considered "typical" of either Christian or African forms of religious behavior.

THE PROCESS OF RELIGIOUS CHANGE

But, although it is not very useful to attempt a sorting out of traits, the perceived similarities aid in the understanding of some of the processes of religious change. In general, religious change takes place by the addition of new elements, the discarding of old ones, or the modification of existing ones. New elements may originate within the culture itself, but they are most frequently borrowed from others. In neither instance are the changes wholly abrupt. In every known case, "new" religions have been continuations of older ones: Christianity incorporated many Jewish elements, Protestantism built on Catholicism, Buddhism sprang from Brahmanism.

In the process of diffusion, the adoption of culture items depends to some extent on whether change is voluntary or involuntary. Voluntary adoption may take place when two cultures have so much contact that they are aware of each other's culture patterns, including religion. Traits will circulate, but the degree of acceptance will largely depend upon their compatibility with existing patterns. Those ideas that fit readily within the system will diffuse with relative ease, although they usually require a certain amount of reinterpretation.

Involuntary change takes place when one of the two cultures in contact is larger, stronger, and technologically more advanced. The rejection of alien traits by the weaker culture is much less easy, and when, moreover, the dominant culture makes strong efforts to enforce religious change by mission work, it is generally successful. As a result, large-scale reinterpretation is necessary. In Africa, there were enough elements in missionary teachings that could be adjusted to existing ones, and the new cults became syncretistic wholes.

Yucatan

In the various examples of religious change discussed so far, the new cults possessed a great amount of internal unity. If one culture is dominated by another, and pressure is brought against its religious customs, extensive reinterpretation may bring about such unity, particularly when superficial similarities between the two religions can be discovered. If not, fusion is not so readily achieved, and a kind of ritual dualism will often result. The Maya village of Chan Kom in Yucatan provides a good example of such a situation. (Redfield and Rojas, 1962). People profess the Catholic faith, go to Mass when they visit the cities, and, at home, attend religious ceremonies that are Catholic in form. But there are other important ceremonies as well, directed largely to the aboriginal gods and spirits. The Maya people themselves make no historical distinction between Catholic divinities and aboriginal deities. Nevertheless, they recognize the differences between the two types of supernaturals because each occurs in a different ritual context, has different religious leaders, and possesses different attributes (*ibid.*:111).

The Catholic aspects are many. Every important village has its own *santos,* whose names, appearances, and attributes are largely those of official Catholic saints. In Chan Kom, the *santos* are San Diego, the Holy Cross, and the *Niño Dios,* the infant Jesus. Together, they protect the village, and any member of the community can pray to them for help. These deities are generally beneficial, and they are not closely bound up with elements of nature. The Holy Cross is a common religious denominator, but each Mayan village has its own patron saint. In Chan Kom, this is San Diego, and one of his functions is to provide village identity.

Services for the *santos* are led by a *maestro cantor,* a man who has memorized prayers from Catholic liturgy both in Spanish and in Latin. Novenas are held on the name day of a *santo* as well as on other occasions. They are made by the whole village, and for the common good. More frequent are the *novenas de promesa,* made in fulfillment of a vow, and held in private houses. Although prayer is the central activity, these are also social occasions, with invited guests, and conversation and food after the service.

The aboriginal supernaturals are much more numerous than the *santos,* and more closely connected with elements of nature. Four *balams* protect the village and its fields, guarding against predatory beasts and driving away evil winds. The *chaacs* are the rain gods and the *kuilob kaaxobs* are forest deities. There are also gods of the bees, guardians of the deer, and guardians of cattle, as well as goblins, demons, and monsters. Rituals are led by specialists known as *h-mens*. They officiate in ceremonies centered around the *balams*, the *chaacs*, and the *kuilob kaaxobs*. The rituals differ from the novenas in several important respects: prayers are always recited in the Maya language; the rituals are taboo to women and to members of other villages; and the ceremonies are not followed by social feasting.

The functions of the two types of rituals overlap. Both are held to cure illness and to insure the fertility of the lands. Novenas, however, are particularly appropriate to baptism, marriage, funerals, and memorial services. Both ceremonies make use of candles, an altar, food offerings, and wooden crosses. Although statues and pictures of saints do not appear in the indigenous Maya rituals, the names of saints are often mentioned in the prayers of the *h-mens*.

The two types of rituals are, to the Maya, parts of one common faith. The *maestro cantors* and *h-mens* are neither opposed to one another nor in competition. Both stand under the ultimate power of *Dios*, who has no image, and thus is not a *santo*. Factionalism came about much later, not because of a split between the two ritual systems and their leaders, but through Protestant mission work in the village (Redfield, 1962:88–112). The schism was, in fact, rooted in a long-existing rivalry between two principal family groups. A most interesting aspect of these developments was that both the Catholic and the Protestant villagers continued to carry on, in common, the rituals requiring the services of *h-mens (ibid.:*107). Thus the native tradition remained the basis for community cohesion.

The type of religious change in Chan Kom was typically one of addition. The *santos* are perceived as not very different from the native gods: both protect the village and guard it against misfortunes, and both need ritual attention and offerings. It was, therefore, not difficult to accept them—who would refuse to have more protection than before? The same attitude is recognizable in other Mayan approaches to cultural change. For example, no definite choice has been made between old and modern curing techniques, for both are tried. Many people have learned Spanish, but they continue to speak Maya at home. Children are breastfed in the traditional manner (*i.e.,* whenever they cry), but their diet is supplemented by strained orange juice.

The situation is by no means unique. Ritual dualism occurs among Negro populations in Haiti, Surinam, and Brazil, where the saints are often identified with African deities. Herskovits notes that, in Haiti, the Dahomean trickster god Legba has undergone fusion with Saint Anthony (both are traditionally associated with poverty) (1965:543). Saint Patrick, often depicted expelling the snakes from Ireland, became identified with Dambella, the Dahomean rainbow serpent. Many Haitian villages do not have a resident Catholic priest. People go to Mass when they visit the city or when a visiting priest stops by. But there are local cult groups whose rituals center on the *loa,* known by Christian names, African-derived names, or both. These vodoun gods are numbered in the hundreds. During the services, both saints and *loas* are invoked. Catholic prayers are sometimes recited or read, but there is little else in the ritual patterns that is reminiscent of the traditional Catholic Mass. Yet, full religious membership in the local cults requires a pilgrimage to the shrine of a saint of the city, as well as long initiation periods. During the cult meetings, the *loas* and saints are called to dance by beating a hollow-log drum, but this drum will not be effective unless it has been blessed and sanctified by a visiting Catholic priest. The cult houses are closed during Lent, for the gods are absent. (In Catholic churches, saints' statues are shrouded in purple cloth, during Holy Week.) All cult houses have altars on which African wood carvings and offerings stand side by side with crucifixes, candles, and colored pictures of saints (Herskovits, 1958:249).

CONCLUSION

What possible significance can be derived from this syncretism? It is a notable fact that when Christianity has made forceful efforts at conversion, its external elements often have been readily accepted. But it remains an open question—and one scarcely studied in detail—how genuine is the incorporation of its symbolic meanings. It appears that, often, it has not been genuine. This shows, in turn, that religious change is not an isolated cultural phenomenon but that a change in symbolic contents can be meaningfully achieved only if the social reality changes as well.

If religion is meaningful as a social institution, it must be related to human experience. Religions do not spring up in order to integrate society or to achieve political independence, and neither do religions necessarily comfort or bestow on man "the gift of mental integrity," counteracting "the centrifugal forces of fear, dismay, demoralization" and assuring "the victory of tradition and culture over the more negative response of thwarted instinct," as Malinowski (1954:53) would have it. Religions can have all these microfunctions and many more, but such romantic confidence in over-all religious efficacy can easily be offset by the realization that religion can also be disintegrative, leading to wars, fears, sufferings, disorder, and demoralization.

The macrofunction of religion is not the "function" of anthropologists and psychologists, but its symbolic affirmation of social reality. Such affirmation does not idealize, does not deny suffering; it attempts to face reality. The religious response is, then, a symbolic image of a social order.

Incongruities between that symbolic image and real life will always arise, and will eventually demand re-examination and redefinition of religious precepts and principles. Some of these redefinitions may be borrowed from those who have caused the incongruities to widen, but the basic realignments will have to come from within. Most religious systems are so rich in symbolic content that they permit flexibility of interpretation and reinterpretation. Should this become impossible, the gods will die, and their religious systems with them.

Bibliography

A

Aberle, David F. 1965. "A Note on Relative Deprivation Theory as Applied to Millenarian and Other Cult Movements," in William Lessa and Evon Z. Vogt (eds.), *Reader in Comparative Religion,* 2d ed. New York: Harper and Row, pp. 537–541.
———. 1966a. *The Peyote Religion among the Navaho.* Viking Fund Publications in Anthropology 42. Wenner-Gren Foundation for Anthropological Research, Inc.
———. 1966b. "Religio-Magical Phenomena and Power, Prediction, and Control," *Southwestern Journal of Anthropology,* 22:221–230.
Ackerknecht, Erwin H. 1965. "Problems of Primitive Medicine," in William Lessa and Evon Z. Vogt (eds.), *Reader in Comparative Religion,* 2d ed. New York: Harper and Row, pp. 394–402 (first published, 1942).
Adair, John J. 1948. "A Study of Cultural Resistance: The Veterans of World War II at Zuni Pueblo," in Bernard J. Siegel (ed.), *Acculturation, Critical Abstracts, North America.* Stanford, Calif.: Stanford University Press, pp. 19–24.
Albright, William Foxwell. 1957. *From the Stone Age to Christianity. Monotheism and the Historical Process.* Garden City, N.Y.: Doubleday Anchor Books (first published, 1940).
Ames, Michael M. 1964. "Magical-animism and Buddhism: A Structural Analysis of the Sinhalese Religious System," in Ed-

ward B. Harper (ed.), *Religion in South Asia*. Seattle, Wash.: University of Washington Press, pp. 21–52.

Anesaki, Masaharu. 1961. *Religious Life of the Japanese People*. Tokyo: The Society for International Cultural Relations.

Atkinson, R. J. C. 1960. *Stonehenge*. Middlesex, England: Penguin Books Ltd.

B

Bächler, Emil. 1940. *Das alpine Paläolithikum der Schweiz, im Wildkirchli, Drachenloch und Wildenmannlisloch*. Basel: Birkhäuser & Cie.

Bachofen, Johann Jakob. 1861. *Das Mutterrecht*. Stuttgart: Krais & Hoffmann.

Balikci, Asen. 1963. "Shamanistic Behavior Among the Netsilik Eskimos," *Southwestern Journal of Anthropology*, 19:380–396.

Barnett, Homer. 1955. *The Coast Salish of British Columbia*. Eugene, Ore.: University of Oregon Monographs No. 4.

Barnouw, Victor. 1963. *Culture and Personality*. Homewood, Ill.: The Dorsey Press, Inc.

Barton, Roy Franklin. 1946. *The Religion of the Ifugaos*. Menasha, Wisc.: Memoirs of the American Anthropological Association No. 65.

———. 1949. *The Kalingas*. Chicago: University of Chicago Press.

Beattie, John H. M. 1960. *Bunyoro, An African Kingdom*. New York: Henry Holt & Company.

———. 1967. "Consulting a Nyoro Diviner: The Ethnologist as Client," *Ethnology*, VI:57–65.

Bellah, Robert N. 1965. *Religion and Progress in Modern Asia*. New York: The Free Press.

Belo, Jane. 1949. *Bali: Rangda and Barong*. Monographs of the American Ethnological Society XVI.

———. 1953. *Bali: Temple Festival*. Monographs of the American Ethnological Society XXII.

———. 1960. *Trance in Bali*. New York: Columbia University Press.

Benedict, Ruth. 1946. *Patterns of Culture*. New York: Mentor Books, The New American Library (first published, 1934).

Bennett, Wendell, and R. M. Zingg. 1935. *The Tarahumara: An Indian Tribe of Northern Mexico.* Chicago: University of Chicago Press.

Berthrong, Donald J. 1963. *The Southern Cheyenne.* Norman, Okla.: University of Oklahoma Press.

Bettelheim, Bruno. 1962. *Symbolic Wounds: Puberty Rites and the Envious Male.* New York: Collier Books (first published, 1954).

Bloch, Raymond. 1956. "Marvels and Divination in Ancient Italy," *Diogenes,* No. 16:39–58.

Boas, Franz. 1894. *Chinook Texts.* Washington, D.C.: Bulletin 20, Bureau of American Ethnology.

———. 1902. *Tsimshian Texts.* Washington, D.C.: Bulletin 27, Bureau of American Ethnology.

———. 1905. *Kwakiutl Texts.* Publications of the Jesup North Pacific Expedition, 3:5–532.

———. 1907. *The Eskimo of Baffinland and Hudson Bay.* New York: Bulletin 15, American Museum of Natural History.

———. 1935. *Kwakiutl Culture as Reflected in Mythology.* Memoir 28 of the American Folk-Lore Society.

———. 1940. *Race, Language and Culture.* New York: The Macmillan Company.

———. 1955. *Primitive Art.* New York: Dover Publications, Inc. (first published, 1927).

Bogoras, Waldemar. 1904–1909. *The Chuckchee.* Leyden: E. J. Brill Ltd.; Memoirs of the American Museum of Natural History, Vol. XI, parts 2 and 3.

Bohannan, Paul. 1963. *Social Anthropology.* New York: Holt, Rinehart and Winston Inc.

Bouché-Leqlerq, A. 1879–1882. *Histoire de la Divination dans l'Antiquité.* 4 vols. Paris: Leroux.

Boule, Marcellin, and Henry V. Vallois. 1957. *Fossil Men.* New York: The Dryden Press (first published in French, 1921).

Bouquet, A. C. 1941. *Comparative Religion.* Baltimore: Penguin Books.

Braidwood, Robert J. 1952. *The Near East and the Foundations for Civilization.* Eugene, Ore.: Oregon State System of Higher Education.

Breuil, H., L. Capitan, and M. Peyrony. 1910. *La Caverne de*

Font-de-Gaume aux Eyzies (Dordogne). Monaco: Publiées sous les auspices de S.A.S. le Prince Albert Iᵉʳ de Monaco.

Brinton, Daniel G. 1868. *The Myths of the New World: A Treatise on the Symbolism and Mythology of the Red Race in America*. New York: Leypoldt and Holt.

———. 1897. *Religions of Primitive Peoples*. New York: G. P. Putnam's Sons.

Brosses, Charles de. 1760. *Du culte des dieux fétiches, ou, Parallèle de l'ancienne religion de l'Egypte avec la religion actuelle de Nigritie*. Paris.

Buettner-Janusch, John. 1966. *Origins of Man*. New York: John Wiley & Sons, Inc.

Bunzel, Ruth. 1938. "The Economic Organization of Primitive Peoples," in Franz Boas (ed.), *General Anthropology*. New York: D. C. Heath and Company, pp. 327–408.

Burkitt, Miles C. 1963. *The Old Stone Age*, rev. ed. New York: Atheneum (first published, 1933).

Burton, Roger V., and John W. M. Whiting. 1961. "The Absent Father and Cross-Sex Identity," *Merrill-Palmer Quarterly of Behavior and Development*, VII:85–95.

Bury, J. B. 1955. *The Idea of Progress. An Inquiry into Its Growth and Origin*. New York: Dover Publications (first published, 1932).

Busia, K. A. 1954. "The Ashanti of the Gold Coast," in Daryll Forde (ed.), *African Worlds*. London and New York: Oxford University Press, pp. 190–209.

C

Campbell, Joseph. 1956. *The Hero with a Thousand Faces*. New York: Meridian Books (first published, 1949).

Cannon, Walter B. 1942. " 'Voodoo' Death," *American Anthropologist*, 44:169–181.

Capitan, L., and D. Peyrony. 1921. "Découverte d'un sixième squelette moustérien à la Ferrassie, Dordogne," *Revue anthropologique*, XXXI:382–388.

Cartari, Vincenzo. 1556. *Le Imagini colla Spozione degli Dei degli Antichi* (The Images of the Gods of Antiquity). Venice: Marcolini.

Castetter, Edward J. 1951. *Yuman Indian Agriculture*. Albuquerque, N.M.: University of New Mexico Press.

Chapple, Eliot Dismore, and Carleton Stevens Coon. 1942. *Principles of Anthropology*. New York: Henry Holt and Company.

Cherbury, Lord Edward Herbert of. SEE Herbert of Cherbury.

Childe, V. Gordon. 1951. *Man Makes Himself*. New York: Mentor Books, The New American Library.

Chowning, Ann. 1964. "Review of *Sorcerers of Dobu: the Social Anthropology of the Dobu Islanders of the Western Pacific* by R. F. Fortune," *American Anthropologist*, 66:455–457.

Clark, Grahame. 1953. *From Savagery to Civilization*. New York: Henry Schuman.

———. 1961. *World Prehistory—an Outline*. Cambridge: Cambridge University Press.

Clarke, Kenneth, and Mary Clarke. 1963. *Introducing Folklore*. New York: Holt, Rinehart and Winston Inc.

Clements, Forrest E. 1932. "Primitive Concepts of Disease," *University of California Publications in American Archaeology and Ethnology*, 32 (2):185–252.

Codrington, Robert H. 1891. *The Melanesians: Studies in Their Anthropology and Folklore*. Oxford: Clarendon Press.

Cohn, Norman. 1961. *The Pursuit of the Millennium*. New York: Harper Torchbooks.

Colby, Benjamin N. 1966. "Cultural Patterns in Narrative," *Science*, 151:793–798.

Colson, Elizabeth. 1958. *Marriage and the Family among the Plateau Tonga of Northern Rhodesia*. Manchester: Manchester University Press.

———. 1960. "Ancestral Spirits among the Plateau Tonga," in Simon and Phoebe Ottenberg (eds.), *Cultures and Societies in Africa*. New York: Random House, pp. 376–382.

———. 1965. "Ancestral Spirits and Social Structure among the Plateau Tonga," in William Lessa and Evon Z. Vogt (eds.), *Reader in Comparative Religion*, 2d ed. New York: Harper and Row, pp. 437–441 (first published, 1954).

Comte, Auguste. 1896. *The Positive Philosophy*. Harriet Martineau (trans. and ed.). London: George Bell and Sons (first published in French, 6 vols, 1830–1842).

Conant, Francis P. 1961. "Jarawa Kin Systems of Reference and

Address: A Componential Comparison," *Anthropological Linguistics,* 3:19–33.

Conklin, Harold C. 1954. *The Relation of Hanunóo Culture to the Plant World.* Doctoral dissertation, Yale University, New Haven, Conn.

————. 1955. "Hanunóo Color Categories," *Southwestern Journal of Anthropology,* 11:339–344.

————. 1957. *Hanunóo Agriculture.* A Report on an Integral System of Shifting Agriculture in the Philippines. Rome: Food and Agriculture Organization of the United Nations.

Coon, Carleton Stevens. 1962. *The Origin of Races.* New York: Alfred Knopf.

Cooper, John. 1946. "The Araucanians," in Julian H. Steward (ed.), *Handbook of South American Indians.* Washington, D.C.: Bureau of American Ethnology Bulletin 143, II:687–760.

Corlett, W. T. 1935. *The Medicine-Man of the American Indian and His Cultural Background.* Springfield and Baltimore: Charles C Thomas.

Coulanges, N. I. Fustel de. SEE Fustel de Coulanges, N. I.

D

Dammann, Ernst. 1963. *Die Religionen Afrikas.* Stuttgart: W. Kohlhammer.

Darwin, Charles. *The Descent of Man,* in *The Origin of Species and The Descent of Man.* New York: The Modern Library, Random House, pp. 387–924.

Davies, B. Trevor. 1947. *Four Centuries of Witch-Beliefs.* London: Methuen.

Dodds, E. R. 1957. *The Greeks and the Irrational.* Boston: Beacon Press.

Dole, Gertrude E. 1962. "Endocannibalism among the Amahuaca Indians," *Transactions of the New York Academy of Sciences,* 24:567–573.

————. 1966. "Anarchy without Chaos: Alternatives to Political Authority among the Kuikuru," in Marc J. Swartz, Victor W. Turner, and Arthur Tuden (eds.), *Political Anthropology.* Chicago: Aldine Publishing Company, pp. 73–88.

Dorson, Richard M. 1962. "Theories of Myth and the Folklorist," in Richard M. Ohmann (ed.), *The Making of Myth.* New York: G. P. Putnam's Sons, pp. 38–51.

———. 1963. "Current Folklore Theories," *Current Anthropology,* 4:93–112.

Dozier, Edward P. 1966. *Hano: a Tewa Indian Community in Arizona.* New York: Holt, Rinehart and Winston.

Du Bois, Cora. 1939. "The 1870 Ghost Dance," *Anthropological Records,* III, No. 1.

Dundas, Charles. 1924. *Kilimanjaro and Its People.* London: H. F. and G. Witherby.

Durkheim, Émile. 1958. *The Rules of Sociological Method.* Sarah A. Solovay and John H. Mueller (trans.). George E. G. Catlin (ed.). Glencoe, Ill.: The Free Press (first published in French, 1895; first published in English, 1938).

———. 1961. *The Elementary Forms of the Religious Life.* Joseph Ward Swain (trans.). New York: Collier Books (first published in French, 1912; first published in English, 1915).

E

Ehrenwald, Jan. 1956. *From Medicine Man to Freud.* New York: Dell Publishing Company Inc.

Ekvall, Robert B. 1964. *Religious Observations in Tibet.* Chicago: University of Chicago Press.

Eliade, Mircia. 1959. *Cosmos and History. The Myth of the Eternal Return.* Willard R. Trask (trans.). New York: Harper Torchbooks.

———. 1963. *Patterns in Comparative Religion.* Rosemary Sheed (trans.). New York: Meridian Books, The World Publishing Company.

———. 1965. *Rites and Symbols of Initiation: The Mysteries of Birth and Rebirth.* Willard R. Trask (trans.). New York: Harper Torchbooks.

Elkin, Adolphus P. 1964. *The Australian Aborigines.* Garden City, N.Y.: Doubleday Anchor Books.

Elmendorf, William W. 1951. "Word Taboo and Lexical Change in Coast Salish," *International Journal of American Linguistics,* 17:205–208.

Engels, Frederick. 1942. *The Origin of the Family, Private*

Property, and the State in the Light of the Researches of Lewis H. Morgan. New York: International Publishers (first published, 1885).

Evans-Pritchard, E. E. 1937. *Witchcraft, Oracles and Magic among the Azande.* Oxford: Clarendon Press.

———. 1940. "The Nuer of the Southern Sudan," in M. Fortes and E. E. Evans-Pritchard (eds.), *African Political Systems.* London and New York: Oxford University Press, pp. 272–296.

———. 1956. *Nuer Religion.* Oxford: Oxford University Press.

———. 1964. "The Divine Kingship of the Shilluk of the Nilotic Sudan," *Social Anthropology and other Essays.* New York: The Free Press, pp. 192–212 (first published, 1948).

———. 1965. *Theories of Primitive Religion.* Oxford: Clarendon Press.

F

Fanfani, Amintore. 1935. *Catholicism, Protestantism, and Capitalism.* London: Sheed and Ward.

Field, Margaret Joyce. 1960. *Search for Security.* London: Faber and Faber.

Firth, Raymond. 1956. *Human Types,* rev. ed. New York: Barnes and Noble, Inc.

———. 1963a. *Elements of Social Organization.* Boston: Beacon Press (first published, 1951).

———. 1963b. "Offering and Sacrifice: Problems of Organization," *The Journal of the Royal Anthropological Institute of Great Britain and Ireland,* 93:12–24.

———. 1963c. *We, the Tikopia,* abridged ed. Boston: Beacon Press (first published, 1936).

Fischer, J. L. 1963. "The Sociopsychological Analysis of Folktales," *Current Anthropology,* 4:235–295.

Fontenelle, Bernard le Bouvier de. 1908. *Histoire des oracles.* Critical edition by Louis Maigron. Paris: E. Cornély et Cie. (first published, 1687).

Forde, C. Daryll. 1934. *Habitat, Economy and Society.* New York: E. P. Dutton and Company, Inc.

———. 1931. *Ethnography of the Yuma Indians.* Berkeley, Calif.: University of California Press.

————. 1950. "Double Descent among the Yakö," in A. R. Rad-cliffe-Brown and Daryll Forde (eds.), *African Systems of Kinship and Marriage*. London and New York: Oxford University Press, pp. 285–332.

Fortune, Reo F. 1935. *Manus Religion*. Memoirs of the American Philosophical Society, Vol. 3.

————. 1963. *Sorcerers of Dobu: The Social Anthropology of the Dobu Islanders of the Western Pacific*. New York: E. P. Dutton and Company (first published, 1932).

Frake, Charles O. 1961. "The Diagnosis of Disease among the Subanum of Mindanao," *American Anthropologist*, 63:113–132.

————. 1964. "A Structural Description of Subanum 'Religious Behavior,'" in Ward H. Goodenough (ed.), *Explorations in Cultural Anthropology: Essays in Honor of George Peter Murdock*. New York: McGraw-Hill Book Company, pp. 111–129.

Frankfort, Henri, H. A. Frankfort, J. A. Wilson, and Thorkild Jacobsen. 1949. *Before Philosophy. The Intellectual Adventure of Ancient Man*. Baltimore: Penguin Books.

Frazer, Sir James George. 1959. *The New Golden Bough*. Theodor H. Gaster (ed.). New York: Criterion Books. (*The Golden Bough* was first published in 1890.)

Freud, Sigmund. 1928. *The Future of an Illusion*. W. D. Robson-Scott (trans.). Edinburgh: Horace Liveright and the Institute of Psycho-analysis.

————. 1938a. "The History of the Psychoanalytic Movement," in A. A. Brill (ed. and trans.), *The Basic Writings of Sigmund Freud*. New York: The Modern Library, Random House Inc., pp. 931–977.

————. 1938b. "The Interpretation of Dreams" in A. A. Brill (ed. and trans.), *The Basic Writings of Sigmund Freud*. New York: The Modern Library, Random House Inc., pp. 181–552 (first published, 1900).

————. 1938c. "Totem and Taboo," in A. A. Brill (ed. and trans.), *The Basic Writings of Sigmund Freud*. New York: The Modern Library, Random House Inc., pp. 807–930 (first published, 1913).

————. 1949. *An Outline of Psychoanalysis*. James Strachey

(trans.). New York: W. W. Norton and Company, Inc. (first published in German, 1940).

———. 1955. *Moses and Monotheism.* New York: Vintage Books, Random House Inc. (first published, 1939).

Fromm, Erich. 1951. *The Forgotten Language.* New York: Grove Press.

Fustel de Coulanges, Numa Denis. 1956. *The Ancient City.* Willard Small (trans.). Garden City, N.Y.: Doubleday and Company, Inc. (first published in French, 1864; first published in English, 1873).

G

Gaidoz, H. 1884. "Comme quoi M. Max Müller n'a jamais existé: étude de mythologie comparée," *Mélusine,* II:73–90.

Gaster, Theodor H. 1953. *The New Golden Bough, A New Abridgment of the Classic Work by Sir James George Frazer.* New York: Criterion Books.

Gebauer, Paul. 1964. *Spider Divination in the Cameroons.* Milwaukee: Public Museum.

Geertz, Clifford. 1960. *The Religion of Java.* Glencoe, Ill.: The Free Press.

Gennep, Arnold van. 1960. *The Rites of Passage.* Monika B. Vizedom and Gabrielle L. Caffee (trans.). London: Routledge and Kegan Paul (first published in French, 1908).

Gerth, H. H., and C. Wright Mills. 1958. *From Max Weber: Essays in Sociology.* New York: Galaxy Books, Oxford University Press.

Gluckman, Max. 1940. "The Kingdom of the Zulu of South Africa," in M. Fortes and E. E. Evans-Pritchard (eds.), *African Political Systems.* London and New York: Oxford University Press, pp. 25–55.

———. 1954. *Rituals of Rebellion in South-East Africa.* Manchester: Manchester University Press.

Goffman, Erving. 1959. *The Presentation of Self in Everyday Life.* Garden City, N.Y.: Doubleday Anchor Books.

Goldenweiser, Alexander. 1931. "Totemism," in V. F. Calverton (ed.), *The Making of Man.* New York: Random House, The Modern Library, pp. 363–392.

——. 1942. *Anthropology.* New York: F. S. Crofts & Company.

Goldman, Irving. 1963. *The Cubeo Indians of the Northwest Amazon.* Urbana, Ill.: University of Illinois Press.

——. 1964. "The Structure of Ritual in the Northwest Amazon," in Robert A. Manners (ed.), *Process and Pattern in Culture.* Chicago: Aldine Publishing Company, pp. 111–122.

Goode, William J. 1951. *Religion among the Primitives.* Glencoe, Ill.: The Free Press.

Graves, Robert. 1948. *The White Goddess.* London: Faber and Faber.

Grey, Sir George. 1841. *Journals of Two Expeditions of Discovery in North-West and Western Australia, during the Years 1937, 38 and 39, under the Authority of Her Majesty's Government.* London: T. and W. Boone.

Griaule, Marcel. 1960. "The Idea of Person among the Dogon," in Simon and Phoebe Ottenberg (eds.), *Cultures and Societies of Africa.* New York: Random House.

Griaule, Marcel, and Germaine Dieterlen. 1954. "The Dogon," in Daryll Forde (ed.), *African Worlds.* London and New York: Oxford University Press, pp. 83–110.

Gulliver, P. H. 1965. "The Jie of Uganda," in James L. Gibbs, Jr. (ed.), *Peoples of Africa.* New York: Holt, Rinehart and Winston, Inc., pp. 157–196.

H

Haeberlin, Herman K. 1918. "SBeTeTDA'Q, A Shamanistic Performance of the Coast Salish," *American Anthropologist,* 20:249–257.

Hahn, Eduard. 1896. *Die Haustiere und ihre Beziehungen zur Wirtschaft des Menschen.* Leipzig: Drucker und Humblot.

Hallowell, A. Irving. 1960. "The Beginnings of Anthropology in America," in Frederica de Laguna (ed.), *Selected Papers from the American Anthropologist 1888–1920.* Elmsford, N.Y.: Row, Peterson and Company, pp. 1–90.

Hamilton, Edith. 1942. *The Greek Way to Western Civilization.* New York: Mentor Books, The New American Library.

Hardy, M. 1891. *La Station Quaternaire de Raymonden.* Paris: Leroux.

Harner, Michael J. 1962. "Jivaro Souls," *American Anthropologist*, 64:258–272.

Harper, Edward B. (ed.). 1964. *Religion in South Asia*. Seattle, Wash.: University of Washington Press.

Harris, Marvin. 1966. "The Cultural Ecology of India's Sacred Cattle," *Current Anthropology*, 7:51–66.

Harrison, Jane E. 1903. *Prolegomena to the Study of Greek Religion*. Cambridge: Cambridge University Press.

———. 1912. *Themis: A Study of the Social Origins of Greek Religion*. Cambridge: Cambridge University Press.

Herbert of Cherbury, Lord Edward. 1937. *De veritate*. M. H. Carré (trans.). Bristol: J. W. Arrowsmith, Ltd. (first published, 1624).

Herder, Johann Gottfried von. 1883. Älteste Urkunde des Menschengeschlechts. In *Sämmtliche Werke*, edited by Bernhard Suphan. Berlin: Weidmann (first published, 1774).

Herskovits, Melville J. 1938. *Dahomey*. 2 vols. New York: J. J. Augustin.

———. 1952. *Man and his Works*. New York: Alfred A. Knopf.

———. 1958. *The Myth of the Negro Past*. Boston: Beacon Press (first published, 1941).

———. 1965. "African Gods and Catholic Saints in New World Religious Belief," in William A. Lessa and Evon Z. Vogt (eds.), *Reader in Comparative Religion*, 2d. ed. New York: Harper and Row, pp. 541–547 (first published, 1937).

Hill, W. W. 1944. "The Navaho Indians and the Ghost Dance of 1890," *American Anthropologist*, 46:523–527.

Hill-Tout, C. 1907. *The Native Races of the British Empire*. London: Archibald Constable and Company, Ltd.

Hobbes, Thomas. 1955. *Leviathan*. Michael Oakeshott (ed.). Oxford: Oxford University Press (first published, 1651).

Hobsbawm, E. J. 1965. *Primitive Rebels*. New York: W. W. Norton and Company.

Hodgen, Margaret T. 1964. *Early Anthropology in the Sixteenth and Seventeenth Centuries*. Philadelphia, Penn.: University of Philadelphia Press.

Hoebel, E. Adamson. 1954. *The Law of Primitive Man*. Cambridge, Mass.: Harvard University Press.

———. 1960. *The Cheyennes, Indians of the Great Plains*. New York: Holt, Rinehart and Winston.

Hogbin, Herbert Ian. 1934. *Law and Order in Polynesia: A Study of Primitive Legal Institutions.* New York: Harcourt, Brace and Company.

———. 1964. *A Guadalcanal Society: The Kaoko Speakers.* New York: Holt, Rinehart and Winston.

Hollis, Alfred Claud. 1909. *The Nandi.* Oxford: Clarendon Press.

Holtom, Daniel Clarence. 1943. *Modern Japan and Shinto Nationalism.* Chicago: University of Chicago Press.

Honigmann, John J. 1947. "Witch-Fear in Post-Contact Kaska Society," *American Anthropologist,* 49:222–243.

———. 1959. *The World of Man.* New York: Harper and Row.

Huber, Hugo. 1965. "A Diviner's Apprenticeship and Work among the Bayaka," *Man,* 65:46–47.

Hubert, Henri and Marcel Mauss. 1902–03. "Equisse d'une théory générale de la magie," *L'Anneé sociologique,* 7:1–146.

———. 1964. *Sacrifice, its Nature and Function.* W. D. Halls (trans.). Chicago: University of Chicago Press (first published in French, 1899).

Hultkranz, Ake. 1953. *Conceptions of the Soul among the North American Indians.* Stockholm: Coslon Press.

Hume, David. 1964. "The Natural History of Religion," in Richard Wollheim (ed.), *David Hume on Religion.* Cleveland and New York: Meridian Books, The World Publishing Company, pp. 31–98 (first published, 1757).

Huxley, Aldous. 1954. *The Doors of Perception.* New York: Harper.

Hyman, Stanley Edgar. 1958. "The Ritual View of Myth and the Mythic," in Thomas Sebeok (ed.), *Myth: A Symposium.* Bloomington, Ind.: Indiana University Press, pp. 84–94.

J

Jackson, John Wilfrid. 1917. *Shells as Evidence of the Migrations of Early Culture.* Manchester: Manchester University Press.

James, E. O. 1957. *Prehistoric Religion.* New York: Barnes and Noble.

———. 1961. *Comparative Religion.* New York: Barnes and Noble.

James, William. 1961. *The Varieties of Religious Experience.*

New York: Mentor Books, The New American Library (first published, 1902).

Jensen, Adolf A. 1963. *Myth and Cult among Primitive Peoples.* Marianna Tax Choldin and Wolfgang Weissleder (trans.). Chicago: University of Chicago Press (first published in German, 1951).

Jones, Ernest. 1951. "Psycho-analysis and Folklore," *Essays in Applied Anthropology,* Vol. 2. London: Hogarth Press, pp. 1–21.

Jung, Carl Gustav. 1938. *Psychology and Religion.* New Haven, Conn.: Yale University Press.

Jung, Carl Gustav, and C. Kerényi. 1963. *Essays on a Science of Mythology.* R. F. C. Hull (trans.). New York: Harper Torchbooks (first published in German, 1949).

Junod, Henri Alexandre. 1913. *The Life of a South African Tribe.* 2 vols. London: Macmillan and Company.

Jowett, B. 1937. *The Dialogues of Plato.* 2 vols. New York: Random House.

K

Kardiner, Abram, and Edward Preble. 1963. *They Studied Man.* New York: Mentor Books, The World Publishing Company.

Kenyon, Kathleen M. 1957. *Digging up Jericho.* New York: Frederick A. Praeger.

Klineberg, Otto. 1935. *Race Differences.* New York: Harper and Brothers.

Kluckhohn, Clyde. 1962. *Culture and Behavior, Collected Essays.* Richard Kluckhohn (ed.). New York: The Free Press.

———. 1964. "Navaho Categories," in Stanley Diamond (ed.), *Primitive Views of the World.* New York: Columbia University Press, pp. 93–128.

———. 1965. "Myths and Rituals: A General Theory," in William A. Lessa and Evon Z. Vogt (eds.), *Reader in Comparative Religion,* 2d ed. New York: Harper and Row, pp. 144–158 (first published, 1942).

———. 1967. *Navaho Witchcraft.* Boston: Beacon Press (first published, 1944).

Kluckhohn, Clyde, and Dorothea Leighton. 1962. *The Navaho,* rev. ed. New York: Doubleday Anchor Books (first published, 1946).

Koch-Grünberg, Theodor. 1916–1928. *Vom Roroima zum Orinoco.* 5 vols. Berlin: D. Reimer.

Koenigswald, G. H. R. von. 1956. *Speurtocht in de Prehistorie.* Amsterdam, The Netherlands: De Spieghel.

Krause, Aurel. 1956. *The Tlingit Indians.* Seattle, Wash.: University of Washington Press.

Krige, J. D., and E. J. Krige. 1943. *The Realm of a Rain-Queen.* London: Oxford University Press.

———. 1954. "The Lovedu of the Transvaal," in Daryll Forde (ed.), *African Worlds.* New York: Oxford University Press, pp. 55–82.

Kroeber, Alfred Louis. 1939. "Totem and Taboo in Retrospect," *American Journal of Sociology,* 45:446–451.

———. 1948. *Anthropology.* New York: Harcourt, Brace and Company.

Kuper, Hilda. 1963. *The Swazi, a South African Kingdom.* New York: Holt, Rinehart and Winston.

L

La Barre, Weston. 1960. "Twenty Years of Peyote Studies," *Current Anthropology,* 1:45–60.

Lafitau, Joseph François. 1724. *Moeurs des sauvages amériquains comparées aux moeurs des premiers temps.* 2 vols. Paris: Saugrain L'Âiné.

Lang, Andrew. 1898. *The Making of Religion.* London: Longmans, Green and Company, Ltd.

Lanternari, Vittorio. 1965. *The Religions of the Oppressed.* Lisa Sergio (trans.). New York: Mentor Books, The New American Library (first published in Italian, 1960).

Lantis, Margaret. 1953. "The Social Culture of the Nunivak Eskimos," in Irwin T. Sanders *et al.* (eds.), *Societies Around the World,* Vol. I. New York: The Dryden Press, pp. 92–128.

———. 1965. "The Religion of the Eskimos," in Vergilius Ferm (ed.), *Ancient Religions.* New York: The Citadel Press, pp. 311–339.

Lawrence, Peter. 1964. *Road Belong Cargo*. Manchester: Manchester University Press.

Leach, Edmund R. 1954. *Political Systems of Highland Burma*. Cambridge, Mass.: Harvard University Press.

———. 1961. "Lévi-Strauss in the Garden of Eden: An Examination of some Recent Developments in the Analysis of Myth," *Transactions of the New York Academy of Sciences*, 23:386–396.

———. 1967. "Genesis as Myth," in John Middleton (ed.), *Myth and Cosmos. Readings in Mythology and Symbolism*. Garden City, N.Y.: The Natural History Press, pp. 1–13.

Leacock, Seth. 1964. "Ceremonial Drinking in an Afro-Brazilian Cult," *American Anthropologist*, 66:344–354.

Leakey, Louis Seymour Bazett. 1965. *Olduvai Gorge 1951–1961*. 2 vols. London: Cambridge University Press.

Lenski, Gerhard. 1963. *The Religious Factor*. Garden City, N.Y.: Doubleday Anchor Books.

Lessa, William A. 1965. "Somatomancy: Precursor of the Science of Human Constitution," in William A. Lessa and Evon Z. Vogt (eds.), *Reader in Comparative Religion*, 2d ed. New York: Harper and Row, pp. 352–363. (first published, 1952).

———. 1966. *Ulithi, a Micronesian Design for Living*. New York: Holt, Rinehart and Winston.

Lesser, Alexander. 1933. "Cultural Significance of the Ghost Dance," *American Anthropologist*, 35:109–115.

Lévi-Strauss, Claude. 1953. "Social Structure," in Alfred L. Kroeber (ed.), *Anthropology Today*. Chicago: The University of Chicago Press, pp. 524–553.

———. 1960. "Four Winnebago Myths: A Structural Sketch," in Stanley Diamond (ed.), *Culture in History: Essays in Honor of Paul Radin*. New York: Columbia University Press, pp. 351–362.

———. 1962. "The Logic of Totemic Classifications," in *The Savage Mind*. Chicago: University of Chicago Press, pp. 35–74.

———. 1963a. "The Effectiveness of Symbols," in *Structural Anthropology*. New York: Basic Books, pp. 186–205.

———. 1963b. "The Structural Study of Myth," in *Structural Anthropology*. New York: Basic Books, pp. 206–231.

Levy, G. Rachel. 1963. *Religious Conceptions of the Stone Age*. New York: Harper Torchbooks.

Lévy-Bruhl, Lucien. 1949. *Les Carnets du Lucien Lévy-Bruhl.* Paris: Presses Universitaires de France.

―――. 1966. *Primitive Mentality.* Lilian A. Clare (trans.). Boston: Beacon Press (first published in French, 1921; first published in English, 1923).

Lewis, Oscar. 1964. "Seventh Day Adventism in a Mexican Village: A Study in Motivation and Culture Change," in Robert A. Manners (ed.), *Process and Pattern in Culture, Essays in Honor of Julian H. Steward.* Chicago: Aldine Publishing Company, pp. 63–83.

Lieban, Richard W. 1962. "The Dangerous Ingkantos: Illness and Social Control in a Philippine Community," *American Anthropologist,* 64:306–312.

―――. 1967. *Cebuano Sorcery. Malign Magic in the Philippines.* Berkeley and Los Angeles: University of California Press.

Linton, Ralph. 1926. *Ethnology of Polynesia and Micronesia.* Chicago Field Museum of Natural History Guide, Part 6.

―――. 1936. *The Study of Man.* New York: Appleton-Century-Crofts, Inc.

―――. 1943. "Nativistic Movements," *American Anthropologist,* 45:230–240.

Little, Kenneth. 1954. "The Mende in Sierra Leone," in Daryll Forde (ed.), *African Worlds.* London and New York: Oxford University Press, pp. 111–137.

Loeb, Edwin M. 1935. *Sumatra, its History and People.* Published in Vienna as Volume 3 of Wiener Beiträge zur Kulturgeschichte und Linguistiek des Institutes für Völkerkunde der Universität Wien.

Lombart, Émile. 1910. *De la Glossolalie chez les Premiers Chrétiens et des phénomènes similaires.* Lausanne: Bridel.

Lowie, Robert H. 1937. *The History of Ethnological Theory.* New York: Rinehart and Company, Inc.

―――. 1947. *Primitive Society.* New York: Liveright Publishing Corporation (first published, 1920).

―――. 1952. *Primitive Religion.* New York: Universal Library, Grosset and Dunlap (first published, 1924).

―――. 1963. *Indians of the Plains.* Garden City, N.Y.: The Natural History Press (first published, 1954).

Löwith, Karl. 1949. *Meaning in History.* Chicago: University of Chicago Press.

Lucretius (Titus Lucretius Carus). 1957. *On the Nature of Things*. William Ellery Leonard (trans.). New York: E. P. Dutton and Company, Inc. (written about 58 B.C.).

Luquet, G. H. 1930. *The Art and Religion of Fossil Man*. J. Townsend Russell, Jr., (trans.). New Haven, Conn.: Yale University Press.

M

Macalister, R. A. S. 1921. *A Textbook of European Archeology*. Cambridge: Cambridge University Press.

Mair, Lucy Philip. 1948. *Australia in New Guinea*. London: Christophers.

———. 1962. *Primitive Government*. Baltimore: Penguin Books.

Malinowski, Bronislaw. 1926. "Anthropology," in *Encyclopaedia Britannica*, First Supplementary Volume, pp. 131–140.

———. 1945. "The Problem of Meaning in Primitive Languages," Supplement 1 to C. K. Ogden and I. A. Richards, *The Meaning of Meaning*. New York: Harcourt, Brace and Company, pp. 296–336.

———. 1954. *Magic, Science and Religion and Other Essays*. Garden City, N.Y.: Doubleday Anchor Books (first published, 1925).

———. 1955. *Sex and Repression in Savage Society*. New York: Meridian Books, The Noonday Press (first published, 1927).

———. 1959. *Crime and Custom in Savage Society*. Paterson, N.J.: Littlefield, Adams and Company (first published, 1926).

———. 1960. *A Scientific Theory of Culture*. New York: Oxford University Press (first published, 1944).

———. 1961. *Argonauts of the Western Pacific*. New York: E. P. Dutton and Company Inc. (first published, 1922).

———. 1962. *Sex, Culture and Myth*. New York: Harcourt, Brace and World, Inc.

Mandelbaum, David G. 1938. "Polyandry in Kota Society," *American Anthropologist*, 40:574–583.

Marett, Robert Ranulph. 1909. *The Threshold of Religion*. London: Methuen and Company, Ltd.

Martin, Paul S., George I. Quimby, and Donald Collier. 1947.

Indians before Columbus. Twenty Thousand Years of North American History Revealed by Archeology. Chicago: University of Chicago Press.

Marwick, M. G. 1963. "A Note on Ordeal Poison in East Central Africa," *Man,* 63:45–46.

Mauss, Marcel. 1904. "Essai sur les variations saisonnières des sociétés eskimos: Essai de morphologie sociale," *L'Année sociologique,* Vol. 9, pp. 39–132.

May, L. Carlyle. 1956. "A Survey of Glossolalia and Related Phenomena in Non-Christian Religions," *American Anthropologist,* 58:75–96.

Mead, Margaret. 1949. *Coming of Age in Samoa.* New York: Mentor Books, The New American Library (first published, 1928).

————. 1950. *Sex and Temperament in Three Primitive Societies.* New York: Mentor Books, The New American Library (first published, 1935).

————. 1953. *Growing up in New Guinea.* New York: Mentor Books, The New American Library (first published, 1930).

————. 1959. "Apprenticeship under Boas," in Walter Goldschmidt (ed.), *The Anthropology of Franz Boas.* Memoir 89 of the American Anthropological Association, pp. 29–45.

————. 1964. *Continuities in Cultural Evolution.* New Haven, Conn.: Yale University Press.

Meighan, Clement W. 1966. *Archeology: An Introduction.* San Francisco, Calif.: Chandler Publishing Company.

Mercier, P. 1954. "The Fon of Dahomey," in D. Forde (ed.), *African Worlds.* London and New York: Oxford University Press, pp. 210–234.

Merton, Robert K. 1957. *Social Theory and Social Structure.* Glencoe, Ill.: The Free Press.

Métraux, Alfred. 1957. "Dramatic Elements in Ritual Possession," *Diogenes,* No. 11:18–36.

Metzger, Duane, and Gerald Williams. 1963. "Tenejapa Medicine I: The Curer," *Southwestern Journal of Anthropology,* 19: 216–234.

Mirsky, Jeanette. 1961. "The Eskimo of Greenland," in Margaret Mead (ed.), *Cooperation and Competition among Primitive Peoples.* Boston: Beacon Press, pp. 51–78 (first published, 1937).

Moodie, Roy L. 1927. "Studies in Paleopathology: Injuries to the Head among the pre-Columbian Peruvians," *Annals of Medical History*, 9:277–307.

Mooney, James. 1965. *The Ghost-Dance Religion and the Sioux Outbreak of 1890,* abridged ed. Chicago: University of Chicago Press (first published, 1896).

Moore, Omar Khayyam. 1957. "Divination—A New Perspective," *American Anthropologist*, 59:69–74.

Morgan, Lewis Henry. 1962. *League of the Iroquois*. New York: Corinth Books (first published, 1851).

———. 1963. *Ancient Society or, Researches in the Lines of Human Progress from Savagery through Barbarism to Civilization.* Eleanor Leacock (ed.). Cleveland and New York: Meridian Books, The World Publishing Company (first published, 1877).

Müller, Friedrich Max. 1870. *Lectures on the Science of Language*. New York: C. Scribner and Company.

———. 1872. *Chips from a German Workshop*. New York: Scribner, Armstrong and Company (first published, 1867).

———. 1885. "The Savage," *Nineteenth Century*, Vol. 17, pp. 109–132.

Murdock, George Peter. 1949. *Social Structure*. New York: The Macmillan Company.

Murray, Henry A. 1962. "Definitions of Myth," in Richard M. Ohmann (ed.), *The Making of Myth*. New York: G. P. Putnam's Sons, pp. 7–37.

N

Nadel, Siegfried Frederick. 1940. "The Kede: A Riverain State in Northern Nigeria," in M. Fortes and E. E. Evans-Pritchard (eds.), *African Political Systems*. London and New York: Oxford University Press, pp. 165–196.

———. 1946. "A Study of Shamanism in the Nuba Mountains," *Journal of the Royal Anthropological Institute of Great Britain and Ireland*, 76:25–37.

———. 1947. *The Nuba*. London: Oxford University Press.

———. 1952. "Witchcraft in Four African Societies: An Essay in Comparison," *American Anthropologist*, 54:18–29.

―――. 1954. *Nupe Religion*. London: Routledge and Kegan Paul, Ltd.

―――. 1964. "Malinowski on Magic and Religion," in Raymond Firth (ed.), *Man and Culture, An Evaluation of the Work of Bronislaw Malinowski*. New York: Harper Torchbooks, pp. 189–208 (first published, 1957).

Newman, Philip L. 1965. *Knowing the Gururumba*. New York: Holt, Rinehart and Winston.

Newman, Stanley. 1964. "Vocabulary Levels: Zuñi Sacred and Slang Usage," in Dell Hymes (ed.), *Language in Culture and Society*. New York: Harper and Row, pp. 397–406.

Nilsson, Martin P. 1961. *Greek Folk Religion*. New York: Harper Torchbooks.

Norbeck, Edward. 1961. *Religion in Primitive Society*. New York: Harper and Brothers.

Noss, John B. 1963. *Man's Religions*. New York: Macmillan.

O

Oberg, Kalervo. 1940. "The Kingdom of Ankole in Uganda," in M. Fortes and E. E. Evans-Pritchard (eds.), *African Political Systems*. London and New York: Oxford University Press, pp. 121–162.

Oesterreich, T. K. 1930. *Possession, Demoniacal and Other*. D. Ibberson (trans.). New York: Richard R. Smith (first published in German, 1922).

Oliver, Douglas L. 1952. *The Pacific Islands*. Cambridge, Mass.: Harvard University Press.

Opler, Morris E. 1941. *An Apache Life-Way*. Chicago: University of Chicago Press.

―――. 1945. "Japanese Folk Belief Concerning the Snake," *Southwestern Journal of Anthropology*, 1:249–259.

Ottenberg, Simon. 1958. "Ibo Oracles and Intergroup Relations," *Southwestern Journal of Anthropology*, 14:295–317.

Ottenberg, Simon and Phoebe (eds.). 1960. *Cultures and Societies of Africa*. New York: Random House.

Otto, Rudolf. 1958. *The Idea of the Holy*. John W. Harvey (trans.). New York: Galaxy Books, Oxford University Press (first published in German, 1917; first published in English, 1923).

P

Park, George K. 1963. "Divination and its Social Contexts," *Journal of the Royal Anthropological Institute of Great Britain and Ireland,* 93:195–209.

Park, Willard Z. 1938. *Shamanism in Western North America.* Evanston, Ill.: Northwestern University Press.

Parkman, Francis. 1892. *A Half-Century of Conflict.* 2 vols. Boston: Little, Brown and Company.

Parsons, Talcott. 1937. *The Structure of Social Action.* New York: McGraw-Hill.

———. 1951. *The Social System.* Glencoe, Ill.: The Free Press.

———. 1961. "Religion and Social Structure," in Talcott Parsons *et al.* (eds.), *Theories of Society,* Vol. I. New York: The Free Press, pp. 645–46.

Petronius. 1960. *The Satyricon.* William Arrowsmith (trans.). New York: Mentor Books, the New American Library (written c. 66 A.D.)

Pettazzoni, Raffaele. 1922. *Dio, formazione e sviluppo del monoteismo nella storia delle religioni.* Rome: Athenaeum.

Péquart, Marthe, and St. Just. 1937. *Téviec; Station-nécropole mésolithique du Morbihan.* Archives de l'Institut de Paléontologie Humaine, Mémoire 18.

Piggott, Stuart. 1940. "A Trepanned Skull of the Beaker Period from Dorset and the Practice of Trepanning in Prehistoric Europe," *Proceedings of the Prehistoric Society,* n.s. Vol. 6, No. 3:112–132.

Pilling, Arnold R. 1962. "Statistics, Sorcery, and Justice," *American Anthropologist,* 64:1057–1059.

Plato. SEE Jowett, B.

Pospisil, Leopold. 1963. *The Kapauku Papuans of West New Guinea.* New York: Holt, Rinehart and Winston.

Prokofyeva, Ye. D. 1963. "The Costume of an Enets Shaman," in Henry N. Michael (ed.), *Studies in Siberian Shamanism.* Toronto: University of Toronto Press, pp. 124–156.

R

Radcliffe-Brown, Alfred Reginald. 1952. *Structure and Function in Primitive Society*. Glencoe, Ill.: The Free Press.
———. 1964. *The Andaman Islanders*. New York: The Free Press (first published, 1922).
Radin, Paul. 1920. *The Autobiography of a Winnebago Indian*. University of California Publications in American Archeology and Ethnology, 16:381–437.
———. 1957. *Primitive Religion*. New York: Dover Publications, Inc. (first published, 1937).
Raff, E. 1928. "Appendix" in F. E. Williams, *Orokaiva Magic*. London: Oxford University Press.
Raglan, Fitz Roy Richard Somerset. 1958. "Myth and Ritual," in T. Sebeok (ed.), *Myth: A Symposium*. Bloomington, Ind.: Indiana University Press, pp. 76–83.
Rasmussen, Knud. 1908. *The People of the Polar North*. London: K. Paul, Trench, Trübner and Company, Ltd.
———. 1930. *Intellectual Culture of the Hudson Bay Eskimos*. Report of the Fifth Thule Expedition, 1921–1924. Vol. 7. Copenhagen: Gyldendal.
Redfield, Robert. 1954. "Introduction" to Malinowski's *Magic, Science and Religion*. New York: Doubleday Anchor Books, pp. 9–13.
———. 1962. *A Village that Chose Progress. Chan Kom Revisited*. Chicago: University of Chicago Press (first published, 1950).
Redfield, Robert, and Alfonso Villa Rojas. 1962. *Chan Kom, A Maya Village*. abridged ed. Chicago: University of Chicago Press (first published, 1934).
Reichard, Gladys A. 1934. *Prayer: The Compulsive Word*. Monographs of the American Ethnological Society No. 8. Seattle, Wash.: University of Washington Press.
———. 1950. *Navaho Religion*. 2 vols. New York: Pantheon Books.
Reynolds, Barrie. 1963. *Magic, Divination and Witchcraft among the Barotse of Northern Rhodesia*. Berkeley and Los Angeles: University of California Press.

Richards, Audrey I. 1940. "The Political System of the Bemba Tribe—North-Eastern Rhodesia," in M. Fortes and E. E. Evans-Pritchard (eds.), *African Political Systems.* London and New York: Oxford University Press, pp. 83–120.
———. 1956. *Chisungu.* New York: Grove Press.
Rivers, William Halse Rivers. 1906. *The Todas.* London: Macmillan and Company, Ltd.
———. 1914. *The History of Melanesian Society.* Cambridge: Cambridge University Press.
Robertson, H. M. 1933. *Aspects of the Rise of Economic Individualism. A Criticism of Max Weber and his School.* Cambridge: Cambridge University Press.
Roscoe, John. 1911. *The Baganda.* London: Macmillan and Company, Ltd.
Ross, Alexander. 1653. *Pansebia: or, A View of all Religions in the World.* London: John Saywell.
Rust, Alfred. 1937. *Das altsteinzeitliche Rentierjägerlager Meiendorf.* Neumünster: K. Wachholtz.
———. 1943. *Die alt- und mittelsteinzeitlichen Funde von Stellmoor.* Neumünster: K. Wachholtz.

S

Sadler, A. W. 1964. "Glossolalia and Possession: An Appeal to the Episcopal Study Commission," *Journal for the Scientific Study of Religion,* 4:84–90.
Sahlins, Marshall D. 1958. *Social Stratification in Polynesia.* Seattle, Wash.: University of Washington Press.
Samuelsson, Kurt. 1964. *Religion and Economic Action. A Critique of Max Weber.* E. Geoffrey French (trans.). New York: Harper Torchbooks (first published in Swedish, 1957).
Sapir, Edward. 1949. "Time Perspective in Aboriginal American Culture: A Study in Method," in David G. Mandelbaum (ed.), *Selected Writings of Edward Sapir.* Berkeley and Los Angeles: University of California Press, pp. 389–462 (first published, 1916).
Schelling, Friedrich Wilhelm Joseph von. 1957. *Philosophie der Mythologie.* 2 vols. Darmstadt: Wissenschaftliche Buchgesellschaft (first published, 1856).

Schmidt, Robert Rudolf. 1912. *Die diluviale Vorzeit Deutsch-lands*. Stuttgart: E. Schweizerbart.

Schmidt, Wilhelm. 1926–1955. *Der Ursprung der Gottesidee*. Münster im Westfalen: Aschendorffsche Verlagsbuchhandlung.

Scot, Reginald. 1930. *Discoverie of Witchcraft*. London: J. Rodker (first published, 1584).

Sebeok, Thomas A. 1964. "Structure and Content of Cheremis Charms," in Dell Hymes (ed.), *Language in Culture and Society*. New York: Harper and Row, pp. 356–371.

Seznec, Jean. 1961. *The Survival of the Pagan Gods*. New York: Harper Torchbooks.

Sheldon, William H., S. S. Stevens, and W. B. Tucker. 1940. *The Varieties of Human Physique: An Introduction to Constitutional Psychology*. New York: Harper and Brothers.

Shimkin, D. B. 1947. "Wind River Shoshone Literary Forms: An Introduction," *Journal of the Washington Academy of Science*, 37:329–352.

Sierksma, F. 1961. *Een Nieuwe Hemel en een Nieuwe Aarde*. 's Gravenhage, The Netherlands: Mouton and Co.

Simoons, Frederick J. 1961. *Eat not this Flesh: Food Avoidances in the Old World*. Madison, Wisc.: University of Wisconsin Press.

Slotkin, J. S. 1965a. "The Peyote Way," in William A. Lessa and Evon Z. Vogt (eds.), *Reader in Comparative Religion*, 2d ed. New York: Harper and Row, pp. 513–517.

———. 1965b. *Readings in Early Anthropology*. Viking Fund Publications in Anthropology No. 40. New York: Wenner-Gren Foundation for Anthropological Research, Inc.

Smith, Grafton Elliot. 1928. *In the Beginning: The Origins of Civilization*. London: G. Howe, Ltd.

Smith, Michael G. 1965. "The Hausa Markets in a Peasant Economy," in Paul Bohannan and George Dalton (eds.), *Markets in Africa*. New York: Doubleday Anchor Books, pp. 130–179.

Smith, W. Robertson. 1956. *The Religion of the Semites*. New York: Meridian Books (first published, 1889).

Sombart, Werner. 1913. *The Jews and Modern Capitalism*. M. Epstein (trans.). London: T. Fisher Unwin.

Speck, Frank G. 1931. *A Study of the Delaware Indian Big House*

Ceremony. Harrisburg: Pennsylvania Historical Commission.

———. 1935. *Naskapi: The Savage Hunters of the Labrador Peninsula.* Norman, Okla.: University of Oklahoma Press.

Spencer, Baldwin, and F. J. Gillin. 1899. *The Native Tribes of Central Australia.* London and New York: Macmillan.

———. 1904. *The Northern Tribes of Central Australia.* London and New York: Macmillan.

Spencer, Dorothy M. 1941. *Disease, Religion and Society in the Fiji Islands.* Monographs of the American Ethnological Society, No. 2.

Spencer, Herbert L. 1876–1896. *Principles of Sociology.* 3 vols. London: Williams and Norgate.

Spier, Leslie. 1935. *The Prophet Dance of the Northwest and its Derivatives: The Source of the Ghost Dance.* American Anthropological Associaton, General Series in Anthropology No. 1.

Spiro, Melford. 1964. "Religion and the Irrational," in June Helm (ed.), *Symposium on New Approaches to the Study of Religion.* Seattle, Wash.: University of Washington Press, pp. 102–115.

———. 1966. "Buddhism and Economic Action in Burma," *American Anthropologist,* 68:1163–1173.

Stannus, H. 1922. *The Wa-Yao of Nyasaland.* Cambridge, Mass.: Harvard African Studies.

Steward, Julian H. 1933. *Ethnography of the Owens Valley Paiute.* University of California Publications in American Archeology and Ethnology No. 33.

———. 1953. "Evolution and Progress," in Alfred L. Kroeber (ed.), *Anthropology Today.* Chicago: University of Chicago Press, pp. 313–326.

Steward, T. D. 1957. "Stone Age Skull Surgery: A General Review, with Emphasis on the New World," *Annual Report of the Smithsonian Institution,* Publication No. 4314. Washington, D.C.: U.S. Government Printing Office, pp. 469–491.

Strehlow, Carl. 1907–1920. *Die Aranda- und Loritja-Stämme in Zentral-Australien.* 5 vols. Frankfurt am Main: J. Baer and Company.

Sundkler, B. G. M. 1961. *Bantu Prophets in South Africa,* 2d. ed. New York: Oxford University Press.

Suttles, Wayne. 1957. "The Plateau Prophet Dance among the

Coast Salish," *Southwestern Journal of Anthropology*, 13:352–396.

Swanson, Guy A. 1964. *The Birth of the Gods. The Origin of Primitive Beliefs*. Ann Arbor, Mich.: University of Michigan Press.

Swanton, J. R. 1905. *The Haida*. Publications of the Jesup North Pacific Expedition, No. 8.

T

Talmon, Yonina. 1965. "Pursuit of the Millennium: The Relation between Religious and Social Change," in William A. Lessa and Evon Z. Vogt (eds.), *Reader in Comparative Religion*, 2d ed. New York: Harper and Row, pp. 522–537.

Tawney, R. H. 1926. *Religion and the Rise of Capitalism*. New York: Harcourt, Brace and Company.

Taylor, Douglas MacRae. 1951. *The Black Carib of British Honduras*. New York: Viking Fund Publications in Anthropology No. 17; Wenner-Gren Foundation for Anthropological Research, Inc.

Thompson, Stith. 1946. *The Folktale*. New York: Holt, Rinehart and Winston.

———. 1955–1958. *Motif-index of Folk-literature*. 6 vols. Bloomington, Ind.: Indiana University Press.

———. 1958. "Myths and Folktales," in Thomas A. Sebeok (ed.), *Myth: A Symposium*. Bloomington, Ind.: Indiana University Press, pp. 104–110.

Thulin, C. O. 1906–1909. *Die etruskische Disziplin*. 3 vols. Gotenborg: Zachrissons.

Train, Percy, J. R. Heinrichs, and W. A. Archer. 1941. *Medical Uses of Plants by Indians of Nevada*. Contributions toward a Flora of Nevada, No. 33. Washington, D.C.: U.S. Department of Agriculture, Division of Plant Exploration and Introduction.

Turner, Victor W. 1962. "Themes in the Symbolism of Ndembu Hunting Ritual," *Anthropological Quarterly*, 35:37–57.

Tylor, Edward Burnett. 1958. *Primitive Culture*, reprinted in 2 vols.: Vol. I, The Origins of Culture; Vol. II, Religion in Primitive Culture. New York: Harper Torchbooks (first published, 1872).

U

Uchendu, Victor. 1965. *The Igbo of Southeast Nigeria*. New York: Holt, Rinehart and Winston.
Underhill, Ruth. 1953. *Red Man's America*. Chicago: University of Chicago Press.

V

Vaillant, George C. 1966. *Aztecs of Mexico,* rev. ed. New York: Pelican Books (first published, 1944).
Vico, Giambattista. 1961. *The New Science of Giambattista Vico*. Translated from the third edition (1744) by Thomas Goddard Bergin and Max Harold Fisch (abridged). Garden City, N.Y.: Doubleday Anchor Book.
Voltaire, François Marie Arouet de. *Essay on the Manners and Spirit of Nations* (first published, 1754).

W

Waal Malefijt, Annemarie de. 1963. *The Javanese of Surinam: Segment of a Plural Society*. New York: The Humanities Press.
Wach, Joachim. 1944. *Sociology of Religion*. Chicago: University of Chicago Press.
Wagley, Charles. 1959. "Tapirapé Shamanism," in M. H. Fried (ed.), *Readings in Anthropology*, Vol. 2. New York: Thomas Y. Crowell Company, pp. 405–423 (first published, 1943).
Wagley, Charles, and Eduardo Galvao. 1949. *The Tenetehara Indians of Brazil*. New York: Columbia University Press.
Wagner, Gunter. 1954. "The Abaluyia of Kavirondo (Kenya)," in D. Forde (ed.), *African Worlds*. London and New York: Oxford University Press, pp. 27–54.
Wallace, Anthony. 1956. "Revitalization Movements," *American Anthropologist,* 58:264–281.
———. 1965. "James Mooney (1861–1921) and the Study of the Ghost Dance Religion," in James Mooney, *The Ghost-Dance Religion*. Chicago: University of Chicago Press, pp. v–x.

————. 1966. *Religion: An Anthropological View*. New York: Random House.

Wallis, Wilson D. 1939. *Religion in Primitive Society*. New York: F. S. Crofts and Company.

Warner, W. Lloyd. 1961. *The Family of God*. New Haven, Conn.: Yale University Press.

————. 1964. *A Black Civilization: A Study of an Australian Tribe*, rev. ed. New York: Harper Torchbooks (first published, 1937).

Wax, Murray, and Rosalie Wax. 1963. "The Notion of Magic," *Current Anthropology*, 4:495–518.

Weber, Max. 1958. *The Protestant Ethic and the Spirit of Capitalism*. Talcott Parsons (trans.). New York: Charles Scribner's Sons (first published, 1904–1905).

————. 1964. *The Sociology of Religion*. Ephraim Fischoff (trans.). Boston: Beacon Press (first published, 1922).

Webster, Hutton. 1948. *Magic: A Sociological Study*. Stanford, Calif.: Stanford University Press.

Welmers, William E. 1949. "Secret Medicines, Magic, and Rites of the Kpelle Tribe in Liberia," *Southwestern Journal of Anthropology*, 5:208–243.

White, C. M. N. 1948. "Witchcraft, Divination and Magic among the Balovale Tribes," *Africa*, 18, No. 2, pp. 81–104.

White, Leslie. 1962. *The Pueblo of Sia, New Mexico*. Smithsonian Institution Bureau of American Ethnology Bulletin 184. Washington, D.C.: U.S. Government Printing Office.

Whiting, Beatrice Blyth. 1950. *Paiute Sorcery*. Viking Fund Publications in Anthropology No. 15. New York: Wenner-Gren Foundation for Anthropological Research, Inc.

Whiting, John W. M., Richard Kluckhohn, and Albert Anthony. 1958. "The Function of Male Initiation Ceremonies at Puberty," in E. E. Maccoby, T. M. Newcomb, and E. L. Hartley (eds.), *Readings in Social Psychology*. New York: Henry Holt and Company, pp. 359–370.

Williams, Francis Edgar. 1928. *Orokaiva Magic*. London: Oxford University Press.

————. 1934. "The Vailala Madness in Retrospect," in E. E. Evans-Pritchard, R. Firth, B. Malinowski, and I. Shapera (eds.), *Essays Presented to C. G. Seligman*. London: K. Paul, Trench, Trübner and Company, Ltd.

————. 1940. *The Drama of Orokolo*. Oxford and New York: Oxford University Press.

Williamson, Robert W. 1936. *Religion and Social Organization in Central Polynesia*. Cambridge: Cambridge University Press.

Wilson, Bryan R. 1961. *Sects and Society*. Berkeley and Los Angeles, Calif.: University of California Press.

Wilson, John A. 1949. "Egypt: The Values of Life," in H. Frankfort, J. Wilson, and Thorkild Jacobsen (eds.), *Before Philosophy*. Baltimore, Md.: Penguin Books Inc., pp. 103–133.

Wilson, Monica. 1959. *Communal Rituals of the Nyakyusa*. Oxford: Oxford University Press.

Wissler, Clark. 1912. *The Social Life of the Blackfoot Indians*. New York: Anthropological Papers of the American Museum of Natural History, Volume 7.

Wolf, Eric R. 1958. "The Virgin of Guadaloupe: A Mexican National Symbol," *Journal of American Folklore*, 71:35–39.

————. 1962. *Sons of the Shaking Earth*. Chicago: University of Chicago Press.

————. 1964. "Santa Claus: Notes on a Collective Representation," in Robert A. Manners (ed.), *Process and Pattern in Culture*. Chicago: Aldine Publishing Company, pp. 147–155.

Worsley, Peter. 1957. *The Trumpet Shall Sound*. London: Macgibbon and Kee.

Y

Young, Frank W. 1962. "The Function of Male Initiation Ceremonies: A Cross-Cultural Test of an Alternative Hypothesis," *The American Journal of Sociology*, 67:379–396.

————. 1965. *Initiation Ceremonies: A Cross-Cultural Study of Status Dramatization*. New York: The Bobbs-Merrill Company.

Index

supreme, 152
of war, 153
Goffman, Erving, 192
Goldenweiser, Alexander, 94–96
Goldman, Irving, 102, 169
Goode, William J., 51, 149, 213, 221, 267, 326, 327
Government and religion, 305–12
Gräbner, Fritz, 66–67
Grave goods, 325
Graves, 111, 132, 134
Graves, Robert, 139
Greece, Ancient, 16, 17, 22, 29, 32, 33, 34, 37, 56–57, 114, 133, 217–18, 224, 240, 286, 292–94, 295, 318
Greek language, 44, 46, 147
Grey, Sir George, 60
Griaule, Marcel, 164, 165
Grimaldi (Monaco), 112, 114, 116
Grimm, Jakob, 45
Grimm, Wilhelm, 45
Grotte des Enfants (Monaco), 112
Grotte des Hyènes (France), 122
Grotte des Rideaux (France), 119
Grotte du Pape (France), 122
Group integration, 58, 291
Guadalcanal (Melanesia), 158, 254
Guardian spirits, 155, 256, 260, 314
Guilt feelings, 248
Gulliver, P. H., 253
Guru, 245
Gururumba (New Guinea), 154, 155
Gwari (Africa), 283–84

H-mens, 356–57
Häckel, Ernst, 69
Haddon, Alfred Court, 82
Haeberlin, Herman K., 256
Hahn, Eduard, 227
Haida (American Indian), 208, 324
Haiti, 358
Hallcists, 134
Hallowell, A. Irving, 91
Hamilton, Edith, 18
Hammer of Witches. *See Malleus Maleficarum*
Hanunóo (Philippines), 247
Harappa (West Pakistan), 140, 141
Hardy, M., 115
Harner, Michael J., 167
Harper, Edward B., 102, 260
Harris, Marvin, 327
Harrison, Jane E., 187, 188
Haruspicy, 219, 221, 240
Hathor, 139

Hausa (Africa), 322
Hawaii, 234, 318
Headhunting, 108, 130, 167
Headshrinking, 167
Healing, 60, 168, 207, 237, 241, 243, 246 ff., 310, 317, 336, 354, 357
effectiveness of, 264–66
exorcism, 50, 249, 259–62, 270
removal of disease-causing objects, 258–59
retrieving the soul, 256–58
Health, 246
Hecate, 286
Heel Stone (Stonehenge), 137–38
Hegel, George F. W., 30, 40
Hepatoscopy, 219
Hera, 150
Herbal remedies, 247, 264
Herbert of Cherbury, Lord Edward, 26–27
Herder, Johann Gottfried von, 37–38
Herodotus, 17–18, 30
Herskovits, Melville J., 159, 167, 220, 314, 322, 326, 354, 358
Hesiod, 18
Hiawatha, 306
Hieroglyphics, 204
High gods, 152, 201
Hill, W. W., 343
Hill-Tout, C., 230
Hinduism, 76, 205, 234, 245, 318, 327
Hippocrates, 224, 251
Historical
method, 19, 42, 48, 76, 93
reconstructions, 81, 93, 94–95
History, 76, 82, 99, 186
Hittites, 224
Hiuen-Tsiang, 24
Hobbes, Thomas, 27–28, 29
Hobgoblins, 155
Hobsbawm, E. J., 330, 340
Hodgen, Margaret, 33
Hoebel, E., Adamson, 153, 247, 248, 304, 316
Hogbin, Herbert Ian, 238, 255, 318
Hohokam (American Indian), 143
Holy, concept of the, 74–76
Holy Communion, 351
Holy Cross, 37, 356
Holy Spirit, 208, 351
Hollis, Alfred Claud, 217
Holtom, Daniel Clarence, 166
Home medicine, 263, 349
Homeopathic magic, 54, 123
Homer, 18, 224